INTRODUCTION

The Sultan . . . was condemned to endure a bizarre sort of apocalypse, a living nightmare so awful he couldn't bear to rest his head on his pillow or close his eyes at any time of day or night, for fear of dreaming of a certain black dog. The dog was a hideous sight: putrid, offensive, with gouged-out eyes. Invariably, it appeared to the Sultan above the hills of dry sand spread beneath Jalo's ramparts. It reared its ugly head, howling in such a crazed state that the hills themselves appeared to drown in its odious inhalations.

SADIQ NEIHOUM, "THE SULTAN'S FLOTILLA"[1]

The late Sadiq Neihoum, Libya's preeminent political philosopher of the 1970s and 1980s, and a onetime adviser to Colonel Muammar Gaddafi, wrote the fable from which the above passage is taken in the late 1970s. The fact that the Sultan was meant to be Gaddafi would have been obvious to the readers even then (which is likely, in part, why Neihoum's writings were subsequently banned and Neihoum forced into exile).

For years, the Sultan searches in vain for a cure for ceaseless visions of being mauled by a rabid black dog. One day, a "wise traveler" arrives with a warning and a solution: the black dog of the Sultan's dreams represents a God-given catastrophe that will occur seven years hence. If the Sultan prepares properly for this cataclysm, by building the equivalent of Noah's ark (the Sultan's flotilla), the black dog will appear only once each year, for seven years, before breaking down the final Palace wall. The Sultan is overjoyed at the news, and as an expression of thanks, marries the wise man to his daughter. The catastrophe arrives as predicted. The people of the kingdom survive, and prosperity returns to the Kingdom. The Sultan, however, does not survive. When viewed from 2011, Neihoum's story proved to be a strangely prescient allegory for Gaddafi's rule and the reform process, which lasted from 2004 to 2011—precisely seven years.

The black dog could represent any number of rising threats, from Gaddafi's domestic Islamic resistance to Libya's disgruntled, disenfranchised youth. The Sultan's flotilla is an apt metaphor for the rapprochement between Libya and the West—a "solution" that proved neither practical, nor effective. The "wise man" might be a composite of Gaddafi's second-eldest son Saif, and intelligence head Musa Kusa, or, better yet, British Prime Minister Tony Blair.

While he was unmistakably a despot, Gaddafi detested the image and took great pains—however manufactured the attempt—to present himself as something altogether more benign: Gaddafi did not rule, the people ruled; Gaddafi did not exercise any formal control, he only offered advice. Libya's "state of the masses" was, in his view, the world's "only true democracy." However he wished to see it, Gaddafi dispensed defective advice, committed heinous crimes against his own people, and set Libya's international identity as a state sponsor of terror and global stirrer of pots.

This is the story of Gaddafi's departure from the Libyan stage. Its roots begin with eighteen years of Monarchy, thirty years of Italian occupation, and before that, successive Ottoman and Byzantine intrusions. The story includes the 1969 coup that brought Gaddafi to power and the decades of international repression, terror, and international notoriety that followed. Yet the narrative ultimately hinges on a few-year period when things had potential to change drastically, for better or worse.

In 2003, Gaddafi signed what many inside and outside his circle had thought an "impossible deal" with the United States (as in, the US would never agree), abandoning his weapons of mass destruction (such as they were) and agreeing to compensate the families of the victims of the 1988 Lockerbie bombing and to share intelligence in service to the West's war on terror. In return, UN- and US sanctions on Libya were lifted, allowing Gaddafi to sell his oil more freely, attract international investment into his ailing oil infrastructure, and assume an altogether more public persona.

For a time, Gaddafi, like the Sultan in Neihoum's story, believed this deal had saved him from his mounting problems—the metaphorical black dog. Yet it was precisely at this critical juncture that Gaddafi lost control of his own destiny, the West lost a few degrees of its moral compass in the Middle East, and the United States and key European countries (the UK and France, in particular) unwittingly set the stage for their own intervention in Libya in 2011. What has been lost in the coverage of Gaddafi's fall from power is this crucial pivot. For even though the Arab

Spring was the trigger of Gaddafi's exit, it was more like the blow of a falling branch from a tree on a house that had only barely survived battering by a violent hurricane.

I ARRIVED IN LIBYA at the cusp of Gaddafi's international makeover, in late summer 2004, as commercial/economic officer at the US Liaison Office (USLO) in Tripoli, a position that appeared on a State Department volunteer list just before I was to take up a position as a Vice Consult in Kuwait. The assignment involved reporting to the State Department and various other interested agencies on all aspects of the Libyan economy and reform process, while facilitating US business interests in the country. I did ask myself if I was comfortable contributing, however indirectly, to a process of reconciliation with a regime tagged with responsibility for the Lockerbie bombing (I had been a college student at the time and knew people who knew some of the victims, many of whom were Syracuse University students returning home for Christmas from study abroad programs). What I learned in pre-departure briefings about the terms of the re-engagement did not settle my mind in this regard, but I reasoned this was a tremendous opportunity for the West (and me personally) to learn more about what was happening on the ground in Libya, how Gaddafi's system did or did not work. Further, tending to seek out the unusual—I had spent most of 1997 and 1998 in Yemen, writing a dissertation on port competition in the Red Sea. There were few places in the region—other than Libya—that could be said to be as exotic. Years before, one hot summer day in 1990, just weeks before Saddam Hussein invaded Kuwait, I had approached the Libyan-Tunisian border, wondering when it might be possible to visit the "Great Jamahiriya" (Gaddafi's made-up word for "State of the Masses").

A few weeks after being cleared for the post, I left for Tripoli, wading through a series of airport security (TSA) agents and airline staff in the US and UK who—despite my visa and diplomatic passport—refused to believe an American was authorized to travel to Libya. I thought it somewhat funny that I was suspect at the borders of my own country but was allowed to move about reasonably freely (even if I was followed) once I was in Tripoli. For whatever reason, I encountered few of the impediments to movement faced by many of my colleagues.

The Libya that I found in summer 2004 bore the markings of a totalitarian state. Phones were tapped and rooms were bugged, foreigners were usually followed. Revolutionary propaganda was ubiquitous. There were few hints of life outside Libya—no advertisements, few foreign products, no signs in any language other than Arabic. Because of the difficult access and lack of standard amenities, many diplomats and businessmen (there were few women) who were posted to Libya for a year or more left with little more than a sense that the country was kooky and yet on the road to reform, as per the somewhat forced proclamations by government officials that "things are different now."

There were advantages to being the person within the US mission charged with talking about the economy and facilitating trade, particularly at a time when the Europeans were already old hat, having returned to the country almost four years earlier, in 1999, when UN sanctions were first lifted. In 2004, I became something of a lightning rod for Libyans who had political agendas of various kinds, and could use commercial issues as a cover to speak with a US diplomat. Further, unlike those above me with weightier responsibilities, I had freedom to travel all over the country, to the southern and eastern deserts; Benghazi and the Green Mountains; the western mountains, Jebel Nafusa—places where American diplomats had not been for more than twenty years. I often stood in for the chargé at protocol events when he was unable or deemed inappropriate to attend. Thus, I found myself hurtling uneasily through the Libyan skies in poorly maintained aircraft with a herd of other diplomats, to Sirte to listen to the Leader's interminable speeches. I witnessed various desert tributes to the Leader, including one massive sound and light show on the edge of the Sahara, was taken to see the cornerstone of the Great Man-Made River, and attended various lower-level diplomatic and cultural events inside and outside the capital.

In a short period of time, I saw the same elements of absurdity that journalists and businesspeople had reported over the years. But I also heard muffled stories and hints of generations of anguish and deeper, systematic human rights abuses—stories that did not really start to surface, and were certainly not mentioned in any official correspondences, until several years later. As the 2011 revolution progressed, many of these stories, a few of which are described in this book, began to resurface with a vengeance. More sustained interaction gave hints of deeper trauma, of lost lives and opportunities. For me, Hisham Mattar's 2007 novel *In the Country of Men* gave voice to an unquantifiable darkness that lurked behind the otherwise benign-looking façade of the new Libya, many Libyans' remarkable and genuine sense of humor, and Gaddafi's vaudevillian distractions.

One thing that struck me most during my two-year assignment was how many times people from different levels of Libyan society, from cab drivers to ex-monarchy ministers and businesspeople, would take me aside and insist that the "US government should know" what they were dealing with in Gaddafi, even as they hoped that the apparent rapprochement would make their lives easier. Now, they would say, is the time for the Americans to push Gaddafi to the wall and exact concessions—or forever hold our peace.

THE US LIAISON OFFICE, the precursor to the US Embassy in Tripoli, was located in a self-styled, five-star hotel. Most of us, including chargé Greg Berry, Deputy Chief of Mission Leslie Tsou, Public Affairs Officer Anne O'Leary, and several temporary administrative and reporting officers (TDY), would put in twelve- to fifteen-hour days in cramped quarters, with few outlets for rest and recreation other than an outdoor pool. In addition to swimming daily laps, with the encouragement of my Libyan commercial assistant, Basem Tulti, I undertook to translate a few Libyan short stories into English. Most were simultaneously depressing and mildly subversive. Noticing that the vast majority of stories contained neither the names of people nor places, we decided to try to find as many stories as possible that contained Libyan geographical references, then visit those places. In retrospect, a good fraction of the 100 diplomatic cables I wrote over the first year were somehow linked, if indirectly, to conversations about or contacts made in the course of researching these stories or attempting to visit the places mentioned. I learned of the stunning Benghazi riots of 2006, as they were going on, from a contact who had helped me track down Sadiq Neihoum's stories. I understood something about the repression of Libya's Berbers after being invited by Berber staff members to visit their homes in Jebel Nafusa, en route to visit the site of Ahmed Ibrahim Al-Fagih's Al Jarad—the story of one town's fight against a swarm of rapacious locusts. Many landmarks of the 2011 revolution—from southern oases to the back streets of Benghazi, I would recognize immediately from these literary forays.

WHEN MY LIBYA TOUR CAME TO AN END in late summer 2006, Libya and the West were in full-blown makeover mode. Out of the sanctions' vise grip, Gaddafi was well on his way to making up for lost time. The Fourth of July party at the chargé's residence was an unusually ebullient occasion, crammed with hundreds of Libyan businessmen, Libyan and foreign diplomats, and artists. It was a testament to the cultural and personal inroads the mission had made with the Libyan people and many of the key administrators. At the same time, on a political/administrative level, a thaw had set in: the narratives each side had set up to justify the reunion were already starting to wear thin, and for all the fanfare, what would happen next in Libya was really anyone's guess.

In 2007, I left the State Department and eventually wound up with then Senator Barack Obama's foreign policy advisory group. One of my assignments was to predict what aspects of the US-Libya rapprochement might come up in the presidential debates with Senator John McCain. While Libya never made it into the debate, the country would soon figure prominently in the political history of both politicians.

In 2008, I joined a Dubai-based multinational company, where I was asked to advise on Gaddafi family squabbles and the prospects for lasting change in Libya. While aspects of the reform process had ramped up since 2006, the Libyans I knew well, who were participating in commercial projects, both large and small, predicted impending turbulence. Dubai, meanwhile, had become a center for both pro- and anti-Gaddafi voices—friends and associates of individual Gaddafi members; traders seeking to expand their business regionally; representatives of the Libyan Investment Authority (LIA), the principal sovereign wealth fund; political dissidents; and ex-monarchy ministers, all of whom were engaged in their own war of words—many months before the 2011 revolution.

In December 2010, while traveling from Dubai to Dakar, Senegal, I flew over the Libyan desert, and appreciated for the first time its true vastness and emptiness. The first object I saw upon landing in Senegal was a Soviet-era Antonov cargo plane with Libyan markings—typically a marker of a weapons delivery, or a State visit by the Leader himself. As I waited in the terminal for my return flight to Dubai three days later, I noticed a Libyan Afriqiyah A340 parked a discrete distance away from the main reception hall. A Senegalese honor guard—barely noticeable—stood on the tarmac, starting up and standing down in line with gestures from a soldier atop the mobile stairwell. The occupant—whom I assumed at the time was either Gaddafi's diplomatic son Saif Al Islam, or the militaristic son Mu'tassim—dallied inside. A figure hurried uncharacteristically down the stairs to a waiting car, dispensing with protocol. After the Libyan revolution, I read that this had been Gaddafi himself, in Senegal for the World Festival of Black Arts (FESMAN), which was to start a few days later. Something about this scene struck me as odd, and I wondered later whether Gaddafi had other, pressing matters on his mind, just days before street vendor Mohamed Bouazizi's self-immolation in Tunisia, the act that launched the Arab Spring. Rumors had been rife in Dubai the weeks before that Gaddafi was preparing a major policy announcement, and that whatever it was, it was not likely to be well received by those with interests in the New Libya.

Once the uprising began on February 15, I became instantly transfixed with events on the ground. After the liberation of Benghazi in March, I looked for ways to get back into the country, even if briefly, to experience the atmosphere of a revolution that, while long deemed a distinct if not imminent possibility, was nonetheless astounding. I was working at the time on a project to establish a network of primary care clinics in port cities in East and West Africa, and I shared an interest with a Libyan colleague in investigating the possibility of applying a similar model to revolutionary Libya—but with a focus on the treatment of trauma—in regions where, despite Libya's riches, the standards of medical care were abysmal. I wanted to know more about how the uprising had spread in Benghazi, and what had happened since I had left. I wanted to look deeper into where the United States and the rest of the West had gone wrong, and right in Libya. After all, I had been sent to Libya ostensibly to help push forward what was at the time the beginning of an interesting transition, if not a warm relationship, one which might have positive effects on the way the United States dealt with other seemingly intractable regional disputes.

UNTIL THE 2011 REVOLUTION, not much had been written about Libya. One obvious reason was the difficulty—particularly for Americans—in gaining access. Journalists would typically have to travel on foreign passports to visit Libya, and were strictly "minded" during their stay. Only a handful of academics—Dirk Vandewalle, Moncef Djaziri, Moncef Ouannes, Hanspeter Mattes, and Ronald Bruce St. John stand out—had devoted more than a fraction of their career to writing about Libya, usually as part of research on oil states and with little expectation that their interest in Libyan politics would become pressingly relevant.

In writing this book, I have tried to fill in the gaps between the academic studies of a dysfunctional state and the more recent journalistic accounts; between the high-level political and economic situations and the local culture; between the pre-2011 history of Libya and the Arab Spring. I draw heavily on my own experiences in pre- and post-revolutionary Libya, as well as a large number of Arabic and French sources.

My perspective is somewhat rare, in the sense that the people who covered the revolution as journalists and diplomats were for the most part different from those who were there before. I benefited from particularly good access to those members of the regime who defected, who were in the know but not known, and wanted to share their insight on the events in which they had taken part. I also had access to many senior sitting and former US and EU officials, many of whom were eager to tell their part of the backstory, even if on condition of anonymity. Many others involved in policy making in current and previous US and UK administrations were unwilling to comment.

In some cases, interviews I hoped to conduct with Gaddafi-era or revolutionary figures were made unnecessary by extensive interviews published in still-obscure local newspapers, before these individuals assumed roles of even greater importance. There was a period in the early days of the revolution during which many of the protagonists were far more open, ebullient, and willing to talk in detail about their experiences.

Much of what happened to Libya over the last few decades is the result of negligence—on the part of Libya's leadership and the international community, including the US and Europe, which paid attention to what was happening in the country only when it was politically or economically expedient. Despite its veneer of irrelevance to US policy makers, Libya had and continues to have a significant impact on the West, even if that impact is diffuse. In the 1970s, Gaddafi sparked a revolution in oil pricing, wresting pricing power away from the major oil companies and putting it into the hands of the oil-producing countries. Gaddafi's money and meddling caused political havoc in Africa, the Middle East, and Europe, particularly during the 1980s, as he supported a range of terrorist groups and revolutionary movements. Libya was almost certainly responsible for blowing up two Western civilian aircraft and their passengers and crew, and for cosponsoring acts of terror that caused Presidents Carter and Reagan to label Libya a "significant threat" to US interests. More recently, Libya became the field on which the West was able to take a decisive public stand in support of the Arab Spring, despite opposition from Secretary of Defense Robert Gates, and others who argued that the United States had no significant policy interests in the country.

I AM ONE OF THOSE WHO BELIEVE that the Obama administration, supported by the Europeans, did the right thing by intervening in Libya, even if the intervention was preconditioned by a host of factors that were not at all transparent. The US did have critical interests in Libya—as poorly explained as they may have been—and also moral obligations. US actions in the years 1998–2004, and the process of rapprochement itself, as I will describe in detail, set in motion a whole series of actions that made a bloodless revolution less, not more, likely. I also believe that had this process been managed differently, the result might well have been different, and the West's strategic and moral obligations to intervene less clear.

What foreigners tend to overlook is that those who fought in the revolution—largely young men between the ages of seventeen and thirty—clearly believed a clean break from Gaddafi was worth the grave risks they took to topple the regime. In other words, even though Libya was looking a bit shinier, and there were promises of jobs and new housing, there was no sense, particularly in Eastern Libya, that this process would benefit any but the top layers of society or that there would be fundamental change. In my many pre-Revolution conversations with Libyans of all kinds, I sensed that, in all this talk of weapons of mass destruction, and foreign investment, ordinary Libyans felt they had been betrayed by perhaps the one country that had the power to save them from further decades of rule by Gaddafi(s).

I RETURNED TO LIBYA for the first time since the revolution, in late July 2011, almost five years to the day after my first visit to Benghazi. My colleague and I arrived on a UN transport literally hours after the assassination of rebel commander Abdelfattah Younes. One had the sense, in this highly charged atmosphere, with multiple hours-long gun battles raging across the city, that the residents of the epicenter of the Revolution were starting to feel—not for the last time—that perhaps they had miscalculated, that the forces of darkness, whether they be embodied in regime "fifth columnists," in foreign meddling, or simply man's morbid attraction to chaos, were possibly too great to overcome. I had experienced this atmosphere of collective angst twice before—in Aden, Yemen, just before the USS *Cole* bombing, and in Asmara, Eritrea, in 1999, during an escalation of the hugely bloody Eritrean-Ethiopian war; the National Transitional Council was struggling to control renegade militias, which it feared remained loyal to Gaddafi. At the same time, the city was alive with as many opinions as weapons. People were proud of what they had accomplished and in the sacrifice of the martyrs and the *mafqoodeen* (the missing), whose images were posted everywhere, along with the newly-revived monarchy flag. My colleagues and I witnessed a country in the throes of shedding the influence of Gaddafi and quickly remaking itself.

The book begins by looking at the historical and sociological context that produced Gaddafi in the first place, his early influences and stated aspirations, and the increasing difficulty he faced motivating a population that moved quickly from ecstasy to apathy to open hostility toward his ambitions. I then look at Gaddafi's turn to rejectionism, and decision to play spoiler to the international (and particularly Arab and Western) community, largely at the expense of the livelihood and comfort of his own people.

I explain how, for the better part of twenty years, Gaddafi became an international pariah, a status reinforced by a series of particularly heinous acts of state-sponsored terror. I describe how Gaddafi managed, for many years, to keep most of his internal and external opposition at bay, even as predominantly Eastern-based Islamists became an increasingly serious threat to the regime. I describe the odd alignment of internal and external circumstances that paved the way for a rapprochement dialogue with the West (and the US in particular). This rapprochement offered real opportunities for Libya and the US, subject to a well-structured deal, for which Libyan reform was not an afterthought. In reality, the process moved forward in an astoundingly ad hoc manner, producing a series of incompatible narratives, that, instead of saving Gaddafi and providing the US with a viable model for engagement with problem states, effectively preconditioned a very messy outcome, once the Arab Spring was under way. In the last chapters I look at how the US and the West came to intervene in the Libyan uprising on the side of the rebels, and why, and what prospects Libya has for becoming a productive, prosperous member of the international community.

PART I

THE MAKING OF TROUBLE

CHAPTER 1

Libya's Lot

If asked what comes to mind when hearing the word *Libya*, most Westerners under the age of sixty would probably say "Gaddafi" and "oil." Reminded of Alan Moorehead's reporting on the famous World War II Allied battles with Rommel's forces at El Alamein and Tubruk, older people might pull up images of a vast, dusty desert—which, in fact, Libya is.

More than 90 percent of Libya's surface area is inhospitable to agriculture and thus to human settlement. Though one of the largest countries in Africa, Libya is home to just over 6 million people. This number is miniscule when compared to neighboring Egypt (81.1 million) and Saudi Arabia (27.4 million). The vast majority live along the coast, concentrated in the two largest cities, Benghazi in the east (approximately 1 million), and Tripoli in the west (approximately 2 million). By contrast, the largest city in the south, Sebha, has a population of only 130,000. Libya is like an archipelago, with a series of population centers along the coast: roads through the southern desert are like shipping lanes, connecting the people to outlying islands in the sand, which themselves link to traditional trading and immigration routes to Sub-Saharan Africa.

The implications of Libya's geographical and demographic features, in the context of an oil state, are more profound than might first appear: water and oil were the two forces that pushed the limits and constrained what

Libya's leaders could do, respectively. The availability of water dictated overall population size, patterns of settlement, and the potential for self-sufficiency in food (and exports). A small population meant that resources could have a great impact: oil money could be spent to increase human capital through education, medical care, or social services; conversely, the money could buy control and loyalty. Gaddafi initially opted for the former, then switched gears to ensure the latter. He certainly tried to exert as much control over both water and oil as humanly possible.

Gaddafi attempted to rectify the fact that Libya has little water with a more than $33 billion project called the Great Man-Made River (GMMR), which brought water from southern underground aquifers to the north at a rate of 6.5 million cubic meters per day.[1] Dubbed the "Eighth Wonder of the World" by Gaddafi, the GMMR was a metaphor for Gaddafi's approach to most things: grandiose, functioning for a while, but ultimately not viable. Gaddafi was so proud of this achievement—implemented by Korean firms under contract to foreign subsidiaries of the US contracting firm Kellogg Brown & Root—that he assigned to the GMMR project its own minister, Abdelmajid Al Ghoud (prime minister from 1994 to 1997). In 2004, Al Ghoud proclaimed at a conference in Tripoli that the aquifers were effectively "limitless," while Libya's most distinguished hydrologist privately predicted the resources would be exhausted within ten years.[2] There were indications that the water was contaminated by nitrate leaching, which some speculated might contribute to Libya's anecdotally high cancer rate.

Apparently aware of the GMMR's failings, in 2005 Gaddafi requested a feasibility study for a proposal to divert water from the Ubangi River (which runs through parts of the Democratic Republic of Congo, the Central African Republic, and the Republic of Congo) and push it over the Tibesti Mountains along the Chad-Libya border using massive turbines. The diversion would simultaneously refill the Tazerbo and Kufra aquifers, turning swampland in the Ubangi basin (encompassing parts of the Central African Republic, the Democratic Republic of Congo, and the Republic of Congo) into vast agricultural areas. All this would make Gaddafi a hero on the African continent by feeding tens of millions of central Africans.[3] The cost of the project was estimated at between $60 billion and $120 billion.[4] The GMMR would reveal something telling about Gaddafi, a future refrain: whatever the cost to himself, the budget, or people's lives, Gaddafi would never admit defeat and would redouble his efforts to outdo himself to make the earlier diversion seem irrelevant.

Oil, of course, played a tremendous role in Libya's development, since the discovery of commercially viable deposits in 1959. The vast majority of Libya's known oil reserves—at 47 billion barrels, the largest in Africa—are located in the Sirte Basin, a five hundred to seven hundred kilometer-wide desert depression separating eastern and western Libya, containing the oil fields Sarir, Messlah, and Bu Attifel. Oil from this region is refined at Ras Lanuf and exported from Marsa Brega, both of which became key battlefields in the 2011 revolution. Libya is rich in natural gas as well, ranked twenty-second in global reserves, with 55 trillion cubic feet in known reserves,[5] or 0.81 percent of the world total (compared with 8.5 percent for Qatar, which is ranked fourth).[6]

While eastern oil dominates Libya's production and exploration, other parts of Libya also have significant resources such as the Ghadames and Murzuk basins in the country's south-southwest and in Kufra to the southeast. The offshore Bouri field, near the Libyan-Tunisian border, is one of the largest in Libya, assessed at 2 billion barrels.[7] The geographic distribution of resources was not fully known at the time of Gaddafi's coup, but would certainly play a subterranean role in the building of resentments in how those resources were applied and distributed.

In terms of religion and ethnicity, Libya, unlike Iraq and Syria with their patchworks of Shi'a–Sunni Muslim and sectarian divides, is quite homogenous: the people are overwhelmingly Sunni Arabs, apart from an 8 percent Berber minority (who are Ibadi Muslims, a denomination shared with the majority of Omanis). One characteristic that Libya shares with Iraq and Syria is a strong tribal tradition: by various estimates, there are more than 140 tribes in Libya. Among the major groupings are the Warfalla, Bani Walid, Obeidat, Ouled Suleiman, Zwei, Megaraha, Tarhouna. Some tribes are large—the Warfalla, number more than eight hundred thousand; others, like Gaddafi's own tribe, the Gaddafa, are quite small. As with oil and water, Gaddafi did his best both to control and to attenuate tribal allegiances.

Geography, resources, population, and tribalism defined Libya's position vis-à-vis the outside world for centuries. Without water and before the discovery (and use) of oil in commercial quantities, Libya was too weak to resist external invasions. Tribal and regional fissures made it difficult for Libya to effectively respond to the invaders, though the regional tribal bond, combined with rough terrain in the east, facilitated the rebel movement so influential in fighting off the Italians. The discovery of oil in commercial quantities in 1959 caused tremendous social dislocation, as the rural poor flocked to the cities in search of work, and encouraged a culture of corruption. These events were directly implicated in the rise of Gaddafi, as well as his demise.

Before Libya

The physical area currently known as Libya was, like much of the rest of the Middle East, a product of Ottoman Turkish empire building and the subsequent scramble by the West to pick up the pieces after the collapse of the Ottoman Empire in the early twentieth century. The rough delineation of three Libyan provinces, Cyrenaica, Tripolitania, and Fezzan, dates from this period. Overall, a steady stream of invaders, each staying for a while, attempted to expand their influence over the coast and, to a lesser extent, the interior, until a combination of local opposition and/or outside aggression pushed them out. Not until independence in 1951 were Cyrenaica, Tripolitania, and Fezzan formally integrated into a single, independent but federated state. Libya played an important role in the history of trade and religion in Saharan and sub-Saharan (Sahelian) Africa and the Mediterranean.

Pre-Islam, the region was the location of several flourishing Greek and Roman settlements. Parts of Libya served as granaries for the Roman empire, as they would for fascist Italy thousands of years later. Writing in the fifth century BC, Herodotus referred to Libyans as "those to the West of Egypt." Ethnic groupings in Libya at that time included the Nasamons in the east to the Gulf of Sirte, the Maces of the gulf to what is today Jebel Nafusa, and the Lotophages (the lotus eaters of Homer's *Odyssey*) on the coast.[8]

The Phoenicians and Greeks mounted the first organized, external settlement of coastal Libya in the seventh to sixth centuries BC. Traders from the eastern Mediterranean first set up seasonal settlements and then more permanent ones along the west coast, all of which were overseen from Carthage, in present-day Tunisia. The Greeks, straying in from the island of Crete some two hundred miles across the sea to the north, established a permanent outpost at Cyrene in 631 BC.[9] The two areas, east and west, came under the same rule for the first time under the Romans.

Byzantine invasions in the middle of the sixth century scattered a few relatively short-lived Christian settlements, before Arab invaders arrived in

Cyrenaica (eastern Libya) from Egypt in 642, under the command of the original Saif Al Islam (literally, Sword of Islam, or divinely-sanctioned conqueror) Amr ibn al As. Inspired by the expansionist ethos of their new religion, Islam, the Arabs made reasonably quick work of the Byzantines, though it took them more than two centuries to pacify the local nomadic-pastoral Berber population, which, according to the great fourteen-century Arab historian Ibn Khaldun, refused them "more than a hundred times," before finally submitting to their rule.[10]

The Berbers had built up the all-important trans-Saharan trade over the previous two hundred years.[11] While part of that trade consisted of legitimate barter, they also made fortunes in the trade in people: historians estimate that over the course of a thousand years, millions of sub-Saharan Africans—most of them women—were transported along these routes and exported to the north and east. The slave trade, which wound down only in the late nineteenth century, conditioned or at least affected in various ways Libya's modern relationship with the rest of Africa, and helped perpetuate links between the northern and southern parts of the country.

Not until the seventeenth and eighteenth centuries did trans-Saharan trade really take off, in no small part due to the expansion of the Senussi order, a puritanical Islamic brotherhood founded by Sayyid Mohammed ibn Ali El Senussi, born in 1787 in Mustaganem, in present-day Algeria. The Senussi order contributed substantially to the stability and connectivity of large portions of present-day Libya by moderating the behavior of the wild tribes, including the Zwei, whose predations made southern routes off-limits to regular trade. Senussi teachings promoted education as a core value and contributed to cross-tribal solidarity, as their lodges *zawaya* (plural of *zawiya*) were intimately interwoven into the tribal leadership structure.[12]

While fundamentalist, in the sense that it advocated a return to the founding principles of Islam, after centuries of "innovations," the Senussi order was never fanatical, in the manner of the Wahhabis of Saudi Arabia. The Senussi, like other mystical and quasi-mystical Islamic movements, stressed the notion of going beyond the actual words of the Koran to discover the subtext or revealed meaning. While it is difficult, if not impossible, to draw a direct connection between the past and continued influence of the Senussi—significantly weakened today—and some form of native immunity or resistance to jihadist ideologies, it is fair to say that the overall tradition in Libya did not welcome extremism, let alone movements that advocated violence against those professing alternate ideologies.

The Ottoman Empire first took interest in Libya in the early 1500s, when an Ottoman Sultan sent a contingent of troops to occupy eastern Libya and Tripoli, largely to keep an option on the region and ward off European powers starting to stake claims in the southern Mediterranean. It was not until the Karamanli dynasty (1711–1835) that the Turks took a more active interest in Libya. Even so, this was empire-by-correspondence. The Karamalis were small-time warlords who paid tribute to the sultan in Istanbul and conducted their affairs as they wished.

The United States' First (Failed) Attempt at Regime Change

Much of the West's—and particularly the United States'—early relationships with the Libyan territories date to the late 1700s, and early 1800s, as immortalized in a phrase from the US Marine' Hymn, "From the Halls of Montezuma, to the Shores of Tripoli."

The Karamanli period overlapped the American struggle for independence and, subsequently, the first American commercial forays into the Mediterranean. European powers had been accustomed to maritime piracy by the North African emirates for years and pursued a dual (and highly ineffective) strategy of combining naval convoys with regular cash payments to protect their commercial ships from North African plundering. Rather than deal with the issue directly, militarily or otherwise, Britain and France chose largely to ignore the problem. One historian notes that "[h]ad London and Paris wished, their warships could have blown the pirate fleets out of the sea and bombarded the capitals of Barbary. But they refrained, in part because it was easier and cheaper to pay tribute."[13] Under President John Adams, the United States followed the same policy, more by necessity than choice. By 1797, the United States had paid out more than $1,150,000 in bribes to the ruler of Algiers, and US envoy Joel Barlow believed, mistakenly, that he had "bought" peace with Tripoli the same year for the sum of $56,486.[14]

When Yusuf Karamanli discovered the discrepancy between what he was receiving from the Americans and what they were paying to the North African emirates, he swiftly abrogated the previous arrangement, demanding a fixed payment of $250,000 with a $20,000 annuity—the former paid within six months—or he would declare war against the United States.[15] While Article I, Section 8 of the US Constitution gave Congress alone the power to declare war, the United States was not willing to rise to Karamanli's bait, largely due to concerns about the budget. Adams's successor, Thomas Jefferson, sent four ships to blockade Tripoli's port, but under closely circumscribed rules of engagement:

> American policy remained fatally inconsistent, for even as a squadron was being dispatched to the Mediterranean to conform the Tripolitans, the *George Washington* was en route to Algiers with timber and other stores, as well as a partial payment in arrears of $30,000.[16]

Jefferson's early preference was for a negotiated solution.[17] As the seriousness of the situation sank in, Congress chose to amend the Tripoli mandate to include the protection of American shipping using "all necessary means," thereby freeing the navy's hand considerably.[18] This would not be the last time Congress would object to presidential action in Libya on the basis of cost and the fear of resulting "quagmire."

The tenor of US-Libya relations changed drastically in 1803, once Pasha Yusuf Karamanli managed to capture one of the American frigates, the USS *Philadelphia*, with its contingent of 307 officers and crew, after it hit a reef while trying to enforce the blockade.[19] Further empowered, Karamanli issued brazen demands that led the Americans to think they might need a more proactive approach, including a seemingly bizarre plan hatched by General William Eaton, a New England military strategist with an unusual determination to learn Arabic and a premonition that he would die young.[20] In 1797, after pulling off an intelligence coup against the Spanish forces in New Orleans at the behest of then President John Adams (in office 1791–1801), Eaton had had his pick of assignments and opted to be US Consul General, based in Tunis.

In the context of growing concerns about the Barbary pirates—Karamanli in particular—Eaton described his plan to Jefferson's Secretary of State James Madison: Eaton would march six hundred miles from Alexandria, Egypt, to Derna in eastern Libya with a small contingent of American troops, defeat the local governor, and then put the "kindler, gentler" brother, Ahmed Karamanli, at the head of a large group of rebels, which would carry him to Tripoli. Channeling the ideas of professor Bernard Lewis and Paul Wolfowitz (two of the "neocon" idealogues associated with the Iraq invasion of 2003) two centuries later, Eaton would declare with conviction that "the defeat of one Barbary state in armed conflict would cause the others to behave more circumspectly."[21]

Eaton successfully took Derna in 1805 with barely a hundred American marines and sailors. In short order, he became the de facto governor of the eastern province, which according to his plan would serve as a platform for raising a local army to march on Tripoli, nominally under Ahmed Karamanli's command. Eaton was counting on starting a revolution against Yusuf Karamanli in Cyrenaica.[22] In fact,

> the people of Derna received Hamet [sic, Ahmed] with greater enthusiasm than the originator of the plan had dared to hope—men from every part of Tripoli began to rally to his banner. The move to depose Yusef had become a reality and it appeared that, with luck and American help, it would succeed.[23]

Madison's endorsement of Eaton's plan created two very interesting precedents—both demonstrated during the 2011 revolution—for future US military action not only in Libya, but globally: a president "engaging in hostilities abroad without a formal declaration of war," and attempted regime change in the name of a "just war."[24] Eaton felt that the stronger a US reaction, the more likely it was Yusuf Karamanli might be coaxed into voluntary exile. Local populations in the west, however—as they would do in many future conflicts—waited to see which way the winds were blowing before they committed to one side or other. As Eaton paused before implementing the final stage of his daring plan, senior navy and consular officials (led by Tobias Lear, principal Consul General of the United States to the Barbary nations of North Africa) negotiated a backdoor deal, paying $60,000 to Yusuf Karamanli to end hostilities against the United States.[25] This capitulation would, in a way, set the tone for future US and Western dealings with Libya.

Constantinople became increasingly concerned with the notoriety of the Karamanli warlords and the West's expansion into North Africa, and reoccupied Libya in 1835, determined to exercise greater military and financial control.[26] Direct Ottoman control provoked violent resistance from the larger tribal groupings, particularly the Ouled Suleiman in the Fezzan and Berber strongholds in the Jebel Nafusa. It took the Turks decades to pacify these regions, as it would the Italians after them.

By the late 1880s, with France having already grabbed most of Algeria and Tunisia, and Great Britain well ensconced in Sudan and Egypt, Libya was the only North African claim open to the Italians, who in any case had been trading regularly with the Ottoman territories for the better part of a century.[27] As the Ottoman Empire began to disintegrate rapidly during the Young Turk revolution in 1908 and the deposition of Sultan Hamid, Libyans began to despair that the Turks would not be able to save them from an Italian assault.[28] The Turks had given the Libyans a rudimentary administrative structure and had established the first inkling of unity across the territories that would become Libya. It was, however, too little, too late.

The Painful Legacy of Italian Occupation: 1911–1947

In the early 1900s, Italy, revisiting millennia-old aspirations, began to see Libya as a potential solution to its demographic and economic problems. Italian companies had spent much of the late 1800s priming the pump, so to speak, through the establishment in Libya of branches of Italian banks, Italian cultural centers, and so on. Libya thus became the object of an Italian version of Frederick Jackson Turner's frontier thesis in the United States. By creating new opportunities and lives for themselves, Italian colonists would reinvigorate a lagging economy at home while fortifying their international prestige. The formal Italian colonization started in 1911. By 1913, various coastal settlements had been established in the provinces of both Tripolitania (the west) and Cyrenaica (the east).

The history of the Italian experience in Libya remains an object lesson in the futility of outside efforts to occupy and tame the country. Stuck in their coastal bases, the Italians made glacial progress in expanding rule into the hinterlands over the course of the first four years of the formal invasion of Libya. The campaign for Tripoli was a case in point: the push began in November 1911, but months later the Italian forces were only ten miles from where they had started.[29] The Fezzan column, led by Lieutenant Colonel Antonio Miani, was sent to take the south, but wound up with hostile tribes encircling them like vultures. By 1915, the invaders had been pushed back to their coastal beachheads at Homs, Misurata, Tajoura, and Tripoli, and were forced to evacuate other posts by sea.

In the wake of the 1918 armistice after World War I, the Italians changed their tactics, leaving troublesome Cyrenaica aside to focus on pacifying the more pliable Tripolitania. General Vincenzo Garioni led a force of seventy thousand men to Libya, bragging that he would take Tripoli "within two months." He did not succeed. For some time, the western rebels were willing to make concessions just to be left alone, that is, letting the Italians keep their bases at Homs, Tripoli, and Zwara, and to claim limited authority over surrounding areas, in return for a measure of self-determination for local Libyan communities. The Italians conceded to the Tripolitanians the right to a parliament and Italian citizenship, and offered the same to the people in Cyrenaica in October 1919. Polling themselves through tribal councils, the easterners flatly rejected the Italian offer, saying dismissively they would "only tolerate Italians on the coast."[30]

The tenor of the Italian-Libyan relations turned sinister in 1922, with the rise to power of Benito Mussolini (Il Duce), who was described much as Gaddafi would be later—variations on "ruthless buffoon." Libyan tribal chiefs repeated their demands for self-rule under a Muslim leader. Italy, for its part, said that if the chiefs wanted peace, Italy would collaborate; otherwise she would assert her rights by force.[31] Mussolini signaled his intentions by appointing the savage Guiseppe Volpi governor of Libya from 1922 to 1925. Sensing a change in Italian resolve, the people in the various subregions of Libya looked for safety in numbers: the Tripolitanians sent envoys to the Senussi leader and future king, Idris, offering to recognize him as their leader in return for Cyrenaica's assistance in holding off the expected Italian onslaught. In 1922, Idris was declared the emir of Tripolitania and Cyrenaica, in absentia. He had left the country for Cairo, where he remained in exile for twenty years.[32]

Volpi underestimated the Libyan rebellion as the "work of a few troublemakers."[33] Though he was successful in putting down the Tripolitanians, he did not foresee confronting as charismatic a leader as Omar Al Mokhtar in the east. Since 1912, Al Mokhtar, a teacher of the Koran and follower of the Senussi order, had been the undisputed mastermind behind an anti-Italian desert and mountain guerrilla warfare campaign. As a means of increasing pressure on Al Mokhtar, Rudolfo Graziani, vice governor and then governor of Cyrenaica from 1926 to 1934 (aka the "Butcher of the Fezzan"), forcibly relocated nearly a hundred thousand residents of the Jebel Akhdar into concentration camps, then sealed the eastern border with barbed wire to prevent relief supplies from entering through Egypt. Graziani also deployed Eritrean mercenaries against the Libyan resistance—neither the first nor the last use of African mercenaries in a Libyan conflict.

Al Mokhtar was finally captured in an ambush in September 1931 and hanged publicly at Sollouq, at the age of about seventy-three. His last words, "We will never surrender, we win or we die," became a common rebel refrain during the 2011 uprising. Estimates are that two hundred thousand people, of a population of less than 1 million (extrapolating from the 1954 census), or nearly a quarter of the Libyan population in 1930, lost their lives as a direct result of Italian policies.[34]

The relationship between Libya and Italy currently remains contentious. Many modern Libyan writers and intellectuals think the Italians decimated indigenous Libyan culture and blame Italian persecution for xenophobia and an ingrained suspicion of central authority, which permeated Libya's relations with the outside world for decades. Others see in Italian repression the roots of creativity in resistance. Interestingly, one of the few and relatively rich outlets for Libyan cultural expression, a magazine called *Libya Al Mussawara* (*Illustrated Libya*) began as an Italian propaganda tool. The fact the Libyans did not turn on the Italians in the wake of WWII and permitted many of those who wanted to stay to do so, unmolested, has been put forth by Libyans in the wake of the 2011 revolution as evidence of a national capacity for forgiveness and reconciliation.

WWII and Independence

Large parts of Libya, particularly the eastern regions, were destroyed in World War II. At the center of a bloody back-and-forth battle between Allied and Axis forces, large parts of Benghazi were reduced to rubble. Libya was, as a whole, decimated, disunited, and dirt poor; while Tripoli was basically spared, the eastern cities were destroyed by relentless bombings (Benghazi alone suffered a thousand air raids).[35] Not only was the country physically in disarray, the lack of a central (or even effective local) administration was a major impediment to reconstruction: "Until its future had been settled and its temporary military administrations replaced by permanent government, there could be little post-war recovery," noted one historian.[36]

If there was a positive side to all the havoc wrought by the colonial powers and the collateral damage of WWII, it was the fact that the war had highlighted Libya's strategic value. Britain and the United States, in particular, wanted to maintain bases in Libya in order to protect vital sea routes leading to the Suez Canal. They found in Libya a small population still uninfected by a growing wave of Arab nationalism and grateful to be rid of the Italians, whom the Allies had forced to cede their former African colonies as part of the Paris Peace Treaties signed in February 1947. At this time, Tripolitanians favored unifying the provinces, while Cyrenaica would only accept Senussi rule; inhabitants of the far less populated Fezzan (some, at least) preferred French oversight, presumably because it would facilitate commerce with other French territories to the west and south.

In the late 1940s, there was widespread consensus within Libya on the need for eventual independence, national unity, and membership in the Arab League, but strong internal dissent about how best to achieve these ends.[37] None of the European powers, each for its own reasons, wanted a united, independent Libya. As of September 1948, the prospective mandatory powers had reached no agreement on Libyan's future. The British and the Italians, in order to ward off a UN decision unfavorable to their interests, drew up in 1949 what became known as the Bevin-Sforza Plan, named for the respective foreign ministers, proposing ten-year trusteeships of each region by its colonial squatter. The French would have the south (Fezzan); and the British, the east (Cyrenaica). Italy would take the western slice of its erstwhile Fourth Shore (Tripolitania). The Libyans were vehemently against the Bevin-Sforza Plan, and the UN dismissed the proposal shortly after it was tabled.

All parties to discussions of independence had grave concerns about how an independent Libya would support itself, as it would immediately join the ranks of the poorest countries in the world: 13 percent of local exports were scrap metal; peanuts, animal hides, and fodder came next. The average annual per capita income was about $25, illiteracy was a staggering 94 percent, and there were virtually no trained local doctors.[38] Given that oil had not yet been discovered, the country had one great untapped resource: the latent (that is, underdeveloped) skills of a small population.

In November 1949, the United Nations General Assembly voted that Libya should become an independent, united country within one year. A National Assembly composed of sixty deputies for Cyrenaica, Tripolitania, and Fezzan each was appointed through leaders in July and charged with writing a draft constitution.[39]

The assembly met for the first time in plenary session in Tripoli on November 25 and spent more than a year debating various models and precedents. The members addressed the thorny issue of the physical seat of government by naming Tripoli, Benghazi, and Sebha (the capital of Fezzan) joint seats of government, with a yearly shuffling of the official capital from one city to another.[40] The Federal Kingdom of Libya came into being on December 23, 1951, under the leadership of King Idris, who had returned from Cairo. The new government was a hereditary constitutional monarchy, with legislative authority vested in a Senate and House of Representatives. In line with this structure, the king nominated a governor for each region, with a group of forty representatives, ten of whom he appointed himself.[41]

While the process behind Libya's bid for independence was chaotic, Libyans were demonstrably proud that theirs was the first North African country to win its independence. As was the case with other states in the Mediterranean basin—Lebanon was a prime example—Libya benefited from the help of successful émigrés, many of whom returned in the 1950s and 1960s to help rebuild the country. There was a genuine desire, encouraged by optimistic returnees, to modernize Libya and to strengthen cooperation with other Arab countries and the West.

Negotiations with the West over rent for military bases began in 1954. Expecting no further discussion, the United States offered Libya $1 million a year for use of Wheelus Air Base in Tripoli. This was far less than the earlier agreement with the interim British authorities, which had paid $15 million annually.[42] US Embassy personnel explained to the Libyans that the prevailing sentiment in Congress was that "host countries" should contribute to the financial burden of defending the free world from Communism. Thus, Libya could rely on congressional "goodwill" in providing development assistance under terms of the Eisenhower Doctrine, which supported countries in staving off Communist influence.[43]

Prime Minister Mustafa Ben Halim proposed the two countries form a Libyan-American council to oversee the application of this development assistance, in line with the terms of the Eisenhower Doctrine. After receiving no response and noticing that the Egyptians had successfully played the Soviets for assistance in building such structures as the Great Aswan Dam, Ben Halim decided to follow the neighbor's example: "We arranged for rumors to circulate about all kinds of aid from the Soviet Union, and watched as the British and American embassies went into top gear confronting this new situation."[44] This elicited an angry response from the Americans, who chastised the Libyans for making such moves without prior consultation with Washington. Having caught the United States' attention, Ben Halim was able to go ahead with his proposed Libyan-American council, and US aid was forthcoming in larger amounts. Vice President Richard Nixon made an official visit to Libya in March 1957 to ensure that Libya had returned to the right path (i.e., anti-Communist).[45] Libyan-American relations improved; from 1953 to 1960, cash transfers amounted to more than $172 million, not including substantial grants of American wheat.[46]

Centuries of relative poverty and hardscrabble existence and concerns about how an independent Libya would make ends meet were suddenly overturned after the confirmation that this impoverished, underpopulated, and undeveloped country was actually rich in resources. It was as if someone on welfare had just won untold riches in the lottery. Virtually overnight, Libya was transformed from a charity case to a country feted by international companies and their governments.

The Discovery of Oil

It would seem therefore that even if the Gardens of Hesperides have faded into oblivion, some of the "golden apples" are still ripe for plucking.

GWYN WILLIAMS, *GREEN MOUNTAIN*, 1963[47]

Commercially viable quantities of oil were confirmed in Libya in 1959.[48] Standard Oil (which later became Esso Sirte and then Exxon), along with W.R. Grace and the Libyan-American Oil Company, discovered or developed most of Libya's large fields, including Mabruk and Amal. Esso built the first export terminal at Marsa el Brega (Brega port), from which the first shipment of Libyan crude departed on August 8, 1961. American independents Continental (Conoco), Marathon, Hess, and Bunker Hunt were among twelve American companies awarded sixty concessions in 1957. By 1969, American companies were producing a full 90 percent of Libyan oil.

In the late 1970s, Esso started to train Libya's first generation of scientists, managers, and technocrats, an effort that would have far-reaching consequences for US-Libya relations. Its accelerated training program focused on grooming professionals from the key oil logistics towns of Brega, Ajdabia, Jalo, and Misurata to take over the maintenance and operation jobs initially staffed by Americans. Further, Esso built a local operations training center to extend Libya's capacity to provide its own technical training. By the early 1980s, more than two hundred sixty Libyans had benefited from Esso-backed fellowships for graduate training abroad.[49]

The new eastern oil economy had immediate significance: it consolidated control within the hands of a new bourgeoisie, based in the east, and it increased the interest of the West in Libya's potential as a provider of high-quality sweet crude, and as a small but potentially lucrative market for consumables, especially cars and electronics. The oil economy provoked massive migrations of people from rural areas to the city seeking jobs. The discovery of hydrocarbons was a boon for those with connections, but created considerable pain for others, as new immigrants from the countryside competed for a limited number of unskilled job opportunities.

The popular response to the resulting disruption was often anger, not only at the foreigners but at those who had let them in. People saw King Idris as an accomplice of the West and therefore of Israel, and as a projection of a newly enriched minority which monopolized revenues drawn from the oil companies. Sadiq Neihoum (the author of the black dog parable) wrote fiery columns in the popular Benghazi paper *al Haqiqa* (*The Truth*) in June 1969, lambasting American materialism:

> Twentieth century culture . . . is a poison which is responsible for the development of both economic and mechanical culture in the United States, and the export to other countries of nuclear weapons and companies of obscene wealth.[50]

Neihoum took further aim at religious hypocrisy, materialism, and a blind dependence on technology, themes that would become Gaddafi's perennial favorites. Many Libyans assumed Neihoum was the source of some ideas expressed much less articulately in Gaddafi's infamous *The Green Book*, in particular, the concept of creating a "Third Way" between capitalism and communism.

Because of its disruptive social impact, the discovery of oil caused the three existing Libyan provinces to decide they would benefit economically under one administration rather than three. In 1963, the federal constitution was quietly revised to abolish the regional governments and include all into the Kingdom of Libya (1963–1969). For a time, King Idris was engaged in state affairs, assisted by Tripolitanian technocrats and the Senussi family itself.[51]

Libya in 1951 was quite different from the Libya of 2010–2011. The role of tribes and, in general, regional solidarity and cohesiveness was far greater. Libyans did not travel widely, and families stayed together. Socially, the country was highly conservative, particularly in the interior, where the Bedouin followed an austere existence, and many still believed in black magic. At the same time, a free flow of people and ideas across the Egyptian border made for a highly fluid and in some ways even permissive subculture, particularly along the coast. In the mid- to late 1960s, Benghazi, like Alexandria and parts of Cairo, was a center for Italian fashion, where women of means dressed in miniskirts and people gathered at night in noisy cafés.[52]

Idris's Kingdom of Libya was not by any means a paragon of virtue. The atmosphere became one of clientelism on a grand scale. While Idris himself lived an ascetic lifestyle, for others, wealth was ensured by access to the king and tribal connections. Ministers, traders, and their acolytes made fortunes, while large segments of the population remained extremely poor.

Free at last from foreign control, Benghazi reasserted itself as the capital of Libyan letters and produced a number of talented intellectuals and writers, including—in addition to Sadiq Neihoum—Mohammed Khalifa Telissi, Miftah Moubarak, Mohammed Hammi, Wahbi Bouri, Kamel Maghur, and others. Many of the intelligentsia also turned their pens into swords, exposing the aforementioned social and political ills.

The Libyan-US relationship deepened in the 1960s with clarification of Libya's position vis-à-vis the Soviet Union, and a feeling on the part of many in the Idris government that the United States was in the best position to guarantee Libya's security, particularly given increasing presence of the big oil companies. At the same time, more and more Libyan citizens (many of whom would have some influence in Gaddafi's Libya) increasingly distrusted the United States and resented its extensive presence in significant aspects of Libyan internal and external affairs, and its support for Israel. This distrust would find a new voice in a twenty-seven-year-old officer in the Libyan army, who was about to change the course of Libyan history.

Gaddafi's 1969 Coup

Your armed forces have toppled the reactionary, backward and corrupt regime. With one strike your heroic Army has toppled idols and destroyed them in one of Providence's fateful moments. As of now Libya shall be free and sovereign, a republic under the name of the Libyan Arab Republic. No oppressed, or deceived or wronged, no master and no slave; but free brothers in a society over which, God willing, shall flutter the banner of brotherhood and equality.

MUAMMAR GADDAFI, BENGHAZI RADIO, 6:30 A.M., SEPTEMBER 1, 1969[53]

The mechanics of Gaddafi's September 1, 1969, bloodless coup remain obscure. Many Libyans still believe it was the work of the CIA and British Intelligence—still concerned by Soviet-Libya contacts—in conjunction with Idris's decidedly hands-off, even disdainful, approach to governing his own country. Indeed, at the time of the coup, Idris was sojourning at a health resort in Turkey.

In many ways, Gaddafi in 1969 was an extremely unlikely potential head of state. He was not well educated, was not from the commercial elite or a senior army officer, and had not served in any government position. He had received a highly accelerated but basic primary education in village schools from Sirte to Sebha, and graduated from the Royal Libyan Military Academy in Benghazi in 1965. Yet, in circumstances that also remain obscure, he was selected for a four-and-a-half-month elite military training course in Britain,[54] and managed to secure an audience with Egyptian president Gamal Abdel Nasser en route back to Libya[55] (which led others to speculate that he, Nasser, was involved or at least had been forewarned of Gaddafi's plans).[56]

Many believe Gaddafi, who was only twenty-seven on the day the Revolutionary Command Council took power,[57] benefited from the Keystone Kops atmosphere engendered by multiple planned putsches; the most promising was to have been orchestrated by Libyan Army commander Abdelaziz Shalhi and set for September 5. The fact that Gaddafi's coup of September 4 was swift and bloodless was at least partly due to ambiguity in King Idris's status as leader. (He had resigned several times previously, most recently on August 4, 1969—at each step, his cabinet and the people of Cyrenaica "refused" his motion.) Other weaknesses included deep resentment at widespread government corruption, and the incompetence of Idris's two praetorian guards, CYDEF [Cyrenaican Defense Forces] and TYDEF [Tripoli Defense Forces], staffed by tribes loyal to the Senussia.)

Attributing Gaddafi's ascendancy solely to the above factors is likely a mistake. Musa Kusa, who became Gaddafi's head of intelligence more than a decade later,[58] claims in a 1978 master's thesis that Gaddafi had begun methodically planning his coup more than eight years before its execution. Gaddafi had spent years identifying potential allies, particularly while living in Misurata from 1962 to 1963, pushed those he trusted into military training, and further cultivated his closest partners (the future Revolutionary Command Council): "[Gaddafi] studied all the weak points in the old regime and formulated new connections between his movement and the Libyan university students. In addition, he built his own political ideology and set forth the political principles of the country."[59]

In 1970, *The Atlantic* magazine said of the coup, "It's the kind of planning operation that would have got a double A-plus at Fort Leavenworth."[60]

CHAPTER 2

Threats and Adaptations

☾

Although the CIA had accreted a thick file on Gaddafi, few profiles of the man have emerged to explain the psychology behind his behavior. Ronald Reagan called him the "mad dog of the Middle East"; Sadat called him "the wild man of the Middle East"[1] Others called him much worse. Many assumed he was simply unstable—yet a man who survived for forty-two years as ruler of a fractious nation cannot be dismissed so easily.

Almost from the moment he usurped Idris's place, Gaddafi had to watch his back. Within a few months, Abdullah bin Abid nicknamed the "Black Prince," a member of the Senussi clan, mounted a countercoup from Chad. This effort was apparently something of a farce, and the perpetrators were quickly neutralized. More seriously, the British MI6—far more concerned with Gaddafi's Soviet sympathies than were the Americans—began plotting what, according to Stephen Dorril's history of the MI6, was an almost equally ill-effected British plan to kill Gaddafi and return Idris to the throne, using a mixture of French and Belgian mercenaries (a ruse to deflect attention from the British).[2] The mercenaries were to break into a Tripoli prison, free the prisoners using plastic explosives procured in Eastern Europe and smuggled into Italy, and employ them to help stage the coup. The mission was scuttled after the Yugoslavian government discovered the plot and confiscated the weapons. The Americans ordered the British to stand down, or they would tell the Libyans and the Italians of the plot.[3]

Perhaps Gaddafi was lucky that these early attempts were soft; they alerted him to the need for vigilance. In an effort to identify a place of comfort—or safety—internally, politically, and in the international sphere, Gaddafi found he had to periodically reinvent himself and hone his coercive powers. Yet, none of these reinventions solved the core problems of ruling Libya and probably confirmed in his mind the notion that ad hoc solutions to government were somehow safer than formal institutions like the Libyan army, which was perpetually the object of his mistrust. Each stage in the political career of Muammar Gaddafi was ultimately an exercise in buying time until the inevitable failure of the current stratagem.

If the 1970s were a period for experimentation and discovering what worked and what didn't, the 1980s were one of churlish intolerance, as Gaddafi cracked down on a population he expected to be more appreciative of his efforts. In the 1990s, it was the people's turn: stymied by international sanctions, Gaddafi found himself locked in a room of snakes—a determined Islamist opposition was effectively in an open war with Gaddafi; and a recalcitrant inner circle was thoroughly tired of the stigma and restrictions resulting from Gaddafi's policies.

Gaddafi's Deck

The constant quest to be the center of attention regardless of the cost explains much of the extreme variance in Gaddafi's policies, as well as his personal behavior. Though clearly an intelligent man, Gaddafi's rougher edges, such as his tendency to extreme, disjointed verbosity and his less than fluid writing style, have been attributed to his lack of formal education. The well-known Libyan writer Ahmed Ibrahim Fagih, who held a number of cultural posts in the Gaddafi leadership, called Gaddafi's mind-set one of "high-school ideas" linked to an accelerated transition at an early age from an essentially illiterate Bedouin child to army conscript: "Gaddafi had most of his primary school education fast-tracked in two years—while the man was not unintelligent, there was no time for intellectual development."[4] US ambassador David Mack, posted to Libya as a vice consul in the early 1970s, confirms Fagih's assessment: "There was an enormous gap between his ideas (increasingly fantasies) and reality—he was young and acted as many young people do, of course with some differences."[5]

Yet Gaddafi also possessed what might be called "selective emotional intelligence." His ability to read the motives and weaknesses of others was among his greatest assets. In his 2012, 585 page exposé on Gaddafi's inner circle, *Ašḫāṣ ḫawl al-Qaḏḏāfī* (*The People Around Gaddafi*) Abdelrahman Shalgam, Gaddafi's former foreign minister and ambassador to the UN, says that Gaddafi had "mastered the art of controlling people, and possessed an exceptional ability to discern people's underlying natures, and dissect their psychologies, and probe their sensitivities."[6] (Shalgam was one of the first of Gaddafi's diplomatic circle to defect.)

Within a decade of taking power, Gaddafi had identified a fundamental set of behavioral strategies that served to keep him safely in power. A core strategy was to sow confusion—the idea that for every issue there needed to be multiple competing interests, none of which was absolute. This applied to associates, to relationships with other countries, to ministries, and even to his immediate family—whom he trusted no more than any other constituency not to dominate or attempt to harm his interests. A related successful strategy was to impute suspicion to others by selectively bestowing favors or taking away privileges. For example, he might issue offers of amnesty to dissident expatriates. If three returned home, two would be imprisoned or killed, while the third would be given a warm welcome and left to his own devices. The result would draw negative attention to the survivor, who would then be suspected of selling out the others.[7]

Stagecraft was another useful tool. Gaddafi was a master of props and timing. He made frequent, theatrical use of his traveling tent and the strategic placement of animals. Goats, for example, would occasionally wander in to high-level meetings with his Western interlocutors. This talent for creating perfectly staged red herrings would play a great role in attracting, repelling, and confusing his own people as well as Westerners. While he was not always original in method, his delivery and his sense for the dramatic were almost unparalleled and are essential to understanding how he managed to stay in power for forty-two years.

Gaddafi's capriciousness and brutality were not, to use one of his favorite words, "latent," nor did they develop slowly and emerge later in his reign. Dr. Fatima Hamrouche, interim minister of health in the Transitional Government, recounted how Gaddafi just after the coup imprisoned her father, one of three senior Libyan judges, for three and a half years. The judge had refused to deliver a stiff penalty on a young soldier who had committed a minor offense, which Gaddafi had taken personally.[8]

Ahmed Al-Zubeir Al Senussi, who became the figurehead of a pro-Benghazi autonomy movement, was one of the longest-held political prisoners in the world, after being imprisoned by Gaddafi in 1970 following a failed countercoup.[9] (The first substantial wave of arrests of those considered to be against the 1969 revolution occurred in 1973.)[10]

In the early years, however, Gaddafi appeared to be more the earnest, naive revolutionary than the rambling, eccentric autocrat of later years, but he and various key members of the Revolutionary Command Council (RCC) often appeared to be wildly out of touch. To illustrate the point, when King Khalid bin Abdulaziz of Saudi Arabia paid a courtesy visit to Col. Gaddafi on September 1, 1979, the tenth anniversary of his revolution, Abdelsalam Al Jelloud (Prime Minister until 1977) asked Ghazi abdel Rahman Al Qasibi, a Saudi court adviser, why Sudan's leader, Jafar el Nimeri, was not responding to Libya's diplomatic initiatives. Al Qasibi had to remind his interlocutors that they had tried to overthrow him in a violent coup a short time before. "But we apologized," said Jelloud, apparently in earnest, "Isn't that sufficient for them?" Al Qasibi came to the conclusion that Jelloud, like Gaddafi, was not playing with a full deck.[11]

Those who closely observed Gaddafi's behavior insisted that clinical pathologies were at the root of his actions. Ahmed Ibrahim Fagih believes Gaddafi was a sociopath, someone for whom the ends are all-important and others' lives are irrelevant. Combined with his sense of impunity was a countervailing paranoia and fear of death. "There is no normal logic in assessing Gaddafi's behavior," Fagih says. "Everything is seen through a prism of paranoia."[12] Wayne White, former deputy director of the US State Department's Middle East/South Asia Intelligence Office, described Gaddafi as having "manic-depressive" tendencies: a brash or instantaneous reaction to either insult or perceived opportunity would be followed by a long period of brooding, fear, and/or regret. As White put it, "If Gaddafi had been forced to take a standard desk job, he would have certainly needed a good therapist."[13]

As he aged, Gaddafi's thoughts appeared to have an increasingly morbid, fetishlike quality. A Wikileaks cable recounted Gaddafi's strange fascination with the sea and his dislike of flying over the ocean (Gaddafi would schedule his flights in order to minimize any time over large bodies of water).[14] Gaddafi seemed to share with Al Qaeda leadership a particular fascination with plane crashes—those he caused, and perhaps one he feared would happen to him.

Gaddafi's attributes—his obsessive need for attention, to have the last word, to assign blame to others, and to be proven correct—are critical to understanding, albeit imperfectly, some of Gaddafi's behaviors. The concept of linkage, which one could define as the necessity to mitigate every accusation or slight with a countervailing claim, threat, or insult, as we will see, was present in almost every dealing with the West. There was certainly no shortage of incidents in which Gaddafi's urge to take the stage trumped reason or morality. Underlying and perhaps accentuating Gaddafi's narcissism were issues of sexual identity, perhaps associated with a fixation on fashion with a feminine touch. As Ronald Reagan famously quipped, "[Gaddafi] can check out Nancy's [the First Lady] closet anytime."[15]

Gaddafi seemed to be an unhappy man. In an interview after the revolution, interim Prime Minister Mahmoud Jibril speculated that Gaddafi lived obsessing about the manner and timing of his own death, just like the Sultan of Sadiq Neihoum's fable quoted in the Introduction:[16] the parallel is presumably not an accident, given that Neihoum knew Gaddafi quite well.

The Early Years, 1969–1975

Gaddafi began his four-decade reign with a five-year period of ruthless experimentation. He purged many of those he had himself recruited to stage the revolution because he feared they were disloyal, precluded the threat of organized rebellion by gerrymandering Libya's administrative units to weaken tribal leadership, and enriched himself and his coterie by appropriating assets of rich traders from the now-defunct Senussi monarchy.[17] In the path to absolute power, the scenario was not a new one.

From 1969 to 1974, Gaddafi ostensibly ruled as part of a junta. There had been about seventy Free Officers (a term borrowed from Nasser's own revolution) behind the coup itself, twelve of whom composed the Revolutionary Command Council (RCC). In addition to Gaddafi, the eleven others were Abdelsalam Al Jelloud, Omar El Muhayshi, Mohammed Megaryaf, Bechir Hawwadi, Muktar Abdullah al Gerwy, Awad Ali Hamza, Mohammed Nejm, Abdelmonem El Houni, Khouildi El Hamidi, Mustapha El Harroubi, and Abu Bakr Younes. This group comprised a varied group of hardliners, conciliators, and pragmatists. Those who did not fall in line with Gaddafi's wishes did not last long, however. The only names that reappear after the 1980s are the three whom Gaddafi perceived to be most loyal—Abdelmonem El Houni, Abu Bakr Younes, and Abdelsalam Al Jelloud.

Just as he eliminated competition with the RCC, Gaddafi moved to contain or co-opt both religious and tribal authority. His first motions toward Libya's religious leaders, or ulema, were conciliatory. By the late 1970s, however, his attitude changed. He did not hesitate to execute imams who appeared to challenge his authority. He was particularly harsh with respect to the Muslim Brotherhood, the prototypical Islamist party founded by Hassan al Banna in 1928, and active followers of the Senussia, pursuing a combination of threats, "re-education" and, failing these, disappearances.[18] In order to channel, mold, and project his own version of Islam (and the notion of his rule being somehow divinely sanctioned), Gaddafi created the Islamic Call Society (Jam'iyat ad'Da'wa al-Islamiya), whose ostensible function was to spread Islam throughout Africa, but which was more of an all-around propaganda tool and mechanism for outing domestic religious opponents, whom he referred to as zanadiq, or "heretics."[19]

Regionally, Gaddafi focused his efforts on trying to convince the Arab states to support his own vision of Arab unity, along the model pursued by Egyptian president Gamal Abdel Nasser, beloved throughout the Arab world for euphemistically "socking it to" the West, by nationalizing the Suez Canal in 1957. Egypt, Syria, and the Sudan agreed to the outlines of what would be a series of mix-and-match political associations, called *ittihad al jumhuriyyat al arabiyya* (the Union of Arab Republics), in April 1971. The ultimately unviable association existed in some form from 1972 to 1977.[20] In 1971, Tunisia's ruler Habib Bourguiba openly mocked Gaddafi for publicly proposing a political merger between Tunisia and Libya with himself at the head.[21] One after another, the Arab leaders came to resent the upstart, thinking his ideas were at best nutty, at worst, dangerous.

Yet for all the purges and political maneuvering, the first five years of Gaddafi's revolution in Libya were a far cry from the brutal, regressive state yet to come. Gaddafi spent more money in the first few years of the revolution on national education and health care than King Idris ever had, building new hospitals and clinics, opening medical schools in Benghazi and Tripoli, and engaging foreign development consultants. Students and doctors trained abroad at government expense.[22] Gaddafi mandated education for all male and female children, and committed to provide basic health care for all.[23] Within a generation, Libya had virtually eliminated illiteracy, while creating a framework for basic, national, free health care.[24] Sheikh Zayed, founder and ruler of the United Arab Emirates, came to Benghazi for an eye operation in the early 1970s—itself a sign of Libya's progress—and was widely quoted in later years, perhaps apocryphally, and then with irony, given the reversed fortunes of the two cities, as saying, "Someday . . . Dubai will be like this [Benghazi]." While Gaddafi managed within a reasonably short time to educate many of his citizens to a level of basic literacy—and increase life expectancy by 20+ years—this achievement should be measured against what he did *not* do, given the vast resources at the regime's disposal and the fact that within twenty years of his assumption of rule, more than 20 percent of the population would be either below international development institutions' measures of poverty, or unemployed, or both.[25]

In these early years, Gaddafi and the RCC appeared committed to righting the social inequities that had come into relief during the monarchy period.[26] Again following Nasser's example, Gaddafi ordered a series of full and partial nationalizations, beginning with the banking and insurance sectors, then moving into the domestic marketing activities of foreign oil companies and the insurance companies.[27] In 1971, he created a series of state-run supermarkets, administered by the national supply company (NASCO). Within ten years, most of Libyans' basic food staples came from these Soviet-style cooperatives.

During this period, he laid the groundwork for the social experiments to come. On January 14, 1971, Gaddafi delivered a speech at the coastal town of Zawiya, twenty-eight miles west of Tripoli, outlining a system of popular committees and congresses, channels through which he envisioned mobilizing the people to advance the goals of his revolution.[28]

Also in 1971, Gaddafi swapped his earlier conception of a popular congress for a single revolutionary party, the Arab Socialist Union (ASU), modeled after Nasser's institution of the same name. The main purpose of the ASU was to dismantle tribal influence and discredit and remove the old monarchist elites.[29] Gaddafi assigned RCC member Abu Bakr Younes to oversee the militarization of high schools and universities, as well as the formation of female military cadres.[30] The ASU clashed with popular apathy and was disbanded in 1976.[31] Conflicts with the Libyan ulema (religious scholars) and Muslim Brotherhood grew, in line with the Brotherhood's influence in Egypt (a radical offshoot of the Muslim Brotherhood assassinated Egyptian president Anwar Sadat in 1981).

In a landmark speech delivered in the main square of the town of Zwara in April 1973, Gaddafi heralded the coming of a Libyan cultural-popular revolution based on something he called the Third Universal Theory, an alternative to capitalism and Marxism.[32] In the five-point program expressing this theory, particularly jarring (and unremarked) were points two and five, which read, respectively:

> All feebleminded individuals must be weeded out of society by taking appropriate measures toward perverts and deviates. . . . A cultural revolution must be staged, to rid Libya of all imported poisonous ideas and to fuse the people's genuine moral and material potentialities.[33]

Even as Gaddafi experimented with various ideological strands, Libya was in the throes of a major economic boom. Oil money was now flowing into the country at an amazing rate, and those who had invested in building up local businesses were making money hand over fist: "Our sales were increasing exponentially," said Omar Benhalim, who, then in his early twenties, was managing divisions of his father's import business. "It was amazing, there seemed to be no limit to growth, and yet the writing was on the wall, in Gaddafi's speeches and behavior. We knew things could not continue. It was just a matter of time. Many who had money to spare sent it overseas, in anticipation of an exit." Benhalim recounts how one day in 1975, just after lunch, he returned to the company showroom to find soldiers standing out front—they remained for a few months, waiting and watching, until the family was told that their services were no longer needed. Within a year Benhalim and many in similar positions had become part of the growing Libyan diaspora.[34]

Gaddafi was clearly disturbed, at least in the early years, by his inability to connect with the people whose interests he insisted he held dear. As the people's apathy became more obvious, Gaddafi hedged his bets by building up his security forces, including the *jihaz al aman al dakhili* (internal security), the Revolutionary Committees, the Jamahiriya Guard, and the *haras as-shaabi* (youth guard). Presumably, he reasoned that if his people did not appreciate the innate appeal of his ideas, coercion would work just as well.

The Gloves Come Off, 1975

Although during the first five years of the revolution Gaddafi had addressed health care, education, and some economic issues, his early initiatives were not enough to stave off popular unrest. The pan-Arab ideology that had instilled such passion in the young Gaddafi had already begun to seem a cruel joke by the time of Nasser's death in 1970, all the more after the Egyptians' disastrous loss of the Sinai Peninsula to the Israelis in the Six-Day War in 1967. The first organized anti-Gaddafi demonstrations occurred in Benghazi in March 1975, and in the same year there were significant protests by Libyan students.[35]

The real shocker for Gaddafi in 1975, and perhaps the most seminal event in terms of what it portended, was an attempted coup from within his own circle. Omar El Muhayshi and Bechir Hawwadi led the coup, supported by other more technocratic members of the RCC. Having now witnessed five full years of increasingly bizarre rulings, many of Gaddafi's former core supporters united against what appeared even then to be a systematic dismantling of the state apparatuses key to efficient economic management.[36] In the wake of the attempt, Abdelmonem El Houni, lightly implicated, escaped to Cairo, from where he directed aspects of the Libyan opposition in Egypt for many years, before Gaddafi "forgave" and invited him back. Originally assigned by Gaddafi to oversee the security and administration of the eastern regions, Mohammed Megaryaf was sidelined and died in a suspicious car accident in 1972. Omar El Muhayshi managed to escape to Morocco, but was ultimately extradited to Libya and killed. Khouildi El Hamidi and Abu Bakr Younes (known for his "unconditional and unswervable devotion" to Gaddafi[37]), Mustapha El Harroubi, and Abdelsalam Al Jelloud were the only "surviving" members of the RCC.

In 1976, continued popular disinterest in Gaddafi's political platform led the self-styled "adviser, guide, and leader" to create a more nefarious organization. Members of the Revolutionary Committees were essentially cadres of well-paid informants, enforcers, spies, and publicists, combined into one. The first Revolutionary Committee was formed at Al Fateh University on April 11, 1976, though Gaddafi claimed to have developed the concept over the previous three years.[38] Suddenly, a person could not expect any kind of advancement or status within Libya, or avoid attracting attention, if he were not affiliated with or seen to be cooperating actively with the committees.[39] By 1985, core Revolutionary Committee members (all well vetted for their ideological verve) were estimated to number three thousand to four thousand.[40] The intrusiveness of the Revolutionary Committees further alienated the people from their wayward leader.

In early April 1976, the nucleus of what would become the Revolutionary Committees initiated a program of persecution against dissidents, mostly students, some who had recently returned from abroad and some who had (or had not) been part of the public protests the year before.[41] Many were rounded up, held, and executed without trial. Some were hung within the universities or forced to beg for their lives on live television before being executed. These student hangings were repeated almost annually for several years, and symbolized Gaddafi's most capricious, violent side for decades.

By 1978, Gaddafi had subjugated nearly all commercial activity to state control. His policy of *Beit li sakinihi* (the house for he who lives in it) created a new generation of squatter-nonowners, displaced families, and led to cloudy deeds of ownership, problems that still plague Libya.

In March 1979, Gaddafi effectively banned private ownership, forcing Libyan citizens to turn in their liquid assets to the Central Bank for a set (much lower) sum. This was the final stage of a systematic asset- and land-grab, which transferred wealth from those with skills to those offering fealty. Though these moves were, of course, highly unpopular among those whose assets were confiscated, those lower down on the socioeconomic scale were either "in favor" or, at least, did not feel strongly enough to object. Whatever the United States might have done, directly or indirectly, to hasten the fall of King Idris, and however much it wanted to see Gaddafi as an anti-Communist, within a short period of time, it came to see his actions as a potential threat.[42]

Gaddafi published his largely incoherent governing manifesto, *The Green Book*, in 1977. Partly a further exposition of the Third Universal Theory, the work was a framework for "participatory government" devoid of political parties. According to Gaddafi, Democracy—according to the Western interpretation—did not truly express the will of the people, as elections were won via majority rule. One of his favorite examples: if 51 percent of the people want to do one thing, and 49 percent another, the latter's desires would be subverted to the former. Gaddafi's solution to this problem was a completely Byzantine structure of committees and congresses.

The fundamental unit of his three-tiered system was the Basic People's Congress (BPC). BPCs, numbering over four hundred in 2009, were regionally anchored consultative units that were to propose legislation and draft local budgets, which were then passed up to higher-level committees for review. At the top of the system was the General People's Congress (superficially resembling a Western parliament), whose committee heads, People's Secretaries, collectively served in something resembling a cabinet, with the secretaries in charge of "ministries." Those who spent much time analyzing how this system was supposed to work were missing the point: most consequential decisions were left outside the purview of the structure under Gaddafi's control. This was all an elaborate subterfuge to detract attention from himself and sow confusion throughout the rest of Libyan society.

Revolutionary Foreign Policy

Even after the failure of his initial forays into quasi-political unions with neighboring Arab states, Gaddafi continued to hunger for influence on the international stage. So he began projecting revolutionary ambitions beyond Libya.

The bulk of Gaddafi's foreign adventures were poorly conceived and ill-advised. Sometime in 1972, Gaddafi had befriended fellow Nasser worshipper and sociopath Idi Amin Dada, then newly installed as president of Uganda. Gaddafi later came to Amin's assistance when Tanzania invaded Uganda in 1979, itself in response to Amin's disorganized attempt to forcibly seize part of northern Tanzania. Gaddafi sent two thousand completely unprepared and lightly trained Libyan troops to Amin's aid. Speaking no Swahili, many of them became lost or were forced by a loose contingent of Tanzanian soldiers into adjacent swamps where they were picked off one by one or eaten by crocodiles.[43]

In the late 1970s and 1980s, Gaddafi backed numerous insurgencies and independence movements in Angola, Niger, Guinea-Bissau, Mozambique, Ireland, Namibia, South Africa, Cape Verde, Liberia, Algeria, and Zimbabwe.[44] A Libyan-backed coup against Nigerian president Seyni Kountché was foiled by the Nigerian government in 1976.

Gaddafi's longest and most expensive foreign campaign was the invasion of his impoverished southern neighbor, Chad, in 1973. Gaddafi made it very clear he considered Chad little more than an extension of Libya. He set his sights early on annexing the Aouzou strip, a one-hundred-mile area straddling the never formally ratified, six-hundred-mile-long Chad-Libyan frontier, via an alliance with the Transitional National Unity government of Goukouni Oueddei. The Libya-Chad border was, to some extent, fair game for negotiation, the result of a hastily executed, never ratified treaty between the French and Italians in 1935. After absorbing the Aouzou strip, Gaddafi effectively annexed the northern half of Chad, which Libya managed to hold, weakly, until the mid-1980s. The situation deteriorated in the 1980s, when the Libyan army failed to pursue and eliminate rebel forces led by French-backed rebel leader Hissène Habré, who forced Libya out of Chad in 1987.[45] While heavily armed, the Libyan forces were abjectly unmotivated. Many veterans of the Chad campaigns would say they had no idea why they were there, whom they were fighting, or why. Ali Abusha'ala, a 27-year-old prisoner of war in 1986, recounts how the other side (the Chadians) would send the Libyans notes saying "they really did not want to kill us, they just wanted us to go back to our country, because the war was a lost cause."[46] Gaddafi himself seemed impervious to the losses and may have used the conflict to purposefully wipe out a generation of senior generals whom he distrusted intensely. Many of these men were from the Eastern cities of Al Beida, Derna, Al Marj, etc.

Not only was Chad a dismal failure, as with many of Gaddafi's foreign gambits, it was enormously costly, both in monetary terms and in Gaddafi's loss of credibility with his own people. Between 1973 and 1994, Libya spent an estimated $23 billion on its southern campaigns[47] and deployed more than fifteen thousand poorly trained troops (of which, between a third and a half were lost). Libya lost a significant amount of military hardware in the process and acquired the stigma of having used chemical weapons in battle.[48] While Gaddafi may have used the war with Chad as an excuse to purge some of his internal opponents, he created many new ones in the process. Many disaffected veterans of the Libyan campaign were easily recruited by foreign agencies to work against the Libyan regime in the following years.

Yet prolific as Gaddafi was in his warmongering, much of his global notoriety came from his evolving and worsening relationship with the United States, effected initially through support for various proxy terror groups and harassment of US commercial interests in-country. Gaddafi had been both fascinated and repulsed by the superpower from the start. The United States had supported King Idris's hated monarchy and was an ally of Israel. However, Gaddafi's dislike of the United States was not just ideological, but also personal. Gaddafi loved to tell, perhaps apocryphally, how he was denied entrance to Wheelus Base by an American GI, and claimed this was a seminal event in his political consciousness.

Once in power, Gaddafi demanded that the US and UK cede their Libyan bases. Having little choice, the US agreed to a low-key handover ceremony on June 11, 1970, with the proviso that there be no crowds and no media. Gaddafi, of course, brought crowds and media.[49] On the receiving end of increasing unpleasantness, and unable to convert Gaddafi to an ally against Communism, the United States removed its ambassador, Joseph Palmer II, in late 1972.

Though tensions rose steadily, commercial interests kept the relationship alive for another seven years. The United States was willing to separate politics from trade to some extent, so long as Libya kept pumping oil for the US market and numerous US-owned multinational corporations could do business there. This relationship was transformed after the 1973 Arab oil embargo. Flexing its muscles in the anti-imperialist struggle that followed the Yom Kippur War, Libya nationalized Hunt Oil and 51 percent of Armand Hammer's Occidental Petroleum, while Libyan diplomats sought unsuccessfully to convince the Saudis to cut off oil shipments to the US.[50] By manipulating the oil companies in Libya, Gaddafi determined the tone of US-Libya relations for decades to come, emulating the earlier strategy of his idol Nasser who nationalized the Suez Canal in 1956. Many analysts have traced Gaddafi's long antagonism toward the West and an ineluctable collision course with the US to this period.[51]

Besides expanding his international profile, Gaddafi was intent on increasing the share of oil revenues that went to the Libyan government. Agreeing with objections voiced a decade earlier by the monarchy's oil ministers, Gaddafi thought the West had been undervaluing Libya's high-quality, sweet crude. Moreover, unlike Persian Gulf crude, Libya's resources did not have to transit the volatile straits of Hormuz and the Red Sea, and were closer to Europe and the US. By shaking down companies like Occidental, an independent operator that relied on Libya for the bulk of its production, Gaddafi successfully broke the global universally accepted fifty-fifty profit split and posted-price system, according to which the large, mostly American oil companies had long bought and sold much of Middle East oil. In the words of Columbia Law professor Michael Graetz, an energy policy expert, "Our problems started with Muammar al-Qaddafi. Before he came along, OPEC (the Organization of Petroleum Exporting Countries) had been an ineffectual and unimportant oil cartel."[52]

Despite—and perhaps because of—Gaddafi's demonstrated ability to affect US global interests, the US chose to treat Gaddafi as if he did not matter. Perhaps its true feeling was that he *should* not matter. Thus, a strange parody of the story of David and Goliath played out, as Gaddafi attempted to goad the US into acknowledging his relevance through entreaties, threats, and then terrorist actions. For the most part, US presidents saw Gaddafi as a nuisance. For whatever reason, Gaddafi got under Ronald Reagan's skin, and the two engaged in an odd war of colorful insults, which while absurd, had far-reaching consequences. Gaddafi's flamboyant "mad dictator" persona and Reagan's demonization of the Libyan strongman seeped into the American consciousness through comedy sketches and works of popular fiction, notably the thriller *The Fifth Horseman*, in which Gaddafi holds the US hostage by smuggling a three-megaton H-bomb into New York in a shipping container.[53]

Life imitated art, and relations swiftly deteriorated. In 1977, the Pentagon put Libya on a list of potential US enemies. Two years later, the embassy chancery in Tripoli was attacked and burned by an angry Libyan mob.[54] American Chargé William Eagleton departed shortly thereafter. In May 1980, President Reagan pulled all remaining US officials from Libya and called for US oil companies to repatriate their employees.[55] Diplomatic ties were officially severed in 1981. The following year, Reagan banned imports of Libyan oil to the US and blocked all exports from the US except for food and medicine. This included, notably, eight Lockheed C130 transports and two Boeing 727-400s purchased by Libya in the early 1970s.

Yet in spite of all the recriminations and theatrics, the US and Libya were tied to each other by common economic interests that neither was willing to forgo. For the Libyans, American technology and expertise (particularly in the oil sector) were virtually irreplaceable. The US found Libyan high-quality, sweet crude an attractive alternative to politically risky, lower-quality oil from the Persian Gulf. US imports from Libya rose from $216 million in 1973 to $2.2 billion in 1976. In 1977, the US was Libya's largest trade partner, running a $3.5 billion trade deficit with the Libyans. In short, according to Ronald Bruce St. John,

> Bilateral economic ties were shaped in large part by mutual economic inertia, but political dialogue was determined by forces external to that relationship. Due to this esteem for American power and prestige, Qaddafi often betrayed a need for U.S. recognition of his position and importance.[56]

Brutality, Incorporated, 1980s

Within fifteen years of Gaddafi's coup, Libya had morphed into a full-blown totalitarian state. The experimental period of incremental social improvement had come to an end, and now Gaddafi's monopoly over power was secured more through fear than patronage. Some Libyans who lived through this period described it as the point at which Gaddafi had given up on his people and declared war on them.

The fabric of Libyan society was beginning to strain under Gaddafi's repression and paranoia. Rifts were widening between those who were members of the Revolutionary Committees and those who weren't. Gaddafi's influence was becoming increasingly pervasive, reaching into homes and families, as the committees recruited ordinary people to spy on their relatives. Anecdotally, by the mid-1980s, an estimated 10 percent of the population had been incorporated through the Revolutionary Committees into a web of informants that frequently spied and reported on family members and each other.

Cracking down on his own people was not enough. Libyans abroad became targets as well. In 1980, Gaddafi launched the infamous "stray dogs campaign," designed to neutralize and make an example of dissident expatriates. This move was analogous to, and perhaps inspired by, the efforts of Iranian leader Ayatollah Khomeini to hunt down former senior officials in the Shah's service. Gaddafi's agents shot influential Libyan dissident Abdel Jalil Aref in a Roman café. Muhammed Mustafa Ramadan, an announcer with the Voice of London, was gunned down after leaving a mosque after Friday prayers. Others were assassinated in Athens, Berlin, and Los Angeles. Gaddafi's aim was to prove that he could get to the opposition members, wherever they were.[57] Yet this wave of state-supported terror was instrumental in the formation of what became one of the longest-lived opposition movements, the National Front for the Salvation of Libya, created by Mohammed Megaryaf in October 1981.

At home, Gaddafi set about systematically destroying each and every possible competing source and symbol of power, whether secular or religious. In 1980, he ordered the leveling of the mosque of Sidi H'mouda, which he said was a base for the Muslim Brotherhood. Gaddafi likewise ordered destroyed a statue of Septimius Severus that stood at a corner of Green Square. This priceless antiquity had previously been pilfered from the Roman ruins at Leptis Magna. Now it fell victim to Gaddafi's desire to eradicate the competing influence of a long-dead empire. To make room for new objects, he ordered obliterated multiple structures of cultural and religious heritage in Tripoli.[58] Gaddafi closed down all theaters and music houses in 1984, declaring the Cinema Qureena/Teatro Municipale in Maidan Al Shajara (Tree Square) "incompatible with the ideology of the Cultural Revolution and the revolutionary spirit." The structure had retained a strong association with Italian influence since Mussolini had inaugurated it in the early 1930s. Once shuttered, the building soon was destroyed by arsonists.[59]

Gaddafi's obsession with extirpating any possible conflicting source of authority or observation was reflected in the state of Libyan arts: writer Ahmed Ibrahim Fagih has remarked that Libya under Gaddafi was one of the few dictatorial regimes to maintain a government unit specifically dedicated to repressing innovation and artistic creation in all forms. Gaddafi thought these activities encouraged "star power" that might detract from his monopoly on public adulation or create alternative social networks.[60] The atmosphere that resulted from such crackdowns was vividly evoked in Libyan novelist Hisham Mattar's *In the Country of Men*. Mattar described systematic tortures and disappearances, gruesome scenes in which suspected traitors were hung in public squares and on university campuses. Libyan poet Khaled Mattawa, in a similar vein, likened Libya during this period to "a helpless teenage girl forced into marriage hoping her groom would be kind."[61]

Gaddafi's domestic policies reversed much of the social good from the previous decade. In a critical blow to Libyan education, in 1980 education minister Ahmed Ibrahim outlawed teaching in English or any language other than Arabic.[62] This act was later cited as a principal factor in the creation of a lost generation of Libyans unable to communicate with the outside world.[63] Ali Omar Eumes, a Libyan artist based in London, recalled that the breaking point was in 1981: "I know many individuals then, some who could have been international movers and shakers in art, literature and culture if they had the right opportunities."[64]

In the end, unremitting brutality proved to be inadequate to the task of ruling Libya. Faced with low oil revenues, resulting from falling prices of international crude, on which his patronage structure depended, and a restive population, Gaddafi intuited that he would have to add new, more conciliatory tools to his dictatorial arsenal. He reached out to various opposition figures in 1987 and, for the first time, freed many political prisoners in March 1988. He employed this "half-hearted" reconciliation tactic repeatedly in coming years.

In June 1988, the regime went so far as to announce another supreme red herring, something Gaddafi called the Green Charter of Human Rights, though its main purpose appeared to be to denounce the use of Islam for partisan or political ends, jabbing once again at the Muslim Brotherhood. In 1987, he initiated a limited consumer *infitah*, or economic opening, the first of a series of periodic measures designed to placate the masses with creature comforts: small-scale joint stock companies called *tasharukiyyat*, which facilitated the import of foreign foodstuffs, appliances, and so on. A large fraction of the goods were defective or adulterated, as Libya had no effective means of monitoring or testing the imports.

As the end of Gaddafi's brutal years drew near, Libya's course would be reshaped by an act of international terror, much more than by any of his domestic pivots.

Lockerbie: The End and a New Beginning for Gaddafi

Gaddafi's gravest single offense against American interests was the December 21, 1988, bombing of Pan Am Flight 103 over Lockerbie, Scotland. Two hundred seventy people were killed aboard the plane, and eleven on the ground. This one event would, directly or indirectly, tie into almost every significant movement in the West's relationship with Libya for the next two decades. Arguably, it also constituted the beginning of the end for Gaddafi himself.

The Lockerbie bombing was not the last of its kind. Less than a year later, Libyan agents detonated a bomb aboard a French UTA DC-10 over Niger's Ténéré desert, killing 170. Though no less barbaric, this act of terror received far less attention than Lockerbie. The French had less international political clout and appeared far less willing to pick a fight with Gaddafi, lest they be put at a disadvantage in the inevitable (and already ongoing) scramble for Libyan resources.

Descriptions of the Lockerbie (and UTA) investigations elicit more questions than answers. Sonia Popovich, then vice president of the organization Victims of Lockerbie, said in a 1999 interview, "The more I have learned of this case, the less I do understand of it."[65] Gaddafi never admitted personal responsibility for any aspect of the bombing, though at times he came close. In an interview with Milton Viorst in early 1999, he remarked, "Whether we were responsible for bringing down the French plane [UTA 772] will be decided by a French court. We don't say anything about it. The same is true of Lockerbie. I can't answer as to whether Libya was responsible. Let's let the court decide."[66]

During the weeks and months following the destruction of Pan Am 103, Libya was not thought to be responsible. Suspicion instead fell, as it would for the UTA bombing, on Syria and Iran. Iran had the most pressing motive. Iranian leader Ayatollah Khomeini had only recently vowed to "retaliate to the maximum" after American cruiser *U.S.S. Vincennes* mistakenly shot down an Iranian passenger plane near Bandar Abbas, killing two hundred ninety pilgrims. Likewise, the West German police had recently broken up a cell plotting the destruction of a US airliner departing from Europe. Investigators tied this cell to the Popular Front for the Liberation of Palestine–General Command (PFLP–GC), which was known to have deep ties to Syria and Iran.

Not until 1990 did Libya emerge as a serious suspect, largely due to the testimony of a Maltese shop owner who had identified Libyan agent Abdelbasset al Megrahi from a set of photos as the man to whom he sold clothing later found at the crash site. This break in the case was bolstered by the discovery, also at the crash site, of a piece of a detonator that investigators were able to tie to bomb-making materials seized in West Africa from Libyan agents.

Even so, not all were swayed by the evidence of Libya's involvement. Pierre Péan, an investigative journalist, argued in his 2001 book on the UTA bombing, *Manipulations Africaines* (*African Manipulations*), that Libya was "framed" (albeit perhaps with Libya's tacit consent and even participation) by the West to avoid inflaming the real suspects, Iran and Syria. Syria at the time was a key member of the anti-Iraq coalition formed by George H. W. Bush, and vital to Israeli-Palestinian talks. Convincingly tying Gaddafi to the Lockerbie bombing would avoid disrupting those shaky alliances, while also serving the US goal of further isolating the Libyan regime. The US State Department took grave offense at various suggestions that it had "steered" the Lockerbie investigation toward Libya.

Gaddafi certainly had plausible motive for both crimes. The Pan Am bombing could have been revenge for President Ronald Reagan's attacks on Tripoli and Benghazi in April 1986; the UTA bombing, retribution against the French for foiling Libyan ambitions in neighboring Chad.[67] Nevertheless, explanations remained elusive. Just as the firm Libyan imprint on UTA circumstantially seemed to bolster the case for Libya's culpability for Lockerbie, the continuing whiff of Syrian-extremist-Palestinian involvement in UTA continued to implicate them with respect to Lockerbie. In interviews after the 2011 revolution, former Libyan

Foreign Minister Abdelrahman Shalgam alleged Palestinian extremist collusion in Lockerbie.

These complexities aside, two years after the Lockerbie bombing, Libya had become the prime suspect. In November 1991, the US and Scotland indicted two Libyan agents, Abdelbasset al Megrahi and Al Amin Khalifa Fhima, for the crime. In 1992, the UN passed Resolutions 731 and 748, which together instructed Libya to comply with a series of requests for information concerning Fhima and Megrahi, support investigations into the Lockerbie and UTA bombings, take responsibility for its actions with respect to the two events, remit the two suspects and cease support for international terrorist organizations. When Gaddafi failed to comply, the UN levied comprehensive sanctions against Libya in 1992.

Gaddafi's adventurous and enormously provocative foreign policies had the effect of drawing condemnation and opprobrium from the outside and increasing a sense of crisis and despair internally, as Libyans feared for their economic future and, frequently, their lives. For many of Gaddafi's advisers, the perquisites of access to the Leader had long ceased to be sufficient compensation for the hardships that accompanied association with a pariah state. All manner of Libyans were at a loss to see how the country could continue on this path without some disaster ensuing, whether in the form of sustained deprivation or war.

More Attempts to Temper Gaddafi, the Early 1990s

As would happen so frequently in modern Libyan history, senior members of Gaddafi's inner circle grasped the severity of Libya's position some time before Gaddafi himself did. Presumably those who had a hand in the planning of Lockerbie and UTA understood that the target countries would see the attacks as declarations of war. This was a dangerous course of action, especially at a time when Libya's resources and domestic support were declining.[68]

Something had to be done. The policies of the 1980s were yielding paltry returns. It was time for drastic measures. If there was one person within the Libyan establishment who could speak with any degree of parity with Gaddafi, it was his former RCC partner, ex-Prime Minister Abdelsalam Al Jelloud. Sometime between 1990 and 1992, Jelloud apparently decided to nudge Gaddafi to do something about the spiral into which he saw Libya falling.[69] If the dedication to his autobiography, published in 1994, is any indication, former Libyan Prime Minister Mustafa Ben Halim seemed to think that Jelloud might have been right, or that the sanctions would have had a quicker effect than they did in reality:

> To the people of Libya, who have paid a dreadful price and have suffered the bitterness of oppression and force, I offer this piece of the true history of Libya, which has long been unknown to them. May it be the proclamation of the good news of the approaching end of a regime which has brought repression and confusion, and may it herald the breaking of the dawn of Liberty.[70]

Jelloud supposedly expressed his concerns to Gaddafi, who challenged him to draw up a national rescue plan. Jelloud set up a series of working groups to craft new policy solutions for the Libyan economy, culture, and youth education and five weeks later delivered a draft report to Gaddafi.[71] The Leader told Jelloud that he could not, in his capacity as a mere "adviser" to the Libyan people, approve the plan. In the spirit of the program of governance laid out in *The Green Book*, the rescue plan had to be put to the masses, via the General People's Congress and Basic People's Congress. When Gaddafi submitted the proposal, however, he framed it not as a national action plan, but as a set of separate concept papers. Jelloud's plan to rescue Libya died by committee, presumably just as Gaddafi had planned.

Perhaps bravely, Jelloud publicly voiced his disappointment. Subsequently, in a speech before the General People's Congress, he opined, "A true Revolutionary is before all a good patriot; a good patriot should know to manage the riches of the country rationally."[72] Gaddafi did not appreciate such criticism, though Jelloud seems to have managed a rare, peaceful exit from government. He was allowed to retreat to his residence in the upscale Tripoli neighborhood of Bin Ashur.

Even though he had dispensed with Jelloud's rescue plan without heeding its warnings, Gaddafi did make some changes in response to Libya's worsening outlook. In late 1990, he reshuffled the ministries, appointing the generally respected technocrat Buzaid Dorda as prime minister, and initiated a process of even more decentralized decision making, effectively circumventing part of the Byzantine budgetary drafting and approval process. The system he had previously created encompassed fifteen hundred self-governed communities, for whom all decisions, even relatively minor ones, could be made only after being funneled through the Basic People's Congresses, then up to the leader or his circle.

The regime later openly acknowledged the failings of its governing bodies. A 2002 document, the *National Report on Human Development*,[73] produced by the Libyan government in consultation with the United Nations Development Programme (UNDP) acknowledged an

> absence of an interactive planning methodology; hesitation in formulating long-term sector development policies. . . . The above situation makes it impossible to formulate local development priorities for each Shaabia [local administrative unit], and evaluate and select projects objectively. It also precludes the inclusion of long-term projections and expectations regarding the direction of development in each Shaabia.[74]

Interestingly, according to this report, Benghazi, Derna, and environs are listed as being "above the national average" with respect to living conditions. The report refers to such regions as Derna, one of the most abjectly poor areas in Libya, as "super-endowed" with respect to quality-of-life indicators, such as education, population density, job opportunities, and the like. It does not so categorize Sirte, Gaddafi's hometown and the recipient of large infrastructure grants over the years.[75]

Gaddafi's piecemeal administrative reforms occurred in the midst of the growing threat of repercussions for Lockerbie. It remains unclear whether these reforms were the result of a fundamental change of strategy, due to internal conditions independent of Lockerbie, or an attempt to prepare for blowback from an eventual indictment. Given Gaddafi's demonstrated impulsiveness, it is possible that reform decisions and Lockerbie formed two separate calculations in Gaddafi's mind, and that he did not, or did not wish to comprehend, that Lockerbie, presumably his response to one set of actions (the US bombings of Tripoli and Benghazi in 1986), would frustrate policy decisions made two years later. A direct parallel can be drawn with the attempted assassination of Saudi Crown Prince Abdullah a decade later—the timing of which was also extremely inopportune, just as the US was about to lift the last of its bilateral sanctions from Libya.

A 1992 article in the Saudi-based *Al Wasat* alleged that verdicts in the Pan Am and UTA cases came as a "shock" to Gaddafi and his closest associates:

> The refusal to hand over the two suspects in Lockerbie, and to cooperate in investigation of accused in French bombing . . . has delayed a "historic opportunity" in front of the Libyan people to remake itself and its positions, and to lighten the heavy burdens on it since 20 years past.[76]

Perhaps Gaddafi had always expected a harsh international response, and this public "historic opportunity" was his vehicle for steeling the people against future hardship. Ali Maghbooshi, a member of the Tripoli People's Committee, described the Lockerbie indictment as a "strange electrical collision" that set off an internal campaign that Gaddafi himself referred to as a "year of big changes."[77]

As consequences mounted, Gaddafi sprang into action. He emptied out the old storehouses of previously procured, substandard goods, closed many of the group supermarkets, and ordered $4 billion worth of new clothes and foodstuffs distributed to the populace as supplementary income, before March 14, 1993, the date on which the UN Security Council was to decide whether to extend sanctions.[78] If this was intended to bolster his popularity, it did not achieve its aim: the vast majority of these goods never found their way to their target populations. Regime clients snapped up the bulk of Gaddafi's handouts, smuggling much of the largesse outside the country to sell at a markup. Matters grew worse once the UN sanctions against Libya started to take hold. Tripoli found itself physically and diplomatically completely isolated.

In 2004, stories still circulated in Benghazi regarding the "highly suspicious circumstances" surrounding a 1992 plane crash.[79] The Libyan government story held that a passenger plane bound for Tripoli from Benghazi, with 157 on board, collided with a Libyan MiG-23 on approach. Libyan authorities reportedly did not allow any foreign investigation of the incident. In 2011, a credible Libyan source claimed that Gaddafi had planned to blow up the plane over the Gulf of Sirte as a sympathy play in advance of imposition of UN sanctions. The flight number had been changed from its previous designation to 1103 to create a not so subtle link with Pan Am 103; the date, December 22, was allegedly chosen for proximity to the date of the Pan Am bombing (December 21, 1988). Libyan security services showed up at Benina airport in advance of departure to prevent certain people (presumably friends of the regime) from boarding the flight.

The bomb apparently did not detonate as planned, so Gaddafi ordered jets to ram the plane several miles from Tripoli airport, lest it crash or explode close to Tripoli and create an international incident. An association of victims of this flight formed shortly after the 2011 revolution, and apparently the National Transitional Council has since opened an investigation.[80] Ahmed Ibrahim Fagih's comment that it was often impossible to assign "normal logic" to Gaddafi's acts would certainly apply here. If the conspiracy is ultimately confirmed, it would add another layer to the Gaddafi psychological profile and demonstrate that, whatever he had planned by changing political course in 1992, Lockerbie was certainly not far from his mind. Here was the concept of linkage, to an extreme never before seen.

The Start of Sanctions

Sanctions hit Libya like a bomb. Between 1992 and 1997, the consumer price index rose 200 percent, while salaries remained fixed by Law #15 of 1981 at between 150 and 500 Libyan dinars (about $100) per month.[81] From 1992 to 1999, Libya's economy grew, on average, a nugatory 0.8 percent.[82]

Unrest and rebellion were perhaps inevitable in such a climate. In 1993, members of the Warfalla tribe (one of four substantial tribes co-opted by the regime) launched a coup attempt. While it ended in failure, this attempt appeared to have greatly unsettled Gaddafi. Opposition groups abroad reported assassination attempts on Gaddafi in August 1995 and 1998, most perpetrated by activists within the increasingly restless Islamist opposition. Between 1995 and 1998, northern Cyrenaica, especially the cities of Derna, Al Marj, and Al Beida, frequent skirmishes took place between government security forces and members of the Islamic opposition. As of 1996, Derna was said to be in a "state of siege," though there were few outsiders in a position to verify this.[83] The Libyan government, loathe to give the locals any credit for the effectiveness of their disruptions, ascribed blame for the uprisings to infiltrators from Egypt and the Sudan.

The international pressure on Libya only increased through the 1990s. With UN sanctions already in place, in 1996, the US Congress instituted a secondary boycott of Libya, the Iran-Libya Sanctions Act (ILSA, also known as the D'Amato Act). ILSA imposed a range of punitive measures on companies that invested more than $40 million in Libyan hydrocarbon projects. Controversially, ILSA was aimed not only at discouraging US companies from investment in Libya, but at non-American corporations as well.

Under pressure from abroad and at home, Gaddafi's regime was struggling to cope. Gaddafi's playbook at this time contained no fundamentally new ideas, only composites of previous strategies. He alternately used carrots and sticks against the Islamic opposition, arresting, killing and beating some, while buying off or releasing less ideologically committed activists. In the late 1990s, he attempted to defray the effects of economic isolation by again turning to economic palliatives, such as allowing more consumables, basic appliances and candy bars into the country. Nevertheless, the public was rejecting his policies in ever more public displays. Interestingly, soccer matches had become a popular venue for an odd kind of proxy war between the regime and its enemies.

Throughout the Middle East, soccer plays a unique role in politics. In Egypt, Hosni Mubarak was known to fix games in favor of teams with regime backing in order to fortify his own popularity. Likewise, in Libya, soccer matches became a channeling mechanism for pro- and anti-Gaddafi elements.

The regime invested directly in several clubs, foremost among them Al Ahly Tripoli, which Gaddafi's soccer-playing son Saadi Gaddafi effectively owned. Time after time, loyalist teams benefited from unfair advantages, never losing a match. Yet the politicking wasn't restricted to the government's side. As popular resentment against the regime grew, games were marked by backlash from the crowd.

Conflict between fans and regime forces often sparked violence. On July 9, 1996, Saadi Gaddafi's bodyguards opened fire on a stadium crowd screaming anti-Gaddafi slogans. On July 20, 2000, in the eastern town of Al Marj, the questionable loss of Benghazi's Al Ahly to rival Al Akhdar of Al Beida (Al Akhdar was allegedly owned by Saadi's mother, whose family was from Al Beida), led bands of roving youth to shout anti-Gaddafi slogans and attack government property. The next day, Gaddafi responded by declaring Benghazi a "rebel city" and sent bulldozers to raze the tomb of Omar Al Mokhtar. This was an astonishing overreaction, even for Gaddafi, given the symbolic value of Mokhtar to all Libyans. In Gaddafi's first official visit to Italy after the reopening of the country in 2003, Gaddafi had worn an outsized button depicting Omar Al Mokhtar. Nevertheless, at that moment, Mokhtar represented to Gaddafi eastern defiance against his rule.[84]

In another incident, Al Ahly Benghazi fans booed Al Ahly Tripoli during a cup final, put Al Ahly Tripoli colors on a donkey, and led it into the stadium.[85] In response, Gaddafi celebrated the Revolutionary Day in 2000 by demolishing the general headquarters of the Al Ahly Benghazi soccer club. Tripoli-based diplomats heard rumors in 2005 that Saadi had reacted to critical comments by the coach of Al Ahly Tripoli by shooting him dead in his (Saadi's) Gargaresh-street mansion in Tripoli.[86]

The soccer wars, while a significant release mechanism for the population at large, were something of a sideshow compared to the escalating conflict between Gaddafi and the eastern, Islamist opposition focused on an organization called the Libyan Islamic Fighting Group (LIFG), many of whose leaders had experience fighting with the Afghan mujahideen against the Soviets. The LIFG suddenly arrived on the scene after an assassination attempt on Gaddafi in 1996, the details of which remain somewhat sketchy. The LIFG served as a model for the establishment and spread of yet other Islamic groups, many of which were supported by colleagues in Egypt.

By 1997, the situation in eastern Libya could be described as undeclared war. Between Benghazi and Derna, members of the LIFG imitated Omar Al Mokhtar's strategy against Italian invaders, using the cave-ridden Green Mountains as their redoubt for a series of guerrilla attacks against regime security forces in the east.[87] The regime responded with napalm strikes against rebel targets that left swaths of denuded landscape, still evident. There were reports of the army battling with LIFG members using helicopter gunships, while the Islamists managed to kill scores of government security officers. Benghazi residents recall the presence of military men with machine guns at intersections, barricades managed by Revolutionary Guard members, all of which stood in stark contrast to the calm, controlled atmosphere in Tripoli.

After an extended series of counterattacks against suspected antiregime agents and their hideouts in the east during the following years, around 1999, Gaddafi announced he had decisively wiped out Islamic opposition, including all traces of the Muslim Brotherhood. It did not take long for events to belie these assertions. Libyan security arrested a number of nationals for planning a car bomb attack in the early 2000s; a couple of months later, a previously unknown group calling itself Al Qaeda in Eastern Libya claimed credit for a suicide bomb attack in Derna. In a way, this was good timing for Gaddafi, for as much as he wanted to believe he had crushed his Islamist enemies, it was becoming increasingly clear that the ability to cite an Al Qaeda threat and suggest some insight into the workings of its networks would be of great value to the Americans. The resilience of the Islamist networks—LIFG and the Muslim Brotherhood, for the most part—strongly suggested that the fighters were far better organized and had much more support within the general population than Gaddafi was ever willing to acknowledge publicly.

Gaddafi's Second Turn to Africa: Winning Friends for D-Day

After years of war against Chad, the International Court of Justice in 1994 awarded the contested Aouzou strip to Chad. Some experts saw this as a hinge moment when the previously aggressive, expansionist Libyan policy toward Africa was replaced by a more subtle and effective soft-power campaign, a few years after Gaddafi had effectively shifted his orientation from the Arab countries, which he felt were ungrateful for his various efforts to promote Arab unity. After 1994, investment, economic patronage, and attempted mediation of regional disputes became key levers to project Libyan influence.[88] One of Gaddafi's main motivations for these maneuvers was to build international political support within the international community, and by extension, the United Nations in the hopes of lifting the international sanctions on Libya.

Through will, coercion, and the promise of large subsidies, Gaddafi transformed the Organization of African States (OAU) into the African Union (AU), and was a founding member of SEN-SAD, the Community of Sahelo-Saharan States. Gaddafi was installed as chairman of the AU at its inaugural conference held in his hometown of Sirte on September 9, 1999, at a cost of $30 million, for lavish accommodations and improvements to Sirte's infrastructure. In 2006, Libya was admitted to the COMESA, the Common Market of Eastern and Southern Africa, augmenting its political influence in the Horn of Africa, including a platform for self-serving mediations in Darfur and Somalia.[89]

Gaddafi used the AU as a channel for various grandiose schemes, including what he envisioned as the AU's ultimate form, the "United States of Africa" (the parallels with the US are obvious). Not all African countries appreciated Gaddafi's largesse and/or meddling and even more strenuously objected to his attempts to co-opt alternative or traditional tribal leaders to anoint himself "King of Kings" of the continent. The date Gaddafi became chair of the AU, 9-9-99, subsequently figured prominently in Gaddafi symbology. The numbers were emblazoned on the tailfins of planes owned by the Gaddafi-financed airline, Afriquiya.

Even so, evidence of Libya's influence in and across Sub-Saharan Africa was clear. The Libya Arab African Investment Company (LAAICO) had offices in twenty-five countries and helped to coordinate investments in a range of commercial activities, from oil to tourism.[90] In more recent years, a downstream marketing arm of the National Oil Company OiLibya, established a network of over 1,250 points of sale (filling stations) in 18 African countries, from Djibouti to Senegal.[91] Gaddafi money financed a prominent mosque in Kampala, Uganda,[92] and an office tower in Dakar, Senegal. Libya signed agreements of economic, military, and cultural cooperation with Gambia, Mali, Eritrea, South Africa, and Ethiopia, to name just a few.[93]

For all his claims to be the continent's champion in the global arena, Gaddafi's hypocrisy regarding Africa was obvious. In 1997, Gaddafi announced Libya's borders "open" to all Africans who wished to live and work in Libya, knowing full well that the main attraction of Libya for most Sub-Saharan Africans was as a launching point for illegal immigration to Europe. Gaddafi used African migrants as his secret weapon to pressure an immigration-phobic Europe into various concessions. Meanwhile members of the regime handsomely profited, ignoring the waves of Africans who sailed from ports like Zwara, bound for the shores of Lampedusa and southern Italy. Whenever Gaddafi wanted to increase political pressure, he would escalate the number of immigrants.

The experiences of Sudanese, Liberian, Eritrean, Ghanaian, and other African nationals headed for Europe have been documented in a fictional account called, appropriately, *African Titanics*.[94] Those seeking passage would typically need to put in a year or more of hard labor to save the average US$1,000 to $2,000 for passage. Thousands died over the years, as overpacked, unseaworthy vessels capsized en route. Farther up the supply chain, the highways linking Niger, Benin, to Sebha, Libya, were at times strewn with the bodies of migrants who perished of thirst or hunger on the early stages of their perilous migrations to the north. Every so often, when Gaddafi was irritated with the crime that proliferated in the refugee camps, he simply decided to empty them out by ordering their inhabitants killed outright or repatriated to their countries of origin. Africans often wound up in jail or under suspicion of committing various crimes. Many were executed without trial, to the weak protests of corrupt regimes that were receiving subventions from Libya to keep them politically engaged on Libya's behalf.

As with most of Gaddafi's grand gestures, the Africa open-door policy generated a sizable domestic backlash from a wide swath of Libyan society. Many Libyan officials felt Gaddafi's Africa policies were making Libya look ridiculous to the Arab world. Workers saw increasing numbers of African squatters as a threat to their livelihoods, sources of violent crime, or, less charitably, a contamination of their way of life. This frustration boiled over most dramatically in the "Zawiya events" of 2000, in which dozens of Sub-Saharan Africans were lynched in that coastal city. According to the Tunisian Libya expert Moncef Ouannes,

> These bloody events . . . evidenced a profound malaise and growing discontent within the population. It was a question of a veritable riot,

> which made the regime very uneasy, because it demonstrated an ability to mobilize a large part of the population of Zawiya (approximately 90,000) and above all, members of the powerful tribe Ouled Sahr, which was strongly represented in the police and the army.[95]

While African migrants bore the brunt of anti-Gaddafi sentiment, the message was clearly aimed at the regime, just as the 2006 Benghazi riots were. While Libyan dissident organizations abroad attempted to build awareness of what had happened at Zawiya, as they did with the 1996 Abu Selim prison massacre, in which more than 1,200 political prisoners were gunned down in a couple of hours, these events never made it into the international political consciousness and as such were not recognized as points of deep vulnerability for the regime.

While very few on the outside understood what was happening within Libya at the time, the late 1990s were clearly a period of high social and economic instability. From Gaddafi's perspective, the priorities were to keep the lid on popular discontent, while using the resources he had at his disposal to create pressure groups that might eventually help him break the sanctions—from recipients of Libyan aid and military support, to African immigrants seeking passage to Europe, to Western intelligence agencies. It seems doubtful, given what happened later, that Gaddafi really understood what would happen once the sanctions were removed, but he also clearly saw that the status quo was not working and was dangerous in its own right.

CHAPTER 3

The Price Is Right

Undoubtedly it was the lifting of U.S. sanctions that was the major watershed in Libya's recent history. Signaling, as this did, that the United States was once again willing to extend the hand of friendship to Libya, it has made all things possible with regard to Libya's reform and modernization.[1]

WANISS A. OTMAN AND ERLING KARLBERG

For decades, Gaddafi alienated his people, baffled neighboring countries, and defied the international community. Each iteration of the Gaddafi program called for a more complex and often more aggressive application of tools of repression and coercion.

Gaddafi certainly had problems. Declining oil revenues in the 1980s and 1990s left him without the usual cash stores with which to placate the masses and cement critical tribal and individual loyalties. Corruption and graft, if not worse in absolute terms, had become firmly institutionalized. Many in Gaddafi's inner circle (and outside it) resented their inability to travel and redeem their ill-gotten gains outside Libya. Young people, faced with poverty and few opportunities, turned to drugs and other asocial behavior. Without the ability to provide for a household, sexual frustration was on the rise, as males (and females) in a highly traditional society were forced to marry later and later—or forgo marriage altogether.

As long as the Libyan people were downtrodden psychologically and without resources, they had limited tools with which they could fight back. The main channels for popular discontent were the relatively well-organized and potentially lethal actions of the Libyan-Islamic Fighting Group (LIFG) and spontaneous outpourings of popular anger. Demonstrations that so far were emblematic of the depth of disaffection had limited combustible power. Libya's expatriate opposition was splintered and largely toothless, and the international powers—the US in particular—were occupied with what they perceived to be more important matters.

In a way, the UN sanctions gave Gaddafi a time-out. While internal threats were substantial and getting worse, at least Gaddafi did not have to worry much about subversion from abroad. As the previous chapter indicates, this had not always been the case. He was also not as easily able to involve himself in foreign imbroglios, which had been a huge drain on the Libyan treasury. Most likely, Gaddafi did not see things this way. An actor needs a stage, and Gaddafi had long demonstrated an almost insatiable psychological need to speak to as broad a public as possible. Whatever it took, Gaddafi resolved, he would break the sanctions.

Thus, even before the UN sanctions hit Libya in 1992, Gaddafi began a long, strenuous campaign to be readmitted to the international community. Most of these efforts had limited effect. He waited almost a decade. In the late 1990s, a variety of factors created new realities outside Libya, a perfect storm whereby some of Gaddafi's problems suddenly interested outside powers.

"Put a Fence Around Libya and Call It a Jail"

For much of the 1990s, many in the US government wanted to leave Gaddafi exactly where he was, somewhat in the same manner that *Tonight Show* host Jay Leno joked about the 1993 Waco, Texas, cult standoff, suggesting the government solve the problem by building a fence around the sprawling complex and call it a prison. Any talk of trying the suspects in the Lockerbie bombing or negotiating with Gaddafi on any issue threatened to disrupt this comfortable equilibrium. Allan Gerson, one of the lawyers instrumental in passing the Anti-Terrorism and Effective Death Penalty Act, which gave the Lockerbie families the right to sue the Libyan government for complicity in terrorism abroad, commented,

> There was, finally the sentiment—never quite expressed in public, but strong within certain offices in the State Department and the National Security Council—that a trial would only serve to disrupt a policy that had been working well for five years; that it would at best result in the convictions of a couple of mid-level operatives . . . and that in either event Kaddafi would be let out of his box, free again to cause mischief in a world that was dangerous already.[2]

This state of affairs couldn't last forever. Perhaps one of the first and strangest of the Libyan efforts for a possible solution to the Lockerbie problem involved former US Congressman and former Democratic presidential hopeful Gary Hart. Libyan agents contacted Hart in February 1992. They requested that he tell the Clinton administration that Libya would consider US demands, and might even be willing to hand over the Lockerbie suspects in exchange for a speedy normalization of relations. Hart followed up by meeting with then Prime Minister Jelloud, who confirmed that pretty much everything was on the table. According to Hart, US Assistant Secretary of State for Near Eastern Affairs Edward Djerejian nevertheless dismissed these efforts, and the talks went nowhere.[3]

The Libyans were persistent, however. They made subsequent approaches through a number of would-be Arab mediators and fringe US politicians, including Louis Farrakhan, the controversial founder of the Nation of Islam,[4] and former presidential candidate Reverend Jesse Jackson, who met with Gaddafi in Tripoli in 1993. None of these attempts panned out, however. In the end, European policymakers turned out to be far more receptive.

Europe had been a precious lifeline to Libya, even during the period from 1992 through 1999, when UN sanctions were in place. European investments in the Libyan oil sector kept the nation afloat throughout the 1990s.[5] Throughout this period, Libyan officials privately held out hopes that the US oil producers would be back soon. Acreage once held by the US oil companies had been held in trust since 1982. The Libyan government would not risk an additional casus belli.[6] But even without the United States, European dependence on Libyan oil was becoming profound. Libya accounted for 21.6 percent of hydrocarbon exports to Italy; 10.8 percent to Germany; 7.6 percent to the UK; and 5.5 percent to France.[7] In 2004, Libya provided a full 41 percent (another source says 75 percent) of Switzerland's oil and gas imports. As we will see later, that situation left Switzerland particularly exposed to Gaddafi's blackmail.

The Libyans were certainly aware of their sway over the Europeans. In 2004, one senior Libyan official taunted the US, saying it would fail in efforts to keep Europe in line with the sanctions, for this very reason. In March 1999, Gaddafi was comfortable enough with the status quo to assert publicly that relations between Europe and Libya were already "very good."[8]

Though the UN sanctions were lifted in 1999, European Union embargoes and US sanctions were still in place. With the odor of commercial opportunities wafting from Libya, the United States found it increasingly difficult to fight European resentment of US legislation designed to prevent the Europeans from deepening their relationships with Libya. Italy was particularly vocal in pushing the United States to reestablish relations with Libya, and for largely commercial reasons. Like France, Italy had kept up surreptitious trade with Libya during the sanctions, and Libya continued to invest in Italy. Tamoil, the downstream marketing arm of the Libyan National Oil Company (NOC), was (and continues to be) a major retail petrol presence in Italy and Switzerland.[9] Dating back to 1977, industrial conglomerate Fiat received large sums from Libyans (Gaddafi bought $415 million in Fiat stock in 1976, for which the Italians paid him $3.1 billion ten years later).[10]

For European investors, the Iran-Libya Sanctions Act, or ILSA, was particularly irking. Technically it mandated severe punishment for any foreign company that invested more than $40 million in the Libyan energy sector. Many of the oil-importing European countries—France and Germany, in particular—felt that this was overreaching. By 1997, even within American policy circles, conventional wisdom was that, in the words of Libya watcher Ronald Bruce St. John, ILSA "had the opposite effect [of what was intended], damaging U.S. political interests. St. John suggested that Libya's standing in United States foreign policy had "grown out of proportion to the threat that Libya posed."[11]

The inevitable breakthrough occurred in 1998, via an aperture created by British Prime Minister Tony Blair's government and the Libyans, who offered as an added inducement the possibility of clarity with respect to the killing of Yvonne Fletcher, a British policewoman who had been felled by shots fired from within the Libyan embassy in London in 1984.[12]

Clinton's Second Term: The Decision to Engage

In 1998, Al Qaeda emerged as a major threat to US security interests after the bombings of the US embassies in Tanzania and Nairobi, followed by the bombing of the USS *Cole* in the Aden, Yemen, harbor in 2000. These acts of terror likely played a significant role in heightening the CIA's and MI6's interest in whatever intelligence Gaddafi might have to offer them. Further, Gaddafi's campaign to buy political influence and position himself as a mediator in various "new" African conflicts, in places like Somalia, South Sudan, Eritrea, and Kenya suggested to many in Western intelligence agencies that Libya could be helpful with information concerning the movements of Al Qaeda and its affiliates in the region, and the actions of other "states and issues of concern," whether Sudan and Darfur or the rise of the Islamic Courts Council in Somalia.[13] To access this information, Sir Mark Allen, alternately head of counterterrorism and chief for North Africa and the Middle East at the British Secret Intelligence Service, led secret talks, in particular with Gaddafi's second son Saif Al Islam, who would play a pivotal role in the US-West rapprochement, in 1999. At least one of the meetings was held at London's Travellers Club, in the presence of British diplomat Nigel Sheinwald, US counterterror and nuclear counterproliferation officers William Ehrman, David Landsman, Stephen Kappes, and Robert Joseph. The Libyans were represented by Musa Kusa, then Gaddafi's head of external intelligence (himself suspected of involvement in Pan Am 103), and former General Secretary of the General Peoples' Committee (Prime Minister) Abdulati Al Obeidi.[14]

The United States and the UK were also newly interested in the Libyan Islamic Fighting Group (LIFG), after one of its members, Anas el Libi (Nazih Abdul Hamid al Raghie's nom de guerre) was linked to the embassy bombings in Tanzania and Kenya, and another member, Abu Layth al Libi, left to join Al Qaeda leadership.[15] Former senior Clinton officials said they doubted a direct link between the new interest in whatever information that Libya might have on Al Qaeda and the embassy bombings, but that it "was not impossible."[16] Even so, as one senior Clinton administration official put it, the US "continued to maintain a healthy skepticism as to the possibility that Gaddafi could be reformed." In 1997, the newly appointed Secretary of State Madeline Albright and national security adviser Samuel (Sandy) Berger seemed favorable to a reexamination of US policy toward Libya.

A fundamental shift in US policy context came in 1998, as key members of Clinton's cabinet and State Department officials expressed the view that continued maintenance of sanctions on Libya would be a costly and ultimately losing battle. In light of increasing pressure from the families of the victims of the Lockerbie bombing, among others, the officials argued that time was right to test Gaddafi's resolve. The underlying goal was, in the words of Martin Indyk, then assistant secretary for Near East affairs, to "attempt to graduate a rogue state," and then use it as a model for the conversion of other problematic states, such as Iran.[17] The British, led by Tony Blair and MI6, had by then already started to vigorously lobby the US and the UN for easing of sanctions on Libya. King Hussein of Jordan and other moderate Arab leaders, including Hosni Mubarak, had expressed to Clinton their view that the sanctions had served their purpose. But it fell to Saudi Arabia, in the person of Prince Bandar bin Sultan, to midwife a new US-Libya engagement.

Saudi and South African Mediation

Gaddafi had sought to involve the Saudis in mediation early on for the influence the kingdom had with the Americans. Rihab Massoud, then political minister at the Saudi embassy in Washington, described the Saudi ambitions: "Anytime we can help an Arab country is our advantage. Domestically, this is during the time when our Prince took over from the King who had been ill [King Fahad]. This was a new introduction to world issues. Also, things were going really badly in the Middle East peace process. We needed something to work."[18]

Rumors abounded that Gaddafi had promised Prince Bandar a hefty sum for his efforts.[19] Another regional power that Gaddafi had lobbied fiercely was Nelson Mandela's South Africa. Gaddafi had funded Mandela's African National Congress (ANC), and the two countries had shared interests on the continent. Indeed, the Saudis and the South Africans would work in concert; there was significant reason to believe that by late 1998, this alliance had tacit approval of at least the UK, and likely the US. In her study on the South Africa–Saudi Arabia mediation, author Lyn Boyd Judson argues that the Western leadership sanctioned Mandela's involvement for its usefulness in quieting expected objections from the left in both the UK and the US. Massoud told Judson in 2004, "We needed someone. What better symbol than Mandela. He is the epitome of morality."[20] Mandela's own motives were described variously as loyalty to Gaddafi for supporting the ANC in its darkest moments and a policy of purposeful, postapartheid evenhandedness in international affairs. There were those who suggested that exigencies of Mandela's upcoming 1999 presidential campaign, that is, Libyan cash, also played a role.[21]

According to Judson, these relationships were not fully known to President Clinton until he was "tag-teamed" by Bandar and Mandela in March 1998. Mandela's chief of staff Jakes Gerwel later said the South Africans were "surprised to find how little Clinton knew about this matter, i.e., the South African-Saudi-Libyan dealings, and what exactly Gaddafi had agreed to regarding turning over the Lockerbie suspects, by this point."[22]

He attributed this to the compartmentalized, multilayered nature of the US government bureaucracies and the fact that Sandy Berger had neglected to brief Clinton.[23]

In 1998, Secretary Albright successfully pitched to President Clinton a "take it or leave it" offer for the Libyans. The main preconditions for dialogue with the Libyans were tripartite: an end to state-sponsored terrorism, acceptable compensation for the Lockerbie victims, and agreement on a mechanism for bringing the accused to justice. Since Libya had already credibly wound down its support for terror since 1994, all that remained was addressing the Lockerbie issue.[24] Less blatant conditions included abandonment of efforts to lobby other states for the lifting of UN sanctions, and a verifiable closing of the military training camps Libya had been hosting on behalf of the Popular Front for the Liberation of Palestine (PFLP), and other radical Palestinian groups.[25] Additional concerns included Gaddafi's attitude toward Israel and the Israeli conflict (Gaddafi, for many years an in line with his early Pan Arab position, had been extremely critical of Israel, and, more or less independent of this, had written a treatise on Israeli-Palestinian relations, advocating a one-state solution he called "Isratine"). On various occasions he had called both the Palestinians and the Israelis "idiots."[26] The US was also concerned about Libya's ambitions in Africa, where Gaddafi continued to stir trouble. Interestingly, Gaddafi's anti-Israel rhetoric did diminish markedly in the wake of direct negotiations with the US.

The US insisted that talks occur in absolute secrecy. It did not want the British to hijack negotiations for their own political and economic purposes; Clinton feared any leakage would hurt the Democrats' prospects in the coming presidential election. Weapons of mass destruction (WMD) were not at the forefront, as the US did not believe that Libya's nuclear weapons or its chemical arsenal posed an immediate threat. Further, since the State Department and the CIA did not share information on Libya's WMD capacity, different agencies had different views of the underlying threat.[27] To the surprise of US negotiators, Libya swiftly responded substantively to all of their requests.[28] "The stance of the Libyans," Assistant Secretary of State Indyk recalls, was one of "we will jump, you tell us how high."[29]

A group of commentators (many of whom later became fixtures within the so-called Republican neoconservative movement) immediately lashed out. John Bolton, the cantankerous, unruly-haired future US ambassador to the UN, accused the administration of "giving in" to Gaddafi.

From his perch at the American Enterprise Institute, he objected to the administration's assurances that it would not allow a trial of Megrahi and Fhima to "undermine" Gaddafi's regime. Those assurances were embodied in a series of concessions on how the suspects could be interrogated in custody, effectively "shielding" Gaddafi from criminal liability. Bolton also took issue with US agreement to the Libyan request that the UN would solely oversee prison conditions for the accused. As Bolton wrote, "this implicit admission that Scottish jails are not up to, say, Libyan standards is breathtaking."[30]

In May 1999, the Clinton administration, represented by Assistant Secretary Indyk and his deputy, David Welch (who held Indyk's position under George W. Bush), began direct negotiations with the Libyans. Indyk was the point person for three meetings at a Saudi guest house in Geneva, Switzerland. Prince Bandar presided over the meetings. Musa Kusa, then head of Gaddafi's external security apparatus, served as the lead negotiator, while the number-two Libyan delegate was regime insider (and former prime minister) Abdelati Al Obeidi. Several US officials described Kusa as looking like the "impersonation of evil." Others said he looked like a university professor, a bit more distinguished than many of his colleagues who "looked perpetually as if they had just rolled out of bed."[31]

At the first meeting, Indyk was impressed that the Libyans were negotiating seriously and reported as much to the White House. However, the second meeting went less well. Around this time, Gaddafi had made public remarks critical of Clinton, to which the US interlocutors objected strenuously, telling their Libyan counterparts that such comments were not only unhelpful, but could end the dialogue. In response, Kusa reportedly threw up his hands and said, "There are limits to what I can do." By the third meeting, the Libyans had returned to their initial conciliatory mode and agreed to more active collaboration on intelligence issues.

Gaddafi's Lockerbie Tactics: A Foreshadowing

For all Gaddafi's powers of persuasion and manipulation, there would still have to be consequences for his support of terror. So the Lockerbie families helped to create pressure and context for both civil and criminal trials of Megrahi and Fhima. Even when many (including in the government) saw the notion of seeking a trial of the two suspects as legally impossible and undesired, the families and their lawyers pressed for and won an amendment to the 1976 Sovereign Immunity Act, governing under what conditions a foreign state may be sued in US courts. The amendment set the stage for a civil trial to proceed, which it did in 2002.

The families' maneuvers helped pressure Gaddafi to agree to a variant of the plan he had proposed in 1993, according to which the Libyan suspects would be tried by a panel of Scottish judges. True to this framework, Gaddafi turned over both Megrahi and Fhima in April 1999, in the process addressing one of the fundamental conditions for the lifting of UN sanctions. Along the way, he had attempted to buy influence in Washington by approaching a series of lawyers to mediate a comprehensive settlement. He then undermined them by trying to pit the families against each other, attempting to bribe them or otherwise disrupt the process.

Until the end, Gaddafi tried to water down the basic conditions governing the trial and rendition, whether by substituting a panel of international judges for the potentially less sympathetic Scottish judges or by stipulating that the sanctions be lifted the moment a deal on extradition had been signed, not after the delivery of the suspects. Gaddafi's main concern was clearly that the trial not be used to undermine his regime.

Gaddafi's concerns appeared to revolve around two primary issues. First, there was no telling what information might be gleaned from the suspects themselves once they had been handed over, or whether the US and other parties would seek further consequences as a result. Second, on the home front, there remained the possibility of domestic consequences if Gaddafi appeared weak on the issue of rendition. Gaddafi got a major concession on the first point from UN Secretary Kofi Annan, who provided him with a sealed letter allegedly assuring him the proceedings would not be used to justify regime change. Further arrangements were agreed to whereby the suspects would not be exposed to those who might try to gain testimony from them that might implicate Gaddafi personally.

To protect himself at home, Gaddafi was said to have struck a deal with at least one prominent dissident to use his good offices with the Megaraha tribe to acquiesce to the transfer of Megrahi (against the protestations of former RCC member Abdelsalam Al Jelloud, a member of the tribe).[32]

By March 2000, George W. Bush was in the White House, and Libya matters appeared to be temporarily frozen while the administration addressed a long list of more urgent matters. One early action President Bush did take was to lift the ban on American citizens traveling to Libya that had been in place since 1981. American oil executives could now pick up discussions with the Libyans about so-called "standstill" agreements, according to which the facilities and concessions of US oil companies previously operating in Libya had been frozen from 1986, the year President Reagan had severed all economic ties with Libya for a period of approximately twenty years. Indyk broached lifting the ban on US citizen travel in 1999 and was told by more senior State Department officials it could not happen as long as the Lockerbie issue remained unresolved.[33] In light of the shifting policy, in early 2004, the State Department sent four consular officials to Libya for a single day to assess safety conditions.[34]

In April 2001, a Department of Energy task force recommended a comprehensive review of sanctions against Libya; about the same time the *Washington Post* published an article arguing that the US would do well to reevaluate its relations with Libya.[35] In the summer of 2001, prior to 9/11, the State Department ceased referring to Libya and Iran as "rogue states," instead using the term "state of concern."[36] Assistant Secretary of State for Near Eastern Affairs William J. Burns met with Libyan chief of intelligence Kusa in London in October 2001—one month after 9/11—to discuss the future of US-Libya relations.[37] President Bush omitted Libya from his 2002 State of the Union "Axis of Evil" speech on January 29, 2002 (naming Iran, Iraq, and North Korea). Between 2000 and 2002, the official attitude toward the Gaddafi regime had transformed dramatically.

Settlement of the Lockerbie claims proceeded on track during these developments. While the financial terms were still not definitively settled, the amount seemed to be a staggering $2.7 billion. Though many at the State Department found this payment "undignified," clearly the agreement itself was in alignment with the plan that the department had laid out for Gaddafi during the Geneva talks. Authors Allan Gerson and Jerry Adler said,

> If Kaddafi were to offer to settle the families' claims on terms acceptable to them—which meant a sum large enough to be considered punitive—and set up an escrow account in Switzerland for that purpose, the administration might have the cover it needed for a comprehensive settlement, consistent with the UN Security Council resolutions.[38]

According to senior administration officials, the State Department took no position on the formula worked out by the two sides, which in effect tied payment of three separate installments of the $10-million-per-family award to specific advances in Libya-US relations: Libya would make an initial payment of $4 million to each family upon full lifting of the UN sanctions; a second tranche of $4 million upon the lifting of secondary (US) economic sanctions and normalization of US-Libya relations; and a third payment upon the removal of Libya from the US list of state sponsors of terrorism—the final barrier between Libya and acceptance by the international community. There were specific dates by which the US government, not a direct party to the agreement, had to meet each of these conditions.

The US may have felt it had scored a major victory. However, Gaddafi and his advisers may have been the ones cheering. Despite the vehemence with which he objected to the terms of the trial and tried to dodge payment of any damages that might imply guilt, the provisions of this agreement implicitly forced the US government to take certain actions in service to the bilateral relationship. In effect, the agreement turned the Lockerbie families, from the principal impediment to lifting sanctions and normalization of relations, into a strong force in favor of resolution. Even so, many of the families said they saw the process as a reckoning. For them, it was a means of producing closure and bringing Gaddafi to justice, in the absence of any other means.[39] In an interview with Fareed Zakaria in 2011, former Deputy Secretary of Defense Paul Wolfowitz said that he believed the Lockerbie families' pressure was the factor that led the US to "mistakenly accelerate the process of peace making."[40] Nevertheless, the Libyan regime saw itself as the ultimate beneficiary of these machinations.

In the end, the UN registered its approval of Libya's decision to remit the two accused to the agreed-on venue in UN Security Council Resolution 1192, strongly encouraging Libya to comply with previous resolutions. On January 31, 2001, after a trial that lasted nine months, a panel of three judges acquitted Fhima and convicted Megrahi of 270 counts of murder, sentencing him to life in Glasgow's Barlinnie prison. The fact that only one of the two accused was convicted and on virtually identical evidence seemed to some like political influence.

On August 20, 2003, the Libyan government accepted responsibility (though not guilt) for Lockerbie and agreed to pay US$2.7 billion to the victims' families.[41] On December 19, 2003, almost four years after the lifting of UN sanctions, Gaddafi announced Libya's "voluntary" abandonment of its WMD program, according to a script that appears to have largely been drafted by the UK and US intelligence agencies.[42]

Libya After 9/11

The Al Qaeda attacks against the US on September 11, 2001, fundamentally changed the dynamics of the Bush administration and forced a radical re-focusing of US foreign policy. With respect to Libya, however, 9/11 simply accelerated (if substantially) forces that were already in play.

The doctrine that emerged to guide George W. Bush's subsequent actions was one of "preemption, military primacy, new multilateralism, and the spread of democracy."[43] Gaddafi knew when to insert the proper emphasis: "We have been terrorized by what happened in America and we express our condolences to the American people who suffered from this unexpected catastrophe," he proclaimed.[44]

Birth of Divergent Narratives

There had been tremendous blowback from the fact that the US was unable to find weapons of mass destruction in Iraq—or a direct link between Al Qaeda and Saddam Hussein. In this context, Libya became doubly useful—if we recall, when US-UK-Libya discussions began in the late 1990s, the US was virtually unconcerned about Libya's WMD program, with the exception of its chemical weapons capacity, and even this was not the primary area of focus. If, however, Gaddafi could be portrayed as having been frightened enough by what was happening in Iraq to unilaterally surrender his weapons of mass destruction, the Bush administration could claim the Iraq operations, however flawed, had salubrious effects. According to one widespread interpretation, Gaddafi's peace offer emerged full-blown just as the US discovered Saddam Hussein in a spider hole in Iraq. Gaddafi, according to this view—and with profound irony, given what ultimately happened to him—was scared witless by the thought of experiencing a similar fate.

While Gaddafi's fear may have been a factor behind his attempts to accelerate talks with the new US administration, it cannot be taken as the central motive.[45] For Gaddafi, the post-9/11 US obsession with fighting Islamic terrorism offered a perfect opportunity to solidify earlier gains. Not only could he claim to possess intelligence that the US desperately wanted, but, should the US accept his offer, he could use the world's superpower to, in effect, wage his own internal battles. No matter that Libya's Islamists were not exactly synonymous with Al Qaeda. Several other Arab states were doing the same collaborative calculus at this time.

Bush administration officials continue to insist that Saddam's fall pushed Gaddafi to make a deal. Condoleezza Rice frames Gaddafi's decision to abandon WMD as a "nonproliferation breakthrough" that was aided by the toppling of Saddam Hussein. In her memoir, she writes, "Despite the trials and tribulations in Iraq, we registered some gains. For instance, the overthrow of Saddam Hussein was beginning to have a salutary effect on other parts of the non-proliferation agenda."[46]

Vice President Dick Cheney made the connection even more bluntly: "[O]ne of the great by-products of what we did in Iraq and Afghanistan is that five days after we captured Saddam Hussein, Muammar Gaddafi in Libya came forward and announced that he was going to surrender all of his nuclear materials."[47]

Martin Indyk would later riposte, "The implication is clear. Get rid of one dictator because of his supposed WMD programs and others will be so afraid that they will voluntarily abandon their weapons programs. Therefore, even if no WMDs were found in Iraq, we still made the world a safer place. The perfect comeback."[48]

While there was significant intelligence to indicate that Gaddafi was highly disturbed by what was going on in Iraq and sped up existing talks about a specific deal that involved WMD, the linkage between Saddam's actual capture and a decision by Gaddafi is specious.[49] As Rice indicates in her memoir, Gaddafi's decision came before, not after Saddam's capture:

> The Saturday before the Libya announcement [i.e., December 13, 2003], I'd called in Dan Bartlett to tell him about the coming good news [the Libya announcement]. I was surprised when he looked disappointed. "I thought you were going to tell me that we had found Saddam," he said. "That will be next week," I said in jest.[50]

As one former State Department official said, "The capture of Saddam was a reinforcing factor that injected some additional vigor into an ongoing process."[51] In further irony, various former US officials, including Wayne White, then deputy director of the Near East/South Asia State Department's office within the Bureau of Intelligence and Research (INR), attested that Gaddafi's worries that he might be next were altogether unfounded. Libya was "nowhere near the top of the US 'hit list' for regime change."[52]

More troubling is the Bush administration's apparent short memory. Rice speaks as if Gaddafi's renunciation of past bad habits had no additional context:

> Even more startling developments were emerging in Libya. In the spring of 2003 we heard through the British that Muammar Qaddafi wanted to open negotiations with the United States and the United Kingdom, with the carrot being an end to Libya's WMD programs. At first we didn't put much faith in the overture but we ultimately decided to send a joint CIA/MI5 team to assess the situation. It returned with a positive report: Qaddafi was serious.[53]

Indeed, Gaddafi had been deemed "serious" by Indyk and his colleagues in the Clinton administration several years before, in 1998.

Just as the US and, by default, its allies in Iraq, had their own explanation for Gaddafi's conversion, Gaddafi had his. He knew what the Americans wanted and knew he could use the international climate to potentially kill two birds with one stone. Not only could he claim to possess intelligence that the US desperately wanted, but, should the US accept his offer, he could use the world's superpower to, in effect, wage his own internal battles. No matter that Libya's Islamists were not exactly synonymous with Al Qaeda. Several other Arab states, including Tunisia and Egypt, were doing the same calculation.

WMD: What Libya Had—and Didn't Have

There is little doubt that Libya had many, if not most, of the pieces needed to make a nuclear weapon. Was Gaddafi anywhere close to actually making a functioning nuclear weapon? The strong majority of international analysts in this domain think not. Gaddafi had acquired a "significant" number of L-1 centrifuges through the notorious A. Q. Khan nuclear supply network[54] as well as "instructions for how to manufacture parts for, and build, a nuclear detonation mechanism." By 2000, Libya had started to install centrifuge cascades at the Al Hashan facility, just outside Tripoli. As of 2003, Libya was also known to have had about forty Frog 7 short-range missiles, three hundred midrange missiles, and eighty Scud B launchers with a range of 280 to 300 kilometers. Libya had tried to build its own short-range missile, first the *Ittisal*, then the *Al Fateh* and *Al Fajr*, and was seeking to build or buy longer-range missiles. International inspections after 2003 found five Scud C missiles and a hundred Russian Scud B missiles. Libya ultimately admitted to maintaining a uranium enrichment program at an initial level and to working on biological weapons, but claimed it had long since abandoned the program and had dismantled its Al Hashan centrifuges by 2002.

However, a large portion of the purchased equipment was defective. Many of the centrifuges were missing rotors, and a key part of the schematics provided by the A. Q. Khan network was missing. These details highlight Libya's principal failure with respect to any WMD efforts—its significant deficit in the human capital required to complete the nuclear weapons jigsaw.[55]

A number of nuclear policy analysts claim the United States was so eager to access Libyan intelligence that it overstated the prospects of the WMD program. Wyn Bowen, author of a monograph on Gaddafi's WMD program, notes that "the Libyan experience highlights the importance of not automatically equating the ability to buy parts and materials with the capability to establish an effective nuclear weapon programme."[56] A well-known French military affairs analyst characterized Libya's 2003 declaration a "pseudo renouncement . . . the exchange of failing or obsolete proliferation programs against the reinsertion of the country in the concert of nations."[57] Elliott Abrams quoted Saif Al Islam, in conversations with US officials, as saying that Libya's WMD were "not that great a threat." A US intelligence estimate around the time of the invasion of Iraq predicted that Libya would have enough enriched uranium to develop a bomb by 2007; this reading was subsequently deemed "very largely overestimated," and Libya's stocks of chemical weapons "far less than thought."[58]

Mohammed El Baradei, then secretary general of the International Atomic Energy Agency (IAEA), claims not only that the Bush administration exaggerated Libya's progress toward WMD, but that the State Department actively withheld information from the IAEA on the progress of this program: "The Americans were unhappy that I characterized the Libyan nuclear program, at first glance, as 'nascent.' The intelligence coup would have seemed more significant if it had been larger or closer to producing a weapon."[59] Baradei says his assessment was confirmed by IAEA inspections in the following months, and accused Energy Secretary Spencer Abraham of staging an "exclusive media show" at Oak Ridge National Laboratory, the temporary storage depot for remains of Libya's WMD program, when the materials first arrived.[60]

The Bush administration fought back against the dissenting opinions of experts. It argued vehemently that Gaddafi had indeed managed to pull together a sophisticated WMD program, that it did pose an "eminent threat," if not to any specific state, then to the nonproliferation regime in general. A US intelligence assessment released about the same time suggested that Libya may have had enough enriched uranium to create a nuclear bomb.[61] During a 2004 visit to the Oak Ridge National Laboratory, President Bush announced, "These materials are the sobering evidence of a great danger. . . . Every potential adversary now knows that terrorism and proliferation carry serious consequences, and that the wise course is to abandon those pursuits."[62]

However, the case for "averted disaster" was much more compelling within the context of biological and chemical weapons than nuclear capacity. Prior to the 2003 deal on WMD, the US and Western intelligence agencies and the IAEA appeared to have some knowledge about Libya's chemical weapons capacity: Libya had indeed managed to accumulate significant amounts of materials required to make biological weapons, including one ton of the neurotoxin tabun, twenty-four tons of yperite, and thirty-five hundred unarmed aerial bombs, useful in the delivery of chemical and biological weapons. In 1988, the CIA expressed concern that the complex at Rabta (which the Libyans claimed was a plant manufacturing insecticides) had the capacity to become "the most important factory of chemical weapons in the third world."[63] Since it had been set up, the factory had produced an estimated one hundred tons of chemical agents.

Nevertheless, debate revolved around the handling of nuclear WMD. Writing in 2011, Baradei was particularly critical of the CIA for holding back information on the activities of A. Q. Khan's network, including that relevant to Libya negotiations, for the better part of a decade. The CIA did so on the grounds that revealing its findings might have compromised efforts to root out other portions of the network. Baradei recalled his reaction to this news: "'Can you explain what was gained?' I wanted to shout. 'Where were all the bigger fish who should now be ready for the catch?'"[64] Still, though he did not agree with the way the Libya conversation had been handled, Baradei ultimately felt the agreement with Gaddafi had been positive in the cause for nuclear nonproliferation. For their part, partisans and former members of the Bush administration continue to argue that liberal analysts and the IAEA purposely downplayed the significance of the administration's achievement on Libyan WMD to serve narrow political ends.

Neoconservatives Say Nay

In the context of the war on terror, and as Gaddafi expected, Libya's extended overtures took on a new light for many within the administration, who saw an interesting potential for collaboration—after all, Gaddafi had been fighting (or supporting) Islamic extremists for decades, and surely had much information to share. Others felt Libya should be rewarded for its newfound "realism," if only so that other rogue states—Iran and North Korea, to name but two—would see the advantages of following suit. This sentiment was echoed by other senior figures within the US government, who took the Welch-Indyk line that there would be no "model," unless the US was able and willing to take yes for an answer. As Meghan O'Sullivan, author of a Brookings Institute study on the effectiveness of sanctions on rogue states, wrote: "By not adjusting U.S. policy in the slightest way to new realities, the United States risks undermining its own sanctions as well as its efforts to encourage other 'rogue' regimes to reform their behavior."[65]

On the other hand, prominent neoconservatives—those most enthusiastically pushing the US invasion of Iraq (particularly Wolfowitz and Bolton, then undersecretary for arms control)—were highly dubious of any benefit deriving from dialogue with Libya. Wolfowitz said, "Look, I think we needed to give some acknowledgment to the fact that he handed over his nuclear weapons program, but it was an illegal program. . . . I thought we were giving him a lot by, in effect, saying you won't suffer the fate of Saddam Hussein. I don't think we had to go nearly as far as we went."[66]

Bolton further believed a Gaddafi engagement would undermine the message of change and the prospect of the demolition of authoritarian regimes in the Middle East by domino effect.

Even so, National Security Adviser Condoleezza Rice and Secretary of State Colin Powell advocated a second look at the relationship with Libya. Both saw benefits to probing the merits of a relationship with Libya that might produce useful intelligence on groups such as Al Qaeda. The neocons essentially felt that "halfway measures" were not worth undertaking. With the upper echelons of the Bush White House leaning strongly toward engagement, the deal seemed to be done.

Even as the US and its allies contemplated and implemented a strategy to release Gaddafi into the wider world, some question whether the West fully appreciated the degree of leverage in its hands, with respect to changing the behavior of the Libyan regime, if not Gaddafi personally—or really cared if it did. (This was, in fact, one of the neocons' points—if one has leverage, one should use it to the maximum.) UK Foreign Secretary Jack Straw, when asked about this very point on the eve of lifting the EU arms embargo in October 2004, said, "[T]his is a very good day . . . for peace and security across the world. [We have not lost leverage over Gaddafi.] In fact, we have gained leverage."[67] It is difficult to see that the EU would have lifted its arms sanctions if the US were not in agreement. This point was important because the lifting of this particular set of sanctions enabled Libya to go on a buying spree over the next few years, with a focus on small arms and gear that was particularly useful in quashing any form of civil disobedience. Britain, France, and Italy were among the powers that sold weapons of all kinds to Libya, until the early days of 2011.

Human Rights

The Bush doctrine that emerged post-9/11 and after the commencement of the Iraq War held that the US would support the cause of "democracy against tyranny." Iraq was intended to be the cornerstone of a hoped-for wave of regime changes. A key talking point became the somewhat indeterminate concept of "transformational democracy," according to which diplomatic and economic rewards (trade agreements, such as TIFAs, for example[68]) would be offered to regimes that pursued change from within, particularly with respect to building democratic institutions and respect for human rights. The British articulated a virtually identical version of this doctrine with trade and engagement linked to responsible international behavior.

In Libya's case, it was hard for many to imagine how human rights could *not* be a central issue in any discussion of rapprochement. Despite the urgency behind the broader policy narrative for re-engagement with Libya, there were senior individuals within the White House, the State Department, the National Security Council, and the Department of Defense (DOD) who felt that Libya still had much to address in the area of human rights before full normalization could be contemplated. Congress saw little incentive for getting involved with Libya, apart from advocating for compensation for the Lockerbie victims, on one hand, and the interests of US oil companies on the other (but, as we will see, as the US-Libya dialogue continued, those factors would become increasingly important). Many within the State Department remained highly skeptical of any prospect of meaningful reform, especially in the area of human rights, as long as Gaddafi remained at the helm. Congress saw little incentive for getting involved with Libya, apart from advocating for compensation for the Lockerbie victims, on one hand, and the interests of US oil companies on the other.

Those in favor of proceeding with Libya included the White House, the CIA, and key individuals at the State Department. They had come to the conclusion that intelligence gains, countering nuclear proliferation, and something that might be called the salubrious impact of Iraq operations on other dictatorships trumped internal Libyan human rights concerns. Those opposed had difficulty mounting an effective countercase because of the profound lack of readily available information about what was actually happening within Libya. Senior State Department officials said they could not remember any discussions of the Abu Selim prison massacre, for example, let alone the Zawiya revolt.

Even without these data, some prominent administration officials opposed any rapprochement. Elliott Abrams, senior director for democracy, human rights, and international operations at the National Security Council for the first half of George W. Bush's first term, and deputy national security adviser for global democracy in his second term, was one of several who felt it was too early to reward Gaddafi. According to Abrams, the Bush administration calculated it was better to be realistic in terms of what one could expect from Libya, take what was possible, and hope that, basically, any contact with the outside world could only work in line with the aspiration of the Libyan people for freedom. (One might call this a *War of the Worlds* argument, after Orson Welles's famous radio play, a hoax live broadcast of an alien invasion of Earth. The aliens, on the verge of vanquishing the human race, begin to die off, are felled by the bacteria that causes the common cold to which the creatures had no resistance.) There were many in Washington, within the departments of State and Defense, and at the National Security Council, who still believed Gaddafi's conversion was about as likely as sticky, three-fingered aliens landing on the White House lawn. Abrams later said, we "won two and failed on the third."[69] By this he meant that the US, in dealings with Gaddafi, scored successes in counterproliferation and counterterrorism policy, but did very little to have an impact on the human rights situation in Libya. As one analyst put it, "The domestic behavior of Qadhafi's [sic] regime was seen as the least urgent issue surrounding Libya."[70]

When human rights concerns did come up in negotiations with Libya, almost inevitably they were focused on Libyan dissident Fathi Al Jahmi. Arrested on October 19, 2002, for calling publicly for free elections, a free press, and the release of political prisoners, Jahmi was originally sentenced to five years in prison on the charge of trying to overthrow the government and insulting Gaddafi personally. He was released on March 12, 2004, largely through the personal intermediation of then Senator Joseph Biden. Hours after being released, Jahmi gave an interview with US-backed Al Hurra TV in which he repeated his previous calls and said famously, "[A]ll that is left for [Gaddafi] to do is hand us a prayer carpet and ask us to bow before his picture and worship him." By upping the ante and making the attack against Gaddafi personal, Jahmi sealed his fate. Very few ever got away with insulting the Leader. Jahmi remained in Libyan custody for almost seven years, from his initial arrest until he fell into a coma in April 2009 and was flown to Jordan for treatment. He died less than a month later.

Former senior State Department officials blamed the brouhaha over Jahmi largely on Gaddafi's misunderstanding of what was good for him, and on Jahmi's brother Mohamed al Jahmy, a US resident, who did his best to keep his brother's situation in front of the media. Assistant Secretary Welch said he repeatedly told the Libyans that their best interests would be served by simply releasing Jahmi or transfering him to a hospital outside Libya (as was eventually done), rather than turning him into a cause célèbre.[71] Natan Sharansky, the famous Soviet Jewish dissident, an ardent supporter of Bush's Iraq policy, recognizes Jahmi in his 2004 book, *The Case for Democracy*, as a dissident deserving of the West's attention.[72]

While Jahmi's case was certainly worthy of scrutiny, the overwhelming emphasis on his plight had detrimental side effects. Most importantly, it detracted attention from the human rights atmosphere in Libya as a whole, obscuring the more severe offenses, which by the 2000s were coming to light. Former US intelligence officials said that there was "some reporting" as early as the 1990s suggesting there had been an ugly confrontation with casualties at the prison[73] (Abu Selim prison in 1996), but the precise magnitude of casualties was unknown at that time. By 2003, however, anyone who claimed not to know about Abu Selim was simply not listening. The

National Front for the Salvation of Libya (NFSL), the primary expatriate dissident group, had been attempting to draw the attention of international media sources for years. Ibrahim Sahad, the NFSL's head in 2011, complained he got nowhere: "The media and governments demanded proof." Sahad said, "We came back with certified testimonials from an eyewitness, but this was still not good enough."[74]

A senior officer with Human Rights Watch said his organization fully realized the deficiencies in the wider approach but decided to work with what they had, using Jahmi as a specific example of a number of different human rights issues, from freedom of speech, to habeas corpus, to torture, etc.[75] At a higher policy level, however, this attention was likely counterproductive, as it only served to increase Jahmi's value to Gaddafi as a lever, exposing the limits of US influence. Gaddafi himself may, in fact, have preferred the spotlight on Jahmi, precisely because it distracted from more wide-scale abuses of power.

The interesting thing about the Libya deal is that there had really never been a consensus within Western policy circles regarding what to do with Libya. There were significant portions of the governing establishment in the US and Europe—even those close to the incumbent heads of state—that were uncomfortable about what was happening. At the same time, there emerged a series of powerful and politically adroit advocates for the rapprochement who were able to keep it moving, while convincing some skeptics that Gaddafi could ultimately be held accountable.

While profit, personal and corporate, was not the primary driver behind the deal, the promise and temptation of large commercial deals were both part of what sealed the advances at each step. The fact that the Lockerbie compensation was tied to specific advances in US-Libya relations created undeniable pressure for the process to keep going, at least until, and unless, something completely untoward happened.

It was the same for the oil interests: once the American oil companies were allowed to start negotiations on a return to their former properties, the lobbying efforts began in earnest. As for Gaddafi, he was looking pretty good—to an anxious, exhausted public (and his closest aides), he seemed to have pulled off the impossible (indeed, a Gaddafi confidante told one Western diplomat in a moment of indiscretion that he and his colleagues were "stunned" the US went for the deal). Some of the most cynical (or realistic, as the case may be) on both sides conceded that perhaps something good would come out of all of this. Others were left with a queasy feeling that, however things proceeded from here, the chances were still good that the ending would not be pretty. The chances of Gaddafi's conversion being sincere were about as likely as sticky, three-fingered aliens landing on the White House lawn. No one, however, predicted that the end was so near—or that the WMD deal itself would be directly implicated. The other main point worth reflecting upon is summarized by the quote at the head of the chapter: The US actions, while they were not an expression of US interests to do harm to ordinary Libyans, were the last barrier between the Libyan regime and a slew of deals that had the potential either to be good, or very bad, for Libya as well as US interests in the region.

PART II

GATES OPEN

CHAPTER 4

The Americans Return

With the 2003 deal in hand, the US and Libya took practical steps to move the relationship forward. As a matter of priority, the Americans sent a team to Tripoli to help with removal of key elements of Libya's WMD program. In early February 2004, the State Department announced the "possibility of assigning a small number of personnel to each other's capitals, in the absence of functioning embassies"[1] and, nudged by the oil companies, lifted the ban on US citizens traveling to Libya.

Soon after, a team of American doctors arrived to assess the Libyan medical and humanitarian-response infrastructure. At Libya's request, the US agreed to host Libyan specialists to explore future educational exchanges. About a dozen senior Libyan educators and administrators arrived in Washington in summer 2004 for consultations and a tour of US universities. Shortly thereafter, a smaller US delegation flew to Tripoli for meetings with the heads of a number of Libyan universities. There was talk of holding a demonstration match between US and Libyan wrestling teams, though this ultimately never happened.[2]

In July 2004, the US presence was upgraded from an "interests section" within the Belgian embassy (a Belgian diplomat passed messages back and forth between the US and Libyan governments and was the point of contact with any US citizen in trouble) to a liaison office, one diplomatic rung below a full-fledged embassy. This action released the second tranche of Libya's promised compensation to the Lockerbie victims' families.

The US Liaison Office-Tripoli (USLO) was housed on the fifth and sixth floors of the newly constructed, sand-colored Libyan-Maltese Corinthia Bab Africa (Gate to Africa) hotel, a joint Libyan-Maltese concern. Completed the year before, the hotel, according to reliable sources, was built on the site of a Jewish cemetery—a hallmark Gaddafi maneuver, in the same vein as installing a sewage drain outside the Libyan Officers' Club, at the beginning of Gargaresh Street (which not only created a foul smell on-site, but polluted much of the Tripoli corniche). These were not-so-subtle reminders of just who had the power to make and unmake, practically anything in Libya.

Walking into a Black Hole

Never between 1993 and 2003 had Libya enjoyed priority attention within US government agencies. Dating back to 1991, the attentions of the State Department's NEA (Near East and South Asian Affairs) Bureau and its Maghreb (North Africa) desk were taken up almost entirely with the Algerian civil war. Though Libya was the next on the list, any resources devoted to it had to be split with Morocco and Tunisia. Wayne White, former deputy director of the State Department's Bureau of Intelligence and Research (INR) estimates that INR had at best a fraction of one man-year devoted to Libya during the years 1992–1997, with the CIA devoting perhaps three full-time people to the country over that same period. A significant amount of the collective effort was devoted solely to tracking Gaddafi's outreach to the West, as opposed to what else was happening within the country.[3] According to White,

> during the period spanning December 2002 to December 2003, 90 percent of my own efforts had been thrown into coverage of Iraq, including countless overtime hours and weekend work—particularly as the situation worsened during the last seven months of 2003. Keeping fully abreast of what was transpiring on the Libyan domestic political scene, in parallel, was highly problematic.[4]

Diplomats newly posted to reporting assignments in Libya would typically "read in" on past reporting on issues in the Libya-US and Libya-

West relationships—the vast majority of this information was limited to details of the early negotiations starting in 1998 discussed above. The more curious members of USLO staff supplemented this information with a small number of academic books on Libya then in print. Academia had virtually ignored Libya, and for obvious reasons: it was isolated; access was highly limited; and there was very little reliable data to be had on practically any related subject of interest.

During its first two years on the ground in Tripoli, USLO suffered both a lack of local capacity and restrictions in staff movement.[5] A typical, fully functioning embassy in a country of modest economic import typically might host a combined team of at least five reporting officers divided among economic, commercial, and political issues. Of course, USLO was never meant to be a fully functioning embassy. It was rather an outpost, meant to scout out the scene and begin to build structures that would ultimately support a full diplomatic presence. Matters were made even worse by the fact that, throughout the first two years, only one or two staff members understood enough Arabic to read a newspaper. This was a critical impediment to information gathering, especially when a large fraction of Libyans, even senior government ministers, spoke poor English.

(Strange) First Impressions

Deposited in Libya after an official absence of more than 20 years, US diplomats had little idea what to expect. There were few other countries at that point—for example, North Korea and, to a far lesser degree, Iran—where the veil had been drawn so closely. We found the capital of Tripoli an austere and crumbling city; much of the newer architecture represented the tastes of low-end ex–Soviet bloc or Korean contractors. The concrete drab was enlivened somewhat by colorful handmade drawings, pastel-green upraised fists, and slogans and aphorisms associated with Gaddafi's revolution. There were few public signs or billboards other than those celebrating Gaddafi: "Libyans' hearts beat as one for you" read one prominent billboard downtown. A single dilapidated movie house catered to expatriate South Asian workers; there were no theaters, no concert halls, and very few public diversions, other than a few threadbare cafés and a couple of restaurants catering excusively to foreigners.

Culturally and architecturally, the Old City was the most interesting part of Tripoli, largely because it was one of the few places with clear links to a pre-Gaddafi past, however neglected: dilapidated homes of members of the Karamanli dynasty, the ruins of the nineteenth-century American consulate, along with a few Roman ruins and Ottoman-era mosques. Circa 2004, the Old City was a warren of leaky residences and tiny groceries, populated by some of the poorest of Tripoli's residents, including many indigent African squatters. The narrow, unpaved alleys, at times marbled with garbage and sewage, would turn into noxious ooze that was difficult to traverse when it rained. It was possible to walk from the Corinthia Hotel clear across the Old City via a breach in the surrounding wall to Green Square, a ceremonial esplanade and the symbolic epicenter of Gaddafi's Revolution. The square was bounded on one side by Al Qasr Al Hamra (the Red Castle), from which Yusuf Karamanli is said to have watched the *Philadelphia* burn back in 1803. Gaddafi had converted the palace into a surprisingly interesting museum containing, among other artifacts, his 1970s campaign car—a powder-blue VW bug, which he had driven across Libya to commune with the masses.

If anything odd happened—and it often did—it happened in Green Square. Two US diplomats were rather stunned, on September 4, 2004, to encounter a late celebration of the anniversary of Gaddafi's Al Fateh ("The Conquering/Victorious") revolution. Rounding the square, the parade included ten large ostriches chained to the back of a flatbed truck, swaying back and forth amid the stop-and-go traffic. Just behind was a truck, the side of which read in Arabic, "Female Revolutionary Veterinary Corps." Another truck carried giant cardboard models of the National Supply Company's refrigerators. To the side, a group of young Tunisian men laughed hysterically while videotaping the proceedings. "This is far more entertaining than anything [Tunisian President] Ben Ali gives us," one quipped.

The Libyan manner of conducting affairs of state posed continual protocol conundrums for the Western diplomatic corps, which by and large was not accustomed to being treated as chits in a battle of egos between Libya and the countries they represented. Gaddafi frequently summoned senior diplomats to hear him speak at various locations in Libya. These speeches were often held at the Italian-built, black marble Ouagadougou Hall in his hometown of Sirte, or in Green Square. Those countries important enough (or whose staff was sufficiently fed up with or informed about Gaddafi's brand of hospitality) begged off. The others would assemble at the requested hour at the old Wheelus Air Base (since renamed Metiga Airport), where they waited hours for the arrival of an ancient Libyan

Arab Airline 727-200, retrofitted with Soviet engines. After the half-hour flight to Sirte, they would be driven around for a while in buses with curtains drawn and then deposited in front of the hall. There they would listen to Gaddafi's three-hour (or longer) speech. Anyone who witnessed such scenes had a hard time deleting the image of Gaddafi's flamboyant minister of protocol, Nouri Al Mismari, stoking the assembled representatives of various Basic People's Congresses into "spontaneous" expressions of devotion for the Leader, using a large, leather whip. (On one occasion, while Gaddafi droned on with the periodic whipping in the background, half of those present in the diplomats box were asleep; the ambassador of a major Asian country was reading James Michener's *Hawaii* in French, while Rana Jawad, an intrepid young BBC reporter, was in a visible altercation on the other side of the hall with Gaddafi's security, who had tried to confiscate her camera.)

USLO requested to see one of the much-vaunted Basic People's Congress in action, in the lead-up to the 2006 General People's Congress. This BPC was held in what looked like a converted schoolhouse. Apathy prevailed, as all the Libyans present appeared to have been dragged away from whatever else they were doing to put on a show for the American diplomats and were not quite sure of their lines. During the hour-long meeting, the local committee extemporaneously praised Gaddafi's revolution and waffled between cautious praise for the new relations with the Americans and warnings of the old tricks of imperialist forces. This scene was frequently repeated in the introductions to an increasing number of foreign think tank personnel and political scientists invited to speak at the Green Book Center, an institution devoted to analysis and commentary on Gaddafi's manifesto.

Throughout the first year, USLO staff people were occupied with a full slate of high-level issues related to the Lockerbie and WMD deals. These included overseeing the removal of surrendered material, passing diplomatic notes back and forth with the People's Secretariat for Foreign Liaison (the Libyan equivalent of a foreign affairs ministry), and arranging visits for Congressional staff (called CODELS), including senior officials from the departments of commerce; health and human services; and the bureau of oceans, environment and science (OES). As part of the WMD deal, the US offered to retrain Libyan nuclear scientists in less threatening fields. The US scientist redirection team, led by Dr. Marie Ricciardone, the wife of then US Ambassador to Egypt, Francis Ricciardone, expressed frustration that the Libyan interlocutor, Dr. Matouk al Matouk, then deputy minister of energy and technology, did not seem to take their meetings particularly seriously.

USLO had a host of other soft issues to take on. The OES department sponsored forty-odd US science delegations from 2004 to 2006. Various officials came to confer with Libya's Environment General Authority about cooperation and training on water and environmental issues. The Department of Defense and veterans affairs departments were interested in securing an American cemetery, which had somehow been "misplaced" since the last US diplomats left Libya in 1980 (though its location was well known to both the Libyans and the other Western missions).

Just as Iraq's promise as a haven for Western technology and services appeared to have disappeared, Libya came into view for many of the same companies as a potential replacement. USLO's capacity to deal with commercial inquiries was quickly outstripped. From a US government perspective, the main priorities were to understand better the environment as it related to oil and gas, and to help large US companies to bid effectively on large-ticket contracts like aircraft, telecoms, and infrastructure projects.

As the Libyans eased up on issuing visas for US officials for a time, Libya became the favorite exotic travel destination for a number of US administration officials, mostly Republican political appointees keen to see George W. Bush's transformational diplomacy in action. After visiting the USLO's offices, they were sure to visit the shops on Rashid Street behind the Corinthia to pick up prized Gaddafi paraphernalia, the most popular of which were "Gaddafi watches"—Chinese-made timepieces with pictures on the face of the Leader in various poses. At the start of the rapprochement, one could even find watches with Gaddafi's image superimposed upon an American flag.

As the Americans worked to catch up on lost time (most of the European embassies had reopened in 1999–2000), European diplomats practically reveled in what they saw as the Americans' "small-time" operation and relative disarray, quipping that the "Americans never entertained, and when they did, they offered hot dogs and paper plates."[6]

Reform Through Commerce

Once the meta-narrative regarding the reasons for the 2003 deal had been set, that is, Libya's giving up WMDs and terrorism for the lifting of sanctions, some of the secondary rationalizations for engagement came into relief. Accordingly, US and Western business leaders were to serve as a "force multiplier," setting the stage for deeper reforms by spreading the gospel of American-style capitalism. Among the earliest advocates of this view was Representative Curt Weldon, mentioned in the previous chapter. After a 2004 CODEL of which he was a member, Weldon announced that his aim was to "promote engagement between American and Libyan business interests, and thus foster the country's free market."[7] The subtext was that commercial deals might accomplish what diplomacy and/or military threats could not: change from within, a velvet revolution, perhaps led by the regime's reformist mouthpiece and Gaddafi's son, Saif Al Islam. The attractiveness of this approach was due presumably to the weakness (or limitations) of the original narrative, which held that, while the US had commercial and strategic interests in Libya, there were no levers with which to compel reform. In retrospect, one has to question whether this was really the case.

So the US and other Western countries were determined to proceed with the opening on the basis of so-called "soft" negotiation, untrammeled by requirements and boundaries. As Wyn Bowen of King's College London noted, "The Bush administration's incremental provision of rewards to Libya in response to the passage of key milestones further smoothed the dismantlement effort, despite the fact that this linkage was not deliberately established at the start and that there was some initial opposition within the administration to 'rewarding' Libya at *all*."[8] As time passed, Libyans with resources who had been uncertain about whether to support the reform efforts began to believe that they had been offered a fait accompli, this time backed by the US and the Western countries. If the US was not willing to push political reform or human rights, they too might as well participate in the process or leave the spoils to others.

Exceptionality

Lurking deep beneath the surface of US-Libya interactions was an interesting, counterintuitive, and potentially useful notion of American "exceptionality" within Libya's worldview. To paraphrase, the idea was that in spite of their history of exaggerated "anti-other" rhetoric, the US and Libya had an odd affinity, built through shared past experiences—those of the Libyan business community in the 1960s and recipients of US educational fellowships are cases in point.[9]

For Gaddafi, exceptionality sprang from a stark reality: the US was the sole (and most important) Western power yet to reestablish diplomatic relations with Libya after the lifting of UN sanctions in 1999. Despite his anti-imperialist rhetoric, Gaddafi was absolutely obsessed with attracting the attention of the US and bringing US leaders to Libya, on terms of quasi-parity. US sanction was the one thing Gaddafi wanted desperately but remained out of reach, tantalizingly so given that the US (as per its historical tendency) did not seem in any rush to consummate the relationship.

Less psychologically complex were latent affinities that a surprisingly high number of Gaddafi's senior advisers, ministers, and National Oil Company (NOC) executives would evince for the US. After dispensing with requisite pro-Gaddafi sloganeering, X or Y minister or his assistant would frequently confide that his years at the University of Arizona or Louisiana State University were "the best of his life." Prime Minister and NOC head Shukri Ghanem was an example of this group, having received his PhD from the Fletcher School at Tufts University. Musa Kusa, the feared head of internal security, held a master's in sociology from the University of Michigan. A large number of these well-positioned Libyans were also products of the Esso-sponsored US fellowships of decades before.

The older generation of Libyans, those with experiences with Americans dating back to the 1960s and 1970s, perceived the US—at least within trading circles—to stand for quality, style, and forthrightness in business. Just as there was a cadre of US-educated technocrats and monarchy-era traders with fond (if outdated) memories of the US and of American customs, there was a community in the US with deep personal attachments to Libya. Every other year since the late 1970s, more than a thousand people have gathered in Texas for a reunion of America-Libyan expatriates, many former oil workers and teachers, to sing the club anthem, "I will be back again Libya."

Not all attempts to capitalize on these past bonds or assumed commonalities were successful. The embassy attempted to reach out, through a couple of social hours, to the US-citizen families of Libyans educated in the states thirty or so years earlier, to explore their numbers and views. Many had married US citizens and returned with them to Libya, with the US spouse typically converting to Islam. In one such meeting, the dynamic quickly turned hostile. Many of these individuals accused the US of abandoning them or of being indifferent to the Libyan condition. Oil hit the flame as a visiting member of the State Department's intelligence bureau,

INR, with little appreciation of the Libyan context, spent most of the meeting simultaneously arguing against and arousing suspicions that he had been sent by the CIA to press them for information.[10] In another display of how far worldviews had diverged in thirty years, Ministry of Labor officials were publicly aghast (and privately amused) when confronted with a pair of female US officials dressed as if they were headed to a cabaret. One proceeded to give a slide presentation suggesting that Libya emulate a certain model of hotel financing recently applied to Afghanistan. The Libyans were taken aback a second time by the presentation itself and felt any hint of comparison with that chaos-ridden, resource-poor state highly insulting.

In an effort to amplify the increasing interest by US oil, aircraft and telecom companies senior Libyans tried to exploit the idea, then current in some American commercial circles, that the Americans had already lost the advantage to the European and Asian companies that had returned shortly after the UN sanctions were lifted in 1999. "The Americans are late," a high-ranking Libyan official told *The Export Practitioner* in 2004.[11]

Certainly, the Libyan oil industry benefited most immediately from European and Asian assistance. In the Americans' absence, a number of countries did good business in oil, construction, and general contracting, including Korea (Daewoo); Germany (Belfinger, Berger, Wintershall, Siemens); Sweden (Skanska); Italy (ENI); Spain (REPSOL); France (Total); and Turkey (various construction firms). Yet the trajectory was not always going up. From 2000 to 2004, Libya's trade with Italy and Germany plummeted, particularly in nonrefined products. Even Italy, which was traditionally Libya's number-one trading partner, experienced large-scale fluctuations in trade linked to political disputes; Italian exports to Libya held steady throughout the 1990s at just over $1 billion per year. The figure jumped about 20 percent in the years immediately after the lifting of UN sanctions in 1999, but continued to wobble until 2008.

By the late fall of 2004, Libya's economic opportunities began to enter the peripheral vision of some American companies outside the oil and gas industry. Particularly interested were those whose hopes of quick riches in Iraq and Afghanistan had been dashed by current events. However, there remained downsides to doing business in Libya, including the continuing stigma of secondary (US-imposed) sanctions as well as the barriers to information both within the country and within the US government in terms of what products could and could not be sold. The Foreign Corrupt

Practices Act (FCPA) discouraged many large companies without clear and compelling interests in Libya from pursuing business opportunities, as Libya figured among the most thoroughly corrupt business environments in the world. Bribes and kickbacks were a recognized way of doing business. General Electric's desalination division opted out of Libya entirely at one point, due to the local subsidiary's inability to get anything done without paying significant bribes. The local agent described the endless requests by Libyan partners and officials for cash or favors like accommodation or other forms of hospitality abroad.

In the early days of the US-Libya rapprochement, it was up to the legislative branch, not the executive, to advocate for US business, with oil notably at the fore. Within the Senate, several veteran members, including Patrick Leahy (D-VT) and Norm Coleman (R-MN), took strong stances in favor of developing US-Libya commercial ties. In August 2005, President Bush asked one of the highest-ranking US officials to visit Libya to that point, Richard Lugar (R-IN), the ranking member of the Senate Foreign Relations Committee, to help speed up the normalization process.

Inevitably, these were not wholly ideological gestures. The oil lobby helped to maintain a steady drumbeat as the 2005 deadline for reactivating "standstill agreements" on concessions left in 1984 approached. A former senior State Department official maintained that US oil company influence was "not as high as one might think," but noted the prominence of ConocoPhillips (one of the original Oasis Group, consisting of Marathon Oil, ConocoPhillips—formerly Continental—and Amerada Hess) in the lobbying efforts. The Sunlight Foundation, whose website describes its mission as "working toward the goal of transparency and accountability in the United States government," published in late February 2011 a list of seventeen companies on the "who's who" list of US and European conglomerates, which actively lobbied the US government. They included Royal Dutch Shell/Shell Oil, ExxonMobil, BP (British Petroleum), Chevron, Caterpillar, Boeing, Dow Chemical, Fluor Corporation, Raytheon, Marathon Oil, Motorola, Halliburton, Occidental Petroleum, and others, between 2005 and 2010.[12]

Corporate lobbying of Congress on Libya issues was particularly intense between 2006 and 2008, coinciding with deliberations about lifting Libya from the terror list and a possible repeal of the Libyan Claims Resolution Act (also known as the Lautenberg Amendment), which made it easier for victims of US victims of terrorist acts on foreign soil to seize the assets of those companies in the US, in the form of the US-Libya Claims Settlement

Act.[13] These efforts declined after Libya paid, in October 2008, $1.5 billion of $1.8 billion to clear outstanding claims unrelated to Lockerbie and the UTA cases. This payment also cleared the way for visits to the US of senior Libyan officials, including members of the Gaddafi family.

Selling the Libyan Private Sector on Reform

For Gaddafi, it was almost as important to convince Libyan expatriates (as foreigners) that the reform process underway was not just another subterfuge, because the regime needed the expertise and commitment of its own small, commercially savvy class to create and sustain the necessary narrative. With this in mind, in June 2003, Gaddafi appointed Shukri Ghanem, a former head of OPEC's secretariat, to the post of prime minister. This move was meant to reassure the Libyans and foreigners alike that the reform process would be handled professionally. A consummate technocrat, at home in both Libya and the West, with an eminently useful professional pedigree, Ghanem was one of the few Libyans who could have implemented the reform process.

Newly empowered, Ghanem sprang into action. One of his first announcements was the imminent privatization of more than three hundred sixty firms. This move was necessary to eliminate more than eight hundred thousand individuals from a bloated, inefficient public sector, and to encourage foreign direct investment. Ghanem's task over the coming few years was to make good on this effort. On the one hand, there was excitement within the miniscule private sector that this signaled a dismantling of Libya's state-run economy. On the other hand, dismantling Libya's state-run economy would have obvious consequences in terms of employment and sinecures for Libyan officials both living and dead (many on the private-sector rolls were phantom names whose pensions continued to be collected by others with connections).

The non-Gaddafi poster boy for Libya's reform efforts, Ghanem literally wrote the book on 1970s Libyan oil policy, entitled *The Pricing of Libyan Crude*. He had a reputation both internally and outside for being pretty much as honest as one could be in Libya. Ghanem had a substantial impact in bolstering the credibility of some reforms, from the time he was appointed Foreign Minister in 2001, to his appointment as Prime Minister, from 2004 to 2006. Within short order, one had a mixed group of "closet capitalist-reformists" (many of whom were members of the Revolutionary

Guards), bona fide businessmen, regime retreads without management skills, and recently returned Libyan émigrés, all chasing newly available agencies and foreign contracts. As a sign of the degree to which Gaddafi's latest, deepest commercial opening (*infitah*) had been internalized, in late 2005, there was a relatively large number of entrepreneurs—youth with connections—in their twenties and early thirties starting up a range of enterprises, from ISPs to marketing agencies and Western-style consulting firms. Many of them saw something of themselves in Saif Al Islam Gaddafi, a bridge between the old dinosaurs and a new, more enlightened regime—not completely free and open, but not completely closed and repressive.

For his part, Saif was starting to play his role with aplomb, reassuring everyone that reforms would continue and that Libya's economic landscape was changing for the better. In late 2004, Saif, with his clean-shaven pate, wire-rimmed glasses, and trademark broad, toothy smile, stood before one audience of about six hundred Libyan, European, and American business-people and diplomats and said that Libya did not need to "continue spending on the military field." He told them that he intended to work to "create sustainable, widespread prosperity for all Libyans, not just a few."[14]

In short order, five or more US-based Libyan friendship societies and/or business councils were formed and began to compete with one another for the favor of US-based multinational corporations and de facto anointment by the US government. On the Libyan side, a somewhat analogous Libyan Businessmen's Council (LBC) was formed and headed by Mohammed Mansouri, the agent for the American company General Electric Healthcare, to channel contacts with approved foreign companies. LBC was in many cases a personal vehicle for well-connected regime apparatchiks looking to capitalize on the new opening. Former members of the LBC insisted later that they truly believed, as did many in Saif's circle, that the regime would make good on its commitments to create a robust private sector and foreign investment framework.

Ambivalence Rules

The dynamics of commercial reform, as it played out in public debates, was both fascinating, puzzling, and at times, highly entertaining. Many of the older commercial agents wavered between loyalty to the homeland (if not Gaddafi himself) and what they saw as the overeager, overcritical (or hypocritical) attitudes of the West, with its newfound interest in Libya. Thus, there were well-connected (both tribally and businesswise) individuals simultaneously arguing passionately for economic reform (observing "red lines," they would rarely say "political" reform) while supporting the regime's position against outside skeptics. There were also those visibly identified with the regime, criticizing others obviously connected with the regime for not paying sufficient deference to prospective foreign investors. Thus, at a late 2004 conference, entitled "Libya: Opportunity and Challenge," Dr. Aref Nayed, an Islamic scholar-cum-engineer whose family held the IBM franchise, and several others publicly challenged UK Ambassador Anthony Layden after a lengthy speech lambasting Libyan progress in opening commercially to the West.[15] At the same event, Saif Al Islam Gaddafi publicly rebuked one of his men for interrupting the speech of a US oil company CEO for a piece of news he thought more important.

Many of those expatriate Libyans (perhaps one hundred) who returned to participate in the latest opening had profoundly mixed feelings. On the one hand, there certainly were opportunities to make money, all the more for those who understood how the regime worked and had expertise that the regime lacked. On the other hand, their actions could be seen to add legitimacy to a regime many of them detested and about whose conversion they were highly skeptical. A few insisted they would not have come back had the rapprochement not happened, solidifying Gaddafi's grip on power. One member of a prominent Misurata-based commercial family avowed, "We were extremely disappointed in the US acceding to Gaddafi's overtures. We fully expected this meant that we would be saddled with the Gaddafi family for another 35 years."[16]

Husni Bey, the chairman of an eponymous commercial group, had, within the span of a couple of decades, become one of, if not the most successful Libyan businessmen, creating and consolidating a mini-empire that spanned consumables, shipping, and logistics, with offices in Libya, Lebanon, Italy, and the UAE. A formidable presence, with an infectious laugh, Bey was among the most willing of Libya's protean private sector (and perhaps able, given the resources at his disposal) to do battle with the regime over key points of reform, even as many grumbled about the profits he was making.

In April 2007, Bey, representing the Libyan Businessmen's Council, participated in a televised debate, held in the context of a conference on economic reconstruction. Sitting by him were Saif Al Islam Gaddafi, Minister of Economy Tayeb Safi, Prime Minister Baghdadi Ali Mahmoudi

(Ghanem was dismissed and named head of the NOC in 2006), and Minister of Tourism Amaar Al Tayef. The government had recently published amendments to the direct investment law (the topic of this particular conference) and looked to Bey and other members of the commercial community to "help them through the sweet talk."[17]

During the conference, Mahmoudi and the other government representatives advocated private investment in underdeveloped regions, including territory west of Sabrata and an area of deep desert called Jarjar Umma in the east (Jarjar Umma, means, literally, "drag your mother around"). "The time has come for us to stop dragging our mothers around," Bey announced, before a crowd of more than fifteen hundred. "What Libyan business wants is not the privilege of investing in the desert, but secure property rights, and legal consideration on par with government or foreign-owned businesses." Bey then turned to Saif Al Islam, sitting in front of him in the audience, and said, "Do not be fooled—these people do not want a private sector." For his troubles, Baghdadi had Bey kidnapped, roughed up and thrown in jail, only to find himself compelled to apologize publicly to Bey some months later.[18] Saif's reformist newspapers, *Qureyna* and *Oea*, documented the scene in a piece entitled "Libyan Businessman Husni Bey: I was kidnapped, and forced to sign a check for millions as a condition of release."[19]

Bey's observations during the conference were largely borne out, as the government immediately enacted new measures to siphon off revenues and state funds through organizations such as the Social Development Fund, the Libyan Investment Authority (Libya's main sovereign wealth fund), and the Africa Fund, among others. The regime also commenced a massive grab of both private (deeded) land and promising small to medium-sized enterprises (SMEs), even while floating publicly the idea of a multibillion dollar fund with which to compensate victims of previous land and asset grabs.[20] As usual, it was far from clear, to quote Aretha Franklin, "who's zoomin' who."

For the returned émigré or homegrown businessman, the vast majority of so-called private-sector activities were ultimately either subsidized or absorbed by the regime. In the case of Buraq Air, Gaddafi's wife Safia was said to have provided much of the start-up capital.[21] For many, patronage came from Saif Al Islam or one of his representatives through organizations like OneNine Petroleum or Libya Al Ghad (Libya Tomorrow).

In spite of all the shenanigans, some of the more powerful returned émigrés insisted it was possible to do clean business in Libya, so long as they steered clear of government contracts. This may have been true for those whose operations were so small that they did not interest Gaddafi family members or key members of the Revolutionary Guard. Anyone visibly making money was susceptible to intimidation and would have to pay for their privileges.

The Primacy of Oil

For foreign companies, and for only a brief time, the money to be made in Libya justified all such difficulties. Bluntly put, if it had not been for oil, associated construction and power contracts, and, later, arms deals, the commercial interest in Libya would have been decidedly weak. Oil was the key resource. In 2004, Libya was ranked first among African countries and eighth in the world in proven oil reserves. It boasted 3 percent of the world total, with estimated reserves of 46.4 billion barrels of high-quality, sweet crude. Additional advantages included the low cost of production and proximity to European markets, eliminating transport costs and associated risk.

In some ways, the period of isolation had made the return to Libya more desirable for foreign interests. When it went offline, Libya had been underexplored relative to other oil-producing countries. Between 40 percent and 70 percent of the territory had been surveyed in the 1970s and 1980s using two-dimensional techniques primitive compared to those available in 2000. There was tremendous potential for bringing updated technology and methods to bear on existing production, which had fallen since previous decades.

In September 2004, the Libyan NOC announced imminent, sealed-bid auctions for exploration and production-sharing licenses (EPSAs) on a scale that had not been seen in Libya for years. EPSA IV contracts were to last for twenty-five years and specified what the winning firm needed to invest in infrastructure in order to maintain the concession. Another innovation, over direct-negotiated contracts were signing bonuses and firm-specified payouts that the NOC could use to determine a winner, in the event of identical bids, specifying what percentage of revenue went to the company and what went to the NOC ("M factor") bids. The NOC appeared genuinely eager to demonstrate that the bidding process was completely fair and transparent. The actual auction *process* may have been, there were various ways the bids might be enhanced or manipulated at the margins—and the results seemed to suggest they were.

More than two hundred fifty firms submitted proposals in the first round. Of those, sixty-eight qualified (NOC accepted bid qualifications), and fifty-seven submitted formal bids, in various combinations. When the results were announced on January 29, 2005, fifteen exploration blocks went to the US firms Occidental (Oxy), Amerada Hess, and Chevron Texaco and their partners. The remainder went to Indian, Canadian, Indonesian, and Australian firms. None of the major European firms won blocks.

Despite the show of transparency, many foreign analysts were absolutely certain the Libyans were favoring the Americans, alleging privately that political factors were at work in the allocation of real estate.[22] The Libyans pointed to the public, sealed-bid auction as proof that there couldn't have been any funny business, but extremely low revenue-factor bids combined with sky-high signing bonuses accentuated suspicion that undue influence had been brought to bear.[23] Transparency aside, it was very much in the Americans' and Libyans' interest for the Americans to be seen to be profiting handsomely from the opening. In 2005, the industry as a whole was anticipating peak oil, a sustained rise in crude prices to above $100 per barrel. The Libyans needed US technology both to discover new reserves and to extract maximum production from aging drilling infrastructure.

The argument can be made that conditions in Libya permitted US companies to bid far higher than their competitors. It would have been an entirely reasonable strategy for a US company with the appropriate know-how (particularly one with past experience in Libya and access to some of the old seismic data) to offer an "unreasonably" good price for Libyan real estate, in full expectation of the "unreasonably" good returns that only it or one of its sister firms could realize. Russian and Chinese oil and gas concerns, while aggressive in Libya at this time, could not match the technology of Occidental or ConocoPhillips. When deciding how to bid, they had to weigh the value they could extract against the prospects of future business and a foothold in Libya. Further, the information advantage with respect to new fields was arguably in the US corner: US firms had done most of the surveying of Libyan oil real estate in the 1970s and 1980s.

As always, personal touches were not lost on Gaddafi. Despite the fact that Gaddafi's squeeze of Occidental in the early 1970s resulted in billions upon billions of lost revenues to American oil, Ray Irani, Occidental's then CEO, took charge of negotiating the company's reentry into Libya, visiting Libya in 2005 to negotiate with Gaddafi face to face. While perhaps not a quid pro quo, the company heavily lobbied Congress and the Commerce Department for an exemption to the 2008 Libyan Claims Resolution Act. The strategy delivered what was expected: of the fifteen ESPA IV exploration blocks, Occidental took nine—far more than its competitors. For his pains, Irani earned a record $460 million in total compensation from Occidental in 2006, much of which was assumed to be compensation for his role in securing the company's wins in Libya and associated booked reserves.[24]

Questions remain as to what it took to secure some of these potential windfall deals. In June 2011, four months after the uprising, the US Securities and Exchange Commission (SEC) began an inquiry into possible violations of the Foreign Corrupt Practices Act (FCPA) by a series of US oil companies, including ExxonMobil, ConocoPhillips, and Occidental, and a number of US investment banks, including Goldman Sachs. The SEC conducted the inquiry in parallel with an investigation by the Libyan general prosecutor's office into "possible irregularities" during the Gaddafi era, many of which allegedly involved influence peddling by entities controlled by Saif Al Islam. The SEC inquiry was soon expanded to cover the activities of France's Total and Italy's ENI.[25] The assumption appears to have been that bribes for oil contracts had been embedded in deals with Libya's principal sovereign wealth fund, the Libyan Investment Authority (LIA).[26]

While US oil companies undoubtedly used Libyan deals to boost booked reserves and shareholder dividends, the companies en masse were also an instrument of US foreign policy. By securing substantial rights to current and future Libyan oil, the companies were enacting the US government's post-9/11 strategy of diversifying the sources of Middle Eastern oil.[27] It looked like a good bet at the time, for the companies were in the market for new sources and sufficiently believed in the Libyan reform narrative that they were willing to pay big money. Within a short time, however, many (those whose compensation structure was longer term) were starting to ask themselves if this had really been such a wise idea.

Honeymoon's Over, 2005–2006

For American diplomats, oil companies, and sundry others interested in the Libyan experiment, the first year back in Libya had been interesting, exhilarating, and exhausting—but largely hopeful. By the second year, the novelty had started to wear off, as both sides felt they were somehow not quite getting what they had bargained for.

Despite the fact that the USLO was still operating in a self-styled five-star hotel, conditions had become psychologically grueling. Embassy personnel were under constant surveillance. Hotel quarters, while well appointed, were cramped, often unbearably hot, and almost hermetically sealed. A joke within the group was that Libya was "Iraq, but without the shooting—for now." The combination of living conditions, "unaccompanied" status (no family members), difficulties in persuading the Libyan government to act on issues critical to moving the relationship forward, and mixed messages from a Washington completely preoccupied with the deteriorating situation in Iraq contributed to a sense of almost perpetual crisis. As a result, USLO gained a reputation within the department as dysfunctional. Key reporting and administrative positions remained unfilled from 2004 through most of 2005.

Of approximately two hundred forty diplomatic posts, the USLO's was rumored to be one with the highest curtailment (dropout or transfer) rate during these years. When questioned, a senior State Department official later said, "Frankly, I was not aware of this. All I can say is that we had our hands full, and while it took a bit of time, we ultimately got better resources out there."[28] The dropout rate, the criticism of Libya by those who left and came back and those who were managing them, and the unaccompanied status made it very difficult to induce anyone with significant Arabic skills to volunteer for Libya, other than on a temporary basis. Further, as the department was exerting stronger pressure on those with Arabic skills to serve in Iraq (many had initially refused on principle), many made the calculation that if an Iraq tour was going to be a condition for advancement within the Near East Bureau, they might as well bite the bullet, as a Libya tour would not count nearly as much when it was time for promotions. Thus, what one would have expected to have been, and in many ways was, one of the most exciting posts in the Near East Bureau, became a pariah post. Even those with serious competencies and the willingness to take risks were so overwhelmed with the magnitude of logistical problems, and complications to their personal life caused by Libya's "unaccompanied" status, that they quickly burned out.

During the first year, "diplomatic notes" (the formal diplomatic process for requesting and approving action) worked reasonably well. Western requests for information and action on a range of issues, even if not satisfied immediately, generated positive responses and some display of willingness to engage. A year later, many of the requests went unanswered, and Gaddafi's men made it clear that certain lines should not be crossed (with respect to human rights investigations and so on), and they reduced access to key ministers. Diplomats' occasional efforts to investigate conditions at Tripoli prisons were met with stern warnings from the Libyan side and threats to make the inquiring officers persona non grata. One member of the team, frustrated with the narrow range of subjects on which he was authorized to report, penned a brilliant three-part essay on the socioeconomic milieu of Moroccan prostitutes in Libya. These cables, entitled "To the Whores of Tripoli," were squelched by the clearing officer, and thus never made it to Wikileaks.

In the middle of 2005, much of the diplomatic community—the US's in particular—found that some of the Libyan government's early receptiveness (if not action) to requests for assistance on both high-level and more mundane administrative issues had been compromised, and that the Libyans were increasingly irritated with what they felt was an unwillingness on the West's part to recognize the "great sacrifices" Gaddafi had made in 2003.

Feeling ever unappreciated, Gaddafi began to chafe. "The more we give, the slower things go," became the Libyan mantra. Officials began responding to perceived (and in some cases, real) slights by imposing quasi-reciprocal penalties on US diplomats and businesspeople. At a time when Libya was ostensibly trying to recreate its image to the West, well-heeled American adventure travelers on international cruises found themselves denied permission to set foot on Libyan soil. Visa restrictions continued to prevent the US from fully staffing the USLO, and often caused some of the larger American oil companies to operate locally using skeleton staffs.

Interestingly, the second EPSA IV auction round, for which twenty-six areas were on offer, resulted in a sweep, not for the Americans, but for the European and Russian firms and the Asian companies like Nippon and Japex. In the third round, covering fourteen areas, the Russians (Gazprom), Canadians, and Germans won exploration rights. ExxonMobil was the lone American company to pick up new real estate. The results likely reflected a message to the Americans from the Libyans that progress in the Libya-US relationship was not going as fast or as deep as Gaddafi wanted or expected. The results also showed the increasing feeling within the industry that Libyan terms (production-sharing demands and expectations of high signing bonuses, and subsequent demands for the incorporation of Libyan nationals in senior positions) were too harsh, given expected returns.

In early 2005, the foreign oil companies began holding collective monthly "awareness meetings" in which to discuss impediments to business that were not specific to any one company. Visas were always at the top of the list. Other issues included more or less incessant demands from the

Libyan government, via Matouk al Matouk, the Libyan minister of labor, for increased quotas in the hiring of Libyan nationals (the vast majority of whom were wholly unqualified). Several companies reported receiving lists of people they should hire directly from Matouk's office.

Frequent changes to tax and investment law as it applied to the oil industry activities were also issues, as were security around oilfields and transport logistics. (Saif Al Islam, for example, at one point canceled all the foreign oil companies' original aviation service contracts and required a Libyan company, whose equipment was not up to international safety standards, to provide service.)

Another issue was the Arab League boycott of Israel. According to a law passed by the US Congress in 1977, US companies would be fined for any collaboration with countries that implemented the boycott. While there was no blanket application of boycott's provisions to US firms at this time, officials within the Ministry of Trade and Investment would selectively put forth proof of compliance to US companies as a requirement for registering a representative office, which in turn would set off a flurry of diplomatic correspondence to Washington. Meanwhile, the General People's Congress began to churn out new, almost weekly, mutually inconsistent laws on various commercial topics, requiring considerable back and forth to determine which law applied and on whose authority.

In late 2006, chargé Gregory Berry, who had held the fort from USLO-to-Embassy for nearly three years, returned to Washington, to be replaced for the better part of the following year by former US Ambassador to Niger, Charles Cecil, as the US Ambassador-nominee Gene Cretz, sat in Washington awaiting clarity on his status, from both the Americans and the Libyans.

Cecil would recall that his time in Libya was marked by the (usual) endless arguments with the Libyans over the granting of visas for US official and business visitors. He described an atmosphere in which all US diplomatic personnel were very closely minded, and contact with ordinary Libyans limited—already a rather dramatic change from the previous three years, certainly since 2004. Cecil noted that the US-Libya relationship had come under tighter control in the months before his arrival, with day-to-day aspects of the relationship moved from the Americas Desk within the Foreign Ministry over to the European Desk, then under the direction of Abdelati al Obeidi, a prominent figure in the Gaddafi hierarchy. Nonetheless, Cecil was one of the very few US diplomats to visit Derna since the rapprochement, and says he also saw no overt manifestation of extreme Islam: "The imam of the town's oldest mosque invited me to his office," Cecil recalled, "The book I saw on his shelf was a copy of Paul Samuelson's introductory Macroeconomics textbook. We had a pleasant chat about the hopeful future of US-Libya relations."[29]

Enter the Gaddafis

My children are like a bag of rats—
when they get out of line, I just shake the bag.

MUAMMAR GADDAFI.[30]

The Western rapprochement coincided with a fateful demographic bulge within the Gaddafi family: the coming of age of many of Gaddafi's nine children. This proved a mixed bag indeed for Gaddafi, who up until now had enforced a near-complete ban on public appearances by or discussions of his immediate family.

While the Gaddafi children certainly had their issues, not all were sociopathic personalities in the Udai and Kusai Hussein mold. Each member of the family had a different persona, with varying degrees of socialization, and different uses for and relationships with Gaddafi himself. The younger sons received a fair share of international press for a range of bad behavior, which was known to have upset Gaddafi; the eldest, Mohammed, and the youngest, Saif Al Arab, got little press attention.

Saif Al Islam (born in 1972) was Gaddafi's second child and the first of his second marriage to Safia Farkash, of the eastern Obeidat tribe. Because of Saif's prominence as a political figure and the fact he was the most interesting, exposed, and public member of the Gaddafi family besides Muammar, Saif took a far greater role in the Libyan makeover than any of his siblings.

Gaddafi's firstborn son Mohammed (born in 1970), known as "The Engineer" for his profession and training, ran the Libyan Telecom and Technology Company (LTT) and on the side presided over the Libyan Olympic Committee and the Libyan Automobile Club. Many staunch opponents of the regime paid a certain respect to Mohammed, evincing grudging admiration for his professional competence and the fact that, for the most part, he managed to avoid politics, the limelight, and the scandals that dogged many of his brothers.

The foreign media painted Saadi (born in 1973) as the black sheep of the family, as it seemed unclear what he wanted to do with his Gaddafi connections. (Perhaps a better characterization would be that he was less wild than his brothers Hannibal and Mu'tassim, less idealistic than his brother Saif, and less focused than Mohammed.) Saadi made his public name early in his twenties as a soccer player, with a stint in the Italian club Juventus, of which the Libyan-Arab Foreign Investment Company (LAFICO) held a minority stake. Later on, he dabbled in film, putting $100 million into a remake of the German thriller *The Experiment*. Married to the daughter of one of the Colonel's senior military commanders, he was rumored to be the target of extortion by the Italian mafia, which allegedly attempted to blackmail him over compromising photos of a sexual nature. To the outside world, Saadi was best known for his partying and paid photo ops with celebrities such as Nicole Kidman.

Gaddafi's fourth eldest son, Mu'tassim Billah (born in 1977), was largely absent from public view from 2004 until 2006. Rumors running the diplomatic circuit held that Mu'tassim was under a heavy cloud, for his role in the alleged attempted coup in 2003 (despite this fact he had been reinstated with military rank shortly thereafter). An altogether more plausible explanation for Mu'tassim's absence was offered by a former senior Gaddafi official in the wake of the revolution: Gaddafi had in mind (again, due to his keen judge of character) that Mu'tassim should be the military backbone of the regime and wanted to send him to Egypt for staff training. He was concerned, however, that Mu'tassim might be the target of Egyptian radicals. He also saw an opportunity to confuse the radicals and potentially gain information about their activities within Libya by creating the impression that Mu'tassim might be "with them." Had Mu'tassim actually been behind an attempted coup, one can surmise he would not have had the opportunity to confront the rebellion in Sirte with Gaddafi fifteen years later. For those who felt Saif was too soft to be Gaddafi's successor, Mu'tasssim was the perfect antidote.

Khamis (born in 1983) began his career as a member of the national police. He was trained in Russia and ultimately put in charge of a group of better-than-average-trained troops, the 32nd Brigade, aka the Khamis Brigade, whose primary mission was to protect Gaddafi and his sprawling residential compound-cum-fortress and command center Bab Al Azziziya (The Splendid Gate), in a southern suburb of Tripoli.

Ayesha, Gaddafi's oldest daughter (born in 1976) was trained as a lawyer and famously served on Saddam Hussein's defense team in the lead-up to his execution in 2006.[31] She was something of a fashion maven; images of her racy Tripoli wedding soon found their way to YouTube. Following on the heels of her brother Saif, with whom she seemed to have the most in common temperamentally, she interacted with the regime and the outside world primarily through the Watassimo charity organization.

Hannibal (born in 1975) oversaw all of Libya's maritime and ports interests as the head of the General National Maritime Transport Company (GNMTC). He was known as "Captain," for having taken a few courses at a maritime academy. Not much is known about Saif Al Arab (born in 1982), other than that he also had some military training. Gaddafi adopted two children: a son, Milad Abuztaia Al Gaddafi, and a daughter, Hanna, who became well known as the alleged Gaddafi family casualty in Reagan's 1986 bombing of Gaddafi's compound at Bab Al Azziziya.

Until 2004, Saif Al Islam was the only Gaddafi child to have developed a quasi-public political persona. By mid to late 2005, other members started to emerge, largely due to a series of foreign scandals (also a direct result of the easing of travel restrictions on members of the regime) and internal disputes that were poorly hidden from Tripoli's diplomatic community. Hannibal was one of the first to draw negative attention to himself. In Italy in 2001, he was involved in a drunken brawl outside a disco, which ended after Italian police officers doused him with a fire extinguisher. He was arrested in Paris in September 2004 for driving at 140 kilometers per hour through the Champs Élysées.[32]

Following Libya's economic reopening, two incidents in 2005 revealed the evolving fissures and tensions within the Gaddafi family to a small group of diplomats and expatriate businessmen. The first involved the ownership of the Coca-Cola franchise; the second involved the distributorship for Caterpillar, the American manufacturer of construction and mining equipment.

Prior to Mu'tassim's alleged banishment from Libya in 2001, he had been the patron for a secondary distributorship of Coca-Cola products, manufactured in neighboring Tunisia. In his absence, Mohammed supposedly moved in to sign a deal with the KA-MUR bottling company, based in Cyprus, and partly owned by the Libyan Olympic Committee, to set up a Coca-Cola bottling plant in Libya proper. When Mu'tassim returned from Cairo in 2003, he demanded the franchise be awarded to him. Mohammed refused to cede control, so Mu'tassim threatened him, the Jordanian managers of the local plant, and various members of the staff, at least one of whom told the US mission he had been stuffed into the trunk of a car and driven around Tripoli for the better part of an afternoon.

All parties had interests in keeping the feud under wraps, as revelation would have put a serious damper on US business interests in Libya. The subsidiary was not American and the Coca-Cola parent company had not requested assistance, so this matter was not under US diplomatic jurisdiction. Nevertheless, after the KA-MUR executives asked the embassy to intervene, the USLO sent diplomatic notes requesting the government, that is, Gaddafi, help diffuse the situation. Ayesha allegedly interceded with her brothers to lower the temperature, as she would do several times subsequently. The Coca-Cola war proceeded over a period of months in soap-opera fashion without the foreign press learning of it.

Even as the Coca-Cola issue smoldered, another even more dramatic contest unfolded. Mu'tassim sent members of his private militia to take over and shut down the local Caterpillar plant for "operating without proper licenses." At the time, it was not exactly clear who was fighting whom or why, but Mu'tassim's private militia was onsite for well over a month.

Much later, Ayesha said that she and her brothers conferred before taking any action that might affect their respective or collective interests. By the end of 2005, Mu'tassim and Hannibal had emerged as the clear bad boys of the family. As Assistant Secretary David Welch related some years later, "At the time, of the possible future leaders of Libya, Saif looked to be the best of the available options,"[33] even though Mu'tassim's style was perhaps more conducive to keeping a lid on Libya.

While it is very difficult to guess exactly what Gaddafi was thinking in the years following these violent outbreaks of sibling rivalry, certain exigencies were obvious. He needed to ensure that his children, now teenagers or adults, did not present a direct challenge to his rule and, more importantly, that one or more of them would be around to continue the dynasty. (It can be argued that there was never really any sign that Gaddafi saw the succession issue as pressing, even at the age of seventy and after forty-two years in power.) Whether at this point he was truly focused on Saif, or Mu'tassim, or looking to Khamis or someone outside the family is completely unknown.

It's All Good

For all the difficulties, there was also progress. The most visible cultural event came in summer 2006, with American participation at the Tripoli

International Fair, a sprawling commercial trade show in the center of town, which had been held—even during the sanctions—every year since the 1970s. While the Libyan administrators were not very cooperative, at one point selling the US space to another country, the USLO was able to rent a modest two-story structure to host exhibitions from twenty or so US companies and their newly appointed agents. As part of the exhibits, the public affairs officer and I collaborated to import an American band, for a concert to be given at the US national day (every country had its own day during the event).

When USA Day arrived, ten thousand Libyans showed up and treated Luna Angel like a rock star, rushing the stage during the hour-long show. While some in the crowd were reluctant to accept the small American flags that were being passed out—for any number of reasons—the moment seemed cathartic in a way. Oddly, while the European press covered this event, there was not a single mention in the US papers. "In how many other Middle Eastern countries at this time," quipped one observer, "would you see thousands of youth waving American flags and singing along with an American band? And yet, it's as if this never happened."

For someone not immersed in the West-Libya political dialogue, social and physical changes in Tripoli were quite visible. Internet cafés and Italian-style cafés were springing up. Downtown, fashionable districts like Ben Ashur and Gargaresh Street were jam-packed with joyriding young men and women, who passed recorded messages to one another on cassette tapes. Green Square sported a shiny new outdoor restaurant and café, Al Saraya, replete with *shisha* (hookah) stations and fancy-clad waiters. This was the place to see and be seen by the new Libyan elite, their protégés, Western suitors, an increasing number of Japanese tourists—and the Libyan government (given the expensive surveillance equipment mounted on the roofs of adjacent buildings).

This optimism and progress was matched by desperation of many informed Libyans. A group of a hundred eight Libyan dissident émigrés produced a white paper entitled, "A Vision of Libya's Future." In it, they demanded a new regime committed to human rights and built upon democratic foundation.[34] The urgency these individuals felt reflected their fear that Gaddafi would actually succeed in reforming himself, at their collective expense. Longtime Libya watcher Luis Martinez characterized the situation: "For those who opposed the Libyan regime, the rehabilitation of Libya seemed to sound the knell for the hopes of democratic change."[35]

In the first few years after the opening of Libya, there was also a modest literary renaissance. Some of this outburst manifested itself in journalistic pieces, but also in poetry and short stories. The newest literary products contained only lightly veiled criticisms of the regime, all the while respecting the red lines by only indirectly mentioning members of the Gaddafi family. Just as Sadiq Neihoum and others attempted to do during the monarchy and the early days of Gaddafi's revolution, the new writers tried to expose the arbitrariness and absurdity of government, and the relative backwardness of some of Libya's traditions.

In one story, "Awdat Caesar" (the Return of Caesar) by Meftah Genaw, a statue of Roman Emperor Septimius Severus (which at one point during the Monarchy had been pilfered from Leptis Magna, and propped up in what became Green Square during the Gaddafi years) is mysteriously brought back to life to marvel at the physical decay that occurred under Gaddafi's rule. Caesar commiserates with a bronze statue "Nude woman with the Gazelle" (an artistic vestige of Italian rule, that sat on a traffic roundabout just off the square), that might have been erotic had she not been encrusted with dirt and rust.[36] (The Statue of the Gazelle would become an objet celebre after the 2011 revolution as a small group of Salafists tried to deface it, for being un-Islamic). In another story, "My Friends When I Die," an older man takes solace only in the thought of staging a proper funeral when he dies, with money he had set aside for his son's education.[37]

Many of the writers had connections in the regime that enabled them to publish, bypass state censors, and even win prizes for their work. Other, less subtle pieces of protest fiction were passed between friends or published outside Libya under pseudonyms in Internet newspapers, such as *Libya al Yowm* (*Libya Today*).

The Final Piece: The Fight to Get Libya off the List

Circa 2005, Libya remained on the list of state sponsors of terror, where it had been since 1979. The designation was a key impediment to full normalization with the US and the lifting of the final US sanctions on Libya—itself the key to a much broader and deeper range of commercial activities with the outside world. This was the prize Gaddafi was after.

Removal from the terror list was important to US-Libya interactions, as the list effectively barred a range of important commercial transactions—

not the least of which was the purchase by the Gaddafi regime of quantities of new weapons to replace stocks made obsolete over the previous decades. It was more important to Gaddafi symbolically, as it was the last measure standing between Libya and full diplomatic rehabilitation, a full stop to the impediments placed on Gaddafi in reaction to his reign of terror in the 1980s. Lifting Libya from the terror list was tantamount to the US giving Libya a clean bill of health.

The primary requirement for a state to be removed from the list of state sponsors of terrorism is the president's certification that:

> (A) the government concerned has not provided any support for international terrorism during the preceding 6-month period; and (B) the government concerned has provided assurances that it will not support acts of international terrorism in the future.[38]

The decision to normalize relations with Libya was technically independent of the decision to lift Libya from the terror list, although in terms of atmospherics, the two were clearly linked. Full normalization of relations (and the upgrading of USLO to embassy status) required the president to notify Congress of the intent to upgrade status, in turn triggering a fifteen-day review period, during which Congress could voice objections.

Those individuals arguing for lifting this last, and highly symbolic, barrier to Libya's reaccession into the international community won out over the diffuse skeptics, as they had in the past. During the congressional review period, the administration was broadsided by a statutory requirement for Congress to publish a list of all countries not fully cooperating in the war on terror. The deadline was May 15, 2005. Given Tripoli's intense cooperation with the US on intelligence, some in Congress and at the State Department felt it was unfair to withhold Libya from the list of countries assisting the US with counterterrorism measures, and, by extension, to retain the state sponsors of terror designation.

Once the office of the President certified a country was in compliance with the terms set for removal from the Terror List, Congress had forty-five days in which to object, via new legislation. The White House was eager to push Libya's removal from the list forward, but was also highly conscious of potential political backlash. Ideally, it would have considered more weightily not only the views of US victims of past acts of terrorism, but various public cases, including that of five Bulgarian nurses and one Palestinian doctor (known as "the medics") charged with infecting (variously) 438–461 Benghazi children with HIV back in 1998, and sentenced to death, under highly opaque circumstances. The medics' case remained unresolved four years after the US and Libya had begun negotiations. The fact that Congress had just forced President Bush to back down on the Dubai port operator DP World's bid to operate several container ports on the US Eastern Seaboard (it was denied), constrained the White House's ability to act, had Congress voiced strong objection to moving the Libya relationship forward. In fact, since Libya had committed to settling the Lockerbie claims, Congress seemed more or less likely to approve of removing Libya from the list. It was the Libyans who appeared to be intent on making it difficult, as an almost unbelievable plot began to surface.

Impulse Buy

Many close to the process said that Libya might have been removed from the list at least a year earlier if not for revelations concerning Libya's 2003 plot to kill then Saudi Crown Prince Abdullah, following a spat between him and Gaddafi at an Arab League Summit earlier that year.[39] The Libyans attempted—successfully—to pass this off as a private matter in which the US was meddling. In support of this view is the fact that the Saudis, while they loathed the Libyans (and vice versa), effectively settled their differences with the Libyans well before the terror list review deadline. As then Assistant Secretary David Welch recounted, "Here they were at each other's throats, the next thing we hear, Mohammed bin Nayef [then Saudi deputy minister for security affairs] is in the Libyan desert falcon hunting with Saif."[40]

Ultimately, a Libya-Saudi reconciliation was effected at the margins of the twenty-first Arab League Summit, held in Doha on March 30, 2009, when Gaddafi unexpectedly apologized in his own unique manner to now King Abdullah, saying, "I consider this personal problem between us to have ended, and I am ready to visit you, and to have you visit me."[41] Musa Kusa purportedly added, off camera, "If we had really wanted Abdullah dead, we would not have failed."[42] With one major roadblock cleared, another popped up. Gaddafi made disparaging remarks about the US and Bush on Libyan television, and Welch was again in the position—and not for the last time—of reminding the Libyans that this kind of sounding off was most certainly not serving Gaddafi well in Washington or with the Bush White House.

Cat's Out of the Bag, May 2006

Despite serious misgivings in various parts of the US government, on May 15, 2006, Libya was finally removed from the terror list. The influence of individual members of the Bush administration and State Department in pushing the Libya-US rapprochement past this last, critical goalpost was substantial. One former official with access to Saif said that senior US officials had reassured Saif, at the point when removal from the terror list looked most in jeopardy, that the Saudi issue would, ultimately "not be an issue."[43]

Gaddafi reveled in his newfound power. Sensing how much the outsiders wanted to strike deals for their own purposes, Gaddafi began immediately to divide and conquer, demanding higher and higher prices. A *Vanity Fair* article quotes a "frequent visitor" to Libya describing Gaddafi's strategy as the "deep stack . . . in which a rich player with mediocre cards intimidates opponents into folding by raising the stakes to levels so high that they dare not call his bluff. And that, says one frequent visitor to Libya, is the way Qaddafi does business."[44]

With Libya off the terror list, Gaddafi felt redeemed and moved quickly to call in previous favors (that is, funding to foreign states) to positions of symbolic importance, such as the rotating leadership of the African Union, something he had craved for years. Much to the chagrin and outrage of the US and Europe, Libya was elected by secret ballot to the chairmanship of the UN's Human Rights Commission on January 20, 2003—three years *before* its removal from the Terror List.[45] The *New York Times* called it an "act of such absurdity that it may finally force some serious thinking about reforming the commission."[46] Even after all of its gestures in service of Libya, the US couldn't help but object to Libya's election, admitting in the process that Libya's human rights record was "horrible."[47] US ambassador to the commission, Kevin Moley, said, "It is especially sad today when America celebrates the birthday of Martin Luther King, a champion of human rights, that a nation which flaunts human rights abuses, would be elected chair."[48] It all served to prove to Gaddafi that virtually everyone could be bought and that, in fact, the Western countries were neither united in policy nor paying careful attention to his actions.

CHAPTER 5

The Great Makeover

The fact that Gaddafi was able to waltz back onto the world stage in such a dramatic manner within a relatively short time after the 2003 WMD deal is a testament to a number of factors, not least of which were Gaddafi's own manipulations, tied to past largesse and the promise of future spending. His success was also the product of an extensive makeover process in which the US and UK were heavily implicated. Many institutions and individuals in the West and Libya participated in this recasting of Gaddafi's regime. Some were believers, in that they felt fundamentally that Libya could be reformed; others, many in the academic community, were reluctant pragmatists, dubious about where Libya was headed, but hard-pressed to turn down an opportunity for involvement in what they saw as an interesting experiment. Others were simply after the money.

Whatever the views of those on the outside, there was never any discernible sign that Gaddafi had fundamentally changed his way of thinking. In fact, to the contrary, there were ample indications that Gaddafi was progressively more "checked out." (During meetings with Western diplomats, Gaddafi often remained awkwardly silent; while he could pull together to deliver marathon speeches, often he appeared under the influence of sedatives.) At the same time, he delegated more of the hard decisions to those around him, while thoroughly enjoying the new opportunities to thumb his nose at enemies and suitors alike. It was almost as though Gaddafi had grown tired of governing, per se, and preferred to indulge his nuttier side.

The question is whether the beginning of Gaddafi's makeover preceded the opening to the West or followed from it. Very likely it was a bit of both. In order to convince the US government (as opposed to the Europeans, who were very much on board with the rapprochement as of 1999) that Libya was serious, Gaddafi's advisers and, to some degree, Gaddafi himself, understood that he had to make some effort to appear reasonable. Saif Al Islam appeared to have played an outsize role in this process, both in communicating this need (and opportunity) to his father and in serving as his effective stand-in during critical periods in the negotiations.

Many internal and external advisers clearly came to the same conclusion. If a Libyan makeover were possible, there would need to be an acceptable proxy for Gaddafi, one who was preferably not too reminiscent of him. There were few candidates better suited to this role than Saif Al Islam Gaddafi. Even as early as 1997, Saif was the most urbane and accessible of Gaddafi's children. He betrayed no noticeable signs of the sociopathic tendencies of many of his siblings, such as Mu'tassim, Hannibal, or Khamis. Even his hapless brother Saadi's acts of rage seemed to come from an inability to "find himself" in Gaddafi's shadow. The fact that Saif seemed genuinely uncomfortable being cast in this role served the purpose even better. Finding the right person to represent the regime was not an easy task, nor was it the end of the story. A whole range of processes had to be set in place in order to lend credence to a strategy that would emerge, again by design, as half-real, half-fantasy.

Of Strategists and Makeover Artists

As of 2003, Libya had engaged a number of parties to help it navigate the critical juncture in Washington. Sandra Charles, a former deputy assistant secretary at the Department of Defense, was head of C&O Resources, a "Washington process" advisory firm that did work for other governments, including the Saudis. A former US congressman on a trip to Libya suggested to Saif Al Islam that he enlist Charles to advise the Libyan government (in fact, Saif himself) on strategic issues related to the US-Libya relationship. Charles maintains that the Libyans and Saif, who was then thirty-one, were particularly uninitiated in the way Washington worked. "While there were many who wanted to jump right into the PR [public relations], we did not see the point of messaging until Libya understood what it was they needed to re-image—"and there were so many things," Charles said.[1] Charles met with Saif in Libya in summer 2004. She conveyed to him the necessity of addressing a range of unresolved issues before making much progress on the US side. Her key recommendations included either deporting or transferring to a foreign hospital the long-standing dissident Fathi Al Jahmi; pardoning the Bulgarian nurses accused of infecting Benghazi children with HIV (see chapter 6); contributing to the African Union Peacekeeping force in Darfur, Sudan; proactively speeding up the dismantling of chemical weapons stocks; and helping resolve remaining administrative issues in order to open a full-fledged US Embassy in Tripoli. Above all, Charles advised the Libyans, if they wanted to make progress, they would do well to "keep a low profile."

The same year, independent of C&O Resources, the Libyans signed a $1.4 million contract with Randa Fahmy Hudome, a former consultant to the Bush campaign on Arab American issues, to become their primary media consultant and lobbyist. After the 2004 election, and while still working for the Libyan government, Hudome was awarded a post as senior aide to Secretary of Energy Spencer Abraham. She was also involved in an Arab American campaign to promote President Bush's efforts in the area of "human rights, democracy and self-determination."[2]

Hudome was criticized in many corners of Washington for her ongoing connections with the Bush campaign and the Department of Energy, even as she served as a lobbyist for the Libyan government. Other Washington lobbyists described Hudome's efforts as "overzealous," citing, among other things, her suggestions that Saif Al Islam be nominated for a Nobel Peace Prize for his efforts to resolve the Lockerbie issue.[3] Another US government official who went back and forth between the Department of Energy and Libya-related consulting contracts was David Goldwyn, the first chairman of the US-Libya Business Association, itself dominated by US oil interests.

For those individuals and entities trying to help Saif and Gaddafi create a more sympathetic image of Libya and its leader, there was an obvious physical stumbling block. Thirty-six-odd years of insularity had physically transformed Gaddafi from a charismatic young revolutionary into a puffy, cranky, vain individual, albeit with a touch of, as *Vanity Fair* put it, "Sartorial Genius."[4] This was something of a mixed blessing; eccentricity was easier to explain away than pure thuggery. It might even provide an engaging distraction from the darker chapters in his past. Still, it would be difficult to make a case that he was a serious statesman, let alone one upon whose word the international community could rely, especially when Gaddafi himself was so transparently desperate to be taken seriously, insisting upon being front and center and speaking his piece however and whenever he wanted.

"Reformists" versus "Reactionaries"

Assuming Gaddafi's real goal was to create only the *appearance* of credible reform long enough for him to decide what to do next, he was very well served by a proxy opposition or, rather, a group that appeared to be pushing him to do things he did not want to do, while in fact being completely under his control.

The creation of multiple warring interest groups was a Gaddafi forte and, in this case, fit perfectly with what the West wanted to see. Just as Saif Al Islam became the designated family reformist, Gaddafi invited (to a large degree, via Saif) individuals with Western training in sciences and administration to play the role of "the reformists" and satisfy the West that all agreements were—at least nominally—being adhered to (while the West itself decided what it wanted to do next with Libya). The outside world saw Gaddafi's appointment of West-savvy technocrats like Shukri Ghanem as prime minister in 2004 and Mohammed Al Badri as head of the National Oil Company as extremely positive moves. At the time, so-styled regime "reactionaries," like Baghdadi Ali Mahmoudi, Tourism Minister Amaar Al Tayef, and former education minister Ahmed Ibrahim, appeared to be losing influence with Gaddafi. In fact, as we will see, not all reformists were really reformists, and not all antireformists had strong views against Libya's opening. As former Foreign Minister Abdelrahman Shalgam notes in his 2011 memoir, while Saif respected Ghanem, in some ways he preferred Baghdadi as Prime Minister, for being far more "obedient."[5]

The legerdemain occurred with the suggestion that this reform-reactionary dynamic had somehow occurred *organically*, that is, that there was indeed a reform movement, per se, that encompassed a group of people with similar uniform ideas and a coherent strategy for implementing those ideas. This was a story the Western media and international diplomatic corps could digest, and it jibed with the previous narrative that Gaddafi had been frightened by the US invasion of Iraq into giving these people a greater voice. The defects in these perceptions arose from the fact that no individual rose to a position of any influence in Libya without Gaddafi's say-so, and that the hand that giveth could just as easily taketh away (which it did, frequently). Further, it was perfectly possible for individuals to be reformist on one issue—economic freedoms for example, which might benefit them personally—and to be completely counter-reformist on others, such as controls on corruption or reforms to the political process, that might threaten their position in the overall patronage structure. It is very possible that Saif was in this latter camp, in that he was pro-change relative to the vast majority of the talentless bureaucrats he called "fossils," but unable to square his own role within this process with an outcome in which the Gaddafi family—or he himself—was not ultimately at the controls. Saif may have had in mind for Libya-sans-Gaddafi Sr. something along the lines of Tunisia under Ben Ali (economically prosperous, but a police state) or, better yet, the UAE, where capitalism ran wild but civil society, social protections, and a robust rule of law were virtually nonexistent.

The rise of the reformists was not wholly a gesture to outsiders; appointing these individuals helped to appease internal constituencies as well. Not just foreigners but also Libyans had to be convinced that something better was coming. As noted, only external and internal pressure on Gaddafi could be eased long enough for him to regroup, he might be able to refashion the Libyan polity into something more modern, though equally totalitarian: a new Tunisia, for example.

The creation of such a reformist-reactionary dichotomy was really a variation on an old standard, an economic *infitah*, or opening, without addressing any of the fundamental political and institutional issues. Yusuf Sawani, recruited to help revamp the relevance of Gaddafi's *The Green Book* in the age of globalization, thus proclaimed the reformist-reactionary distinction *wahmy*, or imaginary, in his postrevolution interview with pan Arab *Asharq Al Awsat*.[6]

The Evolution of Saif Al Islam, 1998–2007

Many outside Libya took the fact that Gaddafi's son Saif played a front-man role in the Lockerbie negotiations as an incremental step toward naming a successor, in the same way that Egyptian president Hosni Mubarak had begun to push his son Gamal onto the public stage.

Saif's transformation into a serious political actor was not instantaneous. His first interviews with foreign media were not an unmitigated success. Saif tried painfully hard to appear affable and in control, despite what was then a very poor command of English. Interviewers were also put somewhat on edge by the jarring proximity of two white Bengal tigers, which he kept as pets.[7]

Saif's higher education was, at least in part, a calculated attempt by Gaddafi to smooth these rough edges. After receiving undergraduate degrees in architecture and engineering at Al Fateh University in Tripoli, Saif completed his first master's thesis, republished by his own publishing house in 2002, under the title *Libya and the XXI Century*.[8] The text is a mixture of Libyan-accented English with denser, more academic prose. Its analysis seemed to have outpaced his academic exposure to date. Saif's thesis explicitly references the theory of competitiveness concepts articulated by Harvard Business School professor Michael Porter.[9] Budding reformist as he may have been, Saif champions an independent judiciary, necessary to "create trust and credibility in the country's laws and regulations," and more investment in education. He concludes, reasonably, "If you want to apply some formal rules, which don't go with informal rules, you get a mess"—which the Libyan state certainly was.[10] There is, tellingly, no explanation of how the mechanisms he proposed might be reconciled with the nonstate state his father had fashioned over the decades. One has to wonder if Saif intended any irony with the placement of a citation from *The Green Book* inserted into the dedication: "Ignorance will come to an end when everything is presented as it really is."[11]

Saif's master's thesis proved very consistent with Gaddafi's *infitah* themes. It used language that was strong but unobjectionable, accompanied by no real analysis as to how to get from A to B. The text also paid careful deference to the notion that whatever happened in Libya, it would be underpinned by fundamental adherence to hidden principles contained within his father's *Green Book*. Thus, he concludes:

> The Libyan economy suffers from many fundamental problems, which grow with the time causing a lot of difficulties. The required reforms must be implemented without any hesitation to avoid more complexities.

The essay catalogues a series of Libya's economic ills, concludes with a list of standard neoliberal reform prescriptions—for reducing barriers to trade, privatizing state-run industry, and fostering a climate of innovation.

It was a valiant first effort, but a dissertation wasn't enough to complete Saif's Western, reformist realignment. He needed to be branded and packaged.

In the years that followed, Saif appeared to have an active role in his own repositioning. Associates described how he pursued Michael Porter, going so far as placing one of his aides in a seat next to him on a flight from the US to London in 2003, with the express purpose of inviting Porter to dinner. Saif was waiting to greet Porter at Heathrow when the plane landed.[12] The subsequent conversations with Porter led to the involvement of the Monitor Group, a Cambridge, Massachusetts–based strategy consultancy run by Harvard Business School professor Mark Fuller, under Porter's oversight.

Saif approached Monitor in early 2004 with a proposal that it assist him and a small group of well-educated Libyan-American academics and businessmen to implement an economic reform and commercial competitiveness strategy for Libya. Accordingly, Monitor executives traveled to Libya in mid-2004, where they met with Saif and various government officials (though not Gaddafi himself), and hashed out the framework for a three-year effort that would be known as the National Economic Strategy (NES), one of the outputs of which was to identify five industry clusters outside oil where Libya might seek to develop a comparative economic advantage.[13] Libya-focused academics, policy analysts, diplomats, and others subsequently heaped criticism on the NES for being light and jargon-filled (a prominent US expert on Libya quipped that one of his graduate students could have written the plan in a few weeks).

In a further attempt to cast himself as an earnest, West-leaning reformist, Saif drew upon the imprimatur of the London School of Economics (LSE). In the months after the beginning of Libya's 2011 revolution, Saif's controversial relationship with LSE was the subject of the "Woolf Inquiry," a 186-page report published by the school in October 2011.[14] The document describes in great detail how Saif, through various intermediaries, attempted to gain admission to various departments for a PhD in the management or government programs, which had rejected him initially in 2001. LSE admitted him to the master's program in philosophy in 2002.

In the following years, various LSE faculty and administration championed Saif's bid for a PhD. Some were sympathetic to Saif or his supporters; some saw potential social value in helping educate and build up the perspective of a potential reformer. Others apparently recognized an opportunity for personal enrichment if they were to advance Saif's interests. Saif, although admitted to the PhD program in philosophy, chose to follow the advice of a senior LSE administrator to pursue a master's. Other sympathetic faculty suggested that Saif pursue a master's in philosophy, policy, and social value (PPSV) to prepare him for subsequent admission to the PhD program. Saif began the program in August 2002 and was finally admitted to the PhD program in the same subject the following year.

LSE's Woolf Inquiry (named for its chairman, former Chief Justice Lord Woolf) documents a range of faculty opinions expressed during Saif's admission and matriculation—that he was getting "undue" outside assistance or possibly not taking his own exams, among other concerns. The report hints at, but does not flag (for obvious reasons), persistent nudging by senior UK government on Saif's behalf. In December 2011, reports in the British press alleged that the Foreign Office had tried to pressure Oxford University to accept Saif into an master's program in development economics in 2002: the head of the department of international development at Oxford told LSE administrators that "the Foreign Commercial Office [FCO] would appreciate help in this case since Libya was opening up to the West again."[15]

The overall picture is of piecemeal and uncoordinated decision making. Individual influence created situations from which retreat was difficult, by either the school or the candidate. The report examines justifications for making an exception for Saif in the admissions process, continuing to support Saif's course of study, and ultimately accepting a large amount of money to support a Center for North African Studies. The authors obliquely blame budgetary pressures for private universities being tempted to accept grants from possibly questionable sources.

Several points stand out regarding the LSE episode and the university's public soul searching after the revolution. First is that the university administration was clearly very happy for the attention and, in particular, the funds Saif brought with him, as evidenced by the ease with which the views of LSE's most distinguished Middle East academic, Fred Halliday (allegedly on good personal terms with Saif), were "rubbished" (dismissed) by senior members of the LSE faculty."[16] In his last formal publication, a collection of essays on various Middle Eastern states, Halliday minces no words about the nature of the Libyan state:

> The outside world may be compelled by considerations of security, energy and investment to deal with this state: there is no reason, however,

> to indulge its fantasies or the fictions that are constantly promoted within the country and abroad about its political and social character. The Jamahiriyah is not a "state of the masses": it is a state of robbers, in formal terms a "kleptocracy."[17]

Second is the fact that practically everyone who touched Saif's file—however inclined they were to support his candidacy—was aware that he would need extra help with his studies, not only because of his relatively weak university-level preparation, but also because he was "far from an ordinary student. He embarked on a challenging academic venture at the same time as he was playing a central role in Libyan, and indeed world, politics."[18]

Third is the obvious involvement of the UK government and Saif's coterie of US-government-endorsed advisers. As with everything else connected with Libya, it was not just LSE and Saif that were benefiting, but a range of other actors, including Saif's advisers (the Monitor Group, among them) and the UK government. Sir Mark Allen, the former MI6 head who is most often credited with leading the earliest negotiations with Libya, maintained a relationship with LSE through LSE IDEAS, a research center, and served as an adviser to British Petroleum.[19] Cherie Blair, the prime minister's wife, was at the time an LSE governor and honorary fellow.[20] LSE's director, Sir Howard Davies, served as the prime minister's economic envoy to Libya while Saif was a student at LSE.[21] Baroness Elizabeth Symons, a close ally of Blair, was appointed to various senior posts within LSE, the UK Trade Office, and the Libyan National Economic Development Board.[22] Thus, LSE was linked through Saif to the highest levels of the UK government and was the principal beneficiary of the prime minister's own lobbying efforts on Libya's behalf.

The worst of LSE's infractions appear to be unconnected with Saif's admission or monitoring of his work (these might be considered customary in private institutions), but linked to the active solicitation by faculty members, including Saif's part-time adviser David Held, while Saif was still a student. In return, the school received £1.5 million to support training programs and to endow the new Center for North African Studies. In this case, at least, one has to somewhat admire Saif's apparent legerdemain in matching the school's request with bribes paid by Turkish, Scottish, and Italian companies to gain access to the Libyan market.[23] According to the Woolf Inquiry, LSE was aware of the likely provenance of these funds, but felt that the process had gone too far for the school to withdraw without considerable embarrassment to all sides.[24]

Saif During and After LSE

Ironically, the brouhaha over his admission notwithstanding, Saif's tenure at the LSE appeared to have been a critical point in his political and intellectual development, whatever his subsequent role in attempting to tamp down the 2011 revolution.

Many who met Saif in the early 2000s and before reported that he lacked gravitas or was not particularly smart. Several of his erstwhile professors, classmates, and advisers have staunchly refuted or revised these characterizations. "Saif . . . was reserved and thoughtful," said one former LSE classmate. "When I first met him I thought he might not be all that smart. His deliberate, measured speech combined with his obstinately practical interests struck me as pedestrian. Looking back, however, I see Saif differently. He spoke slowly because he wasn't confident in English, and he was practical because he was next in line to rule a country of six million people. You could say we had different interests."[25] Another of his classmates recalled Saif to be "chivalrous and thoughtful; someone who did not like flattery, hated personal questions, and was on occasion, fearful of London traffic."[26]

Yehudit Ronen, a researcher at Tel Aviv University and author of a book on Libya, said, "[P]ortraying Saif Al Islam as simply a man of the good life, rushing from one glamorous event to the next, is not accurate. He is busy carrying out missions in the service of the Libyan state, and his influence is prominent in much of its enterprise."[27]

Ronen also referred to Saif as a "Shenkinite," after a street in Tel Aviv known for its Bohemian atmosphere. (Though the term has a meaning Ronen may not have intended. It suggests "intellectual poser" more than "intellectual."[28]) Assistant Secretary David Welch described Saif as "pleasant in person, someone who enjoyed his life, but was rather 'soft' (at least, compared to many of his brothers)."[29] According to some who knew him outside Libya, Saif was painfully aware of the mixed impressions he made on people, both good and bad, as well as the assumptions they made about his motives and intellect. During his time at LSE, Saif confided to a classmate that he was aware that some thought he was "not particularly smart," but that, if he "worried about what people said about him in the shadows, he would drive himself mad."[30] Perhaps tellingly, Saif allegedly added that he thought the perception could be strategically useful, as people underestimated him. Another non-Libyan associate said Saif confessed to feeling as though the Gaddafi name had been a kind of curse, the implication being that he perhaps would have preferred to give up the limelight for a normal life—however he might have imagined this (Saif had never lived a normal life).

While Saif was undoubtedly better educated than his father, his education suffered some of the same holes. It was incomplete and delivered in fits and starts. A senior American consultant and classmates who had extensive dealings with Saif described him as an "intellectual manqué," someone fascinated with ideas for their own sake, and who might have become a professor, if born into different circumstances. Saif was certainly exposed to ideas and people with ideas. He had access to talented PhD tutors, the most erudite and influential thinkers of the twentieth century, and increasingly to heads of state and the pillars of the international financial world, including Lord Jacob Rothschild, Lord Peter Mandelson, and Britain's Prince Andrew, who collectively began to treat Saif as a bona fide colleague, if not peer.

When Saif returned to Libya, he appeared to regress, very possibly due to the proximity of his father. He was criticized within his imported policy circle for associating with childhood friends, whom they described as more "jesters" than serious advisers.[31] Some of Saif's acquaintances speculated Saif trusted the former more than he did the latter, and that the childhood friends entertained and insulated him from the pressure-cooker atmosphere of Gaddafi's "court."[32]

Saif's OneNine Petroleum, effectively an oil services company acting outside the remit of the National Oil Company, was fronted by an individual Saif had publicly rebuked on at least one occasion for buffoonery and who had spent much of his time lobbying the US Embassy with fantastical schemes. Another of Saif's associates was Dr. Omran Bukhres, a visiting associate professor of computer science at Purdue University, with self-described interest in "mobile computing systems, transaction management, concurrency control, and recovery in heterogeneous distributed database systems."[33] All these individuals used Saif's name as a way to gain access, in most cases, more to their own benefit than his.

Saif the Politician

The Monitor Group's 192-page "National Economic Strategy" (NES) was based on the same principles Michael Porter had sold to various other rogue states seeking Western favor, including Iran.[34] Monitor was allegedly paid between $9 million and $11 million to create the NES, an "organization as well as a strategy," whose cochairs were Michael Porter and Daniel Yergin, well known for his Pulitzer Prize–winning book on the history of oil, *The Prize*. Formally, the strategy was meant both to diagnose Libya's economic ills and to create a road map for a globally competitive state:

> This report . . . outlines a vision and presents a comprehensive assessment of Libya's current competitiveness. The project includes an analysis of the macroeconomic, political and social context and the microeconomic business environment; an analysis of key existing and potential industry clusters; as well as an analysis of critical social sectors such as healthcare, education and urban planning. This study informs an action agenda outlining the near-term choices for Libya to create a more participative, productive and competitive modern economy.[35]

Informally, the NES became the primary reform vehicle and training ground for a group of individuals who would help push Saif's reform agenda in the lead-up to the 2011 revolution, and would then form a core group of the rebel leadership in its wake. In this respect one might argue that the NES, and Monitor Group, for their flaws and controversy, played an important—if inadvertent—role in shaping aspects of the 2011 Libyan revolution.

In 2005, the NES had a steering committee run by two UK-educated Libyans, Dr. Abdelhafez Zlitni, one of Saif's most trusted aides, and Yusuf Sawani, previously with the Center for Global Studies of the Green Book. The NES strategy team comprised an executive committee, including representatives of the Monitor Group; the UK-based Adam Smith International, which touts itself as "a leading international advisory firm that works throughout the world to help reform and improve economies and institutions"; and Cambridge Energy Research Associates (CERA, Yergin's parent group). Programmatic work included running training seminars for promising Libyan executives and creating the strategy document itself. Over time, the NES spawned three separate units, the National Competitiveness Council, the Libyan Economic Development Board, and the Libyan Human Assets Office.[36] Mahmoud Jibril, who later became the interim prime minister in the postrevolutionary National Transitional Council (NTC), entered the mix in the third phase, as head of the Libyan Economic Development Board.

While much of the NES, like Saif's thesis, was unremarkable, as with many other quasi-official, objective reports on the Libyan economy, it was deferential (and in the view of many, overly indulgent) to Gaddafi's views and institutions. Representative statements include: "Libya has the only functioning example of direct democracy on a national level." And "BPCs [Basic People's Congresses] provide a meaningful forum for Libyan citizens to participate in law-making."

While many argue that a tainted gesture toward reform like this one was better than nothing, it was very clear to those following Monitor's work that its supporters, whether Gaddafi or the US government or both, had agreed at least tacitly that *political* reform was not part of the deal—at least not now.

The NES coordinated both research and data collection and a training segment, both of which informed the final NES document. The Monitor team claimed to have interviewed and trained some two hundred business and government leaders in various key sectors (health care, tourism, construction, transport and logistics, and entrepreneurship), and polled two thousand small and medium-sized enterprises on attitudes to reform, and competencies (though it is highly doubtful there were that many in Libya at this time).

The NES conclusions were, not surprisingly, very similar to studies done thirty odd years earlier. They noted the need for broad and deep economic reform, for the linking of training to jobs, and for improving the quality of training and education across the board. The most useful or solid prescriptions were those closest to Monitor's and Porter's own core competencies—suggesting ways to shore up the banking sector to increase liquidity and investment, and making a case for self-contained industrial corridors. These would be modeled after other high-visibility clusters and exchange programs, such as the New Economic Cities program in Saudi Arabia, Dubai's International Financial Center, and New York University's Abu Dhabi satellite campus, all of which were in some way meant to create pockets of economic, industrial, or educational activity not subject to all the rules that applied to the rest of the country.

Diplomats based in Tripoli soon realized that Monitor's Libyan engagement was deepening, going beyond policy consulting to assisting Saif with his LSE dissertation and August "youth" speeches, the launching point for most of his signature initiatives—from talk of a constitution, to media and cultural projects, to amnesty for former regime opponents. While this was all "officially unofficial"—Saif still had no formal government position—these communications had a strong policy-making air to them. Within a short time,

Monitor had gone from being the author of competitiveness reports and holding training seminars to steering a good part of Saif's reform agenda and "selling" of the Gaddafis to the Western intellectual and political elite.

One of Monitor's most notable successes was a blueprint for a National Economic Development Board (NEDB). Monitor had highlighted the NEDB as the first in a list of actions for pressing issues in 2006: "Establish and fund a Libyan Economic Development Board—an executive body with strong leadership that is held clearly accountable for driving the reform agenda and for setting up the new governance structure."[37] The idea for the board originated with Maria Al Zahrani, a young American-Saudi consultant and LSE classmate of Saif's, hired to liaise between the Libyan government and consultants from Monitor, CERA, and Adam Smith International. Raised in Southeast Asia, where she was exposed to the workings of the Singapore Economic Development Board and the Malaysian Investment Development Authority, Al Zahrani felt Libya could benefit from an institution dedicated to attracting and expediting foreign direct investment. In the fall of 2005, she arranged a fact-finding mission to these two countries, and introduced Saif to the heads of relevant institutions.[38]

Saif liked the idea of the NEDB and was fascinated with former Singaporean Prime Minister Lee Kuan Yew's notion of Singapore Inc., which had transformed that city-state from backward to "developed."[39] At a time when Saif's political influence was largely limited to the activities of the Gaddafi International Foundation for Charity Associations, the NEDB became a new and more influential vehicle for Saif and his self-selected reform entourage.

In 2006, Saif appeared safely ensconced as the principal regime mouthpiece for economic and social reform, the Monitor Group next undertook what, a few years before, would have been an even more charged assignment. It attempted to remake Gaddafi himself, even to present him as a "world-class thinker."

Monitor's efforts on this front began in 2006 and included visits of renowned academics to Libya for direct conversations with Gaddafi. The dialogues were held with many of the same individuals enlisted to develop Saif's public persona, including American political theorist Benjamin Barber (best known for his 1996 book, *Jihad vs. McWorld*); former London School of Economics director Lord Anthony Giddens (who promoted his own version of a Third Way between capitalism and socialism); political economist and noted futurist Francis Fukayama; Harvard political scientist and former dean of Harvard's Kennedy School of Government, Joseph Nye;

Cass Sunstein (a constitutional adviser to Barack Obama, and the husband of Samantha Power, one of the architects-to-be of the Responsibility-to-Protect rationale for US intervention in Libya in 2011); Robert Putnam, a professor of public policy, also at the Kennedy School; Richard Perle; the list is a long one, and has been repeated in many sources.[40]

The cornerstone of the Gaddafi makeover was to be a book delivered in 2009 on the fortieth anniversary of the Libyan revolution. The proposal, which leaked to the media, would result in

> the definitive text for the international community on the political philosophy of Muammar Qadhafi. . . . As is the case of many individuals who are prominent actors in the world, Qadhafi is well known but is poorly understood, particularly in the West. It is important that he be better understood, particularly so that the West gains a more accurate and balanced understanding of his actions and ideas.[41]

The price tag for this book was to be $2.9 million. While Monitor in its proposal promised Gaddafi authors "with serious credentials, a reputation for fairness," and ideally "those who actually know Qadhafi (sic) and have spent time with him,"[42] Monitor leadership apparently made arrangements to outsource the work to an intern at the US Libya Business Association (which was heavily lobbying Congresss to pressure the Bush administration to speed up normalization of relations with Libya).[43] However, during this undertaking, Monitor ran into increasing difficulties in Libya in 2006 and 2007. The regime designated at least one consultant persona non grata, and rumors emerged of a falling out between the Libyan handlers and Monitor principals. The company ceased operations in Libya in 2007. Company officers attributed the deterioration in the relationship to a number of factors, including their feeling that the reform activities had run their course, and that their services were no longer needed, given the lifting of sanctions, increased infighting within regime circles, and Saif's fundamental lack of influence with his father. The company's headaches with Libya increased in 2008, when documents outlining the extent of Monitor's dealings with the Libyans, raised the question of whether Monitor had been acting as a foreign lobbyist without being registered as such.[44] Monitor would admit the book idea, while well-intentioned, was "a serious mistake."[45]

While maligned within the dissident community and US academic circles for their role in Libya's repositioning, Monitor principals insist they laid the groundwork for meaningful change within Libya (and as I argue, this may well be true, but more in line with the law of unintended consequences). While various senior US officials gave the impression that Monitor was acting fully on its own, senior Monitor officials begged to differ, stopping just short of saying they had been working directly with the US government. One Monitor official related how the company had approached then Secretary of Commerce Donald Evans, a close friend of the president, before accepting Saif's invitation to oversee the NES, to get his opinion about the Libyans' proposal. Evans told them, with a laugh, that they had "every right to do what they wanted, but so did he to slap handcuffs on them when they got back to the States."[46] In other words, they could not count on support from the US government. Several months later, however, a senior CIA official called Monitor's leaders back and asked if they were still in contact with the Libyans. The message was clear: if Monitor wished to pursue the previously mentioned engagement, it was now "very much in the national security interests of the US government for them to do so."[47] Not long thereafter, Liz Cheney, then deputy assistant secretary for public diplomacy within the State Department (and, not irrelevantly, Vice President Dick Cheney's daughter) entered the scene to discuss ways the Middle East Partnership Initiative, the cultural and educational pillar of the administration's transformational diplomacy, might assist with the implementation of the National Economic Strategy.[48]

Remaking *The Green Book*

Given the central role *The Green Book* played in Gaddafi's nonrule-ruling narrative, any significant makeover had to address the blazing inconsistencies between Gaddafi's quasi-conversion to capitalism, and the references to adulterated Islam and Communism that appear throughout his three-part manifesto, which formed the basis of decades of thick internal propaganda.

In late 2002, these reconciliation duties fell to Yusuf Sawani, then general director for the Green Book Center. "Only Sawani," one foreign consultant assisting with the NES said, "could read something intelligent into *The Green Book*, making it sound like a perhaps imperfect expression of profound truth."[49] Indeed, since 2003, Sawani had been behind a series of Green Book Center treatises explaining or reinterpreting statements within *The Green Book* in light of the more aggressive economic opening. One entitled "The Principles of Economic Competitiveness and the Green Book" sets out specifically to establish the "compatibility of Porter's framework" with Gaddafi's treatise: "The competitiveness framework and the Green Book share essential principles: Bottom up approach to competitiveness-building, a commitment to the idea that Libyans control their own economic needs; and a unique model that is 'neutral to state or private ownership.'"[50]

In an interview with the pan-Arab newspaper *Asharq Al Awsat* after the revolution, Sawani claimed that he had been wary of the assignment and that, in effect, it "had never occurred to him that he would wind up at an institution like the Green Book Center," as he had wanted to devote time to academic matters. Moreover, he had been warned against any direct contact with the Gaddafis, as they were "a fire that burns those who get too close."[51] Nevertheless, he had been won over by another Saif associate, who "explained [to me] that the country was in need of reform and change, and training, for which the existing administration was neither appropriate nor acceptable."[52] Others with reformist inclinations, including Gaddafi's cousin, Salma Al Gaeer Al Gaddafi, a pharmacologist with a PhD, who was not herself an unequivocal supporter of the regime, wound up at the Green Book Center in supporting roles. Al Gaeer became a Green Book Center ambassador to the US, in which capacity she criticized both some of the excesses of the Gaddafi regime and contradictory US policies toward Libya.[53] Prior to this appointment, Al Gaeer had been one of the first recipients of a prestigious US Department of State International Visitors (IV) Fellowship, which brought her in contact with leading health practitioners and academics in the US.

Sawani, who later became the executive director of the Green Book Center and oversaw a number of revisions and commentaries on Gaddafi's manifesto, says he rejected an earlier offer to assist Saif during his LSE studies (further confirming various LSE concerns that Saif was getting undue outside help). Sawani was instrumental in the creation, late in 2007, of another institution, the Center for Democracy Studies, whose stated aim was to facilitate "research which aided in the deepening of the understanding of democracy and human rights and the leadership of law and its practical application in Libya, and the development of the political institutions capable of achieving these goals."[54] Sawani claims the idea for the Center came from discussions with Saif and others in his circle about the possibility of "broadening political participation," and correcting the "failure of a number of initiatives connected with political reform, and based in the political leadership."[55] Sawani described Saif as being absolutely "intoxicated" with the idea of unraveling the traditional structure of power and upsetting the traditional balance of power. In early December 2007, Saif, through Sawani, oversaw a series of town hall meetings, *manabir* (literally, podiums), collecting citizens from various Libyan cities to debate reform and constitutional forms. According to Sawani, the idea was to reassure Gaddafi and the revolutionary committees that these various efforts would not replace or circumvent the People's Congresses: "There was strategy to attempt to clothe the idea in theoretical terms, so as not to provoke the ire either of Gaddafi or the revolutionary committees."

Sawani suggested that one of Saif's intentions was to orchestrate a realignment of power away from the Revolutionary Committees: "For that, he had the idea to introduce new levers in the political [scene], all of which were tied to his reform agenda and political ambitions."[56] The permit for the center itself, Sawani says, was obtained through subterfuge and over internal security objections while Gaddafi was out of the country. Gaddafi, it seems, was still very much not on board with these efforts.

All this raises a delicious question, given all that came later: How committed, really, was Saif to reform? How committed were his deputies? While Sawani and others would claim Saif was weak and irresolute, in this regard, the appearance is of a more active hand, even if Saif did see himself as the long-term political beneficiary of a process that took power from his father.

Perhaps the two most interesting things to emerge from the above activities are, first, the degree to which the West, so long keen to punish Gaddafi for his past acts, actively facilitated the appearance, if not substance, of reform. Second, while there are many reasons to question the depth and sincerity of much of the process, it appeared to have made some impression on Saif Al Islam. The reform measures seemed to motivate him to assemble a group of people who would ultimately be in positions to take the process forward farther than he was able or willing to do, given the realities of his situation. As of 2011, those most embarrassed would be the politicians, political appointees, multinational companies, and agencies that stumbled over themselves to help make Libya look almost pristine—something even senior Libyan officials were willing to admit it was not.

CHAPTER 6

Unfinished Business

With the spinning of Libya's transformative narrative and removal from the terror list, Gaddafi wasted no time returning to previous form. The West would soon see the consequences of not making explicit its expectations regarding Gaddafi's behavior, and the penalties he could expect for crossing those lines. The agreement between Libyan state lawyers and lawyers for the Pan Am families (to which the US government was not a formal party) was key to future West-Libya relations and the rapprochement, as it turned Gaddafi's most vocal opponents—the Lockerbie families—into a powerful lobby.

The Case of the Bulgarian Nurses

Because no effective, *comprehensive* mechanism of commitment had been negotiated before the rapprochement, Gaddafi was able systematically to subvert various related transactions to his own advantage, and with highly deleterious consequences for all parties concerned (including, ultimately, Gaddafi). A perfect example is the Bulgarian medics case.

Five Bulgarian nurses and one Palestinian doctor (collectively known as "the medics") had been detained and incarcerated in 1999 for allegedly infecting 453 children in a Benghazi hospital with HIV, the virus that causes AIDS. A Libyan court sentenced them to death in 2004 (six years after their arrest). The international medical community concluded that the pattern of infection did not suggest a deliberate act[1] and was most likely the result of extremely poor hygiene and procedures within the hospital. The case was highly symbolic and emotional, as it involved so many innocent children, an illness for which there is probably no greater taboo in the Middle East; and Benghazi, whose people already felt highly persecuted and underserved by the Libyan regime. The families wanted someone to pay for what they saw as a deliberate crime—and fast.

The matter was left effectively dormant for almost four years, with neither the EU nor the US taking any serious action until 2003–2004 when the issue of dispensing with the remaining US sanctions and normalization of European Union–Libya relations became a more pressing issue. Six years after the jailing of the Bulgarian nurses and the Palestinian doctor, the European Union announced to Gaddafi that it was beginning its new dialogue with him according to a series of principles and specific policy objectives: a policy of active engagement, promotion of human rights, an end to illegal immigration, and a resolution of the Benghazi nurses affair. Written communications with Gaddafi made it "clear" that there would be no "true normalization" without a solution to the latter; yet simultaneously, and without further condition, the EU proceeded with other agreements which contradicted or undermined these principles, such as lifting a key remaining constraint on Libya, the EU Arms Embargo.[2]

Gaddafi complained continuously that various EU officials had come to plead for the release of the nurses, yet no one was concerned with the fate of the infected children.[3] Gaddafi explicitly linked the fate of the children, who were treated like "terrorists" to that of Abdelbasset al Megrahi, who, he pointed out, had to remain in a Scottish prison for life.[4] EU representatives meanwhile attempted to deal with Gaddafi at face value, seemingly blind to the ruses Gaddafi was deploying against them.

Marc Pierini, a senior EU diplomat who assisted with the resolution of the nurses case, describes one early such trap, set during a meeting on May 24, 2005, between European Commissioner for External Relations Benita Ferrero-Waldner and the president of the Basic People's Congress. The latter took them to an auditorium filled with hundreds of victims' family members holding banners denouncing the "criminal acts" of the foreign medics. Pierini said, "The trap was clear: to show to the Libyan public that the foreign visitor had been put before her responsibilities."[5]

To resolve the financial aspects of the nurses issue, the EU created the International Fund for Benghazi, whose administrative council, headed by Marc Pierini, was composed of delegates from the Benghazi Center for Infectious Diseases; the Libyan Red Crescent Society; a Bulgarian non-governmental organization assisting contact with the families; Baylor College of Medicine from Houston, Texas; and the EU Action Plan for Benghazi.

The Libyans initially asked for €10 million in compensation per victim, the exact amount Libya had agreed to pay each of the Lockerbie families but ultimately "settled" at US$1 million, the amount paid the French victims of the UTA bombing.[6] Pierini was not blind to what was going on:

> It is moreover very probable that the amount had been fixed at a very high level of the State for the reasons touching more than prestige of Libya with respect to the payment of 10 million dollars in the affair of Lockerbie, rather than the fate of the families themselves.[7]

Gaddafi, seeing the obvious eagerness of the EU to resolve the issue and open the way to commercial deals, stated his own objective, precisely what the EU had wished to avoid: resolution would be contingent upon Libya's return to the international community, and not the reverse.[8] Gaddafi backed up this point with a not so veiled threat in April 2007, with the reversal of a moratorium (when instituted) on executions, which had been lifted a few years before in order to demonstrate Libya's commitment to human rights.[9]

Regardless of its provenance, the issue of the infections themselves become for Gaddafi an added political liability, less apparently with respect to the West than the regime's relationship with the residents of Benghazi. They understandably wanted to see someone held accountable, however murky the situation appeared to many of them (once again, reminiscent of Lockerbie). One of the more shocking aspects of the case was how little attention it garnered in the international press, within senior levels of the European Union, and even in the Bulgarian diplomatic community, until 2003 when the issue of accelerating bilateral and multilateral relations with Libya (and Bulgaria's application for entry into the EU, which occurred in 2006) made its existence too important to ignore. Indeed, Valya Chervenyashka, one of the captive nurses, in a book published in 2010, alleged that Gaddafi singled out as scapegoats the nationals of countries he was sure would not take a strong stand in favor of their own people. (She also intimates that lower-level Bulgarian diplomats were taking bribes, and that the families of the few local Bulgarian diplomats who came to their defense early on may have been targets of assassination.)[10]

Anthony Layden, UK ambassador to Libya, devised a plan, something vaguely akin to Professor Robert Black's formula for trial of the Lockerbie suspects in The Hague. A "no fault" fund would be established by the EU Commission to provide international assistance focused on technical aid and HIV treatments unavailable in Libya. Soon enough, the Libyans managed to insert conditions whereby the fund would also be used to pay "compensation." Originally, the idea was that no cash compensation would be paid by the West or Bulgaria—if Libya wanted to do this, it was up to the Libyan government; if Libya wanted to solicit voluntary contributions to the fund from a range of public and private sources, this was also acceptable. Gaddafi, however, requested, effectively, that the foreign and Libyan funds for technical assistance and "compensation" be commingled, thereby allowing Gaddafi to say that compensation was coming from this EU-backed fund, and thus that he had forced the West to pay compensation, which was tantamount to an admission that the West (i.e., the nurses) was guilty. While the argument was ludicrous, Gaddafi managed to exploit moments of inattention on the part of the EU to create a "Lockerbie in reverse" and to serve his propaganda purposes in Benghazi.

In the ensuing years, additional questions surfaced regarding how and if the victims and their governments put themselves in vulnerable positions to begin with (again, by not understanding Gaddafi's modus operandi, or being willing to collaborate in atrocities in return for higher-level policy favors). A Bulgarian diplomat told an American diplomat that she felt the Bulgarian nurses had "contributed to the situation" by continuing to work in conditions where children were being infected under either suspicious or negligent circumstances. One of the nurses, Valya Chervenyashka, in her memoir, *Notes From Hell*, criticizes senior members of the Bulgarian mission for effectively ignoring the nurses' case.[11]

In the wake of the February revolution, many in Benghazi continued to believe the infection was deliberate. Many Libyans continue to believe the Bulgarians were responsible, while at least one senior diplomat is convinced Gaddafi himself ordered the infection to "punish" the East for continuing sedition.

Increasing attention to the case of the Bulgarian nurses coincided with Saif Al Islam's rise to public prominence from 2004 to 2007. Indeed, he was positioned as the key negotiator, the good guy who assisted with lifting the ban on executions in 2007. Saif continued to be the "voice of reason," even after the nurses issue had been resolved. "Yes, there was torture," he would admit, contradicting previous official Libyan insistence that the detained medical personnel were treated with proper care.[12]

Setting a precedent for future actions, French president Nicolas Sarkozy played a controversial role bringing the Bulgarian nurses case to a head, before the European Commission had managed to exhaust its processes, sending his then wife Cecilia with Benita Ferrero-Waldner to "take possession" of the nurses and doctor, while carrying on parallel negotiations for the sale of French armaments to Libya. The quid pro quo on the French side, as intimated by Pierini, was the sale of weapons to the regime and an immediate exchange of official visits: Sarkozy would come to Tripoli and would host Gaddafi with pomp in Paris (which he did).

Gaddafi understood that Sarkozy was playing politics with the nurses' case. According to Pierini, "In a sense, the inclusion of the subject in the conclusions of the EU Council of Ministers from October 2004, or Sarkozy's presidential campaign from May 2007, had encouraged the Libyans to 'instrumentalize' a bit more the Benghazi nurses affair."[13] Pierini noted in his memoir that, essentially, the ethical implications of French interference were something France's leaders should work out among themselves.[14]

Indeed, the verve with which Sarkozy courted Gaddafi after his election in 2007 may well have played a role in his ultimate defeat by Socialist candidate François Hollande in May 2012, to the extent that the French believed Saif Al Islam's accusations that he (Gaddafi) had donated £42 million in 2005 to finance Sarkozy's first presidential campaign. The deal was allegedly brokered by a well-known arms dealer with ties to the Sarkozy campaign.[15] Sarkozy admits to a 2005 meeting with Gaddafi in Tripoli, but denies discussing any campaign contribution. The French leader's lack of scruples with respect to deals with Gaddafi perhaps was exceeded only by those of British Prime Minister Tony Blair.

Tony Blair's Affair with Gaddafi

The other major and much better publicized blight on the terms of the explicit and implicit Western rapprochement with Libya was the depth and sketchiness of the commercial dealings between European firms and the Libyan government, as highlighted by the case of now-former UK Prime

Minister Tony Blair. "The first thing that must be understood about the Megrahi affair is the vastness of the entanglements among Libya, the oil companies, and the Blair government," writer David Rose would say in his exposé of the Blair-Libya ties in *Vanity Fair*, just before the revolution.[16]

Blair's interest in Libya and Gaddafi dates back at least to his early days as prime minister. British intelligence played a key role in the Lockerbie deal and the lifting of UN sanctions in 1999; Blair made his first official visit to Tripoli in 2003 and spent the subsequent years heavily promoting Libya-UK commercial deals (recounted elsewhere in the book). The Libya Human and Political Development Forum, a UK group comprising well-known Libyan dissidents attacked Blair publicly for visiting Gaddafi without first demanding "serious human rights reforms."[17]

When Blair made his final commercial pitch to Gaddafi on May 29, 2007, just before the end of his last term as prime minister, he appeared to have been under the impression that Gaddafi was overflowing with gratitude for his personal efforts, dating back to 1998, to ease Libya out of the sanctions. On this trip to Tripoli, Blair had brought with him John Browne, CEO of British Petroleum (BP), and the heads of some other large British companies, including General Dynamics and another defense contractor, MBDA.[18] Blair's clear intent was to seal his exit with some massive contracts for British industry. At stake for BP were exclusive drilling rights for two large onshore fields and one offshore—a deal then thought worth potentially billions of dollars.

Blair's demonstrable eagerness for a "payback," several witnesses attest, was a large part of his undoing. "Blair approached Qaddafi as a supplicant," an aide subsequently noted, allowing Gaddafi to pressure Blair on key issues of interest to Gaddafi personally, as a quid pro quo. The proposed defense deals were less subject to blowback because Gaddafi was equally keen to have the assistance: In 2008, the UK Trade and Industry Defence and Security Organisation, an entity whose mission was to promote the sale of British munitions abroad, finally sealed a $165 million deal with General Dynamics, initiated during Blair's 2007 meeting with Gaddafi. The deal included a contract to supply and train the Khamis Brigade, a ten-thousand-man unit whose raison d'être was to protect Gaddafi from any internal threat.

The connection between Blair and Gaddafi did not end after Blair's tenure. After his retirement from UK public service, Blair made at least six visits to Libya for private commercial reasons, at least two on corporate jets paid for by the Libyan government. During much of this time, Blair was Middle East Peace Envoy for the European Union. As of 2008, Blair was hired by the US bank JPMorgan to undertake business development in Libya. Blair spokesmen asserted that the former prime minister did nothing improper and was only advising Libya on "infrastructure and the future of Libya," and did not engage in "any commercial dealing with Libyan companies or government."[19] In the lead-up to the Libyan revolution, Blair said simply that he had "no regrets" about befriending Gaddafi.

In the wake of the opening of Libya, within the EU, the British, the Swiss, and the Italians were arguably the most brazen in cozying up to Gaddafi. The degree to which these countries' leaders were willing to let themselves be played against one another and to cave in to Gaddafi's increasingly outrageous demands was made patently clear in the wake of the July 2008 Swiss arrest of Gaddafi's fifth-oldest son, Hannibal, and his pregnant wife. Geneva police accused them of beating their servants. The act of arrest led to a vituperative Libyan barrage against the Swiss dubbed "Hannibal's War." Among the many assaults Libya leveled against Switzerland were the withdrawal of €4 billion in Libyan funds from Swiss accounts, the expulsion of Swiss diplomats, and even the imprisonment of a Swiss businessman in Tripoli for over a year on trumped-up charges of visa fraud. Swiss businesses in Libya were shuttered, and oil exports to Switzerland ceased. Amazingly, the Swiss president Hans-Rudolf Merz agreed in late August 2009 to Gaddafi's demand for an official apology, after Gaddafi called Switzerland a "mafia state" at the G8 summit the previous month. This provoked widespread outrage on the part of many Swiss, who accused their government of humiliation, groveling, and "loss of Swiss honor."[20] Adding insult to insult, Libya formally submitted a proposal to the UN proposing that Switzerland be carved up and given to its neighbors, prompting one commentator in the Swiss paper *Le Matin* to object [ironically] that Austria wasn't being given its fair share.[21]

Nor was Switzerland the only country to cave before Gaddafi. Italy's prime minister Silvio Berlusconi allowed himself to be bamboozled into providing Gaddafi surveillance equipment that even the Italians felt was too advanced for Libya to possess in return for promises to stem African emigration. Germany, a heavy participant in the Libyan arms trade, was criticized after the 2011 revolution for having given Gaddafi's youngest son, Saif Al Arab, effective diplomatic immunity and free passage to and from Germany while he was a student.[22]

Why did these individual European countries allow Gaddafi to manipulate them so brazenly? Some have suggested that, in the case of the Swiss, the leaders were simply not used to dealing with a person like Gaddafi (despite the fact that Switzerland hosted a number of Libyan officials, who found the Swiss environment a natural antidote to the Libyan desert and Swiss banking practices highly favorable), and were caught completely off guard by his "wild" reactions.[23]

The Italians were another case altogether. Gaddafi and Berlusconi, whom many Italians saw as an embarrassment symbolizing a marked decline in Italy's international reputation, got along famously. For the first few years after the lifting of UN sanctions, Gaddafi pressed Italy on the issue of reparations for thirty years of occupation, while Italy pressed Gaddafi on lucrative contracts. The two desires were satisfied in an agreement highly controversial among the Italian people and externally. According to the text of the Friendship Treaty, signed in 2008, Italy would pay Libya $5 billion in reparations for colonial actions in Libya in annual US$200 million increments, which would then be used to hire Italian contractors to rebuild, among other things, the coastal highway from Tunisia to Egypt.[24] The agreement included significant extensions to ENI oil and gas contracts. It also authorized US$500 million in purchases of materials from the Italian government to help Libya guard 1,056 miles of coastline against illegal emigration to Italy. Here again, Gaddafi used the very real threat of waves of African emigrants as a lever to obtain monetary concessions and access to technology to track (presumably prevent) the exodus of African emigrants to Europe, but also to follow the movements of his own people.[25]

Gaddafi's threats aside, Italy's relationship with Libya was substantively very different from those between Libya and other European states, and perhaps bears some similarity to the relationship of Germany to Israel—the former brutalizer whose prey had managed to escape and make good. Not only did Italy feel some collective guilt for what it had done in Libya, it wanted to profit from good relations. The two countries fundamentally had, despite the past ugly history, more in common than not on some levels.

As Alan Friedman observed in his history of the former CEO of the Italian conglomerate Fiat, which had ample dealings with Gaddafi's Libya, "It is essentially difficult for the Italian mind to accept that an American journalist working for a British newspaper in Italy might simply find a subject extremely interesting and then—without any promptings or payoffs—he might choose to investigate."[26]

In examining these deals from a postrevolution, post-Gaddafi perspective, it seems that one of the most lethal consequences of the deal making and rapprochement was the escalation of arms trade between Europe and Libya. According to Andrew Feinstein, an expert in international arms tracking, between 2006 and 2009—the years for which the most detailed statistics are available—EU governments authorized arms exports to Libya valued at more than €834 million, well over a billion US dollars, of which €276 million accrued to Italy, €210 million to France, and €119.35 million to the UK, for matériel including military-ready helicopters, riot-control gear, small arms, ammunition, and jamming technology.[27] French military correspondent Jean-Marc Tanguy claims that €160 million worth in small arms and jamming systems alone were sold by EU countries to Libya after 2004, including €79.7 million in small arms from Malta, and €18 million in assorted military hardware from Belgium.[28] In the years preceding the revolution, French companies Thales and Amesys sold radar systems, and a range of jamming and Internet filtering and tracking systems, respectively. Mobile land-to-sea radar sold by Thales apparently posed a serious threat to French forces during the initial stages of their attack on Libyan air defenses.[29]

While trade in arms to Gaddafi had been limited prior to the US-Libya rapprochement, it became frenzied after the lifting of the UN arms embargo in 2003, and then the EU embargo 2004. While the US was apparently not involved in major arms sales to Libya during this time, Russia, China, and the ex-Soviet states made full use of the opportunity to restock the Gaddafi regime.

Libya spread these contacts across multiple vendors, both to gain goodwill and to avoid raising eyebrows.[30] The events of the first few months of the uprising and many revelations thereafter revealed just how deeply Libya had exploited the open door to arm itself against potential insurrection.[31]

Undercutting "Victory": The Blight of Rendition

US policymakers continued to disagree about what exactly to do with Libya and how quickly to move forward. Those on the fence about the merits of the Libya reengagement insisted weakly that economic entrée to Libya would have a trickle-down effect on Libyan freedoms. The oil companies, such as the Oasis Group (Marathon Oil, ConocoPhillips—formerly Continental—and Amerada Hess), were very happy to pursue their reentry arrangements, while they and new entrants went after new exploration rights under the EPSA IV process.

Meanwhile, the clandestine services of both the US and UK were exploiting the new relationship with the Libyans to ramp up their antiterror campaigns, most notably by involving Libya in a complex web of extralegal renditions of so-called enemy combatants, captured in places like Afghanistan and Pakistan, to Guantanamo Bay, Cuba, and cooperative states—first Egypt and Tunisia, now Libya, for interrogation (which appears in many cases to have involved direct torture). In 2007, information about "ghost flights" began to surface: a breach-of-contract dispute filed in New York in 2007 revealed some details of the commercial contracts for a Gulfstream V jet based at Washington Dulles airport that made numerous flights to Europe, Asia, and the Middle East around the same time that terror suspects were flown to various cooperating countries.[32] Documents uncovered by Al Jazeera after the fall of Tripoli to the rebels in August 2011 appear to confirm that Libya was one of the countries involved and to provide details of UK complicity.

The Al Jazeera documents describe, with respect to Libya, a degree of closeness among the US, UK, and Libyan intelligence services previously out of the public view. "Your achievement in realizing the Leader's initiative has been enormous and of huge importance," a British official wrote to a senior Libyan intelligence counterpart. "At this time sacred to peace, I offer you my admiration and every congratulation."[33] The discoveries prompted the British government to convene the Gibson inquiry, named for its chairperson, a prominent British judge, in September 2011. The panel subsequently announced that MI6 and CIA cooperation with Libya was "much closer than previously acknowledged" and included at least eight separate renditions.[34] In January 2012, UK Justice Secretary Ken Clarke announced that the inquiry had been abandoned in light of Libya's own police investigations.[35] Human rights groups had boycotted the inquiry from the start, after intelligence agencies' insistence that most of the proceedings be held in secret.

Former CIA counterterrorism specialist Michael Scheuer has explained that the rendition program originated in the agency during the Clinton years as a means to bring Osama bin Laden to justice (and presumably to extract information) without "having to grant terrorism suspects the due process afforded by American law."[36] Cofer Black, then head of counterterrorism at the CIA, testified before the House and Senate Intelligence committees that 9/11 was, effectively, the year the rendition program came into its own.[37] After 9/11, the Bush administration deployed a group of politically appointed lawyers within the Justice Department and the White House. They were to prepare legal opinions supporting the notion that, within the context of the war on terror, the US was not bound by either the Geneva Conventions, which governed treatment of prisoners of war (the solution would be to create a new category of stateless warriors, "illegal enemy combatants") or the 1984 UN Convention against Torture and other Cruel, Inhuman or Degrading Treatment or Punishment, ratified by the US in 1994. Regardless of who else in the government knew of the program, senior officials at the State Department disavowed any information concerning what the CIA was or was not doing.

Egypt had been the most obvious first implementation partner for rendition policies, given its government's close relationship to the US, the fact that Egypt received some $2 billion a year in US aid, and its own long-standing reasons for wanting to extract information from Muslim extremists. Libya shared the same animosity for Islamist groups and thus was presumably also amenable to participating in any project that would deliver enemies of the state straight to Libya for questioning—and worse.

Embarrassingly for the West, some of individuals "rendered" emerged to play significant roles in post-2011 Libyan politics. Libyan nationals Sami Al Saadi and Abdelhakim Belhaj accuse the UK of involvement in their involuntary repatriation to Libya in 2004. Belhaj, one of the founders of the Libyan Islamic Fighting Group, Gaddafi's nemesis Islamist organization, led the final assault on Bab Al Azziziya in August 2011 in coordination with NATO forces. Belhaj claims he was apprehended in Malaysia in 2004, transfered to Thailand for CIA interrogation, and then rendered by the CIA back to Libya's Abu Selim prison.[38] In April 2012, the BBC revealed that the UK government had agreed to assist with the Gaddafi regime's request for Belhaj's rendition in 2004 and informed "foreign intelligence agencies" (i.e., the CIA) that Belhaj was in Bangkok.[39] "We are planning to arrange to take control of the pair [Belhaj and his then pregnant wife] in Bangkok and place them on our aircraft for a flight to your country [Libya]," one of the CIA handlers wrote. Communications regarding other rendees carried the banal proviso, "Please be advised that we must be assured that [the prisoner] will be treated humanely and that his human rights will be respected."[40] Another Libyan national targeted by the rendition program was Ibn al-Shaykh al Libi, a paramilitary trainer for Al Qaeda, who was captured in Afghanistan by Pakistan and turned over to the FBI, from whose custody the CIA sent him to Egypt for interrogation.[41] Al Libi was later identified as the source of a critical piece of flawed intelligence senior Bush administration officials used to establish a link between Al Qaeda and Saddam Hussein, and thus to justify the 2003 invasion of Iraq.[42] The Libyan government claimed al Libi committed suicide in his cell in May 2009 (but never allowed an outside investigation).[43] The testimony of another Libyan-born rendee adds further color to this process. Abu Sofiyan Bin Qummu says he was captured in Pakistan and delivered to the Americans, who kept him in a cell in Kandahar (Afghanistan) where he was interrogated while naked and set upon by trained dogs. The Americans, he claims, then flew him to Guantanamo, Cuba, where he was held for six years in a barred cage and subjected to "all kinds of inhumane torture," before being extradited back to Libya in an American plane, via the Yemeni capital of Sana'a, and hand-delivered to the Libyans, who put him in the Abu Selim prison until he was released in 2010, as part of Saif's Islamicist rehabilitation program. Abu Sofiyan Bin Qummu denies ever having been a member of Al Qaeda and says his journey to Pakistan had to do with escaping incidents back in Libya: "Had I actually been with Al Qaeda, the Americans would have left me alone," he says. While Belhaj has publicly said he bears the US no permanent grudge, Abu Sofiyan Bin Qummu is less forgiving: "I still have problems with the Americans."[44]

At the time Belhaj was rendered, both the current US State Department Human Rights Reports and Human Rights Watch had detailed extensive domestic human rights abuses in Libya. These specifically included torture, poor conditions, impunity, arbitrary arrest, incommunicado detention, lengthy political detention, denial of fair public trial, and so on.[45] Indeed, many officials within the State Department were well aware of what was going on at the Justice Department and the White House, and were "horrified" by what was happening:

> Some took active steps to stop the new rules and practices from being adopted. When their efforts failed, they alerted others with leaks to the press. . . . Temporarily, however, it was the Yoo's and the Bybee's and the Gonzales's of the administration [the primary authors of the pro-torture legal opinions], that prevailed.[46]

It is unclear whether specific individuals were targeted for rendition because the West had reason to believe they had information, or whether the Libyans, as the Egyptians were thought to have done before them, simply drew up a list of people they wanted for their own purposes (dissidents, for example) with the cover that their interrogation would produce information pertinent to the war on terror. Former State Department officials said these arrangements mirrored those Washington had carried out a few years before with the Algerian regime. That regime had also attempted to exploit Washington's obsession with Al Qaeda to have members of the military arm of the principal opposition, the Islamic Salvation Front (FIS), delivered to Algeria.[47] In the case of Libya, the fact that the George W. Bush administration had declared the Libyan Islamic Fighting Group (LIFG)—whose primary target was Gaddafi—a terrorist organization in 2003, assisted in justifying renditions of LIFG-affiliated members back to Libya.

After these policies came to light, Jack Straw, the UK foreign minister under Blair, attempted to defend himself in 2011: "No foreign secretary can know all the details of what intelligence agencies are doing at one time." Secretary of State Condoleezza Rice did not have the (however implausible) deniability of Straw, after verbally approving a CIA request to employ waterboarding and other interrogation techniques as early as July 2002.[48] In a similar vein, a CIA spokeswoman said simply, "It can't come as a surprise that the Central Intelligence Agency works with foreign governments to help protect our country from terrorism and other deadly threats. . . . [T]hat is exactly what we are expected to do."[49]

Human Rights Watch countered, "It remains a stain on the record of the American intelligence services that they cooperated with these very abusive intelligence services."[50]

While the US media treated the ghost flights as a relatively insignificant coda to a long list of other human rights abuses occurring during the Bush watch, this collaboration is highly relevant and significant to the nature of the US-Libya relationship at this time because it severely hampered efforts by the US and participating nations to put serious pressure on Libya to respect human rights or any reform. All Gaddafi (or his advisers) had to do—and perhaps did do—when asked to moderate his behavior on any number of outstanding issues, was remind his handlers that he was doing some of their dirty work.

What Terror Dividend?

Given the lack of information about the intelligence that might have come to light, it remains difficult to quantify whether the CIA's dealings with Libya benefited anyone but Gaddafi himself. Sources in the public domain allege that the gains were, in fact, not negligible, and included information on Libyans who fought or were trained in Afghanistan and/or who had been associated with the Libyan Islamic Fighting Group (LIFG), including Anas el Libi and Abu Layth al Libi,[51] files on LIFG assets in Britain, and other LIFG operatives with suspected ties to Al Qaeda.[52] Information provided by the Libyan regime was to have led to the formal US designation of LIFG as a "foreign terrorist organization."[53] Musa Kusa, perhaps acting as a double agent, was supposed to have provided valuable intelligence to the Americans and British, including names of black market suppliers, transporters, and dealers in nuclear parts.[54] Libyan intelligence was to have enabled international authorities to shut down portions of A.Q. Khan network operating through Malaysia and the United Arab Emirates.

Yet other sources cast doubt on the depth and usefulnesss of the intelligence payoff. While former senior LIFG members are known to have defected to Al Qaeda, I have been unable to find any sources attesting to anything but a weak operational link between Al Qaeda and LIFG—or confirmation of the overwhelming operational value of the information provided by the Libyans (of course, much of the material was classified). Other sources suggest that a good fraction of the information derived from Libya on this count was, to borrow a line from former Defense Secretary Donald Rumsfeld, "known unknowns." Retired State Department officials with access to intelligence on these issues confirm their understanding of the primitive nature of the Libyan WMD program at the time ("less developed than the Iraqi program before bombing of the Osiris facility by the Israelis in 1981"), and more generally, the fact that while Libya had an extensive intelligence bureaucracy, it was operationally weak, ill motivated, and incompetent.[55]

The years after Libya's removal from the tightest tethers of the international sanctions straitjacket demonstrated very clearly the consequences of the West not putting together a robust road map or formal agreements to govern Gaddafi's rehabilitation. The US and the UK, principally, were so obsessed with completing other narratives regarding terror and nuclear proliferation, all bolstered by significant commercial interests, that they simply never stated what Gaddafi was expected to do, in fact *must* do, in return to remain in their good graces. As a result, there were major, known human rights abuses continuing long after Libya had been removed from the terror list, from the EU arms embargo, and so on—including the killing of dissident Daif al Ghazal, the continued incarceration of the Bulgarian nurses, etc. Further, the US actually had to coax Gaddafi to pay the last tranche of damages to the Lockerbie families—which legally, it was not obligated to pay because the US did not meet the deadline for full normalization of relations, codified in a document that committed the US government to certain actions, but which the US government did not have a direct hand in drafting.

Further, because these troublesome items, like the case of the Bulgarian nurses and the release of convicted Pan Am bomber Megrahi, for example, had not been part of or covered by the original deals, they were susceptible to pressure by commercial and political interests that inevitably had insinuated themselves into the dialogue during the intervening period. In many ways, Gaddafi had performed brilliantly, turning negatives into positives and liabilities into assets, all at the expense of the West. He was now free to purchase as many weapons he wanted, from the same people who were trying to quarantine him.

The WMD-terror deal was perhaps the weakest link in terms of enforcing anything, as cooperation effectively turned the US and Western intelligence agencies into collaborators with Gaddafi in the repression of his own people. In this context, any possible good that could have been done, in terms of sustainable reform, was all but stillborn. As Saif Al Islam discovered—again, in the absence of a clear reading of his intentions—in this atmosphere and without his father's precommitments to the West, he would be practically toothless. Further, lack of precommitment enabled those who wished to see Saif's efforts buried—Mu'tassim, and Ahmed Ibrahim, to name two—to fight back. Yet for all of Gaddafi's masterful manipulations and talk of a new Libya, the irony was that there were serious fissures in the asphalt with which Gaddafi's Libya had been repaved.

CHAPTER 7

Cracks Apparent

That a certain buckling of the Libyan social fabric took place within the first years of the rapprochement is no accident, for one of the promises Gaddafi made to his Western interlocutors was the appearance of progress, which meant loosening the reins in key areas of interest—economic reform, press freedoms, human rights, and so on—just enough to suggest good faith, but not irreversible empowerment of the people. Further, while the reform narrative sold well outside Libya, large constituencies simply did not believe anything that came from the regime and were furthermore suffering from both the cumulative effects of Gaddafi's repression and some particularly deep wounds. As far as those in eastern Libya, for example, were concerned, there would be no redemption for Gaddafi, or his clan. For those who participated in Gaddafi's crackdowns as implementers, enforcers, or direct beneficiaries, the new openness posed serious uncertainties and threats. What does a professional thug do once the mafia don has decided to turn state's evidence? In 2005–2006, the magnitude of the challenge was perhaps just starting to become clear to Gaddafi. How could he accommodate his victims and his collaborators after years of mistreatment and mutual dependence, respectively? While Gaddafi tried, largely through the offices of Saif Al Islam, to reach out, for many it was just too late.

The Abu Selim Massacre

One of Gaddafi's most unforgivable acts, and most galvanizing event in the history of the Libyan resistance to Gaddafi was the Abu Selim massacre, which took place in an eponymous prison in Tripoli on June 29, 1996, in which more than 1,250 prisoners were killed in about two hours. Many of the Abu Selim victims had been imprisoned since 1989, or 1995, when more mass arrests took place, and were predominantly from the eastern population centers of Benghazi, Al Beida, and Derna. The killing of so many individuals was destined to galvanize public opinion in a region in which everyone knows everyone else.

The proximate spark of the killings was a protest against poor living conditions. The disturbance turned into a near revolt in which the prisoners allegedly took two guards hostage (one died of unknown causes). Guards shot at the prisoners, killing six of them and injuring many more. Gaddafi's Head of internal security, Abdullah Senussi, arrived on the night of June 28 to hear prisoners' demands, which included an end to torture, better medical care, family visits, and more time in open-air quarters.[1] Human Rights Watch interviewed several former prisoners and one guard, all of whom claimed to have been in the prison at the time of the massacre, Senussi assented, and 120 sick prisoners were taken away that night (they were never seen again, and presumed shot).[2] The following morning, men with machine guns systematically exterminated most of the inmates, in an operation that took two hours and five minutes and left few witnesses.[3]

Rumors concerning what had happened took some time to percolate through the region. Families continued to apply for visits and to deliver care packages for years after, ignorant of the fate of their loved ones. Sometime in 2002, the regime decided that its interests would be better served by releasing information piecemeal, in the process trying to buy out families with blood money. This was the same strategy Gaddafi had used in other major cases that involved large groups of family claimants, whether Lockerbie or the Bulgarian nurses case (the nurses, the doctor, and the victims and their families). In 2002, one Abu Selim family received a death certificate; others were sent in batches over the following years. Thus began a process whereby the families, certainly those based in eastern Libya, began to form networks both to support one another and to coordinate protests. By 2007, Abu Selim families in Benghazi were holding protests each Saturday. In particular, Fathi Terbil, a Benghazi-based lawyer whose three relatives had been killed in the massacre, emerged as a prominent advocate for the families.

Survivors' accounts of life in Abu Selim appeared in force after the 2011 uprising. One described the prison after the 1996 massacre: "The area of Bu Sleem [sic] prison was surrounded by high walls, ringed with armed wire. Garbage surrounding it on all sides, and from within poured the stench of corpses."[4] Along with second-hand stories of the massacre itself, there were accounts of multiple-year detentions in solitary confinement and medical neglect. Mohammed Al Mujarib, a former inmate, said that once he had arrived at Abu Selim, "life as I knew it ended."[5]

Opposition in the Age of the Internet

In the two years after Libya's reopening, between 2004 and 2006, Internet usage in Libya grew from practically nothing to about 20 percent penetration. Informal estimates in 2006 suggested there were about twenty thousand to forty thousand Internet users in Tripoli, of a population of two million. While, again, reliable statistics are unavailable, Internet usage was clearly growing at a very fast clip, facilitated by increasing points of access—Internet cafés—direct satellite access, and interest in social networking sites, Facebook first among them. In these early days of the Internet in Libya, Libyan government censorship was still somewhat primitive, and illicit satellite hookups allowed those with influence to bypass censors entirely.

Around 2004, Libyan exiles began to set up opposition sites, which IT-savvy Libyans were able to access without much difficulty. As the postrevolutionary magazine *Al Libii* (*The Libyan*) reported in spring 2011, "since sanctions were lifted in 2004, a handful of UK-based websites set up by Libyans who fled their country in the 1970s are playing a much greater role in fostering awareness of domestic politics in Libya." Some of the sites offered the "straight dope" on political and economic developments in Libya; others were directed at rallying opposition to the regime. *Libya Al-Yowm* (*Libya Today*) was one of the former. *Akhbar Libya*, by the Libya Human and Political Development Forum (LHPDF), mixed opinion with targeted information campaigns, some of which aimed to expose specific Libyan officials for corruption. One such campaign succeeded in ousting the head of Al Fateh University in Tripoli, after it published evidence of her "illicit practices."[6] Opposition political parties, such as the National Front for the Salvation of Libya (NFSL), maintained websites that facilitated contact with members who were sympathizers within Libya. Also notably, a few scant blogs appeared from within Libya; one in English—libyans.blogspot.com—whose members posted from Tripoli. When using exile sites or other forms of Internet posting, either within or outside Libya, many Libyans wrote using pseudonyms.

Meanwhile, violent uprisings continued to ignite. On February 17 and 18, 2006, crowds of angry youth in Benghazi launched a two-night rampage. The events began as a government-organized protest against the wearing of a T-shirt by Italian reforms minister Roberto Calderoli that depicted the Danish cartoons published the previous September, which many Muslims had found offensive to Islam.[7] Eleven people were killed in the events and scores wounded; the Italian consulate was gutted, but more significantly, the protestors quickly turned against obvious manifestations of regime control, including the offices of the Social Security Fund, which owned most of the real estate in eastern Libya. Violent protests moved to Sebha in the south the following day.

The 2006 riots were far from isolated. When juxtaposed against the 1993 coup attempt, the soccer wars of the late 1990s, and the 2000 lynchings-cum-riot in Zawiya, we can discern a growing pressure-cooker atmosphere in which popular discontent increasingly manifested itself in large-scale acts of public disobedience.

Though the regime continued to fight violence with violence, it attempted to use some of the tools from its reformist arsenal as well. From 2009 to 2010 the regime released several groups of high-profile "Islamist" prisoners (there were 946 in all, largely emptying out the Abu Selim prison, which, the regime announced, would be closed). The release was spearheaded by—who else?—Saif Al Islam, assisted by Sheikh Ali Sallabi, a Libyan Muslim cleric whom Gaddafi had also imprisoned in Abu Selim and who was an associate of Yusuf Qaradawi,[8] as part of a dialogue and reconciliation initiative.[9] In March 2010, the regime released 214 prisoners. Thirty-four among them were from the Libyan Islamic Fighting Group (LIFG), including three of its senior members: Abdelhakim Belhaj, de facto leader of the group and one of the American "rendees," who would become a notable figure in the forthcoming rebellion; Khaled Charif, head of military operations; and Sami Al Saadi, an ideologue. Many of these released prisoners assumed leadership or fighting roles in the 2012 uprising.

Saif Al Islam announced additional prisoner releases on September 1, 2010, including that of an ex-Guantanamo detainee, Abu Sofiyan Bin

Qummu, another person rendered by the Americans for interrogation in 2007. These releases were typically preceded by debates organized within Libyan prisons between representatives of the regime and young Islamic militants, including veterans of Afghanistan, Iraq, and Somalia conflicts, who the regime felt were inclined to jihadist or neo-jihadist thinking.[10] In April 2009, Colonel Kama El Dib described to representatives of Human Rights Watch a series of training programs he ran at the General People's Committee for Public Security in 2004. He claimed that up to sixty thousand Libyan officers had been trained in this context in "human rights concepts, nondiscrimination, security and legitimacy, the torture convention, how the policy should deal with citizens, and the Great Green Charter on Human Rights." Human Rights Watch said that while it could not evaluate the impact of these measures, it felt it was important to be as encouraging as possible.[11] Even so, not much had changed.

For all the steps forward, there were (or appeared to be) steps backward. In March 2006, Shukri Ghanem was sacked as prime minister and replaced by a known opponent of the reform process of which Ghanem had been a prominent symbol, Baghdadi Ali Mahmoudi. Ghanem was made the head of the National Oil Company, replacing Mohammed Al Badri, another technocrat with a strong reputation for competence. Given Ghanem's expertise in oil and experience as former senior OPEC administrator, the shuffle gave outsiders the feeling that higher-level reforms might be in danger, but that the focus on attracting foreign oil investment might continue at an even greater clip.

Talk of a New Constitution—and the Stating of Limits

Two thousand seven was the year Saif appeared to have been anointed, if not by any formal paternal dispensation, then in the absence of strong objection by the Leader, as Libya's primary reform icon. In a speech on August 20 (CK) entitled "Libya—Truth for All," Saif announced his plan to draft a new Libyan constitution, and launched two new newspapers *Oea* and *Quryna*, and, a TV station called Al Wasat (The Middle), and a radio station. This public address would become an annual event, sponsored by the Libyan Youth Association, and the venue for all significant announcements related to Saif's reform platform, which he styled "Libya Al Ghad (Libya Tomorrow)."

Linked to the question of a constitution and the rights of minority groups in Libya was the contentious issue of Libya's Berbers. In 2007, the regime, through Saif, for the first time reached out to the Berber communities, whose demands for linguistic and cultural recognition Gaddafi had long ignored. (Berbers and mixed Berber-Arabs are variously estimated at 5 percent to 20 percent of the population, and are heavily concentrated in communities like Yefren and Gharyan, in western Jebel Nafusa. The Yefren rebellion was ultimately critical to the formation of a western front against Gaddafi in the post-February 2011 hostilities.)

As part of the "rapprochement within a rapprochement" in 2007, Gaddafi hosted a session of the international Imazighen (Berber) Congress to discuss "education and social integration of Berber communities" in Libya, and subsequently allowed limited expression of Berber culture in country, notably via a website called *Tawalt* (*Word*), which rapidly became a hub for information on Libyan Berber language and heritage, as well as related discussion groups.[12] Members of the Berber community hoped that these new overtures, including visits to Berber communities by both Saif and Prime Minister Baghdadi Ali Mahmoudi, might lead to an explicit mention of "protected cultural rights" within Saif's proposed new constitution. This would be in stark contrast to Gaddafi's statements in the *1969 Constitutional Declaration* and *1977 Declaration of the Establishment of the Authority of the People*, which insisted on the "absolute" Arab and Arabic character of Libya.[13] Yet Berber hopes were swiftly dashed. In December 2008, the regime (and, allegedly, members of Saif's Libya Al Ghad) organized at least one sizable and menacing anti-Berber protest in Yefren. *Tawalt* was off line by February.

This mini Berber Spring is a telling example of the limits Saif the reformist had in mind and is perhaps a clue to the limits of how far he was willing to go. While the releases and the minority rapprochement were happening, Saif increasingly peppered his public statements with reminders of the "limits" to expression. The sensitivity of the Berber issue was underscored—and contributed substantively to tensions with the US—by the expulsion of a US diplomat by the Libyans, after he met with members of the Berber community while on a personal trip to the Jebel Nafusa.[14]

Not long after, in 2008, Gaddafi named his son Mu'tassim Libya's national security adviser, an appointment that signaled to many that Gaddafi had far more confidence in his fourth-eldest son than they had previously suspected. Many analysts saw this as an indication and a public sign that—

however he felt about Saif, and Saif's reformist stance—Gaddafi was ready to play hardball if things got out of hand. It might also have been, as author Dirk Vandewalle posits, that Gaddafi had made the overall limits of reform—and in particular, the distinction between economic and political reform—clear when he removed Ghanem as prime minister in 2006.[15]

Regime's Attempts (Again) at "Quiet Compromise"

In the context of the general opening and under the ostensible leadership of Saif Al Islam, the Libyan regime undertook a series of actions that ultimately proved momentous. It notified 112 families of Abu Selim victims of their relatives' deaths between 2001 and 2006 and offered them incremental amounts of compensation: first, Libyan dinar 120,000 (US$98,590) if single; LD130,000 (U$106,800) if married. The regime then increased the offer by June 2009 to LD200,000 (US$164,300).[16] As with the case of the Bulgarian nurses and the Lockerbie and UTA families, the offers came with conditions; victims had to renounce all internal and external claims against the government. Notification was carried out in stages, with a stepping-up in the first half of 2006 and verifications provided to, of the 351 families, 160 from Benghazi, and others from Tripoli, Derna, Al Beida, and Misurata. In some cases, officials in Tripoli provided death certificates, but no formal apology.

We must understand the context of the growing opposition: of the 1,235 killed most were political prisoners, and of those, most were from Benghazi and neighboring cities and towns. Benghazi's population—minus the 150,000 to 200,000 foreign laborers, mostly Egyptian—was under 700,000. If we assume 1,000 of the Abu Selim victims were from Benghazi or nearby towns and villages, this means at least one person of every thousand, in a highly insular society with large extended families living in close proximity. Every person in Benghazi would have known at least one and likely several of the "disappeared."

In March 2007, thirty of the victims' families took the unprecedented action of filing a claim against the Libyan regime in North Benghazi Court to try to force the government to reveal the fate of the Abu Selim detainees.[17] Equally, if not more unprecedented was the fact that the government in April 2008 acquiesced to the creation of a Coordination Committee of the Families of the Victims, led by Fathi Terbil, a well-known name in Benghazi, who would attain almost heroic status during the Libyan revolution, and a lawyer colleague Mohammed al Ferjany. This body proceeded, under more or less formal cover, to organize sequential demonstrations in Benghazi, in front of the headquarters of the security services, beginning in June 2008 in Benghazi, and in Al Beida and Derna, growing in size from 150 on November 30, 2008, to more than 200 subsequently. This was more than the regime had bargained for, and there are indications that at this point that more hardline forces within the government thought the appeasement campaign was going very wrong: the attempt to repress or intimidate various members of the committees, and singling out the Terbil, who was arrested and then released on March 30, 2009.

That same month, the Coordination Committee publicly released, via opposition websites, a list of demands on the Libyan government, including the identification and prosecution of those responsible (which, of course, meant Gaddafi's head of internal security, Abdullah Senussi), full hand-over and identification of remains, an official apology, and the release of all other detained family members. This would not be the first appearance of Senussi, who had in recent years become Gaddafi's undisputed "iron fist."[18]

On June 29, 2009, there were sizeable protests in Benghazi by Abu Selim families, including many women and children. Then minister of justice, Mustafa Abdeljalil (who soon became head of the National Transitional Council after the 2011 revolution), seemed to encourage a legal process and establishment of a legal process through the courts as the way for those who did not accept compensation to go forward. Abdeljalil told Human Rights Watch in April 2009, "The offers of compensation were made in the context of reconciliation. Around 30 percent of the families who had so far been informed of the death of their relatives have accepted the offer of compensation, 60 percent have refused because they believe the amount is insufficient, and 10 percent have refused on principle."[19] Perhaps in an attempt to end the process, on August 10, 2009, Saif Al Islam's Gaddafi Foundation issued a public statement saying that 569 families had been compensated (and, implicitly, had accepted the government's terms), and that negotiations were continuing with the families of 598 victims.

Gaddafi (or someone with his ear, whether Saif or someone else) had apparently concluded that it was necessary to come clean, at least to a degree, about Abu Selim. It would be better to resolve the claims, as with all the external victims' families, than let this issue further motivate revenge against the regime. One of the issues, of course, was that short of implicating those directly responsible—notably, Abdullah Senussi—trying them, and fully compensating the families, half-measures were likely to have the opposite of the intended effect. Further, Gaddafi probably felt he could not risk implicating one of his own (Senussi) without weakening and delegitimizing himself and his power structure. A similar calculus was presumably behind Gaddafi's obsession with bringing Megrahi home from Scotland, for the Lockerbie bomber was a significant remaining source of dirty laundry hanging outside Libya proper.

This extended process of tying up loose ends with respect to internal abuses proved significant, because, like the National Economic Strategy and its associated ventures, it created a series of intermediaries who would work together on behalf of the victims and their families and communicate with other groups, such as lawyers and other officials working on the Benghazi HIV infections, and Saif's appointed reformists. There was, therefore, a social network around "rehabilitation" disproportionately located in the eastern Libya.

Lockerbie's Back

On August 20, 2009, Abdelbasset al Megrahi was released from his Scottish cell after eight and a half years of incarceration, by order of Scottish Secretary of Justice Kenny MacAskill, on "compassionate grounds" stemming from local physicians' determinations that he had less than three months to live.

The Blair government made this decision, contravening assurances given by the UK to Washington that Megrahi would serve his full sentence in Scotland. The timing was significant, as the release coincided both with Saif's now-customary August Green Square address and, more importantly, with the fortieth anniversary of the Al Fateh revolution on September 1, 2009, for which Gaddafi wanted to see Megrahi back in Tripoli.

The circumstances behind the return of Megrahi are not completely known, but a January 27, 2011, *Vanity Fair* exposé by David Rose presents a complex layering of deals and quid pro quos among Gaddafi, the Blair government, the UK's then Foreign Minister Jack Straw, the Scottish Justice Minister Kenny MacAskill, and Scottish First Minister Alex Salmond, all in the name of UK interests. Those interests were primarily the BP oil and gas deals Blair thought he had secured with Gaddafi in May 2007. Gaddafi had since made clear that he wanted Megrahi back before he died in prison of advanced, terminal prostate cancer, which would have had disastrous effects on the Libya-UK relationship.[20] Told of the foreign secretary's recommendation to MacAskill that a prisoner transfer agreement (PTA) be signed, but with an exclusion for Megrahi, Gaddafi was allegedly furious[21] and held up official validation of the oil contracts. This resulted in a flurry of conversations in the UK between senior UK officials and Scottish officials regarding how to secure Megrahi's release. Rose argues that the Scottish government, originally vehemently against any PTA, may have assented to a quid pro quo (again phrased "in the national interests") whereby London would put a statute of limitations on tort claims filed by non-Scottish UK prisoners who alleged mistreatment in Scottish jails. (Scotland was facing a spate of such claims, which threatened to be very costly.)

Senior UK and Scottish officials deny the claims. Lord Peter Mandelson, UK Business Secretary in 2009 and erstwhile friend of Saif, called suggestions of a trade-related quid pro quo "offensive."[22] Whatever the claims, Rose points out, Megrahi was freed, and the tort law was amended. These eleventh-hour wranglings over Megrahi illustrate the growing bilateral insidiousness of a ratcheting-up process that Gaddafi had turned into an art: once an individual or government made one compromise in service to a commercial interest, other deeper compromises were necessary in order to preserve the original interest. This was Gaddafi's hook-and-bait game. In the 1990s, when the US and Britain were calling the diplomatic shots, handing over Megrahi for trial was the first condition Libya had to meet before normal relations could be restored. Once Megrahi was convicted and sanctions began to be lifted, pressure was exerted in the other direction. As far as Qaddafi was concerned, Megrahi's return to Libya was the price of fully opening up Libya to the bankers and the oilmen.

While Obama criticized the Brown government for Megrahi's release, many in the administration, as well as many of the Lockerbie families, believed the US position should have been much stronger, and that President Obama's and Secretary Clinton's relatively soft responses indicated the administration must have been informed of the deal in advance.[23] To the extent that the US was disapproving, it only had itself to blame: the Bush administration (and in truth, the Lockerbie families) had chosen not to continue to isolate Gaddafi and opened the floodgates to an endless number of such transactions across multiple countries.

Megrahi's Return

Megrahi arrived by Libyan Afriquiya Airways jet at Tripoli's Metiga Airport on August 20, 2009, at 8:45 p.m., flanked by Saif, wearing traditional dress. At the airport, there was a reception of about a hundred young people.[24]

According to a US State Department cable, "a much larger throng" had been removed subsequent to President Obama's statement demanding that Megrahi be placed under house arrest. The same cable described press coverage as "low key"; simultaneously, a large rally was being held at Green Square, under patronage of the Gaddafi Development Fund, that "created the perception of a hero's welcome" despite the fact that many of those present seemed unaware of Megrahi's release. Libyan TV did not carry the event live, and Saif did not speak as he had in previous years. The spokesman of reform had made several comments during this period that were not appreciated—to put it mildly—in the US or the UK.

At a press conference, Saif specifically thanked the Scottish government for its efforts to help free Megrahi and proclaimed, "Our efforts have succeeded." Text messages sent to Libyan phones announced the release of "the national hero Megrahi." As the State Department cable notes, the Libyans seemed to be trying to "manage the optics" for two audiences, while "technically" sticking to the agreement.[25]

Subsequently, Saif was "rewarded" by the General People's Congress (at Gaddafi's behest, of course) with the offer of an official post, that of General Coordinator of the People's Leadership Committees, a new body Gaddafi had created to manage the regime's relations with various national tribal leaderships. Many external analysts read into the nomination and Gaddafi's remarks that he might retire to consider more "global matters" as tantamount to announcing that the succession issue had finally been put to rest: Saif was Gaddafi's man.

As with many things hatched in Gaddafi's mind, Saif's anointment as heir apparent may well have been the opposite of what it appeared: an effort by Gaddafi to "tame" Saif's agenda by giving it a more mainstream channel. Indeed, Saif was remarkably unclear about whether he would formally accept the post, choosing instead to make a series of bold, reform-minded statements, some with more overt political content: "We will have a new constitution, new laws, a commercial and business code and now a flat tax of 15 percent." "We can be the Dubai of North Africa." With regard to a new role within the regime, he said, "I will not accept any position unless there is a new constitution, new law and transparent elections—everyone should have access to public office. We should not have a monopoly on power."[26]

About this time, rumors began to percolate that Saif's actions—his support for Benghazi victims' associations, prisoner amnesties, talk of a new constitution, for example—were making Gaddafi, Saif's brothers Mu'tassim and Saadi, and members of Gaddafi's inner circle decidedly nervous. Gaddafi had supposedly heard something on one of Saif's television stations that he did not like and showed up at the studio in person to harangue the staff and order the station closed.[27] In late January 2010, Saif's pro-reform newspapers *Oea*, *Quryna*, and *Cyrene*, announced they would publish only online, before resuming print copies that July. On November 4, 2010, Prime Minister Baghdadi Ali Mahmoudi (one assumes, axiomatically, with the approval of Gaddafi senior) closed down all Saif's media outlets after an op-ed appeared alleging government incompetence and calling for a "final assault" on corruption.[28] A few days later, the regime arrested between ten and twenty-two journalists in "Saif's camp."[29]

By November 2010—a few months short of the 2011 revolution—the Revolutionary Committees, supported by Mahmoudi (whom Saif had previously referred to as a "fossil"), appeared to have tilted Gaddafi decidedly against Saif, whose public charges of government ineptitude seemed to have pushed his father too far. Saif thus retreated to his £10 million Hampstead, London, mansion, which he had bought in July 2009. He told his friend and adviser Benjamin Barber he was "tired of Tripoli, that he had too many enemies there,"[30] echoing statements that he would retire permanently from Libyan politics to live in London that he had made earlier in the year.[31] Many in the political and business circles saw this as a concession that his brother Mu'tassim had "won."

Gaddafi Bites the Hands That Feed

The issue of what to do about or how to respond to developments in Libya entered, peripherally, the Obama presidential campaign in 2008. Advisers to the campaign prepared briefing notes on the evolution of the relationship and a set of talking points for debates, in case some aspect of the "rehabilitation" arose in sparring with other Democrats or Republican nominee John McCain. (The issue of US involvement in Libya never came up in the debates, even though the next step in the US-Libya relationship proved to be a critical moment in the Obama presidency.)

Those who held out some hope that Gaddafi would moderate his behavior in the wake of his diplomatic coups—notably, extricating himself from the terror list—did not have long to wait before understanding that this was not part of his plan. Gaddafi was remarkably restrained in his public comments between 2004 and 2006, limiting his speeches largely to marginal topics for a domestic audience. They were rambling discourses on the evils of genetically engineered organisms, for example.

As soon as the last of the bilateral US-Libya sanctions were removed, however, the old Gaddafi quickly reemerged. According to one observer, Gaddafi—or his handlers—may have begun to feel "safe" in speaking his mind once he realized how desperate various commercial parties were to secure deals with the new Libya. Tony Blair's infamous 2007 meeting in the desert was a case in point. From 2007 to 2010, Gaddafi's performances became more and more bizarre.

In one strange and rather forced attempt at bilateral cultural diplomacy, the Middle East Institute and Columbia University hosted call-in conferences with Gaddafi on two occasions. The first conference, entitled, "The Prospect for Democracy: A Libyan-American Dialogue," was held March 22–23, 2006, at the Columbia campus. It was sponsored jointly by the Green Book Center, Columbia, and the Center for Strategic and International Studies (CSIS). US Assistant Secretary for Near East Affairs David Welch attended the event.[32] The brother of now-famous Libyan dissident Fathi Al Jahmi would write in the lead-up to the conference that "both the university setting and the presence of senior State Department officials are a gift to Qadhafi [sic]), who will use his monopoly over all Libyan television and newspapers to declare this a sign of U.S. support,"[33] which of course it was, and he did. Libyan News Agency JANA reported that Columbia was "grateful for the opportunity to exchange ideas and thoughts around [Gaddafi's concepts of] Third Universal Theory and Direct Democracy."[34] The conference generated an outcry among the Columbia student body and a scandal for the then dean of Columbia's School of International and Public Affairs, Lisa Anderson, a Libya expert.

On March 31, 2008, the Middle East Institute in Washington, DC, hosted another planned Gaddafi call-in conference, cosponsored by Exxon Mobil and the Green Book Center. The Libyan panelists, who included Yusuf Sawani and Mohammed Siala, former head of Libya's Department of Foreign Cooperation, were noticeably on edge throughout the event, fearing that they might say something that Gaddafi might not like. At one point, Sawani, in response to a question about the fate of Fathi Al Jahmi, exploded in rage, inviting the US to come "pick up the 'crazy old man' Jahmi, put him in an orange jumpsuit, put him on its 'flying prison' aircraft and take him to Guantanamo."[35] The backlash against and chaos engendered by both conferences presumably squashed the hopes of any repeat performances, though Georgetown University undertook another such conference in 2009 (at which Gaddafi did speak).

Gaddafi was clearly feeling on a roll. In a June 2008 speech on the anniversary of the US strikes against Libya, he said:

> It has been proven that there is no democracy in [the US]. Rather, it is a dictatorship no different than the dictatorships of Hitler, Napoleon, Mussolini, Genghis Khan, Alexander the Great, and the rest of the tyrants. In the days of crazy Reagan, the American president issued a presidential order to launch a war against Libya, for example, a presidential order to besiege Libya, a presidential order to boycott Libya, and so on. Is this a democracy or a dictatorship?[36]

During a November 2009 visit to Italy, Gaddafi asked Prime Minister Silvio Berlusconi to find two hundred Italian "models" for whom he paid £53 each to listen to what was described as a "solemn discourse on the role of Muslim women" (twenty of the models were invited on an all-expense-paid trip to stargaze and drink warm camel's milk).[37] Some of them apparently accepted the offer.

After President Obama took office in 2009, Gaddafi made various plays to meet the president, most of which Obama's staff managed to parry. He did shake the president's hand on July 9, 2009, at a G8 Summit in Italy, less than three months after Secretary of State Hillary Clinton welcomed Mu'tassim al Gaddafi to the State Department. "We deeply value the relationship between the United States and Libya," Clinton said on that occasion. "We have many opportunities to deepen and broaden our cooperation, and I'm very much looking forward to building on this relationship."[38]

Less than a month later, in a speech before the UN General Assembly on September 23, 2009, Gaddafi could, apparently, no longer contain himself. Characteristically, he spoke long beyond his allotted fifteen minutes and chastised the UN and implicitly the US for violating the sovereignty of member states:

> The Preamble states also that if there is a use of force, then it must be the United Nations' force, or the United Nations as military interventions, according to the joint ventures of the United Nations, not country, or one, two country, or three country, using the force or the military power.[39]

The Security Council "should be called the Terror Council," he said, after ripping up a copy of the UN Charter. To underscore the point, Gaddafi explained the Western action in Iraq:

> Then we come to the Iraqi war, the mother of all evils. The United Nations also should investigate. Iraq is an independent country, member in this General Assembly. How this country is attacked and how this country how we have already read in the general in the charter that the United Nations should have interfered and stopped.[40]

As if to soften the meaning of his words, he added, "We are content and happy if Obama can stay forever as the President of the United States of America."

If Gaddafi really thought that Obama would be his guarantor of peace, he would soon be very disappointed.

In part, Gaddafi's performance may have had something to do with a few indignities that had come with his first trip to the United States. Contrary to the hospitality afforded him by Sarkozy on his first official trip to France in 2007, Gaddafi was denied permission to set up his tent in Manhattan—or even in rural New Jersey—and banned from visiting the World Trade Center site. Libya's delegates to the UN desperately tried to find a place for their leader to stay. Thoroughly insulted by his reception in the US, one of Gaddafi's first acts upon returning to Tripoli was to refuse to allow the Russians to take back spent uranium—part of the original understanding on the disposal of components of Libya's WMD program.[41]

Saif, uncharacteristically, had been the first to thumb his nose at Libya's key allies when he accompanied Megrahi on his return to Libya in 2009, saying "In all commercial contracts for oil and gas with Britain, al-Megrahi was always on the negotiating table."[42] In 2010, during an interview with British press, he raised eyebrows by bragging that the now former prime minister, Tony Blair, was a "personal family friend" of the Gaddafis and had visited Libya many times since he left office.[43] The origins of these comments are unclear, but they certainly appeared to have been made with the intention of embarrassing Blair, who was already under scrutiny for his postretirement dealings with Libya. Was this an instance of hubris or a veiled threat, a reminder, to one of the individuals who had benefited most and personally from the rapprochement, that he needed to be circumspect in how he characterized his relationship with Libya? Blair described, in

September 2011, his role in Libya in almost the same terms he had used to justify his role in the Iraq war: "I have no regrets."[44]

Saif's Limits

Had the rigged dichotomy of "reactionaries versus reformists" become a hard reality, as some aspects of the makeover began to look a bit too lifelike for Gaddafi's taste. Interviews of some of Saif's "implementers," from Yusuf Sawani to Mahmoud Jibril and others, suggest some disillusionment with Saif's personal stake in, and commitment to, a process he professed to champion, and which they claim they originally felt was sincere.[45] Sawani, who after the revolution assumed a post as professor of political science at Tripoli University, maintained that Saif did not pay enough attention to the process, and "was more concerned with attracting the attention of foreign experts and advisers," than making firm progress toward his stated goals.[46] At the same time, Sawani suggests that regime supporters, those with revolutionary committee credentials, were alarmed by some of Saif's maneuvers, noticed his vulnerability, and worked to undermine individuals in his orbit. Jibril, the "sheikh of the Muslim Brotherhood in Libya" is one example. In a further, critical move, Mu'tassim had by this time aligned himself more forcefully against Saif, a development that individuals in Saif's orbit confirmed indirectly. According to Sawani, "Mu'tassim was completely opposed to the plan of Saif Al Islam."[47]

Many of Saif's former assistants or aides described a process in which Saif sought to pursue his own agendas, without having to directly confront his father, such as asking others to float opinion pieces and watch the results, all the while making a show of the fact that it was *he* who would suffer at least part of the consequences. Thus Gaddafi and his son seemed to be waging an indirect and believable contest, via third parties. Fathi Baja, a journalist and professor who wrote for Saif in *Quryna*, described in an interview with the postrevolutionary, Benghazi-based paper *Miyadeen* (*Public Squares*) how he was challenged by Gaddafi about an article entitled, *Libya Ila 'ain* ("Libya's Going Where?"). In the article, he challenged what he described as the "Michael Porter/Monitor" thesis that reform should start (and could be limited to) economic reform, and advocated strongly for the drafting of a new constitution, which Saif had intermittently been promoting.[48] Shortly after the article came out in 2009, Baja, a bespectacled academic who bears some resemblance to American actor John Goodman, was summoned to meet with Gaddafi in Tripoli. It was a surreal spectacle in which Saif Al Islam, Musa Kusa, and Khamis Gaddafi made cameo appearances.

Baja described how Gaddafi explained he had summoned him to "protect" him from those who felt his article had been disrespectful and wanted to "eliminate" him, and that his son Khamis, who had been Baja's student in the university, had "put in a good word." Baja went on, "Gaddafi said to me then, I want to protect you now, because these words [you have written] have displeased many, and they want to kill you." After listening to Gaddafi for two and a half hours, Baja was then released to the beaming Khamis, who took him out to dinner and let him go. Saif was present at the Tripoli meeting with Gaddafi, but apparently neither intervened nor said anything to Baja, perhaps, in Baja's estimation, because Baja had implicitly criticized Saif for not moving far or fast enough:

> [My] article was a response to Saif's program, which he said stemmed from Porter's argument [in the context of the National Economic Strategy] that economic reform alone [was sufficient]: Porter told Saif that Libya's lack of progress was due to economic and management deficiencies. In a nutshell, the point of [my] article was that politics was the key to solving the crisis, assuming the intentions behind the reform were robust.[49]

Sawani attributes the experience to the fact that Saif could not go against his father on any matter that was critical to progress, such as a constitution, which Saif first proposed in 2006. Even in the area of economic development, many of Saif's projects—however well intentioned—suffered from being scatterbrained, influenced at least in part by fear of his father's reaction. A former Department of Defense official and later adviser to Saif said that it was apparent, in her many conversations with Saif, that he was "fixated" or "obsessed" with his father on one hand; on the other hand, Saif tried to dispel the perception that Gaddafi held sway over him or that he needed to clear every decision with Gaddafi.[50] Sawani alleges that he was himself increasingly targeted by members of the revolutionary councils, who suspected him of being a foreign agent sent to undermine the regime. Sawani says he was likely saved (perhaps the only person to have been "saved" in such a manner) by Wikileaks cable revelations of "tense relations and differences between him and Saif."[51]

Mustafa Ben Halim described an episode that provides an interesting parallel. In his memoirs, he questions whether he should have been more bold in resisting then prime minister Hussain Yusuf Maziq in pushing for a change from a monarchy to a republican form of government, in the late 1950s.

> Perhaps I should have ignored the arguments against it and accepted the post [Prime Minister] when the King made the offer and then formed a strong government and pushed the reforms through with determination right away, even getting very tough if need be with some of those resisting regime, who were the beneficiaries of a corrupt system.[52]

Ben Halim ties weak-hearted or incomplete efforts, or the fear of insufficient resolve by both the king and reformists to combat corruption and devolve power to the lower house and the cabinet to an atmosphere conducive to Gaddafi's 1969 coup.

Of course, circa 2009, the cast of characters was quite different. Instead of a kindly, paternalistic monarch who hated to say no to any supplicant, there was Colonel Gaddafi, who had an entirely different approach than mild-mannered King Idris. At the same time, many more of Saif's contingent were clearly asking themselves what might have transpired if Saif had either the will or, perhaps more relevant, the ability to push his father harder to accede to the creation of a new constitution and concrete steps to devolve power from the Gaddafi regime to more formal organs of state. Ben Halim notes that during both the monarchy period and the rehabilitation, the US and the West had chosen the side of the status quo over attempting to encourage change:

> [T]he British cautioned strongly against the change to a Republic, and warned of the dangerous consequences of such a change. The Americans were more flexible and merely suggested less haste and a deeper study of the question, while preparing the people gradually.[53]

The years following the 2003 WMD deal were mixed for Gaddafi. Suddenly, he had to cope with any number of issues that he probably had not anticipated and for which he had not developed a consistent plan. Saif had played his role well, regardless of how committed he was—or could be—to making sure the reform program was implemented. Those in his orbit, hearing his transient confessions, said he felt he had committed himself to an impossible task; the combined forces of his father, his ambitious and violent brothers, and his father's regime fanatics were not conducive to a smooth transition. While these elements had appreciated or been told to appreciate the role of very circumscribed signaling reforms, Saif had clearly gone beyond what those invested in the regime were willing to stomach. Again, regardless of his exact feelings and motives—which were likely complex—Saif had over the course of six years managed to provide some cover to those demanding acknowledgment of past abuses (like the Abu Selim victims and their lawyers) and academics and journalists who criticized the excesses and financial abuses of regime figures. By antagonizing those opposed to real reform, giving the masses a heightened sense of political awareness, and cultivating a group of people who appeared willing to follow this path, Saif had clearly demonstrated the limits to reform, as well as a tantalizing glimpse of "what might be."

The Contenders

With Saif spending increasing time in London, and voicing both public and private doubts about his political future in Libya, foreign diplomats began to pick up the thread that Saif was, in fact, losing the battle for reform with his brothers and the murky group of regime reactionaries with strong tribal connections.[54] It was, after all, Mu'tassim, not Saif, whom Gaddafi sent on the first official trip to the States in 2009, as a minister no less. By some standard logic this would suggest that, indeed, Saif was on the outs: the Colonel perhaps had given Saif as much rope as he was comfortable giving, or ever wanted to give, or was being pressured by those who had done his dirty work for the previous three-plus decades to pull back, before Saif created a situation that the regime could not control. Or perhaps Gaddafi was just enjoying playing the games he always played.

From 2008 to 2010, Gaddafi apparently had given Saadi another chance to prove his leadership credentials, or, alternately to occupy himself respectably, entrusting him with the overall management of a multibillion-dollar initiative informally called the "Zwara Corridor," encompassing a 40-kilometer stretch of coastline between Zwara and Ras Jedir.[55] Following the spirit of Monitor's "economic clustering" recommendations, the Zwara Corridor was to serve as a hybrid industrial/export zone, and include a quarantine zone for alcohol-guzzling, beach-going tourists. (Unlike in Dubai, where foreigners can drink alcohol in hotels, Gaddafi had been adamant that Libya remain officially dry.)

In 2010, a number of foreign firms considered investing in this area, less for what they could do there, than as a lever into more promising contracts elsewhere in the country. The Zwara project put Saadi on a collision course of sorts with Saif, who was far more powerful, and Hannibal, whose fiefdom was maritime and port affairs. Saif had been actively courting (and been courted by) the Port of Houston for a series of port management contracts (one of which involved a proposed port at Homs, within the corridor); Saadi had done the rounds of the Gulf-based port operating companies, attempting to secure their support. Senior Libyan businessmen would confess in winter 2010 that the Zwara project was a complete mess, not only for these heightened family rivalries, but for Saadi's failure to find investors for the cornerstone refinery. Saadi did not have nearly the clout of Saif, and indeed would have needed Saif's support to move these projects forward—and yet Saif's own long-term position in this constellation was far from clear.

Meanwhile, Mu'tassim was pressuring various of Gaddafi and Saif's men—Shukri Ghanem first—to transfer state money into his own personal accounts so he could augment his personal militia (the one he used to shut down the Caterpillar plant back in 2005), and outgun that of his brother Khamis (the 32nd Brigade). Even as those on the outside saw Saif's star falling, Mu'tassim may well have been chipping away wildly at whatever increased confidence he may (or may not) have won from his father. Abdelrahman Shalgam, in his post-Revolution memoir on the people within Gaddafi's circle, claims that Mu'tassim had tried to intimidate Prime Minister Baghdadi Ali Mahmoudi into linking the budgets of various ministries, including Foreign Affairs, into his [Mu'tassim's] new Ministry of National Security.[56] Shalgam says he urged Baghdadi to overcome his hesitation and inform the Leader of Mu'tassim's actions. Shalgam says he believes that conversation took place as Gaddafi sacked Mu'tassim sometime in late 2010, months or weeks before the Revolution. This could, in part, explain Gaddafi's subsequent reliance on Saif during the Revolution to make certain decisions (still unclear) and what appeared from television interviews and his actions to be highly varying emotional states. Anecdotal accounts paint a picture of chaos in the Gaddafi household, with Gaddafi quasi-catatonic, Mu'tassim out of control, and no one Gaddafi firmly in charge. As of February 15, 2011, Saif may well have found himself, suddenly, ruling Libya, with very little real life preparation, and under the worst circumstances possible.

CHAPTER 8

On the Eve of Revolution

Politically, Libya is a stable country. There is currently no viable challenge to Qaddafi's leadership. The security risk to business in Libya is very low. . . . [B]y far the greatest risk to foreign companies operating in Libya is its business environment.[1]

CONTROL RISK GROUP

In the few months leading up to the revolution, the situation in Libya was almost as mysterious as before the rapprochement. On a macro level, Libya was growing fast; there had been some symbolic, if not always meaningful, economic reforms. At the same time, Gaddafi was clearly unleashed and exercising little restraint in his words and deeds. Many of the principal advocates of deeper, structural reforms, from Saif down, appeared to have been stopped in their tracks, while more aggressive family members, Mu'tassim in particular, and old-guard regime agents pressed their case that Gaddafi was taking the country down a dangerous path. Libya was moving forward with some bilateral relationships, such as with Italy (largely by dint of Gaddafi's close personal friendship with Silvio Berlusconi, arguably Europe's most flamboyant prime minister). But relations with the US were suffering a potentially dangerous malaise, also linked to personal issues, largely Gaddafi's feelings that the US—and the US president—was not only ignoring but outright disrespecting him.

Assessing the health of Libya in 2009–2010 depended highly on one's perspective. To the Western commercial community, the country appeared to be entering a kind of postpartum optimism. In an era of economic stagnation, "[a]t a time of global gloom, Libya is a rare source of light," wrote Heba Saleh in a 2010 feature for the *Financial Times*.[2] The economy had been booming for four years, fed by high oil prices and rising foreign direct investment. From 2004 to 2010, average growth in GDP hovered around 5 percent; foreign reserves rose from $20 billion in 2003 to $170 billion at the end of 2010.[3]

The Libyan government announced it would be spending $46.6 billion on infrastructure in 2010, up 32 percent from 2009, and a commitment of $66 billion to new infrastructure between 2010 and 2012. Of that, $10 billion would go to upgrade Libya's ports; $5 billion for industrial development; $2.5 billion for civil aviation and upgrading airports in major cities of Tripoli, Benghazi, and Sebha; and $1 billion for a new rail system.[4] The US construction company AECOM, which had entered the country in 2007, was by 2010 overseeing 265 contracts, covering 146 infrastructure projects in 41 cities and towns in Libya, with 300 more planned by 2020.

The Old City, long a reminder of the neglect that the regime had inflicted on the Libyan population and culture, was in full bloom, its bidonvilles or shanty towns cleared forcibly to make way for boutique hotels, shops, and restaurants; the skyline started to resemble that of Dubai in the early 2000s, with building cranes everywhere. The range of consumer goods and outlets available continued to increase, with the addition of boutique outlets like Marks & Spencer. (The agent for Marks & Spencer was Husni Bey; Gaddafi's men forced the closure of the upscale boutique at least once, on the grounds that it was a Jewish enterprise, or that Bey had not paid the proper taxes.)

In 2009, more than five years since Libya had been reintroduced to the international community, progress had been made on many fronts. While Libya did not experience the depth of privatization promised in 2004, there was progress in some non-oil sectors, including banking, where six of sixteen national banks had been privatized. In 2006 the original 1998 investment law was amended, lowering minimum requirements for foreign direct investment from tens of millions of dollars to a far more reasonable figure. The Ministry of Investment and Trade appeared to be adding constantly to both commercial and labor laws, although much of the legislation was open to interpretation, given contradictory statutes and the lack of a unified code.

Upon closer examination, some of Libya's economic successes were considerably less impressive. Overseen by Saif, with the help of his close friend Mustafa Zarti, the Libyan Investment Authority (LIA), which for a time effectively managed Libya's estimated $200 billion sovereign wealth fund, made a series of very poor calls during its first foray into international capital markets just before the global recession hit in 2008. Goldman Sachs allegedly lost more than $1 billion in LIA funds on risky trades (the Libyans allegedly threatened to put a "hit" out on the young trader responsible).[5] Weeks before the venerated US investment bank Lehman Brothers collapsed, an internal effort was made to broker an LIA-backed rescue, but when the LIA representative showed up, Lehman Brothers rebuffed the approach on the grounds that Libya did not fit the company's "investor profile" (i.e., Libya's was dirty money). As the crisis progressed, a few weeks later, Lehman executives reconsidered and tried to get LIA back into talks, but it was too late—LIA would have nothing to do with the rapidly failing Lehman. The Libyans apparently by this point felt Lehman was itself "dirty money."[6]

A Nervous Breakdown in the Making?

Beneath the impressive economic numbers, those in a position to advise the Gaddafi family (particularly Saif) became concerned. In an interview with *Asharq Al Awsat*, Mahmoud Jibril said that, while he had been head of the economic development board, he had urged Gaddafi to push forward the opening at a faster pace or risk an implosion: "I went to him in Ramadan 2009 and spoke with him for an hour and 45 minutes. For most of this he said nothing, then he said: 'We will cancel the government and distribute the wealth. Be patient: two months and everything will be finished.'"[7]

Elsewhere in the region, individuals with ties to Libyan opposition in exile noted that Gaddafi's confidantes had been alerted to a new campaign, the bare outlines of which sounded ominously like a repetition or reformulation of the Revolutionary Committees, a reactionary, not a progressive maneuver. On a more hopeful note, there were other rumors floating in these circles that Abdelsalam Al Jelloud was resurfacing, either to promote the new, obscure Gaddafi vision or to head off another disaster.[8]

During the period 2004–2010, many Western leaders had the opportunity to observe Gaddafi up close. Gaddafi's public persona was typically what might be described as animated. Some foreign diplomats and a few businessmen saw Gaddafi in a more indisposed state. Officials described him as looking heavily medicated, sedated, and puffy. Prolix in public, he could be stone silent for lengthy, uncomfortable periods in smaller groups. Gaddafi's behavior in 2009 and 2010 again led outsiders to focus on the question of whether he was fully in control of his actions, or whether he was simply reverting to his usual antics. His UN General Assembly speech appeared to be within the range of vintage, provocative Gaddafi.

The accounts of various aides who tried to warn him of upcoming disaster, however, suggest he had retreated into a depressed or less than functional state, even prior to February 15, 2011. One source suggests that Gaddafi was "trailed on a weekly basis" by an Italian psychiatrist.[9] Given the personality traits enumerated, we might question the degree to which the arm's-length response of the US and the West to Libya post-deal might have set Gaddafi off in ways to which the Western leaderships had not drawn connections: for example, Gaddafi, as he was wont to do, may well have taken local (New York City) refusals to allow him to pitch his tent in Central Park, or visit the site of Ground Zero, as grave insults, justifying subsequent rants and retributions. Tales emerged from Gaddafi's UN team about their desperate efforts to find a ground-floor, luxury accommodation in New York for Gaddafi's UN General Assembly visit—as no one would have him.[10]

In that same year—2010—there were some very strange signs, which in retrospect might have been harbingers of turbulence: Gaddafi's hints that he might consider nationalizing the oil industry—combined with lower price expectations for crude, made Western oil companies nervous. Diplomatic relations with the US had suffered a blow after the Wikileaks scandal and associated revelations. There were a couple of strange defections and rumors of vague new policy proclamations by Gaddafi, which seemed to suggest that he might be regressing in his plans for Libya's new orientation. In short, strange things were happening in Libya many months before the start of the Arab Spring. Many observers passed these off as par for the course, but the fact is that a number of diplomatic missions and oil companies started to draw down their staff until things calmed down.

Wikileaks

In late 2010, a bolt from nowhere rocked US-Libya relations as 250,000 confidential, but not top-secret State Department diplomatic cables from 274 embassies were leaked in what was known as the "Wikileaks" scandal. Included were a series of cables written by US Embassy-Tripoli and USLO personnel about Gaddafi and the family dynamics, and Gaddafi's fears and foibles, particularly during his UN General Assembly visit to the US. The latter were credibly said to have infuriated Gaddafi, not only for the personal insult, but likely more critically for his loss of face with his own people: so *this* was what the Americans really thought of Gaddafi.

As expected, the scandal unleashed a torrent of retaliatory measures. Ambassador Gene Cretz, the author of many of the cables deemed most sensitive, was rendered ineffective. A State Department official noted, "The Libyans made it clear he [Cretz] was unwelcome." Cretz admitted to receiving a number of phoned death threats, and State Department officials noted that he was not the only one within the embassy so threatened. The State Department recalled Cretz to Washington for consultations in late 2011, with the expectation that he would remain there until another ambassador was appointed.[11] Other countermeasures included the Libyan declaration of the then political reporting officer as persona non grata for meeting with members of the Berber community. As is always the case during times of strain in bilateral relations, visas became an issue. Once the officer had left, the department was unable to get a visa for a replacement. Effectively, Wikileaks had frozen US diplomatic activity with and within Libya, and created a situation reminiscent of US-Libyan relations in the early 1970s, just after Gaddafi's coup.

Beyond Wikileaks' immediate impact, the outside world and Libya's community were interested in the leaked documents, not only for the rare glimpse they provided of what American diplomats thought, but also how little they really knew—and how little they had learned since 2006. One section in the documents on Gaddafi could have been written ten or twenty years earlier:

> Qadhafi is a complicated individual who has managed to stay in power for forty years through a skillful balancing of interests and realpolitik methods. Continued engagement with Qadhafi and his inner circle is important not only to learn the motives and interests that drive the world's longest serving dictator, but also to help overcome the misperceptions that inevitably accumulated during Qadhafi's decades of isolation.[12]

One cable on the Islamist presence in Derna, quoted heavily in outside news reports and later used as evidence supporting a strong presence of Al Qaeda in eastern Libya, was in fact a summary of unconfirmed statements made by a dual US-Libyan citizen to the deputy chief of mission.[13] Since 2004, there had never been a full complement of reporting officers within the embassy, and events in the eastern part of the country were, as a result, still largely unknown. Other cables mentioned the names of longtime embassy contacts in the context of information that could reasonably be said to be prejudicial to their safety (though some said the lack of information helped exonerate them with those in the regime who suspected they were giving the Americans too much information).

The release of yet more cables further strained relations between the US and some of its better in-country sources, whose statements—and identities—could be guessed, even if the actual names were redacted. To these individuals, the State Department could only respond with weak mea culpas.

Worry in the Oil Sector

By December 2011, there had been talk for over a year about how disappointing the Libyan oil environment had proven, relative to the huge expectations that followed the opening of the EPSA IV rounds. The international media were full of panicked reports about Libyan oil in 2009. In one article headlined "Libyan Promise Falters," its author wrote, "Five years after Libya reopened its oil sector to global participation, it has not matched its billing as a 'new El Dorado.'"[14] Increasingly, Libya was receiving press with titles such as "Libya: A Mixed Bag."[15] Gaddafi, perhaps inspired by Venezuelan strongman (and friend) Hugo Chavez, floated the idea of re-nationalizing parts of the Libyan oil industry—a major red flag.[16]

In early October 2010 came the announcement that American oil companies Chevron and Occidental Petroleum, after making no major new finds, were leaving or not extending the licenses for which they fought so vigorously in 2005.[17] Verenex and Medco had made some finds in a zone called Area 47 while Shell, BP, and Exxon pushed on, betting on large-scale gas finds.[18]

Though barely reported, this news was explosive, given how much Occidental had invested in the Libya relationship since 2005. Also not extended were the licenses of Woodside Petroleum (Australia) and Liwa Energy (Abu Dhabi). A smattering of other international oil companies did extend their concessions, including the American company Amerada Hess, Brazil's Petrobras, Indonesia's Medco Energi, Oil India Ltd., and Algeria's Sonatrach. The US oil companies ConocoPhillips, Marathon Oil, and Hess were in much different positions, being partners with the National Oil

Company (NOC) in existing production (Waha, or Oasis fields). Various majors were saying that their expectations of strikes within Libya had been vastly downgraded. In all, foreign companies operating in Libya had discovered 2.16 billion barrels of crude oil and 7.87 billion cubic feet of gas in five years. Further, legislation governing Libya's oil industry had not changed much since the original law in 1955 and was very much out of line with current industry practice and technology.[19]

The business environment was also becoming less welcoming. In a relentless effort spearheaded by Matouk al Matouk, who was equivalent to a labor minister, the Libyan regime continued a campaign to encourage managers to hire unqualified Libyans and to appoint local Libyan general managers to run Libya-based operations. Obtaining visas was a problem as well.

Other disconcerting events in 2009 included the establishment of the Supreme Council for Energy Affairs, which stole the power from NOC to negotiate contracts and set production and development targets. While NOC head Shukri Ghanem was sent out to promote this development, describing it as a "positive" event, Prime Minister Baghdadi Ali Mahmoudi, and Saif's brother Mu'tassim were to oversee this new authority,[20] further ensuring that contracts were upheld. Many found this situation far less comforting, as it suggested direct interference by Mu'tassim in the oil ministry policy and budgets (which did happen), even with Ghanem officially at the head of the NOC.

Some of the oil companies' frustration had to do with a structural preference on the part of the Libyans, which affected both Libya's ability to make a profit and the oil companies' ability to sell. Due to wear and the lack of replacement or repair resulting from the sanctions, Libyan fields were old and poorly functioning, losing production capacity precipitously. The incentives for the Libyan government motivated it to push for exploration contracts, EPSA (Exploration and Production Sharing) agreements, at the expense of existing fields. Despite the rumors of imminent development, exploration and production-sharing agreements (DEPSAs—contracts focused more on developing existing capacity), these never materialized, and Libya's overall oil infrastructure capacity continued to decline. The problem rested with the culture of corruption and an institutionalized stinginess: intermediaries needed their palms greased, which was far easier with earlier EPSA contracts that allowed for large bonuses.

In its annex to the NES, Cambridge Energy Research Associates (CERA) exhorted Libya to invest deeply and quickly in production capacity in order to take advantage of a relatively short window of higher prices. In a speech, Daniel Yergin, chairman of CERA, commented:

> [Libya's] resource base allows much higher production. The tendering of exploration rights is booming, but exploration by itself can take far too long for Libya to take advantage of its window of opportunity. If your country doesn't raise its production in the next few years, other countries will be glad to do so in Libya's place.[21]

In 2006, many analysts like Yergin believed oil would soon rise above $100 a barrel. By 2007–2008, the oil industry anticipated a different scenario, that of an oil and gas glut, provoked by the emergence of natural gas, superseding oil. Simply put, regardless of the oil in the ground in these fields, the economics of oil looked very different in 2010, compared to 2006.

Though many of the nuisances described may have contributed to the overall annoyance factor of work in Libya, we cannot discount the possibility that insiders had become increasingly alarmed about some aspect of Libya's risk profile, perhaps related to issues of succession or corruption. Given that most of the same big oil companies were in Saudi Arabia, it is conceivable that the Saudis had inside information about Gaddafi's internal rivalries and had warned off the American companies. Whatever the case, the Western oil companies were watching internal schisms with keen interest. A Reuters reporter wrote in November 2010:

> The rivalry in oil exporter Libya is watched closely by Western oil majors including BP, Eni and Exxon-Mobil. They have poured billions of dollars into Libyan oil and gas projects and some analysts say their investments could be jeopardized by shifts in the political landscape.[22]

Just as the diplomats' and oil executives' antennae had been raised, an unusual event occurred, which had many outside Libya guessing what exactly was happening within Gaddafi's inner circle.

Off and On the Reservation

In November 2010, Nouri Al Mismari, Gaddafi's longtime chief of protocol, left Libya for France on the pretext of treatment for an allegedly chronic ailment. Mismari had handled the logistics for Gaddafi's international visits and speeches for more than twenty years and knew most of his secrets. It is unclear if regime charges of embezzlement against Mismari had been prepared before or after he fled.[23] Not surprisingly, the circumstances behind Mismari's departure are obscure. There were rumors that Mismari and Mu'tassim Gaddafi had crossed swords sometime after 2004 about a business deal, that the latter had had Mismari's son killed in 2007, and that Mismari, despite having benefited financially from his work for the Gaddafis, such that he could afford "a luxurious home in France, fancy sports cars and jewels," had been biding his time for an opportunity to deliver a counterpunch.[24] Meanwhile, about the same time, late November to early December, Saif was said to have returned to Libya.

The French debriefed Mismari in the course of an asylum application and were apparently ready to send him back to Libya, when they changed their minds. According to one source, in addition to a furious response to France and Sarkozy personally, Gaddafi immediately confiscated the passports of other senior officials who he thought might be flight risks.[25]

There have been allegations that Mismari had been carrying information about unrest in Benghazi and that he would help the French pave the way for French action against Libya once the Arab Spring was under way.[26] It seems highly unlikely that Mismari had foreseen the Arab Spring, but the timing of his defection reflects the heightened level of turbulence and concern within Gaddafi's inner circles prior to the new year.

As an indication of how seriously Gaddafi took Mismari's defection, he sent a host of people—including Mu'tassim—to convince him to return, as late as February 5, to no avail.[27] Abdelrahman Shalgam, in his 559-page postrevolutionary treatise on the "people around Gaddafi," said that he met with Gaddafi about the same time and that the two discussed deteriorating morale within the Libyan leadership. Gaddafi was "intensely bitter" about increasing ridicule heaped upon Prime Minister Baghdadi Ali Mahmoudi and what he sensed was similar chatter about the incompetence of his sons.[28]

Contingency Planning?

What was the Western policy establishment thinking about all this? Had some agencies started to plan actively for contingencies, predicated upon further dramatic declines in Libya's orientation or Gaddafi's mental state? It was apparently known (to the Italians, at least) that Gaddafi had been seeing an Italian psychiatrist (there are no other public reports that Gaddafi had ever seen a Western doctor for mood disorders). If so, the assumption is that this doctor was passing information on Gaddafi's condition to the West. Alexander Najjar, in his 2011 book *Anatomy of a Tyrant*, speculated that Nouri Al Mismari provided French authorities with a trove of information on Gaddafi, which may have alerted the French and their Western allies to "something" coming, in time for the French to send aid to the "future insurgents."[29]

Given a lengthy history of the kinds of actions Gaddafi was capable of executing when he was down or felt affronted, some in Washington (and other European capitals) may have begun to conclude that Gaddafi might soon become a serious problem. While there is a big leap between these observations and the suggestion that the West somehow divined or was involved in what was about to transpire in Libya, the coincidence is rather striking. And it is reminiscent of the kinds of discussions the British had in the years after Gaddafi's coup about his potential to be become a liability that should be addressed.

After pulling all the above threads together—difficult to do at the time—the events that followed seem somehow far less out of the blue. By the same token, they strongly underscore the argument that the Libya conflagration contained significant elements that were independent of the Arab Spring. We have no idea, of course, what would have happened had neighboring Tunisia and Egypt not ejected their leaders in popular uprisings during the following months. At the same time, contrary to blasé security assessments from leading security companies, Libya was not stable; foreign commercial interests looked increasingly at risk; US-Libya relations were effectively frozen; and the principal reformists appeared to have been neutralized, at least for the time being.

Setting the Stage: Extremism, Regionalism, and Tribalism

As January 2011 came and went, and a Libyan version of the Arab Spring appeared ever more likely, Washington-based policymakers, steeped in the Iraq experience, began to wonder aloud about the risk of a no-holds-barred civil war, stoked by tribal, regional, and extremist-ideological schisms. Implicitly and explicitly, these would be the three dysfunctions to watch. Even if subsequent events appeared to substantiate these fears in different ways, it is worth elaborating on the situation.

TRIBALISM

With respect to tribal influence, Libya in 2011 was certainly not Libya of 1950 or 1960, an era when tribal affiliations were still quite strong. In the intervening years, Gaddafi had done much to attenuate tribal affiliations on a national scale, in part by creating new administrative districts that cut across tribal lines. As he did this, however, he increased patronage links to those tribes closest to his own clan (the Gaddafa), including Warfalla, the Megaraha, and the Mujraba, from among whose ranks came key associates Abdelsalam Al Jelloud (Megaraha), Abdullah Senussi (Megaraha), and Abu Bakr Younes (Mujraba). Mahmoud Jibril, head of the former Libyan Economic Development Board and future rebel prime minister, was a member of the favored Warfalla tribe, and his studies in the US were alleged to have been linked to tribal privilege. Despite the fact that members of all of these tribes defected to the rebel side in 2011, there remained large numbers who would not abandon their loyalty to Gaddafi. Each tribe tended to provide services to Gaddafi in professional clusters; thus the Warfalla were typically heavily represented in Gaddafi's security force, and the Megaraha more in senior finance and commercial positions.[30]

Despite Gaddafi's half-hearted attempts to settle the Bedouin in townships outside the cities, the exodus from the rural regions to the main cities of Benghazi and Tripoli sped up under Gaddafi, as he had never built sufficient infrastructure or jobs to keep people in rural areas. There was also large-scale migration from Benghazi to Tripoli in the 1980s and 1990s, as the economic opportunities were predominantly in the well-funded West. While the east-west cultural divide persisted, and Benghaziites complained frequently of discrimination in Tripoli based in part on their accents, there was a fair amount of intermarriage, which further attenuated linkage to place and tribe.

One prominent Arab columnist wrote:

> The potential impact of Libya's much-discussed tribes as a disruptive force in post Gaddafi Libya should not be exaggerated. Their role in conservative Libyan society has traditionally been limited to the social sphere. It is unlikely that this would change substantially to play a prominent role in politics in the future.[31]

Libyan political commentators cited a poll taken in the lead-up to the revolution, which demonstrated that tribalism, while important, was not all important: 90 percent of one thousand male respondents felt an "attachment" to their tribe,[32] with 45 percent describing this as a "very strong" link;

45 percent, an active/present connection; and 15 percent identifying themselves as more or less indifferent to both tribal connections and context. According to a survey conducted in six districts in eastern Libya in the fall of 2011 (i.e., after the revolution), only 1 percent of more than fourteen hundred respondents indicated "membership in tribe'" as their principal affiliation.[33]

In a way, all of this was splitting hairs; much the same could have been and was said about Iraq pre-2003. Tribalism is, to use a favorite word of Gaddafi, "latent," and however much it has been attenuated by time, mixing, and so on, it flares up under conditions of uncertainty as a social security net of last resort. What Libya did *not* have was the complicating factor of Shi'a–Sunni divisions, which rent post-Saddam Iraq and were an obvious factor in Bahrain's Arab Spring. The relevance of tribalism to the post-revolutionary Libya was tied to the magnitude and duration of the disruption; in other words, the more chaos Libya endured in transition from Gaddafi to whatever came next, the more likely tribalism, regionalism, and religious extremism would emerge as problems.

EAST-WEST DISPARITIES

The existence of separate regional identities in a country like Libya is far from surprising. As we have seen, the vast majority of the population is concentrated in the west around Tripoli and in the east around Benghazi. Historically, these regions and cities evolved somewhat differently; the tribal affiliations and political traditions were somewhat different. Members of each region are readily recognizable to the others by both accent or dialect and often appearance. For the same factors described—migration, economic dislocation, increased travel, and intermarriage—the almost absolute link between tribe and region had been very much weakened from the 1960s to the present, which was not to say that regional prejudices do not continue to exist. On the other hand, the main cause of regional discord (the east-west split) had less to do with these factors directly than to the escalating tension between the east and the Gaddafi family, which was linked to feelings of mutual distrust and a historic restiveness, to the tradition of opposition to the Italians, and even to King Idris. The easterners, one might say, were naturally disinclined to submit to outside authority. As the Islamist-flavored opposition grew and became increasingly effective, Gaddafi pursued a policy of collective punishment, depriving Benghazi—a commercial hub at various times in Libyan history—of its dynamism and even basic infrastructure.

Of course, Gaddafi's policies of collective punishment created new animosities, also regionally centered. Unemployment was much higher in the east than in the west, a situation exacerbated by a large number of Egyptian expatriate workers, mainly in the East (by various estimates, at any given time one sixth of the people in Benghazi were Egyptians in the service and transit trades). Benghazi's port, once the country's lifeline to the outside world, had been operating far below capacity for decades, and there were few tourist facilities. Symbolic was Benghazi's central, picturesque lagoon, which had been sealed off, its waters fed by effluent from an abattoir, producing a noxious stench that literally sucked the oxygen from the center of the city.

During the makeover period, the Gaddafis had said much about the improving conditions in Benghazi as a way to soften the east-west divide. The 2002 *Libya Development Report* cites Benghazi as one of the most prosperous regions in Libya. From 2009 to 2010, there had indeed been some improvements—the effluent to the central lake had been cut off. The twelve-hundred-bed Benghazi medical center, mothballed for well over a decade, opened in 2009, albeit at one-sixth capacity. Low-income, low-standard housing developments constructed by Turkish firms were going up, under the Saif Al Islam reformist banner. Even so, Benghazi residents saw it as an attempt to effectively place all potential regime opponents in places where they could be controlled.

Even though Tripoli was the seat of government, many innovative ideas and people—as witnessed in the provenance of those who participated in the National Economic Strategy sessions—came from Benghazi, which, like Derna and other centers in the east, was known as the "place where people (actually) read." While Bernard-Henri Lévy could be forgiven for underappreciating the intellectual history of Benghazi, he misspoke when he said: "I noted, during the passage, and once more, that only art, and more particularly, the art of letters, could give life to stone and that a town without writers, however beautiful it might be—and God knows Benghazi is beautiful—will never know other than a second-rank existence."[34]

EXTREMISM

As with Western notions of the strength and relevance of tribal affiliations in modern-day Libya, there is some support for the idea that eastern Libya had become a bastion for extreme ideologies. Anyone who had studied Libyan opposition groups knew that the most effective elements were both Islamic (as opposed to secular) and based in the east. Further, these groups, the LIFG first and foremost, had been fortified by the experiences some of its members had had as fighters in Afghanistan and Iraq. A cache of documents discovered by US forces on computers at a safe house along the Iraqi border with Syria in 2007, known as the "Sinjar records," offered a rare demographic snapshot of 595 foreign fighters in Iraq. The shocking find in the documents was the relatively high percentage of individuals that were Saudi and Libyan nationals.[35] The absolute numbers were not as important as the per capita representation: 52 of the sample of 595 records (those that included nationalities) came originally from the Libyan town of Derna, with a population of 80,000.[36] Some speculated their impetus might have been the Libyan Islamic Fighting Group's (LIFG's) "increasingly cooperative relationship with Al Qaeda."[37]

The Sinjar records were publicized in a 2007 *Newsweek* article entitled, "The Martyr Factory: Why One Libyan Town Became a Pipeline for Suicide Bombers in Iraq."[38] Wikileaks drew attention again to the Sinjar records in 2010 by publishing a June 2008 US Embassy-Tripoli cable, erroneously quoted describing Derna as a "wellspring of Islamic terrorism."[39] The cable did not offer a direct assessment of the situation in Derna by embassy personnel, but rather recounts the assessment of an unidentified American-Libyan national. Among the more interesting reported observations was the notion that local religious leaders "encourage jihad" through coded messages during Friday prayers.[40]

The provocative title of the *Newsweek* article notwithstanding, the author noted that he found no evidence in the Dernawi population of any "blind commitment to some overarching, jihadist ideology," but that "personal factors like psychological trauma, sibling rivalry and sexual longing" were prevalent. Reports issued by a few Western reporters who showed up in Derna after late February 2011 further supported previous (albeit inconclusive) onsite assessments. A Reuters correspondent reported on the local residents' efforts to counter the widespread external impression that Derna was somehow linked to Al Qaeda:

> For a long period Derna [was] thought to be sympathetic with the "Islamists," but the residents of Derna strongly deny any connection with al Qaeda, and there is no proof that al Qaeda ever had a presence in the East despite statements by Gaddafi that the LIFG had al Qaeda members in its midst.[41]

Bernard-Henri Lévy later wrote that his and colleagues' attempts on March 2 to verify claims that an "Islamic Emirate" had been created in

Derna by Abdel Hakim Al Hasadi (another Libyan veteran of the US detention center at Guantanamo) turned up nothing obviously incriminating: Al Hasadi was apparently "at the front" fighting. Lévy says, "We did not see there anything resembling either an emirate or a burka." (Hasadi supposedly mandated the wearing of the burka by all Dernawi women.)[42]

On the one hand, the radicalization of young people in the East was felt to be a natural reaction to harsh conditions of chronic unemployment and regime harassment. However, most Libyans in heavily populated areas appeared to believe that the primary motivator for Dernawi youth fighting in Iraq was not sympathy with jihadist ideologies, per se, but that they saw it as an opportunity to fight Gaddafi by proxy, gaining skills in the process that could be useful in the struggle back home. Further, groups like the Libyan Islamic Fighting Group (LIFG) and associated smaller groups had strong ties to the local commercial elite—also long repressed by Gaddafi—all of which contributed to the formation of a kind of popular sympathy with "the rebellion," just as Omar Al Mokhtar had during the counter-Italian insurgency in the 1920s and 1930s.[43]

Missing from most of these Western reconnaissance missions is reference to Derna's modern history, specifically its role, above all the cities in the east, in producing more of Libya's intelligentsia and political elite than any other city or region in Libya. This fact was itself the subject of much more speculation and was presumably linked both to its culture of resistance to Gaddafi and to what happened subsequently. Mohammed Al Mufti, author of several informal books on Libyan culture, asked many of the older generation in Derna why Dernawis had established such a culture of education and valued learning. Older residents attributed this emphasis to a mixture of factors, the root of which was that it was a farming community—*fellahin*—and as families had more children, they confronted the problem of how to divide land. To ensure that the children were able to support themselves, the families pushed them (including girls) to attend school and to pursue their studies abroad. Mufti credits Dernawi's "intellectualism" to one of the Italians' few positive acts in Eastern Libya, the establishment of a local school.[44]

How Gaddafi Ruined His Remake

As we have seen, the prevailing impression of Libya in Western policy circles in the few years (if not the few months) before the revolution was one of a success. Despite the fact that the pace of economic reform was slower than wished for, Gaddafi had basically served his purpose and could be left on autopilot. The US and UK governments still referred to reconciliation with Libya occasionally as a model counterproliferation and counterterror initiative, but with far less verve. The US and UK intelligence communities appeared to be getting what they felt was some useful information out of the arrangement (exactly what has not been disclosed, even if information on some of the methods has been exposed), and huge commercial opportunities were lurking within reach.

As time went by, however, Gaddafi seemed to be going more and more off the rails—again. Indeed, it is hard to think of anyone Gaddafi had spent much time and energy courting while sanctions were in place that he had not personally embarrassed or insulted. In the same way, he was compelled to try to prove his righteousness by exploiting "unfinished business" like the remaining Lockerbie payments, the Bulgarian nurses case, and various unconsummated commercial deals to extort return reparations from the West. There appeared to be no way that Gaddafi's mind could let him "forgive" an exogenous event like the Wikileaks scandal and let its trove of personal slights go unpunished, just as he was not able to prevent himself from pulling together a team to assassinate Crown Prince Abdullah, during the very time when he was trying to strike a deal with the West.

Thus, rather than spending his golden years enjoying the fruits of a tremendously successful rehabilitation campaign, Gaddafi chose, again, to try to resurrect his "honor" at the expense of his personal and Libya's national interests, unsettling the foreign oil companies, and embarrassing his closest allies. At the same time, he was deepening relationships with the West's strongest competitors, especially Brazil, Russia, India, and China (the BRIC countries) and universally loathed foreign rulers, like Venezuela's Hugo Chávez, who had spent the previous few years chasing out many of that country's foreign investors.

Gradually, those individuals who had assisted with Libya's transformation—those who were still alive or in office—came to realize that they might have a problem on their hands. The State Department further drew down embassy staff while trying to figure out the next move. No one, at least outside government and intelligence circles, seemed to know what to make of Mismari's defection and rumors of Saif's apparent decision to remove himself from Libyan politics. Some felt the best course of action was simply to wait out the storm; a new ambassador might smooth things over. Or maybe not.

The fact remains that both Gaddafi and the West shared responsibility for this state of affairs, which had direct roots in the 2003 WMD deal and subsequent rapprochement. As we have seen, the conditions for Gaddafi's rehabilitation were framed largely in terms of compensation for past acts of terror (the Lockerbie bombing), "declarations" (abandonment of WMD), and "willingness to cooperate" on high-level issues, like counterterrorism.

Still, very little attention was paid to more systemic problems of human rights and trying to control Gaddafi's natural, disruptive tendencies. So, while the West was able to crow that it had succeeded in "flipping" Libya from the dark side, it was not long before Gaddafi started to complain that he had been swindled by the West, which was not living up to its various implicit promises of proper respect for a major world leader with continental influence (i.e., Gaddafi). With nothing to anchor them to an objective reality, the narratives spun by the West and Libya about the reasons for the rapprochement and their respective obligations allowed both sides to revert to traditional adversarial positions, with increased righteousness.

Gaddafi had another, problem, however. Just as he had been constrained by key associates and tribal leaders in responding to the Western demands for Libya to turn over Megrahi and Fhima for trial, he was constrained to some degree by the needs and wishes of those people within his circle who had been the pillar of his repressive apparatus for more than three decades. These people had done his dirty work, had been compensated for it, and would have a very hard time finding a role within any new, more open, more respectable Libya.

So Gaddafi found himself between a reform process and narrative he knew was necessary to maintain on some level in order to continue to buy time—before he had another plan. Those who had fought his previous battles for him were increasingly unhappy and were becoming recalcitrant, if not an outright danger. The overriding anxiety and paralysis Mahmoud Jibril had seen in Gaddafi months earlier may have made it impossible for him to do anything other than what he had always done—try to play all sides against the middle. Yet the rules of the game had fundamentally changed. The West, unwittingly, may have simply added too many balls to Gaddafi's already immensely complicated juggling game—such that it was only a matter of time before he would lose his grip.

PART III

FITNA (CHAOS)

Like so many of its utopian counterparts in the 20th century, this was a regime likely to self-destruct.

LISA ANDERSON[1]

CHAPTER 9

Benghazi: The First Five Days

It has become almost a matter of course that the end of war is revolution, and that the only cause which possibly could justify it is the revolutionary cause of freedom.

HANNAH ARENDT, ON REVOLUTION[2]

The Libyan uprising, was undoubtedly a youth-led popular revolt, initially centered on (and sustained by) a series of rather amazing, and still somewhat unexplained, actions that took place in Benghazi and environs from mid-February through end of March 2011 and beyond, against a regime that had long considered the East the equivalent of a province under revolt. Interviews with numerous Benghazi residents in summer 2011 revealed pride in "spontaneous public action," but also acknowledged that the roots of rage went back a long time; the regime's reaction to protests in January and February were simply the final straw in a series of deep insults and organized deprivation. While this is all very true, the role of individual leaders, and the actions of a core group of individuals—some courageous citizens pushed to acts of incredible heroism, others who had held high office under Gaddafi but whose loyalties remained to the East, academics who took part in Saif's reform process as aides or trainees, or their local interlocutors—played a critical, and thus far underestimated, role in steering the people and articulating their cause.

Egypt and Tunisia

The ultimate trigger for the movements subsequently known as the Arab Spring is widely acknowledged to have been the self-immolation on December 17, 2010, of Mohammed Bouazizi, a twenty-six-year-old fruit vendor in the Tunisian town of Sidi Bouzid, 265 kilometers south of Tunis, following humiliation at the hands of a female police officer the previous day. The question of how a lone act, however intense and gruesome, could have mobilized a nation to overthrow the leaders of a seasoned police state is a good one. One would have expected, in a state with one of the most controlled medias in the world, that news would take time to spread, that there would be confusion regarding what had happened, and why. Much credit is due to the Qatari TV channel Al Jazeera, which was for days literally the only global network to cover the unrest (and in so doing, to goad popular action); the Western press did not catch on to the fact that these events could have significant consequences until a day or two before Tunisian strongman Zinedine Ben Ali was forced to abdicate, on January 14, 2011. Ben Ali and his cronies had ruled Tunisia since he ousted Habib Bourguiba in a bloodless coup in 1987—not without similarities to Gaddafi's rise to power. From Tunisia, the Revolution initially skipped over Libya and landed in Egypt.

The Egyptians called Tunisia's revolution a "Tunisami," which inspired activist and a much more technologically savvy youth to use social media such as Facebook to call for a Day of Rage (*yowm al Ghadab*) for January 25, a week after Ben Ali fled Tunisia. Eighty thousand Internet-users registered online and took to streets to demand reform and express alienation and not-so-veiled resentment at Hosni Mubarak's increasing indications or preparations for his son Gamal to succeed him. It would be the largest act of civil disobedience in Mubarak's thirty-three-year rule. Egypt's Day of Rage encompassed mass protests in Cairo, Alexandria, and several other cities.

As in Tunisia, and Libya subsequently, protestors at first had rather vague demands, including, in Egypt's case, an end to repressive emergency laws, the sacking of the interior minister, and an increase in the minimum wage. Protestors took control of Tahrir Square, while Mubarak's regime, shocked by the scale of the demonstrations, sought to confront the waves of protest with shows of force and censor coverage of what was going on. Egypt's interior minister Habib al Adly banned all protests, clamped down on social networking sites, blocked cellphone coverage in Cairo, and had more than a thousand arrested.[3]

While the riots were still under way in Tunisia, and just gearing up in Egypt (i.e., before the Egyptian "January 25th Revolution") the Libyan towns of Derna, Benghazi, and Bani Walid, saw primarily economic-driven protests from January 13 to 16. In several cases, demonstrators took over abandoned construction sites, which they proclaimed symbolic of the Libyan reformists' failed promises to improve living conditions.[4] These actions coincided with another set of Wikileaks revelations on the decadent lifestyles of the Gaddafi children ("Qadhafi Children Scandals Spilling Over into Politics" and "A Glimpse into Libyan Leader Qadhafi's Eccentricities," filed in September 2009 and February 2010). These reportedly led Gaddafi to cancel all soccer games in the country, fearing that the soccer clubs and fans themselves would become a vector for protests, as they had in Egypt.[5]

In early January—almost a month and a half before the Libyan uprising started—Khamis Gaddafi cut short his trip to the US. On January 15, he wrote a letter to the CEO of weapons manufacturer General Dynamics, complaining that "promised munitions had not arrived,"[6] an indication that he, and one must presume the Gaddafi clan, was preparing for the worst. The close relatives of certain high-placed individuals said that by the third week of Tunisian protests, they were convinced "Libya's next."[7] In interviews with *Asharq Al Awsat*, Dr. Fathi Baja recounted a meeting on February 14 with exiled journalist Mahmoud Shammam (the future spokesman for the National Transitional Council), Ali Tarhouni (the NTC's future finance minister), and other Libyan colleagues in Morocco, where they were attending a conference. Baja predicted that on the day Egyptian President Hosni Mubarak stepped down, Libya would likely see a repeat of the 2006 Benghazi riots, but not more: "[T]he people would go into the streets, the security forces would confront them, and things would die down after a day or two. I didn't expect it to continue because the people are not ready for killings after [the] *buslaim* [Abu Selim] massacre]."[8]

Fathi Baja said Ali Tarhouni disagreed, saying that he felt something deeper was happening, even though "we all expected it would be bloody." This was particularly the case after Gaddafi had mocked the Tunisian and Egyptian popular uprisings.[9] Baja noted that Al Jazeera—and, to a lesser extent, the US-Congress-funded Al Hurra ("Freedom" in Arabic) Satellite TV channel—played a key role in informing and rallying the Libyan people.[10] According to the American Broadcasting Board of Governors, Al Hurra's value lies in "presenting in-depth discussions that are not addressed in the Arabic-language media, such as human rights and freedom of speech and religion."[11]

Individuals suspected of disloyalty or connections to dissidents abroad reported being under close surveillance as early as February 6 and 7.[12] A noted Libyan painter, Mohammed Bin Lamin, the brother of a London-based dissident, had just returned from an art exhibition in Managua, Nicaragua, when he was picked up by Libyan intelligence and taken to Abu Selim prison, where he was held and tortured for eight months, until he was liberated by rebel forces in the final assault on Tripoli. In an interview with a Nicaraguan newspaper, Bin Lamin said some five hundred like him had been arrested and of that number perhaps only a hundred twenty survived.[13]

The regime, somewhat belatedly, increased censorship of Libya-focused foreign news websites such as *Libya Al-Youm*, *Al-Manara*, *Jeel Libya*, *Akhbar Libya*, *Libya Al-Mustakbal*, and *Libya Watanouna*, on January 24, 2010. The next day, Gaddafi ordered YouTube videos of continuing and growing unrest in Benghazi, protests by families of Abu Selim victims, blocked.[14]

Jamal al Hajji, a journalist and political commentator, was one of the first—if not the first—to call for local protests in late January for which, according to Amnesty International, he was arrested on February 1.[15] On February 5, Ibrahim Sahad, the secretary general of the National Front for the Salvation of Libya (NFSL), for many decades the principal seat of Libyan opposition abroad, issued a "call to action" against Gaddafi, helping to organize anti-Gaddafi protests in Washington, DC; Doha, Qatar; and various European capitals, to attract international media attention to a "prospective" Libyan revolt. "We knew," Sahad said, "we likely had a single shot, a limited window in which to cripple the regime—if it failed, the blowback from the regime would be decisive. We would not have a second chance."[16] Sahad dates NFSL preparations to the moment Tunisia's Ben Ali had been deposed. He and others were determined to compel the international press "not to ignore Libya," as it had ignored or distorted "seminal" events in Libya's recent history, the 1996 Abu Selim massacre and the 2006 Benghazi riots.[17] According to Sahad, the NFSL had been training groups within the Jebel Nafusa just prior to the February explosion, and had sent members across the Tunisian-Libyan border to support rebels in the western mountains at the start of the conflict.

The external opposition website *Libya Al-Youm* reported that Taqi al Din al Chalawi and Abdel Fattah Bourwaq, who together ran the local news site *Irasa*, had been arrested February 16, along with blogger Mohammed Mismari, after he sent dispatches to Al Jazeera and BBC Arabic. Idris Mismari, a Benghazi-based journalist and colleague of various other intellectuals and professionals upon whom Saif Al Islam had relied to help implement his reform program, called reporters at Al Jazeera in Doha to exhort them to send a crew to Libya, as "something huge was going down." Internal security promptly picked him up at home and drove him to Tripoli, where he was allegedly tortured, with a large group of others. Mismari was left for dead, revived, and then asked to recant on public television.[18] Buzaid Dorda, the former "technocrat-prime minister-turned-head of external intelligence," was said to have attempted to defuse this particular incident, by apologizing to Mismari for the poor treatment—as if it had all been a mistake.[19]

While Western social media has been recognized as an assisting force in mobilizing the masses—particularly the youth—during this period, in Libya credit was always given more directly to traditional media, Al Jazeera broadcasts in particular, and cellphone texting, as the numbers with access to Facebook, for example, were still relatively small. In Egypt, the role of social media appears to be being revised downward, for similar reasons, as "Almost 80% of the people in Egypt had cellphones, relatively few access to Facebook."[20] Activists had access to Facebook, which facilitated their communication with one another, but also made it easier for their movements to be tracked by governments with sophisticated monitoring software.

Credible sources in Benghazi maintained that in early February, as the first stirrings of revolt were underway, Musa Kusa (now foreign minister) assembled Gaddafi's security forces and instructed them explicitly to prevent people from congregating in large groups. In Libya, Kusa was to have said, there would be no Tahrir Square. Kusa allegedly oversaw meetings in Tripoli of the *kasshaf* (revolutionary boy scouts), and Revolutionary Guards and Revolutionary Committees—instructing them how to disperse and repel street mobs. Simultaneously, the regime began to release criminals from jails on the condition that they bear arms against the protestors. As a last-ditch palliative, Gaddafi offered grants of $800 per household to cover food expenses, a 150 percent salary increase to those working in the public sector, and a doubling of the effective minimum wage.[21] It was far too little, too late. Following the example of Tunisia and Egypt, small groups of Libyan dissidents, some inside the country, some outside, called for a "Day of Rage" on February 17. The timing was significant, as this was the anniversary of the anti-Gaddafi riots of 2006. In anticipation of more actions, Saif Al Islam announced the regime would release 110 eastern-origin prisoners held for their connections to the Libyan Islamic Fighting Group (LIFG).[22] Muammar Gaddafi allegedly met with a group of senior activists, telling them they would be "held responsible for any ensuing chaos."[23] Gaddafi sent a variety of unlikely envoys to Benghazi. In addition to Senussi's and Saif's men, there was the unfortunate presence of Saadi Gaddafi, who had already done his share to rile resentment among Benghazi residents during the infamous soccer slayings of 1996, in which his bodyguards had fired on spectators.

An audibly nervous Saadi Gaddafi spoke on Benghazi radio on February 17 to try to calm the situation with promises of money and development assistance for the eastern regions, to develop a proper airport and other infrastructure for the region (allegedly $24 billion worth).[24] Saadi's statement was an explicit admission that Benghazi was, in fact, in terrible shape. He promised that the regime "meant it" this time:

> I have taken permission from my father so he can give me Benghazi, no one will come near it, I am coming to live there, I am even bringing my clothes . . . now we will give you all of what you want. I promise good money (*meezaneeya kwaysa*) and whatever you want you will get. I will take care of the young people and infrastructure.[25]

The First Five Days

On the evening of February 15, Benghazi military security (Gaddafi's men) responded, at least in part, to one of several Facebook "calls to action" by arresting Fathi Terbil, one of the lawyers representing the families of the Abu Selim victims. Until then, Terbil had continued to represent a contingent of the families and enjoyed a degree of protection due to his "official" involvement with Saif Al Islam. Abdullah Senussi had arrived in Benghazi earlier on the 15th, by some accounts to arrest Terbil, by other accounts to order those holding him to release him immediately.[26] Terbil is widely viewed as a hero for his actions both before and during the revolution, and in particular for pushing the case of the Abu Selim families. Some prominent Benghazi residents agree, but fault Terbil and others—before Terbil's arrest—for allegedly agreeing to a proposal put forth by Saif, i.e., that if they would help calm the situation in Benghazi, he (Saif) would make sure they had a role in writing a constitution for Libya, and that he (Saif) would speed certain other political reforms.[27] Even if that had been the case, Terbil might have reasoned that some concessions were preferable to a bloodbath. His arrest, however, and the popular reaction to it, quickly changed the situation on the ground irrevocably.

Terbil was held for only a few hours; the security apparatus released him at 9:30 p.m. Later, in a scene reminiscent of the rooftop protests by Iranians against their regime in the wake of the (unsuccessful) 2009–2010

Green Revolution in Iran, Benghaziites screamed from apartment buildings and rooftops. There was shooting in the streets, and rocks being thrown at government premises. Eyewitnesses described a sense of mixed rage and fear. Until then, the protests had been predominantly peaceful, with no deep organization and no unified calls for other than basic reforms. Abdel Salam al Mismari, a lawyer and one of Terbil's humanitarian colleagues (not to be confused with Nouri Al Mismari in the previous chapter), claimed he and others used Facebook to discuss the kinds of placards and slogans protestors would use, and whether and at what point they would call for Gaddafi to step down.[28]

Subsequent to Terbil's arrest by varying accounts, thirty to sixty young men, joined by members of the Abu Selim families (perhaps a total of a hundred fifty people)[29] appeared at the *Mudiriyyat al Amn*, the interior security offices in the Hwari section of town, chanting, "Wake up, wake up Benghazi, this is the day you've been waiting for." The protestors proceeded to Maidan Al Shajara (Tree Square, in the city center), where they were joined by yet others.[30] Baja noted that news of Terbil's arrest spread like wildfire and as groups of revolutionary youth moved toward city hall, then Pepsi Street (named for a bottling plant), and then on to Gamal Abdel Nasser Street.[31]

The morning of February 16 was calm. Many Benghaziites went to work as usual. Asma al Fitouri, author of a Libyan account of the stirrings of revolution, described how the people of Benghazi had been ruminating on the events of the previous day and night, and as the afternoon approached, there were spontaneous protests in Maidan Al Shajara, which were more "insistent, adamant, and courageous."[32] When these spilled out into Gamal Abdel Nasser Street, the regime spared no force in putting down the crowds. There were many casualties.[33]

News of what had happened thus far in Benghazi on the 15th and 16th spread to other cities in the east. Clashes with government forces that left four dead and eighty injured in Tubruk and Al Beida triggered larger street protests.[34] In Mismari's view, it was this combination of rapid escalation of interlocking movements against the heady background of the events in Tunisia and Egypt that allowed the people to "break the barrier of fear."

Baja further described the demonstration of solidarity in front of the Benghazi courthouse on February 16: "[There] I found Abdelsalam al Mismari and Jamal Bilnour. A group of lawyers went with them into the meeting. Things [were] very random, not well organized." Baja stressed that the intention at this point "was not to create a revolution" (in line with assertions that there were negotiations under way between Saif and his former reformist allies).

On the 17th, the awaited "Day of Rage," witnesses described armored vans driving through Benghazi, barreling through makeshift roadblocks, as groups of residents congregated on the street corners downtown, perhaps thirty at the end of every block, watching what was unfolding before them.[35] Amateur video shows groups of "yellow hats" (mercenaries, a mixture of revolutionary committee members and imported Africans, who identified each other by wearing yellow hard hards) in groups, attacking protestors with knives, guns, and cleavers.

Mismari says Abdullah Senussi, Gaddafi's head of internal security, asked him to help to stop the protests, all the while denying that there was any violence: he had not heard of any shootings in Souk al Hout (the Fish Market), nor had he any knowledge of the protests and killings in Al Beida. He denied the bloodbath in Benghazi. Mismari said he told Senussi "we will remain until our demands are met."[36] Next, someone claiming he represented Saif Al Islam came to the courthouse and asked: "What will it take for the protests to stop? We want a compromise." Mismari said the group's demands were categorical:

> [A] stop to the killing, the right to peaceful protest, freedom of expression and a quick trial for those responsible, freedom to print and to broadcast over the Internet, the opening of an immediate investigation into the circumstances of the aggression and the permitting of peaceful demonstration and the people to express their demands.[37]

Saif's emissary left, only to return half an hour later with Saif's response which was that any and all demands must be put to the General People's Congress for consideration.

At some point during the course of February 17, the Benghazi Rubicon was crossed. Protestors gathered along the corniche and around Al Manar, the city's distinctive lighthouse building. "Chants are loud and organized!" reported Libya17Info, a blog that emerged as one of the principal sources of information on events in Benghazi.[38] The scenes that followed were both chaotic and disturbing—as children were seen jumping off the Guiliana Bridge to escape the grasp of security forces, paid thugs drove around in cars shooting at demonstrators, and people were taken from their homes and hospital beds—during the nights of February 17 and 18.[39] While breaking into the local headquarters of the interior ministry, protestors discovered a document, signed by Abdullah Senussi, ordering an attack on them early on the morning of February 19. The attack was to use four hundred members of the security forces from the Katibat Fadeel (the Katiba), known as "fist of Gaddafi," a massive security complex in the middle of the city that housed what one resident called Gaddafi's "occupying army," noting, "You did not want to go near that area on foot or by car, as those who entered rarely came out alive."[40]

Mismari described the courage of ordinary people, the youth in particular:

> We survived the first critical days; the bloody events and the killing increased very quickly; people did not give up, even in the face of bullets. "Mu'tassimeen" (guardians/hard-core supporters) spent the night in the square, but were then attacked with guns or arrested. Surrounded, we tried to defend the courthouse building, as it represented the symbol of the city and was the repository for the national archive.[41]

On February 18, soldiers opened fire on a funeral procession of four hundred to five hundred people as it passed the Katiba. There were cries of "the regime must fall" and a melee ensued. One witness said, "The people could not be 'calm' until they had avenged themselves on the Katiba, and seized its secrets. . . .[42] A volcano erupted in every corner of Libya."[43] Between five hundred and six hundred protestors gathered in front of the police headquarters in Benghazi and fought with security services, leaving thirty-eight injured.[44] In Al Baida and Zintan (Western Libya), hundreds of protestors chanted for Gaddafi to go, and set fire to police and security installations. In Zintan, protestors set up tents to express "peaceful protest." In Benghazi hundreds congregated in Maidan Al Shajara, where they were initially scattered by water cannon.[45] Yet, Mismari said, ordinary people kept coming out into the streets, "*like butterflies to the flame*."[46] According to Dr. Adbelnasser Saadi, an attending surgeon at Benghazi Medical Center, one of 6 medical facilities in the city, he and his colleagues saw more than 2,000 injured patients from the 17th to the 20th, and that of 580 admitted to the hospital, 110 died. He described the situation in the city as absolute, bloody chaos.[47]

One of the most singularly heroic acts of the Benghazi uprising occurred on the afternoon of February 20. Mehdi Ziu, forty-nine, an oil engineer and father of two, had participated in protests the day before when he apparently had the idea of filling a car with propane tanks and gelatina (explosives used typically in blast fishing) and ramming it into the walls of the Katiba, which was filled with hundreds of soldiers and the antiaircraft batteries firing on demonstrators. Cellphone video captured the explosion as Ziu's bombing created a breach that allowed the Benghazi masses to rush in, followed by trucks and bulldozers. Many people died.[48] Rebels then burned police stations and army barracks and looted government arsenals.

Within a few days of the start of the uprising, the 17th February Coalition [the precursor to the NTC] issued some specific demands on behalf of the movement, including fulfilling Saif's promises of a constitution and some limited reforms.[49] Soon thereafter, "the ceiling [of demands] was raised" to include Gaddafi's removal from power and a full amnesty for revolutionaries. A week later, the Coalition felt it needed to publish a formal statement, or bayan, of goals for the revolution as a whole.

Members of the 17th February Coalition helped shape the nucleus of a rebel governing body by establishing temporary committees to address specific urgent needs related to provisioning, relief, and military affairs (the *majlis askari*), the local governing councils in the liberated towns and cities, and ultimately, the transitional council (*majlis intiqali*) itself.

Baja describes the circumstances of writing the *Bayan*:

> After the first week of the revolution we had the idea to publish announcement [of] what we want from the revolution and its general goals. . . . [T]hen myself, and Mohammed Al Mufti, and Saleh Al Ghazaal to write the *Bayan*. . . . It was an opportunity for us to summarize our vision for Democratic freedom, and a constitution, and general freedoms, and to express that our problem, or the quandary with Gaddafi was not only economic, but a question of freedom and respect.[50]

As many recalled several months later, during the preparation of the postrevolutionary draft constitution, the coalition's *Bayan* explicitly stated the founders' hopes and intention to create a democratic and unified state. Around this time, Abdelhafiz Ghoga was chosen as the coalition's official spokesman; he requested the *bayan* be given to "citizen reporter"

Mohammed Nabbous (later killed by the regime) so he could send it to Al Jazeera. A senior US diplomat later said that it was this document, written by Baja, Mohammed Al Mufti, and Saleh Al Ghazaal, that gave outside powers (the US in particular) some measure of confidence that there was an "organization" at work, there were legitimate interlocutors, and that they could be trusted.[51]

Bombshell: Saif's Speech

On the evening of February 20, Saif Al Islam, the reformist son, negotiator, compromiser, and his father's foil, appeared on state television, transformed. Unshaven, he wore an ill-fitting suit and mismatched tie. To most Libyans, the meaning of the words he spoke was irrelevant. Saif had gone, apparently overnight, from being the compensator for his father's lunacy, to a replica of it, expressing himself in the same disorganized, rambling fashion. In a disjointed forty-minute discourse, Saif played good cop—"I will tell you the truth only. . . . We want . . . freedom, democracy and real reform"—fearful cop—"What is happening in Al Beida and Benghazi is very sad. How do you who live in Benghazi, will you visit Tripoli with a visa?"—conspiratorial cop—"There are those who sit and drink coffee and watch TV and laugh at us when they see us burn our country"—and bad cop—"Instead of mourning eighty-four, we will be mourning hundreds of thousands . . . and the oil will stop."[52]

While it is difficult to know exactly what Saif was thinking, the performance had a distinctively harried and improvised air to it. Had he indeed just lost a heated argument with his brother Mu'tassim and his father, and been ordered to toe the family line, as some of his former associates would claim? Was there any truth to the rumor that he had tried to escape the country just two days before, and been apprehended and dragged back to Tripoli on his father's orders?[53]

Professor David Held, Saif's part-time adviser at the London School of Economics, said, "Watching Saif give that speech—looking so exhausted, nervous and, frankly, terrible—was the stuff of Shakespeare and of Freud: a young man torn by a struggle between loyalty to his father and his family, and the beliefs he had come to hold for reform, democracy and the rule of law. The man giving that speech wasn't the Saif I had got to know well over those years."[54]

The reaction to Saif's speech, predictably, was abysmal. His crowd of erstwhile acolytes tried to distance themselves and their bank accounts from

Saif. Some of the first to turn on him were, of course, those who profited most from the relationship: former supporters at the London School of Economics, such as Held. Cherie Blair was another; one observer said she looked as if she wanted to run when Saif's name was mentioned. A scant few stood up for him in print. Benjamin Barber was one, though only after removing himself from the governing board of Saif's charity on February 22.[55]

It is unclear what exactly had happened in Tripoli in the late afternoon of February 20. Saif apparently did meet with a group of his closest friends outside Bab Al Azziziya earlier that evening and gave them the impression that he would confront his father, with the aim of getting him to agree it was time for him to go into a "respected retirement."[56] Saif's friends said they drove with Saif to Bab Al Azziziya, watched him enter the compound, and could even see Saif speaking with the assembled siblings and his father. The next time they saw Saif, he was on television delivering the now-famous, rambling finger-wagging diatribe. Others in Saif's former inner circle asserted they were fired upon as they tried to leave the compound and narrowly escaped with their lives.[57] One of these individuals wound up giving preliminary testimony against Saif before the International Criminal Court (ICC), after the international body issued warrants in late June 2011 for the arrest of Gaddafi, Senussi, and Saif on charges of crimes against humanity.[58]

We can only speculate about what actually happened during that family séance at Bab Al Azziziya. Indications are that had Saif even attempted to propose alternate scenarios, his brothers—and Gaddafi—would have been very much opposed. Another question is whether Saif, at this point, had any choice. He was the family spokesman. Perhaps the assembled relatives felt that both the Libyan people and the West would respond better to a strong message from Saif—it appears very possible that the others were too distraught or otherwise incapacitated to speak publicly. As noted, the speech was Saif's Rubicon. For whatever reasons, he presumably understood that there was for him, as for the rebels, no turning back.

Mohammed Al Houni, Saif's confidante and one of the Libyans who facilitated his introductions to the rich and famous in Europe, told the Arabic press in the days after the speech about an "alternate speech," which Houni had written in the preceding days, expressing deep regret for the loss of life in the East and laying out a specific program for expedited reform, à la what the leaders of Morocco and Jordan had done. However, an article in *Vanity Fair* by European lawyer Phillipe Sands casts doubt on this last-minute scenario, quoting International Criminal Court sources as saying Saif had chosen his path days if not weeks before, when he allegedly helped procure African mercenaries to keep Tripoli and Benghazi under Gaddafi rule.[59] According to this view, Saif's speech, and his refusal to call off Abdullah Senussi from his using Katiba troops to suppress Benghazi, were part of a consistent, premeditated pattern of behavior. ICC Chief Prosecutor José Luis Moreno Ocampo asked specifically if he thought the speech could have gone differently, responded, "No, that is not what my evidence is saying. The information shows that he was involved well before that, that he was involved from the beginning, in the planning before the 15th of February."[60] Saif, according to this view, had made his mind up long before.

News of the events unfolding in Benghazi spread through Tripoli like wildfire. Residents were initially emboldened to stage their own impromptu demonstrations, with impunity; on February 17, 18, and 19, Tripoli residents staged protests in and around Green Square, with no police or army in sight. Just before February 20, the date of Saif's speech, however, Gaddafi's forces seemed to have recovered from their initial paralysis, and members of the Revolutionary Guards and army troops were sent into the streets of Tripoli to crack down on the protestors. As in the Green Revolution in Iran just a few years before, pictures were taken of crowds, and sophisticated e-mail, voice, and social network filtering and face-recognition software were used to identify some of the participants.

The crackdown soon became absolute. Snipers drove around Tripoli in cars and taxicabs, shooting at anyone who looked like they might be a rebel sympathizer. According to Dr. Issam Hajjaji, a noted Libyan physician who supported the relief effort by running clandestine treatment centers, "We all thought the regime would fall within days. However, Gaddafi had a mercenary army in Tripoli. They quickly quelled demonstrations there and in Zawiya [the third largest city] by firing directly at crowds. People taken to hospitals or private clinics were arrested if their injuries were firearms related."[61]

There were many reports of snipers shooting at those who came to collect dead bodies from the street. Tear gas and live ammunition were used in at least one mosque in Tripoli after Friday prayers. Per Kusa's alleged instructions, "Roving patrols of mercenaries and militia used live fire to clear and control streets and prevent demonstrations from forming."[62] *Asharq Al Awsat* reported that Gaddafi loyalists drove into anti-Gaddafi neighborhoods like Fashloum (a poorer neighborhood in Tripoli) with cars draped in the monarchy flag; when residents assembled to express sympathy, loyalists sprayed them with bullets.[63]

Abdel Salam al Mismari described the core group of Benghazi lawyers' early efforts to reach out to Commander Abdelfattah Younes, who at that point had not formally thrown in his lot with the rebels.[64] The group entreated Younes to use the *sa'aiqa*, crack troops under his command, to take down the Katiba and defend the people from Gaddafi's militias and mercenaries. Many Benghaziites credit Younes with doing this, others said his role was more marginal, and yet others continued to suspect that he was still aiding the regime.

On February 22, one of the Abu Selim lawyers entered the Benghazi courthouse, which had become the rebel organizational center, the *matbah* or kitchen, of the revolution, to announce that Younes had promised he would protect the Libyan people and would not waver from this obligation (*wajib*). The group had said, effectively, it was time for Younes to "make the right decision, and in an open way," said Mismari. He was aware that Gaddafi had infiltrated the protest movement, and that someone within it had been tasked with killing Younes, as a means of "sowing chaos between the tribes and the revolutionaries." Within two days, the lawyers' group discussed with Younes a strategy for setting up a national army. They questioned his delay in joining the revolutionary cause. Mismari noted that Younes gave a convincing answer: he [Younes] said he wanted to avert a bloodbath in Benghazi, and Gaddafi was preparing through various channels to send more mercenaries and *Keta'ib* [militias] to Benghazi by air. According to Mismari, Younes told National Transitional Council members that he had tricked Gaddafi, telling him he could contain Benghazi with the forces available to him, without reinforcements, and had requested the immediate evacuation or standing down of forces sent by Gaddafi from outside, as they were a dangerous provocation.

Widespread Defections/Resignations/International Sanctions

On February 21, Libyan representatives to the UN threw their support behind the rebels and called on the Libyan army to help unseat the "tyrant" Muammar Gaddafi." The first Libyan ministers to resign were Ali Errishi, minister for immigration and expatriates, on February 20; Mustafa Abdeljalil, justice minister, followed on February 21; and Abdelfattah Younes, interior minister, on February 22. Ahmed Gaddafadam, a close cousin and aide of Gaddafi, resigned two days later, on February 24. Libya's chief prosecutor, Abdelrahman Al Aybbar, resigned on February 25.

The Libyan ambassadors to India, the Arab League, Belgium, US, France, Sweden, and Poland, and the head of the mission to the EU, left their posts in protest on February 22; on February 25, the Libyan ambassador to Portugal, Bangladesh, Belgium, China, France, India, Indonesia, Malaysia, Nigeria, Poland, Portugal, and Sweden did the same.[65] Abdelsalam Al Jelloud, had apparently by this point already escaped to Rome. During the start of the uprising, Ahmed Ibrahim Fagih, a member of the Libyan delegation to the Arab League, was in Tripoli. He rounded up his family and went to the airport, where he found a scene of mass chaos. Fagih managed to board a plane to Istanbul. Abdelmonem El Houni, then Head of the Libyan delegation to the League, based in Cairo, had made the decision to go over to the Rebel side, and polled individual delegation members whether or not they would join him.[66] The Arab League barred Libya officially from its meetings on February 22 for "crimes against the current peaceful popular protests and demonstrations."[67]

Former Egyptian minister of culture Dr. Jaber Usfoor declared on February 26 that he was giving back the €50,000 citation he had received from the Gaddafi World Literature Prize in 2010 in protest to "the massacres which it [the regime] had committed."[68]

The UN General Assembly and Security Council voted strict sanctions on the Libyan regime and referral of key individuals to the International Criminal Court, under suspicion of crimes against humanity, also on February 26.[69] The UN decisions were followed by EU sanctions on individuals within the regime, and an arms and travel ban. On March 1, the UN Human Rights Council suspended Libya's membership.

Gaddafi Regime Reels

A senior Libyan government spokesman, in an exercise of supreme understatement, admitted during a press conference that the government's "handling of the first days of the rebellion was a big failure for the government diplomatically and with media also." Yet in parallel with the compromising words, the regime consolidated its hold over the capital in raw, brutal fashion. When even these efforts failed to stop the momentum of the unrest, Gaddafi senior sent Khamis and his 32nd Brigade to forcibly quash the now open rebellions in Misurata and Benghazi, and to back up the Benghazi barracks, the Katiba.[70]

Underscoring the spirit of no compromise, Gaddafi himself appeared in Green Square on February 22 to deliver what became famous as the "*zenga zenga*" speech, after a memorable passage in which he uses the term, Libyan slang for "neighborhood street or alley." Whether due to the camera angles or dim lights, Gaddafi gave the impression of being isolated and weak. The defiant speech, however, was vintage Gaddafi:

> You are presenting to the world, the true picture of the Libyan people, gathered around the revolution without exception . . . and you from the Green Square, present the truth which transforms/changes the apparatus of betrayal, the brokerage houses, the depraved, and the regressive and cowardly elements that surround it and distort your image in front of the world.[71]

From there, he proceeded to describe how much the world respected and considered Libya a beacon:

> And today when you say "Libya" they say to you ah, Libya of Al-Gaddafi; Libya of the Revolution. All the peoples of Africa, and the peoples of Latin America, and Asia, consider Libya their *qibla*[72] . . . and the governments of the world, all of them including the big nuclear powers, look up to Libya, to your country, to Tripoli, Sirte and Benghazi.[73]

Gaddafi hit all the expected notes, evoking the image of Omar Al Mokhtar, a symbol of resistance against the Italians. He criticized the traitorous Americans (who, he said, had tried to assassinate him many times), castigated Berlusconi's government for its perfidy, and said that the various tribes of Libya would stand united against the enemy:

> Libya will become a new Afghanistan, there will be a civil war. . . . I and millions will cleanse Libya inch by inch, abode by abode, house by house, alley by alley [*zenga zenga*], person by person, until you [sic] have cleaned the country from filth and contaminants.

He ends with a call to action: "*ila amam, ila amam, thowra, thowra* . . . [forward, forward, revolution, revolution]." (Gaddafi might have thought later about being more precise—*which* revolution exactly?)

Humanitarian Crisis

By the end of February, thousands of people had converged on Tripoli's international airport—businessmen, diplomats, African day laborers, and workers from the Philippines, Korea, and Turkey. Within days, there were tens of thousands of people. In impromptu camps, they waited for flights that in some cases never came. The Philippine ambassador managed to get ten thousand of his nationals out by boat; fifteen thousand Chinese workers boarded a ferry to Crete. The British Embassy was heavily criticized for its poor organization in evacuating its citizens. Meanwhile, the US sent a ship, the *Maria Dolores*, to evacuate American citizens from Tripoli on February 25.[74]

Within weeks, medicine and food were becoming scarce.[75] Tripoli's residents described an eerie situation in town, where the remaining people attempted to maintain some kind of normalcy by going out to cafés in the evening. Things were relatively quiet in Tripoli until the night of Sunday, February 20, when crowds started forming in public spaces. Several eyewitnesses said they could hear the roar of demonstrators "like a freight train" from miles away.[76] Many others, locals and foreigners alike, fled for the Tunisian borders. By February 25, an estimated four thousand people had crossed the border,[77] as the International Commission for the Red Cross (ICRC) warned of increasingly dire conditions.[78]

Rebels and their sympathizers set up a clandestine medical support network in Tripoli to treat those wounded during clashes with regime forces. Issam Hajjaji relates the story of volunteers who supported those who tried to battle the regime there:

> (The regime) looked for injured with gunshot wounds, to take them away. A clandestine medical network sprang up, with doctors treating people in their homes or safe houses. Casualties would be sent by members of my extended family, using simple code words on the telephone. The towns of Zintan, in the Nafusa mountains, and Misurata were under siege. I managed, through gunrunners, to smuggle insulin, intravenous fluids, and antibiotics to Nafusa but not to Misurata. This smuggling was widespread.[79]

Hajjaji credited the Libyan diaspora for helping organize relief efforts: "Expatriate groups organized themselves in the UK, elsewhere to buy medicine and smuggle them into Libya, across the Tunisian and Egyptian borders, sometimes hidden in the tyres of cars."[80]

Rebel Onslaught

The apparent ease of Gaddafi's rout left many in shock or disbelief. Within a week of the Benghazi Day of Rage, the regime had effectively lost control of the eastern half of the country, with twenty-two cities along the coast and in the interior caught in the wave of uprisings in Tubruk, the Jebel Nafusa (February 21), Misurata (February 24), and Zawiya (February 26).[81] By the end of February, Gaddafi's regime had lost control of large parts of the country, including Benghazi and environs, Misurata, Ras Lanuf, and Marsa Brega.[82]

At the start of the rebellion, Gaddafi's often-repeated claims that Libya's tribes would rush to his support appeared to be without merit. By February 20, the Touareg, Warfalla, and Hasawna tribes had gone over to the rebel side. In an interview on Al Jazeera, Akram al Warfelli, a leader of the Warfalla, called on Gaddafi to stand down; Sheikh Faraj al Zuway of the Zuwayya tribe, which was positioned to guard the southeastern oil fields, threatened to cut Libya's exports until and unless the regime's violence against opponents ceased.[83] Gaddafi's circle attempted to counter these setbacks by holding conferences where members of Libyan tribes publicly offered their support to the regime. French reporter Delphine Minoui, who covered events in Tripoli throughout much of March, recounts the following exchange with a tribal sheikh:

> "Whom do you represent, exactly?"
> "Uh, we are here under our . . . personal authority. We do not represent our tribes."[84]

A pro-Gaddafi website, covered a pro-regime rally, held by the "Libyan Tribal Council," purporting to speak for "Libya's 2000 Tribes," one of whose issues was a "complete rejection of what is called the Transitional Council in Benghazi, which hasn't been nominated nor elected by Tribal representatives but rather imposed by NATO."[85]

While Gaddafi was struggling for domestic support, the eastern rebels were already moving onto the international stage. The process of assembling a representative body for the nascent rebel movement began with the naming of Abdeljalil as rebel leader on February 17. The Transitional National

Council (TNC) (*al majlis al watani al intiqali*) was hastily formed on February 27 with a base in the Benghazi courthouse, but was officially proclaimed at the Tibesti Hotel in Benghazi on March 5.

One of the more politically astute moves of the new body was the drafting of a statement of principles in late February and early March, which served as a kind of road map for what would come next, and a more formal document in April. Among the first critical acts of the TNC was to call for a no-fly zone and strikes against Gaddafi and his compound, in the process reversing statements the rebels had made just weeks before (prior to Gaddafi's counteroffensive) warning off any outside intervention.

The propaganda machine went into action, attempting to play to traditional Western fears of Al Qaeda and loose weapons. On February 23, Libya's vice minister of foreign affairs claimed that Al Qaeda had established an "Islamic Emirate at Darna [sic]," under the leadership of Abdel Hakim Al Hasadi, also a former Guantanamo prisoner, and that the burka (face covering) would be imposed on Dernawi women.[86] On February 28, Gaddafi said Libya had been "betrayed" by Western leaders calling for him to step down.[87] In late February, a pro-Gaddafi contingent left Sirte and headed east. It attacked Marsa Brega on March 2, but was repulsed. Community-based youth groups (some vestiges of Gaddafi's Youth Scouts) filled gaps in public services, helping out at hospitals and directing traffic.[88] Oil industry workers at eastern facilities like Marsa Brega, the offloading point for European-bound crude oil, threatened to stop work, destroy pipelines, and sabotage facilities if the West did not intervene against Gaddafi.[89]

Gaddafi Punches Back

At the end of February, many felt it was a matter of days before the regime fell, that the Libyan revolution might mimic that of Tunisia after all, with a reasonably quick removal of Gaddafi and his immediate supporters. However, after a period of confusion and regrouping, the Gaddafi regime staged a comeback that appeared to change the game.

Gaddafi voiced his threat in a speech on March 6: "There will be a jihad Islamic front on the Mediterranean. You will see a return to the time of Barbarossa, the pirates, and the Ottomans imposing ransoms on boats."[90] In very few words, Gaddafi cast himself as the antidote to an allegedly ingrained feature of Libyan people to turn to the dark side in times of stress.

He was effectively siding with the West against his own people, that is, claiming, "I can't control what happens next," while reminding the US of a particularly dark period of US-Libyan relations and the threat of piracy, then synonymous with Somalia. Al Qaeda couldn't be far behind. This notion of Libya becoming a launching pad for a new generation of Mediterranean pirates—completely without basis—appeared in several security reports published early in the conflict.

Within a matter of days, Gaddafi's forces had retaken the initiative. Checkpoints sprung up throughout the capital with sporadic demonstrations in Fashloum, Tajoura, and other poor Tripoli neighborhoods.[91] There were reports, as the weeks went on, of the regime using revolutionary flag–draped cars to incite anti-Gaddafi elements in the streets, whereupon armed men would jump out of the cars with machine guns, shooting anyone in the vicinity. Claims of a mini-rebellion in the Janzour neighborhood appear to have been exaggerated.[92]

On or about March 2, Gaddafi forces started their push toward Benghazi. The apparent strategy was to create a swath of coastal control from the Tunisian border to Marsa Brega, with a focus on the cities.[93] Loyalist forces employed brute strength and fear tactics—bombing and helicopters—more for effect than for their destructive power. Brave as the opposition forces were, they scattered in the face of massive firepower.

On March 6, Gaddafi launched military strikes against the "oil crescent" towns of Ras Lanuf, Marsa Brega in the east, and Zawiya in the west. US Secretary of State Hillary Clinton said the US was "far from deciding what to do" about the no-fly zone.[94] By March 7, the port and industrial capital of Misurata, 118 miles to the east, became the focus of a brutal counterassault as the regime pounded the city with airplanes and tank-fired mortars, killing at least eighteen.[95]

In stark contrast to the situation when he gave the desperate *zenga zenga* speech two weeks earlier, Gaddafi appeared to have pulled a rabbit from his hat. "In going after the rebels, suddenly Muammar Al Qaddafi is winning," *The Economist* lamented.[96] In a matter of days, loyalist forces retook Zawiya and Zwara, both of which were critical nodes on the eastern supply route from Tunisia to Tripoli, and prepared for a long siege of Misurata. Gaddafi forces rolled back the rebels along the coastal road, taking back the critical oil export and refining facilities of Ras Lanuf and Marsa Brega, subsequently seizing the equally strategic junction at Ajdabia, a stone's throw from Benghazi.

Increased Attacks Against Civilians; Requests for Help

NATO intervention in Libya was predicated first and foremost on the need to protect innocent civilians from their own government. Agencies such as Human Rights Watch (HRW) documented significant acts of violence against civilians through videos and interviews with eyewitnesses and victims. Mainstream international media appeared to accept that Libyan forces killed "Libyan civilians in their homes and in the public space, repressed demonstrations with live ammunition, used heavy artillery against participants in funeral processions, and placed snipers to kill those leaving mosques after the prayers."[97] At a minimum, it was undisputed—even by the regime itself—that "hundreds of unarmed protestors" had been killed; Saif attributed this to overzealous and untrained security services.[98] Nor was the use of imported mercenaries to quell rioting in Benghazi in any doubt. The regime appeared to be using helicopter gunships and aircraft to fire on protestors (later confirmed), and highly imprecise weaponry, such as cluster or spider bombs in areas where there were many civilians.[99] The international media reported tens of thousands of dead in the first few months of the conflict. The International Criminal Court Chief Prosecutor José Luis Moreno Ocampo later claimed (and at the time of writing was still trying to prove) that the regime distributed Viagra to troops as part of a deliberate effort to use rape as a tool of war).[100]

Other atrocities were clear, including the use of Red Cross–marked helicopters to fire on aid convoys attempting to relieve the siege of Misurata.[101] The Human Rights Watch 2012 Report on Libya documented the use of low-metal mines, mortar-fired cluster munitions in residential areas in Misurata, and parachute antivehicle mines fired by GRAD rockets.[102] The report added to this list the execution of prisoners by Gaddafi forces before the fall of Tripoli, the execution by the Khamis Brigade of forty-five detainees in a Tripoli warehouse about the same time, and likely regime complicity in scores of deaths in and around Tripoli, Al-Qawalish, and Bani Walid.[103]

In most of these cases, it is difficult to say who actually ordered the attacks, or if they were coordinated by the highest echelons of the regime. If Saif and Abdullah Senussi make it to trial, the claims of "intent" presumably need to be addressed, though by early May 2011, the ICC's Ocampo decided that he had enough evidence to proceed with formal charges of crimes against humanity, including forced disappearances, firing on unarmed civilians, wide-scale arrests, and the use of torture, to issue arrest warrants for individuals within the regime—Muammar Gaddafi himself, Saif Al Islam, and Abdullah Senussi.[104]

The Threat to Benghazi: Real or Rhetorical?

With control reasserted over much of the west by early March, Gaddafi was free to refocus on what was happening in the east. Forces and a substantial fraction of Gaddafi's armaments, led by Khamis's 32nd Brigade, were collected and sent out to roll back rebel advances, en route to a showdown in Benghazi.

While some continue to question Gaddafi's intentions with respect to Benghazi, others have no doubt that he intended a bloodbath. First, Gaddafi had a long and violent history with respect to Benghazi; second, Gaddafi habitually signaled his intentions in advance and had made it clear that he was sending his best generals to finish the rebellion. In a March 17 radio address,[105] Gaddafi warned the eastern populations of an imminent operation to free those being held "hostage" by the rebels, who would be shown "no mercy."[106] Third, the combination of these events with the sheer size of the force sent against the east suggested the intent was to slaughter, not to intimidate. The US State Department received "many, many" calls daily from the Libyan community in the US, as well as people within Libya, pleading for the Obama administration's action before it was too late.[107] One Libyan-American said he and his friends, hiding in Tripoli at the time, felt they were watching a climatic image from *Lord of the Rings*, as the forces of evil amassed to destroy the forces of good.

The majority of the Gaddafis seemed to believe that the US and other Western countries were bluffing, and that the NATO coalition would fall apart before it could take any meaningful action. One of Saadi's former Western business advisers later claimed that Saadi alone among his siblings understood the magnitude of his father's tactical mistake. Saadi had pleaded with Gaddafi to reverse his assault on Benghazi, lest the UN vote to authorize the no-fly zone. At the same time, he was attempting to contact CNN to dispute claims that Gaddafi would carry through with his threats against the east.[108]

CHAPTER 10

The Debate over Intervention

The proximate debate in the West over intervention in Libya was clearly conditioned or perhaps framed by President Obama's "New Beginnings" speech in Cairo in 2009. It had set the tone for what many hoped would be a new approach by the US and its allies in dealing with the Middle East, one based on respect for human rights and democratic ideals:

> I do have an unyielding belief that all people yearn for certain things: the ability to speak your mind and have a say in how you are governed; confidence in the rule of law and the equal administration of justice; government that is transparent and doesn't steal from the people; the freedom to live as you choose. Those are not just American ideas, they are human rights, and that is why we will support them everywhere.[1]

America is not, Obama said, "the crude stereotype of a self-interested empire."[2]

The speech eerily foreshadowed much of what came next in Tunisia, Egypt, and Libya—the people asking the US to join them in supporting these very ideals, including human rights and the pursuit of democracy;

the need to act in concert with other nations, collaboratively; the need not to engage in excessive force or to resort to force when other means would be preferable; of working with moderate Islamic elements to diffuse rejectionist strands; and the need to provide funds to support reconstruction and nation building in war-torn regions.[3]

While the speech did not figure heavily in media reports—Western or Arab—during the early months of the Arab Spring, it had become an implicit standard against which people in the region judged US actions. The speech became more relevant as the US was seen to be waffling between its support for established, friendly regimes—Egypt, Bahrain—and policy consistency. According to journalist Michael Hastings, "[O]nce those governments actually began to fall, the Obama administration was slow to distance itself from the oil-rich autocrats the US had supported for decades. In Egypt, Vice President Joe Biden downplayed the democratic revolt, saying that he didn't consider Hosni Mubarak a 'dictator.'"[4] Defense Secretary Robert Gates came out early against US military involvement in Libya, based on, in his assessment, the likelihood of escalation and resulting US commitments, and the nonessential nature of US interests in Libya. Testifying before Congress, he argued specifically that a no-fly zone would require taking out Libya's air defenses and would be a "big operation in a big country."[5] Clearly, Gates's main concerns were cost and mission creep—particularly given ongoing US commitments in Afghanistan and Iraq, and the real possibility of hot conflict with Iran. The State Department, true to its mission (not the size of its budget), would prove more useful in examining the broader policy implications of nonintervention.

Gaddafi's bounceback was problematic for the West, and all those who were secretly and not so secretly hoping for Gaddafi's quick exit. The fact that Gaddafi could mobilize not just hundreds or thousands, but hundreds of thousands of supporters begged the question of how uniform the opposition to the regime really was.

Civil war was a term avoided in the West and NATO circles, as it detracted from the cleaner notion of a unified popular rebellion. However one cut the conflict, however, several things were increasingly obvious to those with some knowledge of Libya: (1) there was a pronounced east-west divide, with far more support for Gaddafi in western Libya than in Eastern Libya; (2) western Libya benefited from an early unfair advantage in the form of mercenaries and heavy weapons.

Views Outside the Beltway

The mainstream American press and pundits, including Nicholas Kristof at the *New York Times*, argued in April there was a need to support the Libyans in a "noble cause," but not get too deeply involved.[6] In late August, post-Liberation, he removed any hesitation in an op-ed entitled "Thank You, America!"[7] Dirk Vandewalle, the academic with the longest consistent focus on Libya,[8] cautioned the US and the West against falling into a "Gaddafi trap," that is, supporting narratives of external domination and knee-jerk reactions that could easily lead to a dismemberment of the country, or that could be perceived as a partisan move in a country where tribal loyalties remained keen, and memories long."[9]

Gaddafi's fixation on making a bloody example of Benghazi was probably his single largest strategic error. Prior to this, the European press had been decidedly soft on intervention. The Economist on March 3 published a lead piece noting that "Muammar Qaddafi [sic] has enough military power at his disposal to make dislodging him a bloody and uncertain business. . . . His air defenses include nearly 100 MiG 25s and 15 Mirage F1s, equipped with Soviet era air-to-air missiles and a huge arsenal of Russian surface to air missiles."[10]

The International Crisis Group (ICG), a nongovernmental research organization based in Brussels, published a statement on March 10, 2011, calling for an immediate ceasefire and negotiations toward transition to a post-Qaddafi, legitimate and representative government. "Military intervention," the statement continued, "should be viewed as a last resort, with the goal of protecting civilians at risk, and nothing should be allowed to preempt or preclude the urgent search for a political solution."[11] The statement did not specify how these negotiations would proceed. Indeed, it was highly unclear whether Gaddafi was in any mind to accede to such negotiations, or would respect whatever agreements issued from them. The ICG report neatly summarized underlying fears:

> Determined Western intervention could help topple the regime but at considerable political as well as human cost and would risk precipitating a political vacuum in which various forces engage in a potentially prolonged and violent struggle for supremacy before anything resembling a state and stable government are re-established.[12]

As of March 10, neither the US or NATO seemed any closer to a decision on what to do about Libya, despite the fact that on March 8, the Gulf Cooperation Council took the bold step of calling specifically on the UN Security Council to implement a no-fly zone:[13] "The White House remains locked in talks with its European allies over potential action against Libya amid divisions in Congress and in the US national security establishment about how to respond to the violence."[14]

Some members of Congress, including Senator John Kerry, challenged Defense Secretary Robert Gates's bleak assessment of the desirability of US intervention and called for broader and more active intervention. Senators Mitch McConnell (R-KY) and John McCain (R-AZ) also lent their support to the concept of a no-fly zone.[15] Meanwhile the White House appeared to be groping for a coherent explanation as to what the US was doing with respect to Libya. Chief of Staff Bill Daley, when pressed by the moderator of Meet the Press on March 6 to explain whether US intervention in Libya and Gaddafi's departure were in the United States' national interest, was reduced to saying that intervention was "in our interest as human beings."[16] All of which was consistent with Clinton's own statements at the time that the US was "far from deciding" what to do about a no-fly zone. Benghazi-based Internet sites such as Feb17.info proclaimed themselves appalled at the lack of external support from the US and the West.[17]

The split over Libya policy crossed partisan lines. Democrats such as Virginia Senator Jim Webb warned against "giving weapons to people we know nothing about," while McCain was one of the first to advocate for American intervention in Libya. Onetime Democrat, Senator Joseph Lieberman (I-CT) spoke of a basic decision between casting support for the rebels or watching them be destroyed: "We are not talking about large-scale military action—we are talking about giving the opposition to Gaddafi a fighting chance of unseating him."[18] Many in the Republican Party were quick to seize on Libya as falling clearly outside the range of US interests. Sensing a vulnerability, Tea Party members like Michele Bachmann (R-MN) and other contenders for the Republican presidential nomination, Mitt Romney included, argued that Obama was doing the opposite of his campaign promises, i.e, getting the US into another costly war (but without the "strategic interests" of Iraq).[19] During an October presidential debate, Bachmann famously said, "Now with the president, he put us in Libya. He is now putting us in Africa. We already were stretched too thin, and he put our special operations forces in Africa."[20] Another Republican contender, Herman Cain, demonstrated how little he knew about Libya: "I do not agree with the way he [Obama] handled it for the following reason," Cain told the *Milwaukee Journal-Sentinel*, before cutting himself off. "Nope, that's a different one. . . . I got all this stuff twirling around in my head."[21] Mitt Romney, who ultimately became the Republican nominee, was "wildly difficult to pin down on Libya," but accused Obama in an interview with the *National Review Online*, of creating "another example of mission creep and mission muddle."[22]

It is interesting to note the strong consistency of Bush-era positions and the divisions between the Bush "moderates" (those both for the Iraq War and in favor of engaging Libya) and the neocons (who were consistently against engaging Libya, on the grounds that, if anything, the regime should be removed in the same manner as that in Iraq). While Tea Party supporters were eager to criticize Obama for violating his antiwar stance (in effect, replicating Bush's mistakes in Iraq and Afghanistan), Paul Wolfowitz and Elliott Abrams "sharply criticized" Obama for being "too slow" to condemn Muammar Gaddafi.[23] In late March, Ex-Vice President Dick Cheney's former national security adviser, John Hannah, urged Obama to act fast:

> If President Obama acts now with boldness and resolve, a window does exist for avoiding a long-term US military commitment in Libya and achieving a rapid end of Qaddafi's regime. But the opening is narrow and could close fast. . . . If he does, Obama will have succeeded in limiting the suffering of the Libyan people and significantly advancing America's national interests and global standing, a pretty good day's work that all Americans would rightly applaud.[24]

In August, Abrams rued,

> Had the White House acted sooner and more resolutely Qaddafi could have been brought down sooner, and with fewer Libyan deaths. Moreover, the lingering damage to NATO could have been avoided. . . . So the certain drumbeat from the White House and its supporters—"This shows how wise the president has been"—should be rejected. Winning in the end is great, and it sure beats losing. Winning sooner and smarter, winning with your alliances intact, would be far better.[25]

Musing about the Libyan Spring and Gaddafi's end, Condoleezza Rice said, in her memoir, "I was very, very glad that we had disarmed him of his most dangerous weapons of mass destruction. There in his bunker, making his last stand, I have no doubt he would have used them."[26]

Secretary Gates came out early and strongly against US support for a no-fly zone, arguing before Congress that this would require taking out Libya's air defenses and would be a "big operation in a big country."[27] Such a no-fly-zone argument would presumably not have gone far at all if Gaddafi had not shown signs of resiliency, defying numerous predictions from those on the inside and out that he would be gone within days.[28] As of early March, Secretary Clinton said the US was "far from deciding" what to do about a no-fly zone, as Libyan opposition elements proclaimed they were "disgusted at the perceived lack of external support from the US and the West."[29]

Even as the Washington policy apparatus continued to squabble internally for a consistent view, quasi-mainstream voices started to suggest that Libya was all part of some precooked American plan, as unlikely and unmotivated as that would be. A good portion of this emerged from a *New York Times* piece claiming that "clandestine operatives (were sent) into Libya (early in the conflict) to gather intelligence for military air strikes, and make contact with rebels."[30] A Yale literature professor extrapolated from this article in the widely read online *Huffington Post* that the Obama administration "had in fact precipitated the rebellion by providing expertise and human intelligence around the time that the rebellion was getting started," citing as further evidence stories that Obama had signed a presidential finding, authorizing covert assistance to the rebels.[31] While the date of the finding was not publicized, secondhand reports suggested it was "immediately" after hostilities broke out (news reports were vague about the exact date, but placed it two to three weeks before, or the first week of March).[32] The *New York Times* quoted a US military official indicating that "small groups of CIA operatives have been working in Libya for several weeks as part of a shadow force of Westerners that the Obama administration hopes can help bleed Colonel Gaddafi's military."[33] According to a respected French military digest, the US and UK were engaged in cyberpropaganda campaigns in the early days of the NATO campaign, broadcasting messages by SMS to Libyan naval commanders, for example, to stay in port.[34] None of this is particularly surprising—and appears to ramp up sufficiently slowly that it contradicts the above insinuations that the US somehow knew what was coming, or somehow incited it.

Crafting Libya Policy, on the Fly

The group that was credited with having the most impact on evolving Libya policy, other than the president, was, in addition to Hillary Clinton, National Security Council (NSC) directors Samantha Power, who covered multilateral engagement, and Gayle Smith, global development; and Susan Rice, the UN ambassador, on one hand, and on the other, Defense Secretary Robert Gates, and Mike McFaul, who covered Russia at the NSC. The three at NSC were in favor of intervention, specifically the establishment of a no-fly zone. Against were Gates, National Security Adviser Tom Donilon, Deputy National Security Adviser Denis McDonough, and Obama's chief of counterterrorism John Brennan, who argued against a "vital interest" and cited the very real possibility of "mission creep."[35] A major factor governing debate over Libyan intervention was the domestic economic situation and severe budgetary pressures on the military, still recovering from a more than $1 trillion campaign in Iraq and an expanding effort in Afghanistan. It was widely felt within the defense establishment that the US simply did not have the wherewithal to wage another major campaign in the region or, more precisely, to put itself in the position where this might become be a possibility. (It is perhaps interesting to recall that the US was unwilling to take on the Barbary pirates at the turn of the nineteenth century, for very similar reasons.)

A few in the pro-intervention camp expressed concerns that intervention would fuel "conspiracy theories" that the US somehow had a hand in either sparking or stoking the Arab Spring.[36] *The Nation* referred to the four female members of the group as "Warrior Women"[37] styling them as a somewhat self-contained advocacy group that stood up to their male counterparts, including the commander in chief, to define a set of working conditions for intervention, and "collected the information to make their case and persuade the President to take military action."[38] While an appealing image, this does not appear to be a completely accurate characterization of the dynamic.

Certainly, those who worked on Libya policy were an odd mix of people who had all worked in some way with (or in some cases against) one another previously. Samantha Power had built a reputation as an uncompromising defender of humanitarian intervention in cases where genocide was a possibility, elaborating her thoughts in a Pulitzer Prize–winning book *A Problem from Hell: America and the Age of Genocide*, which was extremely critical of both the George H. W. Bush and Clinton administrations for what she saw as "sitting on their hands for years" while massacres of Muslims in Bosnia continued. Power argued that recent American history was marked by intervention in favor of "promoting a narrowly defined set of US economic and security interests, expanding American markets, curbing nuclear proliferation, and maintaining military readiness, not 'squishy humanitarian' social work."[39]

Susan Rice had been an adviser to President Clinton on Africa during the Rwanda genocide (she joined the Obama campaign early, with Gayle Smith moving over from the Clinton camp subsequently). Despite their crossover loyalties to the Clinton and Obama administrations, these women worked together in different ways to understand action on Libya and were "adamant and public supporters of the implementation of the third pillar of the Responsibility to Protect" doctrine, which includes the use of military force, if necessary. Rice, Power, and Smith had other ties in common: in addition to being senior NSC hands, they all had advised Obama on Darfur-related issues, while he was still a senator, and then a presidential candidate.[40] Hillary Clinton and Power were said to have mended fences reasonably early in the Obama administration, thanks in part to the intervention of senior diplomat Richard Holbrooke, who had also been a senior advisor to Hillary Clinton's presidential campaign.[41] Smith had worked for Bill and Hillary Clinton, and then "defected" to the Obama camp. Clinton in the past had often been in agreement with Robert Gates on other defense issues. According to one correspondent: "Obama's Tuesday night decision to push for armed intervention was not only a defining moment in his ever-evolving foreign policy, but also may have marked the end of the alliance between Clinton and Gates—an alliance that has successfully influenced administration foreign policy decisions dating back to the 2009 Afghanistan strategy review."[42]

Overcoming Baggage

While his subsequent media efforts left much to be desired, Gaddafi had been quick to play on Western fears that Libyan instability would lead, as it had in Iraq, to uncontrolled chaos. His and Saif's early speeches were littered with references to the archetypal failed state: Somalia. On February 22, Gaddafi asked the international community, "Do you want Libya to be like Somalia? It [intervention] will lead to civil war."[43] In a statement on

February 26, Saif said Libya "risks becoming like Somalia[44] and warned, subsequently, that Libya without Gaddafi would be, again, "a new Somalia," splintering into tribes and clans.

Of course, Somalia, like Bosnia and Rwanda, was a loaded word for the Americans, and for Democrats, in particular. It was Bill Clinton's ill-fated humanitarian and military campaign in Somalia in the early 1990s—dramatized in the film *Black Hawk Down* with the spectacle of fallen US marines dragged through the streets of Mogadishu—that put Somalia on the map.[45] In a March 2 speech, Gaddafi added the threat of piracy into the mix, evoking a return of the days of the Barbary pirates: "In the Mediterranean Sea there will be piracy, like in Somalia. . . . They will say that the ships of the Christians are infidel ships, and cannot sail in the Mediterranean unless they pay. This is what will happen if Libya is not stable."[46]

The Western foreign policy establishment, still unsure what was happening on the ground, appeared to take the bait. On March 2, Secretary Clinton, speaking before the Senate Foreign Relations Committee, said, "[O]ne of our biggest concerns is Libya descending into chaos and becoming a giant Somalia." Clinton, no doubt heavily briefed on the Islamist opposition in Libya, relied on the Sinjar records (documents found in Iraq with demographics of foreign fighters) to question whether Al Qaeda and other groups might exploit a power vacuum to establish a new foothold in the region, such as happened in Somalia.[47] Saif and his father amplified these points further in speeches on March 8,[48] Foreign Minister Musa Kusa—less than two weeks after his defection March 31—cautioned that Libya was headed for civil war and could turn into a "new Somalia."[49]

At this time, the Libyan rebels, Al Qaeda, a range of Islamist organizations, and the West formed an odd collection of cheerleaders for Gaddafi's removal. On February 21, the Egyptian-born, "celebrity" Al Jazeera Islamic affairs commentator Yusuf Qaradawi, issued a fatwa (religious enjoinder) to "All Libyans, to shoot a bullet at Gadhafi if they could do so." The Libyan Islamic Fighting Group, not to be outdone, issued this statement:

> It is with the grace of God that we were hoisting the banner of jihad against this apostate regime under the leadership of the Libyan Islamic Fighting Group, which sacrificed the elite of its sons and commanders in combating this regime whose blood was spilled on the mountains of Darnah, the streets of Benghazi, the outskirts of Tripoli, the desert of Sabha, and the sands of the beach.[50]

Al Qaeda in the Islamic Maghreb (AQIM) posted on one of its websites: "[It] is time for the 'imposter, sinful, hard-hearted bastard Kaddafi [sic]) to meet the same end [as Ben Ali and Mubarak].' . . . We declare our support and aid to the Libyan revolution in its legitimate demands, and we assure our people in Libya that we are with you and will not let you down."[51]

Gaddafi's deputy foreign minister countered by claiming that jihadists had proclaimed Derna an Islamic emirate (which never actually happened).

On February 28, British Prime Minister David Cameron and French President Nicolas Sarkozy jointly floated the idea of a no-fly zone–exclusion zone to stop attacks by mercenaries and Gaddafi's warplanes against civilian targets within Libya. While the French papers were lambasting Sarkozy for allowing his foreign minister to offer advice to the "soon to be deposed" Tunisian dictator Ben Ali, Britain's *Financial Times* was questioning whether the prime minister—who had studiously distanced himself from Tony Blair's joint ventures with the Americans in Iraq and Afghanistan, highly unpopular with the British public—was set to take the UK down another risky and potentially expensive path at the height of a global economic downturn.[52] For Cameron, however, Libya had since become a matter of personal contention with his predecessor, whose government he excoriated for "appallingly dodgy dealings with Libya."[53]

The French Catalyst

While 10 Downing Street weighed Britain's response to the unfolding events, Sarkozy made the first move, suspending diplomatic relations with Gaddafi's government on February 26.[54] Two days later, France sent two cargo planes filled with medical supplies to Benghazi.[55] French participation dated effectively from March 9, with the deployment of AWACs aircraft to monitor events in Libya.[56] Saif lashed out at Sarkozy personally for these actions, threatening to expose the extent to which Libya had financed Sarkozy's 2007 election campaign.

Meanwhile, in one of the more astounding diplomatic interludes of the conflict, flamboyant French intellectual Bernard-Henri Lévy, while visiting Egypt in early March was following events in Libya. He said he felt compelled, watching the revolution unfold there, to travel overland to the rebel capital: "It was an accident of history," he wrote.

> I happened to be in Egypt when Gaddafi sent his planes to shoot at the pacifist demonstrations in Tripoli. It seemed to me such an enormous, unprecedented thing, and I felt the Egyptian democrats around me were so horrified by it that I decided on instinct to go to Libya straight away.[57]

Lévy requested and was granted an interview with Mustafa Abdeljalil, in which he offered to use his good offices with the Élysée Palace to request an audience for a National Transitional Council delegation. Lévy described in his Benghazi memoir published in November 2011 how, with essentially no plan and without prior authorization from any French government officials, he found himself speaking by satellite telephone with a president he didn't vote for and with whom he had been on "fragile" terms for several years, requesting him to meet a delegation from the newly formed "Benghazi Commune."

"I would find it extraordinary if France would be the first to take action," Lévy claims to have asked Sarkozy. "Absolutely," Sarkozy responded, "as if [in Lévy's words] he found it perfectly natural to receive a proposal for the official recognition of a newly formed power of which nothing, to date, was known other than it was rebelling against the all-powerful government in Tripoli."[58] Lévy claims he advised Sarkozy to keep Alain Juppé, the French foreign minister, out of the loop, since he was hostile to the idea of intervention in Libya: "One is reminded," Lévy recounts, "of the manner in which he [Juppé] conducted himself during the crisis of Bosnia, and then Rwanda. He will be absolutely against intervention in Libya. He would not be Juppé if he were not against." The French media had a field day with Juppé's sidelining by the philosopher-statesman, and Juppé's understandably nonplussed response.[59]

Adbul Jalil selected Ali Essaoui, Gaddafi's ex-finance minister, and Mahmoud Jibril, the former head of the National Economic Development Board, to travel immediately to Paris to meet with Sarkozy—with the condition that France commit to a formal recognition of the council as the sole legitimate representative of the Libyan people, which it did, in a statement on March 10. There would be obvious parallels between the French and US decision-making processes, at least to the degree key individuals were pitted against the defense establishment. According to *Le Nouvel Observateur*, the "Élysée and the ministry of defense are split over the way forward after four months of bombing efforts." According to the same article, Defense Minister Gerard Longuet objected to the lack of an exit strategy and was "in favor of allowing Gaddafi to stay if [he] gave up civilian and military responsibilities."[60]

Lest anyone had forgotten, Sarkozy was second only to Tony Blair and perhaps Italy's Berlusconi in his contributions to Gaddafi's rehabilitation. As we saw, he participated in the dramatic photo-op end of the Bulgarian nurses' case, to the point of being accused of rewarding Gaddafi with promises of future diplomatic receptions in Europe in a way that undermined EU efforts to keep Gaddafi within bounds. One of those quid pro quos was an agreement to host a lavish reception at l'hotel de Marigny, the official residence of guests of the French government, from December 10 to 16 2007, just after the nurses' release.[61]

Sarkozy's volte face was presumably far less blasé and unplanned than Lévy intimates in his description of his conversation with the president from the Tibesti Hotel in Benghazi. Sarkozy, far more than Obama, had been accused early on—while the Tunisia crisis was unfolding—of taking a regressive stance on the Arab Spring. The fact that France's foreign minister, Michèle Alliot-Marie, was discovered in Tunis offering soon-to-be deposed Tunisian leader Ben Ali intelligence assistance proved a major embarrassment to the French government.[62] The French press raised the possibility that Sarkozy was in danger of losing French policy leadership over the Arab revolutions, which until then had been "dubious if not catastrophic."[63] Other prospective motives floated were the need to demonstrate leadership within NATO and the Euro-Mediterranean partnership, as well as to show that its armaments were working.[64]

Sarkozy, moreover, was facing record low opinion ratings in the early stages of the run-up to the 2012 French presidential election, in which polls had him behind even Marine Le Pen of the Far-Right National Front. This was also before the spectacular meltdown of the former head of the International Monetary Fund and French Socialist Party Candidate Dominique Strauss-Kahn on May 15 (the expected winner). As several commentators suggested that the Libyan crisis offered Sarkozy the perfect opportunity to regain the initiative, despite the fact that his actions appeared highly hypocritical and given his eagerness to cozy up to Gaddafi in 2007 by intervening in the Bulgarian nurses' case, the subsequent hosting of Gaddafi at the Élysée, and the fact that France was the first European country to sign an agreement to supply Libya with arms the same year.[65] Several sources suggest that Sarkozy met with Gaddafi in Tripoli while he was Interior Minister in 2005 specifically to discuss a 50-million euro contribution to Sarkozy's upcoming presidential campaign.[66] All of this would be forgiven, as the French warmed to the idea of an activist France, leading EU policy under a decisive leader. As one French blogger framed it:

> The French have perceived their country as having a leading role in the hierarchy of nations. It is for this reason that Sarkozy's actions have been met with cross-party approval. The crisis in Libya fits seamlessly with the laudable ideals immortalised in the triptych of "liberty, equality, fraternity."[67]

Sarkozy's intentions aside, France could be credited with taking the first tangible, decisive steps toward isolating Gaddafi and creating an actionable international consensus.

The Wider Spring

By early to mid-March, the Middle East was metaphorically and, in many cases, literally on fire. The timing of the subsequent revolts had no little bearing on international actions in and attitudes toward what was happening in Libya. Saudi Arabia and other Gulf States sent troops into Bahrain to quell a Shi'a-led uprising against the Al Khalifa dynasty there on March 14, and on March 18, protests turned deadly in Syria. The arc of rebellions was unfortunate for Gaddafi. Had Syria exploded sooner, or so conventional wisdom holds, attention would likely have been deflected from Libya, and the question of "why Libya and not Syria" would have proven far more prickly. Bahrain was the main concern of the Gulf Cooperation Council countries, Saudi Arabia and Qatar in particular. The Bahrain event and possibilities of local infection clearly conditioned both the Saudi and Qatari actions in Libya, in ways that are still being sorted out.

The US Takes a (Public) Position

Foreshadowing her key role in defining US policy on the Libya conflict, Hillary Clinton told the UN Human Rights Council in Geneva on February 28 that it was time for Gaddafi to go: "Through their actions, they have lost the legitimacy to govern. And the people of Libya have made themselves clear: It is time for Gaddafi to go—now, without further violence or delay."[68] In the same speech, she hinted that exile might be an option for Gaddafi, but that he must still be held accountable for his actions—a potentially mixed message for Gaddafi, who, according to those in his circle at this time, suggested that he was convinced the US was "out to get him," no matter what.[69] President Obama weighed in publicly for the first time on the Libya conflict on March 3 during a White House press conference with Mexican president Felipe Calderón, saying that Muammar Gaddafi had "lost legitimacy to lead, and he must leave."[70]

A critical step in the formation of US policy toward the evolving situation in Libya was the articulation of a set of specific criteria in support of intervention, including legitimate local leadership that could convincingly articulate their needs; strong regional (Arab) support; and a clear legal mandate, i.e., a UN resolution supporting external action. Sources close to President Obama say the Secretary played a key role in formulating and selling these criteria to the President.[71] In *A Problem from Hell*, Power described the tendency of government bureaucracies (here, she takes direct aim at the State Department) to dilute the messages and warning of lower-level analysts, and to refer to past intractable situations ("quagmires") as an excuse for inaction. She also said she believes such crises typically come with warning and that the perpetrator(s) always counted on the inaction of the outsiders. While some diplomats with past Libya experience complained they had not been consulted by the Department or the Administration, Clinton appeared to have reached deep enough into the bureaucracy, and outside of it, to understand that nonintervention in Libya specifically was not an option if the US wanted to preserve credibility in the region.

Gaddafi's explicit threats to make Benghazi "suffer," seemed almost ready-made to play to the R2P case-in-waiting. "What Power and her supporters want is to solidify the principle of 'responsibility to protect' in international law," wrote one critic. "That requires a 'pure' case of intervention on humanitarian grounds."[72] "In our best judgment," Power later said (the failure to set up a no-fly zone) would have been "extremely chilling, deadly and indeed a stain on our collective conscience."[73] The latter phrase "stain on our collective conscience" is a direct and presumably deliberate reference to Obama's 2009 Cairo speech: "And when innocents in Bosnia and Darfur are slaughtered, that is a stain on our collective conscience. That is what it means to share this world in the 21st century. That is the responsibility we have to one another as human beings."[74]

Tuesday, March 15, 2011

The critical policy meeting on Libya occurred on the evening of March 15, Washington time. Not all of the most interested parties were present, and the secretary of state called in from Paris. The meeting was described by various sources, including the *Washington Post* as "highly contentious."[75] Hillary Clinton was said to have made up her mind in favor of intervention two days before, but had not revealed which side she was leaning toward either to G8 foreign ministers or Mahmoud Jibril, whom she met on March 14, so as not to "get out ahead of US policy."[76] Obama made the final decision and instructed Rice to push the UN Security Council for "giving the international community broad authority to achieve Qaddafi's removal, including the use of force beyond the imposition of a no-fly zone."[77]

On the evening of March 17, Gaddafi spoke on the radio, calling Benghaziites his "sweet people" and entreating them to "come back to him"; then vowed that those who did not (comply) would be shown no mercy. Saif derided the UN resolution, saying, "Within 48 hours it will be all over. . . . Whatever the decision, it will be too late." The rebels, after earlier saying no to intervention, were now pleading with the West and NATO to establish a no-fly zone. Foreign Minister Musa Kusa,[78] still in office, had announced unilateral truce, yet this was clearly a ruse, as Gaddafi's troops were pushing to within twenty miles of Benghazi, and regime jets bombing targets within the city. By the morning of March 16, thousands of Benghazi residents had already left, either to stay with relatives in neighboring towns or to travel by car to the Egyptian border.

An armored column had progressed from Ajdabia the previous night and was able to attack the upscale neighborhood of Tabalino just before dawn, taking Gar Younes University, where they were held loosely by a group of *shabab* (youth) and Islamist fighters.[79] News spread quickly, "They're in the city," people texted each other furiously. Many saw people crying openly in the streets; others tell of families boarding themselves up in their houses boiling pots of water with which to defend themselves.[80] A former member of the monarchy parliament described how he and others "too old and too stubborn," were more or less at peace with the notion that the end was near. Others—many who had already left for Al Beida and Derna—were said to have started preparing for a long guerrilla war, à la Omar Al Mokhtar.[81]

Statements by prominent Arab bodies, most importantly, the Arab League on March 12, aligned with Clinton's and Obama's purported "list of must haves," and galvanized a flurry of last-minute diplomacy. On March 13, Clinton met in Paris with the G8 and Gulf ministers. What the Russians would do was still a big question, but Clinton's meeting with Russian Foreign Minister Sergei Lavrov apparently secured Russia's abstention in the UN Security Council vote on Resolution 1973. France's involvement also posed issues. France had argued strongly against NATO as the implementing command authority behind the multinational operation that would ultimately be called Unified Protector, saying the international body was unprepared and member states unequipped to play substantive roles. France also wanted to leave out recalcitrant states such as Germany, Turkey, and Italy. The latter, by contrast, insisted on NATO command, proclaiming France was harboring "ulterior motives" and "hidden agendas."

Lévy had assisted in bringing Mahmoud Jibril to meet with Clinton in London on March 14. He recalled that Jibril was "furious"—at himself—when he left that meeting for having ostensibly failed to move Clinton. In fact, he had done the opposite "A 'source' in Hillary's entourage told me that Jibril hadn't understood," Lévy wrote, "that the esteemed diplomat [Jibril] was somehow a bit out of touch with the situation he had helped create, that he had reached Hillary on a very fundamental level; that he had caught the attention of Clinton the political animal, but also, very simply, the female instinct within her"[82] (a loaded statement, certainly).

Many Libyans steadfastly refuse to give Jibril any credit on this score, believing in effect that the situation sold itself. This may have been a function of the persistent ambivalence about former Saif associates now advocating for the transitional government. Yet Jibril's lobbying may have been necessary even at that. Many in the administration at this point were in fact not convinced that a major massacre in Benghazi was either inevitable or a casus belli.

If there was to be a Libya intervention, or so the Western nations reasoned, they needed cover from the Arab governments. On February 24, the foreign ministry of the United Arab Emirates (UAE), part of the GCC, issued an uncharacteristically strong statement, condemning violence against the Libyan people:[83] "[We are] following with concern the developments in Libya . . . [and are] shocked at the suffering of the Libyan people and strongly condemn the violence, the killing of the Libyan people and the damage to Libya's infrastructure."[84] This was followed the next day by the politically even more significant development, when the Arab League took the (also unprecedented) step on March 8 of endorsing the imposition of a no-fly zone and calling for the setup of safe areas in places being shelled by government forces. Syria and Algeria were the two Arab League countries to vote against the Arab League resolution urging the UN to impose a no-fly zone. On March 12, the GCC took the striking initiative to urge Arab League foreign ministers "to shoulder their responsibilities in taking necessary measures to stop the bloodshed." Several Arab states floated the possibility of an Arab–African Union coalition to provide the Libyan rebels air cover as a means of averting a politically undesirable American intervention.[85]

Part of the strength of the Arab reaction to the Libya crisis came from the fact that Gaddafi, while tolerated, was widely loathed, particularly in the Gulf, whose leaders were a favorite target of Gaddafi's ridicule (covered with glee by Qatar's Al Jazeera channel). However much they would have loved to be rid of Gaddafi, most of the Gulf countries were constrained in their actions for fear of encouraging incipient protests in their own backyard. Oman, which historically played the role of mediator within the GCC, might have preferred to sit out the debate over Libya, given its own (highly rare) internal unrest, but nevertheless lobbied the Arab League and the GCC to urge the UN to take action against Libya. Iran, somewhat comically, given its own successful crackdown on the Green Revolution two years earlier, attempted to take the high road, condemning Gaddafi for subjecting his people to a "shower of machine-guns, tanks and bombs."[86] With the passage of the UN Resolution 1973 on March 17,[87] Saif allegedly turned to a group of confidantes and said, "We gave up our nukes, and they screwed us."[88]

Algeria

Because of its complex and extremely bloody recent history, Algeria was something of a missing actor in the Arab Spring—the only North African state in which the earthquake had not had serious, immediate reverberations. Algeria's position is a function of its own brief experiment with democracy, in which a predicted Islamist victory at the polls in 1991 was headed off by a last-minute military "countercoup" that plunged the country into a ten-year bloodbath, which killed at least 100,000 people. The populace largely supported the military junta against depredations committed by Islamist extremists (though the government was far from innocent). While

Algeria's relations with Gaddafi were never perfect, President Abdelaziz Bouteflika's government clearly was interested, if not in keeping Gaddafi in power (the Algerians were also not tremendous fans of Gaddafi), then neighboring Islamist influence at bay. Thus Algeria funneled supplies and arms to the loyalists and provided safe haven to Gaddafi family members, who would use the country as a base for loyalist propaganda. From late 2010 to the present, Algeria's principal role has been to serve as something of a ghost of Christmas past and future rolled into one: it is an example of what could happen if the Islamists are denied their say and of what might happen if extremist Islam is allowed to spread unchecked.

Qatar

Among the reactions of the Arab states with respect to the Libyan revolution, the actions of the Qataris appeared for a time—and perhaps still—impenetrable. As we have seen, Qatar's Al Jazeera was in effect the only foreign media presence in Libya in the early weeks of the conflict, and was critical in building international awareness of what was happening on the ground. In sum, the Gulf emirate provided over $2 billion worth of assistance, including on-the-ground training (to cite one example, Qatar created a task force to provide technical and logistical assistance to rebels in the East at Tubruk, Benghazi, and Al Beida, and in the West in Zintan),[89] munitions, humanitarian aid, and, perhaps most importantly, helping the rebels market eastern oil when there was no other source of income—all of which garnered the Emirate tremendous support in-country. Subsequently, Qatar was responsible for helping build Libya's postrevolutionary television media, which had an unmistakable Qatari imprimatur.[90] Many believe the emirate's contributions to the Arab Spring countries—and Libya in particular—were simply an extension of a policy of opportunism, a desire to be punching in foreign affairs at a level commensurate with the country's financial weight, a strategy Emir Hamad bin Khalifa al Thani had been pursuing since deposing his father in June 1985. Since then, the Al Thanis had been mediating—with less than stunning success—in Yemen in the Houthi rebellion; in territorial disputes linking Djibouti, Eritrea, and Yemen; in the Palestinian-Israeli question, and so on. The Qataris had even offered to mediate in the Bulgarian nurses' case in 2007.[91]

Looking around at all the Arab Spring movements, Qatar presumably saw and continues to see an opportunity to project regional leadership and influence, consistent with its attempts to mediate various Middle Eastern and African conflicts over the previous decade.[92] The differences in this case were that, first and foremost, the gambit worked; second, Qatar put its military jets, not just its money and diplomats on the table; and third, while it chose to spread its funds, on-site military training, and humanitarian assistance liberally amongst the opposition—Islamist, traditional, and liberal—it unequivocally backed the rebels. While the Emirates received much credit in Libya for its early support of the rebel cause, the fact that Dubai was a base for both powerful pro- and anti-Gaddafi elements made the net impact less clear.

Others attributed at least part of Qatar's position vis-à-vis the Libyan revolution to its animus toward its direct neighbor, Saudi Arabia, which had been trying to undermine Qatar's position in the Gulf for decades. According to this hypothesis, by supporting the Libyan rebels, Qatar could not take the moral high ground over Saudi Arabia (vis-à–vis its support for crackdown against Shiite protestors in Bahrain) while hedging its bets in any future conflict between the Saudi leadership and its home-grown extremists. Others opined that Qatar's motives were primarily economic, and designed to obtain some degree of future influence over Libyan gas, which competed with Qatar's primary resource. Indeed, Qatar Gas and Qatar Oil were expected to profit handsomely in future contracts with Libya.[93] In any case, Qatar's small population and massive wealth gave it a strong measure of immunity in the Arab Spring. Whatever the exact mix of motives, Qatar would top, by a large margin, the list of countries with which Libyans felt they had the best relations, in an October 2011 poll.[94]

March 17: The UN Vote

On the night of March 17, the UN Security Council was set to vote, based on a very shaky consensus, for implementation of the resolution authorizing a no-fly zone. Ten countries voted in favor of UN Resolution 1973. Brazil, Russia, India, and China abstained, along with Germany. The proceedings at the UN were broadcast live to multitudes near Maidan Al Shajarah and the Benghazi courthouse. As it was clear the resolution would pass, cameras caught people weeping with relief and joy. The joy quickly turned to increased angst, as nothing had yet changed on the ground; the resolution had passed, but had not translated into necessary relief. Indeed, the resolution only increased Gaddafi's determination to beat NATO to Benghazi.

The March 19, 2011, issue of *The Economist*, changing its own tack, published a strongly worded editorial under the title "No Illusions," exhorting the West to act before it was too late:

> Are countries content to sit on their hand and watch rebels die? And if they feel they must step in, what exactly can they do? In Libya a moment will soon have passed when a no-fly zone designed to stop Colonel Qaddafi from using his air force could offer civilians much protection. . . . If he [Gaddafi] arrives at the city, its people will need more than just air cover to save them in what could be a bloody and long-drawn-out-battle.[95]

Two days later, the French jumped the gun. At 5:45 p.m. on March 19, Sarkozy launched Operation L'Harmattan (desert wind)—the French analogue to the American Operation Odyssey Dawn—several hours before the official start of the operation. The strikes, launched by eight Rafale jets, blew up one or more tanks (different French sources give different accounts) on the edge of Benghazi. Subsequent air raids flown by mixed-nationality fighters destroyed sections at the front and middle of the convoy, effectively immobilizing the bulk of the force moving east.[96]

According to one French military analyst, the Americans, accustomed to orderly campaigns, were "stunned" at France's forwardness, because for them, it was simply "out of the question" that NATO enter into the fray without first having "softened the opposing side (Gaddafi's) defensive forces"—despite the fact that, at this point, every hour was critical.[97] Presumably the Americans knew of the French intentions and gave their tacit assent, so that it would not seem to be obviously controlling the operation (which, of course, it was). All Benghazi knew was that French planes had come to the rescue. In response to the French action, Italy's Berlusconi immediately threatened to pull the country's bases for NATO use.[98] The French attacks were immediately followed by more than a hundred US Tomahawk missiles, which in a matter of hours turned the remnants of Gaddafi's coastal forces into cinder.

Gaddafi Pleads Peace—for a Moment

True to form, as soon as plans for intervention began to crystallize, Gaddafi switched gears, promptly announcing he was willing to talk about a cease-fire. Just as quickly, the fresh Arab resolve abruptly began to dissipate, as Amr Moussa, head of the Arab League, announced he had misgivings about NATO strikes.[99] Several Arab states, hitherto supportive of NATO action, began to balk, fearing high numbers of casualties and an increased likelihood of a ground campaign. Secretary Clinton again jumped into the diplomatic fray, speaking with a series of Arab ministers, including Hamad bin Jasim al Thani, the Qatari foreign minister; the UAE Foreign Minister Abdullah bin Zayed al Nahyan; and King Abdullah II in Jordan, collectively concerned about US criticism of Saudi Arabia's intervention in Bahrain. The Western press echoed these sentiments: in a March 21 editorial, the *Financial Times* urged Arab leaders to stay the course behind military action.[100] On the sidelines, Gaddafi tried desperately to threaten former supporters. To sway French resolve, he promised to publish documents proving that Libyan contributions to Sarkozy's presidential campaign had been "decisive."

The UN resolution and subsequent NATO actions provoked a short-lived rally among anti-Gaddafi elements within Tripoli: after three days of strikes, residents renewed protests, and were emboldened to speak with foreign press. Shopkeepers and restaurateurs in the Old City seemed to be of one mind, that Gaddafi must go. But the regime tightened its grip, putting down the new outbursts, including one in the Souk Al Jumaa area within two weeks of the start of the NATO strikes, and reinforcing its actions with a relentless propaganda campaign via state television.[101] Following this, there appeared to be renewed efforts to try to unhinge Gaddafi from power, even as some of his strongest allies melted away.[102] On March 31, Musa Kusa, long suspected of having a hand in the Lockerbie bombing, left Libya on the pretext of illness for the Tunisian island of Djerba, where British Intelligence spirited him to London for debriefing. Many in the Western political and intelligence circles hoped that Kusa's defection would bring about a quick collapse of those around Gaddafi and/or create the conditions for someone with access to the Leader to assassinate him. It was not to be.

The members of the Arab league continued to work against Gaddafi, largely behind the scenes. The Saudis, while still demonstrably upset with Obama for "forsaking" longtime ally Hosni Mubarak, were said to have supplied the rebels with arms, at American request, all the while working to avert regional or domestic "contagion."[103] Meanwhile, the UAE, though quick to express solidarity with the rebels at a national level, could be seen to be hedging its bets behind the scenes. The UAE had made significant progress in the previous year with the Gaddafi regime, signing a number of high-level trade agreements.

The Saudi-financed *Asharq Al Awsat* claimed in summer 2011, that the Algerians had helped smuggle arms to loyalist forces through the port of Djen Djen, 267 kilometers east of Algiers (run by Dubai port operator Dubai World). Loyalists and rebels, were known to be using the Emirate as a center for the transfer of weapons, money, and humanitarian supplies, via Dubai. A ranking Libyan businessman and diplomat both maintained that Dubai authorities either did know about these shipments, or "chose to look the other way"[104] (the ship in question was Libyan-flagged and arrived July 19[105]).

The Omanis, while experiencing an unprecedented level of domestic protest, condemned Gaddafi's actions against his own people. The Egyptians and the Tunisians offered some of the most direct assistance of the war to the Libyan people, mainly on a grassroots level (though the Egyptian government is strongly suspected of having helped funnel arms to the rebels).

Diplomatic Strategists versus Military Pragmatists

"Success has a hundred fathers, and defeat is an orphan," goes the saying. Since no one in the US administration was fully confident how things would turn out in Libya, there was naturally an escalating procession of fathers. For all France's (and Sarkozy's) plausible ulterior motives, the French and Sarkozy personally deserve a good deal of credit for galvanizing the campaign. On the French side, much credit was given initially to Bernard-Henry Lévy for convincing Sarkozy of the moral imperative to act in Libya. In the US, early public credit for articulating the same "moral imperative" was given to NSC director Samantha Power.[106]

It seems the formation of US policy toward Libya as a whole was a more frenzied process, in which no clear direction was evident until the last minute. While Power and Susan Rice appear to have done much to lobby the UN and NATO for an implementation of an infrequently evoked Responsibility to Protect (R2P) doctrine (according to which the international community has a responsibility to intervene to protect civilians when their own government either fails to, or is the perpetrator of atrocities, like genocide), Secretary of State Clinton, by dint of her position and external investigation, seems to have played the most substantive role in shifting Obama to yes on the issue of intervention or the no-fly zone, with the R2P doctrine becoming a convenient, necessary, and sincerely assembled "casing" for a more complex set of rationales.

NATO had its own set of informal criteria for implementing military action under R2P, including seriousness of risk; whether the action is primarily meant to neutralize the threat (as opposed to something else "like bananas or oil"); whether this is truly a last resort action; proportionality of response; and balance of consequences, or how likely are the people in question to be better off as a result of the action than inaction. Gareth Evans, former Australian Foreign Minister, in an October 6, 2011, speech at Chatham House on NATO and RPT, said he felt "If you apply those tests to the Libya case back in March when the Resolution (UN Resolution 1973) was passed, I don't think you have any difficulty at all about ticking every one of those boxes."[107] While many took issue with NATO's evaluation of these kinds of criteria (while not about oil or bananas, it is not realistic to say that NATO intervention was *solely* about protection of civilians—certainly not after Benghazi had been secured and the campaign went into multiple months), it is curious to see the large number of books that emerged in the wake of the Libyan revolution condemning NATO action in strident terms—and in the process, effectively passing over the all-important, and morally complex, context of the intervention.

In the case of France, it is likely that Sarkozy took an altogether more opportunistic approach to Lévy's call, based on a prior sense of how he wanted to play Libya. Sarkozy had a firm reputation for going it alone and circumventing institutions of state. As one pundit put it, "In France today, there are no conventional politics. There is only Sarkozy."[108]

According to this narrative, once the decision to intervene had been made—for which the R2P doctrine would be a supporting pillar—the US administration had two critical tasks. First, the building of support for the no-fly zone itself (largely within the ranks of the US cabinet, and against Secretary of Defense Gates's views), partly on the grounds that it would increase US standing on the Arab Street. Clinton was said to have put in multiple hours of damage control with NATO allies to ensure the mission proceeded as planned.[109] Critically, she successfully lobbied Russian Foreign Minister Lavrov and Chinese diplomats for an abstention on the UN vote authorizing the no-fly zone, even though both repeatedly called upon NATO to exercise restraint. She calmed Berlusconi and Italian

Foreign Minister Franco Frattini, who had been seeking a German-Italian compromise behind the scenes.

Sarkozy had clearly made up his mind about the Libyan crisis, while Obama allowed those around him to make their respective cases before agreeing to the United States' military contribution to the allied Libya campaign, code-named Unified Protector. In both France and the US, the view of the military establishment was not heeded. One can also exaggerate the influence of the "humanitarians," however useful and relevant their views. This makes sense, in many ways, because the military looked at the conflict in terms of how it would affect active commitments in Iraq and Afghanistan (with the specter of a hot conflict with Iran very much in mind). At the same time, Clinton and Obama appeared, to their credit, to be looking at Libya as a key piece in convincing the Arab Street that the US interests and commitments, while rooted in security and economics, also included a moral dimension—that, in fact, US ability to influence events in the region as a whole would be seriously compromised if the Obama administration could not establish credibility with the Arab people.

In Obama's March 28 speech to the American people explaining US action in Libya, the linkage to his 2009 Cairo speech was clear:

> Born, as we are, out of a revolution, by those who longed to be free, we welcome the fact that history is on the move in the Middle East and North Africa, and that young people are leading the way. Because wherever people long to be free, they will find a friend in the United States.[110]

CHAPTER 11

Stalemate Looms

In the first few weeks after the start of the NATO campaign, the rebels were understandably elated. After Friday prayers, Libyans held placards aloft expressing appreciation for the West in general and specific people they felt had been critical in marshaling support for the rebel cause. Just weeks before, Gaddafi's forces had recovered from their initial disarray and seemed likely to crush the revolt and exact their revenge. Now the rebels had a new chance to end Gaddafi's reign.

The rebels did their best to put on a good show for foreign observers. Signs posted around the country read: *"Libya: la sharquiyya la gharbiyya"* ("Libya: No Easterners, No Westerners"), and *la lilqabaliyya* ("no to tribalism").[1] Regional, religious, tribal, or ideological differences within the rebel camp were neatly papered over.

Yet by mid-April, as Hillary Clinton admitted later, a bit of "buyer's remorse" began to seep in.[2] Though John McCain visited Benghazi and called the rebels "my heroes," the cautions of the naysayers already appeared to be becoming reality. Words like "quagmire" or "stalemate" were entering the discourse, to the distress of the sitting politicians. Meanwhile, many within and outside the anti-Gaddafi coalition began to assert that the NATO actions had surpassed the R2P mandate and taken sides in what looked increasingly like an all-out civil war.[3]

Dealing with the Opposition and Congress

President Obama caused a ruckus within Congress by not consulting the body formally and directly before engaging in military support for UN Resolutions 1970 and 1973.[4] According to the War Powers Resolution of 1973, a federal law, "The President may not introduce US Armed Forces into hostilities for periods exceeding sixty days without Congressional authorization." Against the advice of White House counsel, Obama chose to read US actions as not falling within the definition of hostilities, as intervention was framed as a defensive not an offensive operation. This situation had obvious parallels in the Barbary wars, in which President Jefferson set the precedent for nonhostile hostilities, for which he felt Congress's assent was not required.

Robert Gates, the sole senior Republican holdover from the Bush administration, continued, even after the launch of Operation Odyssey Dawn, to scoff at US interests in Libya, telling the *Wall Street Journal* that the country was "not a vital national interest of the United States," and NBC's *Meet the Press*, "I don't think it's a vital interest of the United States, but we clearly have an interest there."[5] Gates offered weak support for the mission already underway by couching US intervention as an assurance that a Libyan "civil war" would not destabilize Tunisia or Egypt.[6] Gates, who previously held positions as interim director and then director of the CIA, was no stranger to previous and ongoing US military operations in the Middle East and knew more about Libya than most, given a direct role in drafting threat estimates supporting US action against Gaddafi in the late 1980s, under Reagan.[7] Gates's primary interest, presumably, was in guarding American commitments in Iraq and Afghanistan, which any dramatic increase in US involvement in Libya would of course threaten.

Senator Richard Lugar (R-IN), the ranking Republican on the Senate Foreign Relations Committee, also not a newcomer to Libya issues (Lugar had been sent by George W. Bush to Tripoli in 2005 to effectively put a point on the 2003 deal with Gaddafi), amplified Gates's statements: "I personally don't think we should be engaged in a Libyan civil war."[8] Lugar, with Speaker of the House John Boehner (R-OH) led a bipartisan group within Congress pressing the president on the War Powers Resolution.[9]

Explicit in the varied debates over intervention was the question of US national interests and some notion of both proportionality and consistency. Many pointed to what they saw as inconsistencies in Obama's approach to

Libya, with respect to a passive approach to uprisings in Bahrain or Syria. Obama ultimately predicated US intervention or support on moral and humanitarian grounds—the protection of Libyan civilians. One argument that was never articulated very strongly in the lead-up or even well into the NATO operations was that of the danger a wounded, exiled but not dead Gaddafi, with access to weapons, supporters, and large amounts of undisclosed liquid assets, could potentially do to US interests. After all, this was a regime that in the past had not hesitated to use lethal force against civilians in any number of guises. The State Department implicitly acknowledged this in announcements of continuing states of emergency with respect to US-Libya relations, both during and after the fighting was over:

> [T]he situation in Libya continues to pose an unusual and extraordinary threat to the national security and foreign policy of the United States and we need to protect against this threat and the diversion of assets or other abuse by certain members of Qadhafi's family and other former regime officials.[10]

Critique of Leading from Behind

For all the complex factors at play in the assembly and execution of operation Unified Protector and the White House's attempts to explain to the American people—and Congress—why the US was not more obviously out in front (it was cost effective, inclusive, put the fewest American lives in danger), and on the other hand, why the US was in the game to begin with, reviews of evolving US Libya policy and Obama's speech went from mixed to worse.

Opponents of the Libya intervention continued to insist the US had no firm, significant interests in Libya and had a field day with the unfortunate characterization by a State Department spokesman of US strategy as one of "leading from behind." To many, this seemed to be a metaphor for indecision and even outright abdication of a US leadership role in Middle East policy. The Abu Dhabi–based *The National* called "leading from behind" a "paradoxical strategy of aggressive multilateralism, tempered by a deep sense of America's limitations," with Obama as an "eloquent progenitor and paladin of American imperial decline."[11] Many proximate to the European decision-making process on Libya felt similarly: the French military journal *DSI* described the European contribution to the NATO mission as "not reassuring," as France and the UK seemed equally muddled over its ultimate objectives.[12]

A number of commentators thought the policy, while eloquently put, simply would not work, as it left open any number of significant questions, from the need for an eventual ground force, conditions under which the UN might be engaged, to who would effect an eventual reconstruction, should Gaddafi be deposed. *New York Times* columnist Thomas Friedman, while acknowledging he had little knowledge of Libya, said Obama's speech was well phrased and "sincere," but it was "naïve to think that we can be humanitarians only from the air."[13] There appeared to be a contradiction between White House statements that "Gaddafi must go" and the failure to field sufficient force to get rid of him if he refused.

Even in France and the UK, where the Libyan operation received favorable public opinion, analysts questioned the long-term objectives and the decision-making methods. Sarkozy was taken to task for his "evasion" and lax decision-making process. The respected French military journal *DSI* opined:

> When Bernard-Henri Lévy made his presentation to the Élysée he was received by the President and his special advisor: the ministries of Defense and Foreign Affairs did not seem to be at all informed of what was happening. Is the president the only person who would know the possible military options?[14]

Others argued NATO had quickly surpassed the mandate given by UN Resolution 1973 and called into question the ethics of a NATO-rebel collaboration, in which the rebels were effectively telling NATO "what targets to hit."[15] A common question from journalists would be, how could NATO be assured civilians would be "definitively protected," as long as Gaddafi was in power?

Even as these debates were raging in Western capitals, many Libyans (still in Tripoli at the time) continued to insist they were "elated" by the NATO bombings and in fact were worried on nights when they did not hear the sorties.[16] Within Tripoli, people in neighboring houses erupted in cheers whenever they heard flights and explosion of ordinance, telling themselves it was "one less day" until Gaddafi's ouster, despite the obvious physical danger to themselves.[17] A poll conducted after the revolution confirmed resounding popular support for NATO action, in spite of US and EU doubts.[18]

The Conflict Unfolds

What many in the East referred to as a "motivational divide" between east and the west (meaning, mainly, Tripoli) was clear from almost the beginning. Eastern Libya was effectively autonomous by February 23. Once a center of power was defined there, eastern rebels held their own against loyalist forces for many months, particularly as Gaddafi focused on reabsorbing, with considerable casualties, other defecting regions. The retaking of western strongholds like Zawiya, Zwara, and Misurata, and pockets in the western Jebel Nafusa were each particularly violent.

In the east, the attitude toward Tripoli appeared initially to be one of sympathy, as word trickled back about the atrocities and deprivations experienced by those who tried to fight back against high concentrations of loyalist fighters there. Clearly, Gaddafi had a home-field advantage, and the diversity of populations within the west—particularly in Tripoli—deprived western rebels of the natural cohesiveness of the east.

Fighting in the east came to be characterized by rapid, chaotic retreats and the retaking of deserted villages by pro-Gaddafi forces. This was particularly the case in the eastern oil cities of Marsa Brega, Ras Lanuf, and Ajdabia, where tribal loyalties also came into play.[19]

As the months went on, however, and substantial progress was not made in rolling Gaddafi back in the west, many in the east began to feel that the western regions were not pulling their weight. There were murmurs that the westerners did not want liberation as badly as the east had.

This notion of western Libyan apathy could not be sustained, however, as Gaddafi's forces staged lengthy, brutal sieges to retake the major towns of Zawiya and Misurata, shelling both cities for months, often indiscriminately. The eastern fighters themselves had difficulty holding oil towns on the far outskirts of Benghazi, including Ajdabia, Marsa Brega, and Ras Lanuf. Lack of progress on the western and eastern fronts stemmed from a number of factors, foremost that they were outgunned and outtrained. Despite many army defections, loyalist forces demonstrated an early ability to adapt to new conditions created by NATO strikes, switching to light vehicles with mounted mortar launchers once their tanks became easy targets.

In the early days of the revolution, several western towns and cities had been able to convert momentum from protests and sit-ins into self-control. The most significant of these were the port city and industrial capital, Misurata, to Tripoli's east, and the town of Zawiya, to Tripoli's west, along the key coastal road to Tunisia. Misurata fell to the rebels on February 23, whereupon it was immediately set upon by loyalist forces using heavy weapons. The fight for the coastal city of Zawiya started as it did in Misurata, on or about February 24 or 26, as rebel forces were joined by a large number of defecting army troops, and government forces fired upon a sit-in at a mosque.

The tanks of the Khamis Brigade turned the tide against the rebels. Zawiya rebels had managed to hold off pro-Gaddafi forces in thick fighting with many casualties until about March 10, when the brigade assaulted the city. Its tanks took a week to regain Zawiya, before moving on to Misurata. A state of bloody siege prevailed for almost three months, despite NATO's assistance.

The tide had turned against the rebels on March 20. After days of softening with artillery fire, loyalist armored units entered Misurata and held central Tripoli Street. Loyalist snipers picked off demonstrators from within the city. Government forces staged several massive attacks on March 28, the Khamis Brigade in particular firing upon civilians indiscriminately. By early April, the rebels had lost much of the city and were holding only the north and northeast sections of the city and the port.

With Abdelfattah Younes imploring NATO to do more, the situation was deemed sufficiently dire by April 18 that the EU made plans to send up to a thousand ground troops on a "humanitarian mission." Loyalists continued indiscriminate mortar shelling and GRAD rocket attacks on residential areas of Misurata. However, by April 20, the rebel forces managed to turn things around and retake half the city. On April 22, Gaddafi's troops announced they were withdrawing and leaving resolution to local tribes. After a short hiatus, loyalists returned to shelling on April 24, hitting the city center and residential areas. During another massive loyalist assault on April 25, rebel forces countered effectively, pushing their attackers to the city perimeter by the following week. Rebels retook the airport on May 10 and secured coastal roads a few days later.

The battle for Misurata was intensely bloody. Tens, if not dozens, died each day from snipers and mortar rounds. Reports emerged that Gaddafi forces were using munitions banned by international treaty and cluster bombs, booby trapping bodies, and indiscriminately shelling residential areas. There were widespread reports that loyalist forces used helicopters painted with Red Cross insignia to attack the city. The ferocity of the battle demonstrated, first, the strength of the resolve of the Misuratan resistance, and second, the importance the regime attached to making sure Misurata did not slip into rebel hands. Gaddafi clearly hoped to forestall such a devastating blow to overall morale and security in the west, as well as any hope of regaining territory in the east.

Once Misurata was secured, the rebels expected they would be able to retake the initiative. Instead, they fell into a phase of seeming paralysis, making few if any new gains on the western front for months.

Strange Envoys and Failed Mediations

During the first few months of the revolution, many different parties offered their services to mediate the Libyan conflict. Some were covering their bets with a not yet defeated patron; others had lucrative markets and strategic attachments to protect. Still others foresaw a protected bloodbath to which they felt a negotiation solution—even one that kept the Gaddafi family in place—would be far preferable.

On March 10, the International Crisis Group, a Washington, DC–based research group—just days before Gaddafi's onslaught against Benghazi—called for "complete cease-fire" and negotiations, aimed at "replacing the current regime with a more accountable, representative and law abiding government." For the rebels, such a stance would amount to capitulation, if not certain death; Gaddafi himself showed absolutely no inclination to negotiate himself out of power.[20]

Russia and China, as per tradition, attempted to stand as long as possible with authoritarian regimes that were loyal customers for arms and other commercial deals, and good friends in a region where their influence was waning. In one of the stranger efforts, Kirsan Ilymzhinov, the Russian head of the World Chess Federation, arrived in Tripoli allegedly to try to convince Gaddafi to step down over a game of chess, as NATO bombs crackled around them. This was a vintage Gaddafi propaganda tactic that supported Gaddafi's assertions that "everything is fine."[21]

Through the end of April, the US had kept diplomatic channels with Libya more or less open on the chance that compromise might still prove to be the only viable future to the bloody conflict. Once the NATO campaign had hit full swing, however, Western governments were increasingly loathe—officially at least—to pursue these leads, feeling that they would be of little use, if not actively counterproductive. Libya discovered that many of those who had helped facilitate the relationship at its early stages were either no longer in positions of influence or unwilling to help. Tony Blair appeared to want to be as far away from Libya as possible. Of the American officials who had originally championed Libya, few were still in their original positions. David Welch, notably, had left the State Department for the international energy contractor Bechtel, California representative Tom Lantos died on February 11, 2008; Curt Weldon had lost his seat in Congress in early 2007.

Many of the African countries and their rulers were far less active in their backing of Gaddafi than he might have hoped or expected and far less supportive than his former allies in the Bush administration. South Africa, Burkina Faso, and Senegal all offered to broker cease-fires, individually and through the offices of the African Union. An African Union (AU) delegation, led by South African President Jacob Zuma, also included President Mohamed Ould Abdel Aziz of Mauritania, Amadou Toumani Toure of Mali, and Denis Sassou Nguesso of Congo-Brazzaville. They arrived in early April to try to broker a cease-fire. Gaddafi accepted the plan, while the rebels rejected any deal that would leave Gaddafi or any of his family in place. When the same delegation arrived in Benghazi to meet with NTC officials, they encountered hostile demonstrators outside the Tibesti Hotel. Lévy described how he jumped on the back of a truck with a microphone, under the eye of US envoy Chris Stevens (who had no recollection of the event), and announced to the crowd, "I am French, a friend of Libya, and I beg you to stop. The world is watching you, following you with admiration. If you give your movement an air of brutality, of violence, you will lose the advantage of your admirable revolution."[22]

Ugandan president Yoweri Musevini and Rwandan president Paul Kegame were far more circumspect. In an interview with the pan-African *Jeune Afrique*, Musevini rattled off a balance sheet of Gaddafi's good and bad deeds in Africa. While there were things to admire, such as a bold vision for African economic union and confronting the Western oil companies in the early 1970s, Musevini intimated that Africans on the whole detested Gaddafi's meddling. Particularly offensive were his attempts to rally tribal rulers, "local kings," against governments to stir up domestic opposition, exploiting religion to political ends and even attempting assassinations. In Gaddafi's mind, Musevini said the "ends justified the means."[23]

In an op-ed entitled, "Rwandans Know Why Gaddafi Must Be Stopped," Kegame argued that the AU should have been more actively consulted, if only to help prevent more such disasters within Africa: "While the support may not have been military, the AU could have offered something far more valuable—political support and moral authority for the coalition's actions on the ground."[24] Nevertheless, Kegame did not raise his voice in support of Gaddafi staying in power.

Libya still had its advocates. Curt Weldon, the former congressman, was one of the first to return to Libya. He was invited by a senior Gaddafi staff aide and, with at least the tacit backing of the US government, he sought to convince Gaddafi to step down.[25] In an op-ed published in the *New York Times* in April, Weldon intimated that he felt US had let the Libyan people—not Gaddafi—down, by not supporting the opening more forcefully:

> Sadly, in the years since my first trip, Washington has squandered many opportunities to achieve that goal without bloodshed. And unless we begin to engage with the country's leaders—even those close to Colonel Qaddafi—we may again lose our chance to help build a new Libya. . . . While American companies have made billions of dollars in Libya since 2004, they have failed to engage with anyone but the Qaddafi regime itself.

Curiously, Weldon laid the blame for the failure of the "opening" on US business:

> There's nothing wrong with American companies profiting from business with Libya. But did they also consider their larger responsibility to American interests? And where were the White House and Congress in all this?[26]

Saif Al Islam reached out to various parties in the weeks and months following his disastrous speech of February 20 and was, despite his public rhetoric, said to have tried to convince his father and brothers to compromise.[27] Though he called Libya's erstwhile champion Tony Blair, the former prime minister reportedly firmly rebuffed him. On March 18, he called Secretary Clinton to talk her out of intervention. She refused to take his call and had Ambassador Cretz tell him that loyalist troops needed to stand down immediately and Gaddafi needed to relinquish power.[28] Saif tried to send messages to Sarkozy via Bernard-Henri Lévy, who apparently told him that without decisive action on the ground favorable to ending the conflict, he was wasting his time.

Here a detail emerges that may be critical in understanding Saif's (and Gaddafi's) overall calculus. Lévy told Saif's emissary that Saif would do himself and his family well to "negotiate an exit." The emissary pointed to the television, at that moment broadcasting images of Hosni Mubarak being carted off to his jail-hospital. His point: the Gaddafis could not hope for so merciful a fate. "Mubarak," Lévy's interlocutor said, "did not have blood on his hands, he had accepted to leave power without spilling blood. . . . There's no comparison with Saif, who, himself has much, much, blood on his hands."[29] With the regime crumbling around him, Saif may have believed that there simply was no exit for him.

As the months wore on, however, the West's optimism for a somewhat neat exit for Gaddafi began to fade. While the siege of Misurata had been broken by mid-May, rebel forces appeared to be losing the initiative. Intensive NATO strikes had not dislodged Gaddafi, nor had they decisively weakened his support in the west. There had been no palace coup.

David Welch's successor at the State Department, Assistant Secretary for Near Eastern Affairs Jeffrey Feltman, met with Gaddafi advisers in Tunisia on July 17. Feltman and other State Department officials insisted there was no talk of a deal (as Gaddafi's spokesman claimed): the meetings were solely to convey to Gaddafi that he must step down. At the same time, there were indications that Washington was growing weary of stalemate and had started to explore "outs,"[30] including those that might leave Gaddafi in Libya, perhaps even in some position of influence.[31] A Gaddafi spokesman framed the meeting with three US officials in Tunis as a path to a possible "arrangement." The Russians continued working, as they would later with Syria, on a compromise to secure a cease-fire and little else.[32]

In mid-July, Gaddafi senior sent four representatives via Paris to Israel to meet influential Israeli parliamentarians, Tzipi Livni and Meir Shitreet.[33] During the meeting, the Libyans allegedly broached the possibility of providing Israeli Jews of Libyan descent funds with which to start a pro-Libya Jewish party. According to Al Jazeera, the visit was meant to "improve the Israeli view of Gaddafi" and signal Gaddafi's inclination to support normalization of relations with the Jewish state. The Israeli interlocutors were said to have described the idea simply as "strange."[34] The fact that these meetings took place at all seems to lend credence to the notion that the question of Israel had played a role in the earlier rapprochement, and that perhaps Gaddafi felt the Israelis either "owed" him or would see some use in mediating with the Americans.

On the heels of Assistant Secretary Jeffrey Feltman's meeting with a Libyan delegation in Tunis, the Libyans apparently held out hope for help from some of those who drove the original US-Libya rapprochement. Former Assistant Secretary David Welch met with two Gaddafi envoys at the Cairo Four Seasons Hotel on August 2, 2012, a few days after the assassination of rebel military commander Abdelfattah Younes (but into the final stages of the NATO campaign).[35]

Details emerged from a cache of documents found in government offices by an Al Jazeera crew after the fall of Tripoli in August.[36] The Libyans, Fuad Abu Baker Al Zleitny and Mohammed Ismail—one a Gaddafi aide, the other a close associate of Saif—wrote in their minutes that Welch had requested the meeting (Welch maintains the opposite, that the two men had contacted him about the meeting). *Asharq Al Awsat* claims Welch opened the discussion by saying, "The situation is very serious, and I say this without exaggeration, as a friend who is well informed of the situation. It is necessary to take matters in all seriousness, and with responsibility and care."[37] The article claims Welch then proceeded to outline a series of steps that the Libyans could take to help their position vis-à-vis NATO and the Americans, because even though there was "little love for Libya in the US," there was opposition to US intervention within Congress and the administration, and among some intellectuals.

The Libyans say Welch enumerated a list of "confidence-building measures" that Gaddafi might use to focus US attention on a "solution" acceptable to all sides. Welch and sources close to him insist that many of these statements were either exaggerated by the interlocutors to make his comments "more palatable" to Gaddafi, or else were taken out of context. Among the alleged "prescriptions" were that Gaddafi provide critical intelligence about links between specific members of the rebel National Transitional Council (NTC) and Al Qaeda and other extremist elements (information that might then be delivered to the Americans through the good offices of countries like Egypt, Morocco, Jordan, or Israel), and provide specific information about the probable location of munitions, particularly shoulder-launched missiles.[38] Welch allegedly encouraged the Libyans to exploit the evolving situation in Syria to their advantage, and said that what happened in Libya "would not have happened under a Republican administration," and that the US leadership was surrounded by "inexperienced advisers."[39]

After the story broke on *Al Jazeera* English and in the US press, Foggy Bottom distanced itself from Welch. A State Department spokeswoman stressed Welch's meeting was "personal," while some US officials questioned whether Welch had obtained proper approvals. A State Department official said Welch was frequently in Libya after he joined Bechtel, but was, "like any good diplomat-turned-businessman, exploiting his contacts."[40]

Welch insists he cleared the meeting with the Libyans with the Department in advance, and that the Department had confirmed this in a late Friday press briefing, where it attracted little media attention.[41] This claim is borne out by a September 1 briefing in Paris, in which State Department officials confirmed that Welch was in touch with the Department "both before and after" the meeting.[42]

The idea that the Department knew of and sanctioned the meeting is further bolstered by the fact that both the US administration and NATO were, in late August, and with no obvious end to the conflict in sight, beginning (privately, not publicly) to consider some form of negotiated solution.[43]

Regardless of who said and recorded what, and on whose authority, during the Welch-Libyans meeting, the encounter is interesting in its consistency with the statements and actions of others who had been at the center of the rapprochement process, whether Democrats or Republicans: Many clearly felt protective of the structures and relationships they had worked to build. Former Assistant Secretary Martin Indyk, a Clinton partisan, once-senior American-Israel Public Affairs Committee (AIPAC) staffer, and Welch's predecessor, said after the 2011 Libyan revolution that he felt the US had violated its commitments to Gaddafi, and that—while this was an obvious loss for Gaddafi—the "loss" of Libya would prove harmful to broader US regional interests, particularly the prospect of averting conflict with Iran.[44]

NTC Leadership Under Strain

The NTC had been a target for those in the US and EU who doubted the rebels' political competency and/or ability to influence Libyan popular opinion or manage whatever might happen after Gaddafi stepped down. Contrary to the complaints of many foreign policy observers and intervention skeptics, the NTC was not led by a group of complete unknowns. From the beginning, the public leaders of the NTC were in fact well known to the US and its European allies through various previous dealings with the Gaddafi regime and its reformist elements.

Mahmoud Jibril, the NTC's alternating prime minister–foreign minister, had a PhD from the University of Pittsburgh, and since 2007 had been a prominent member of Saif's team as head of the National Economic Development Board. Fathi Terbil, who held the Youth Affairs portfolio, was one of the key advocates for the victims of the Abu Selim massacre. Fathi Baja was known for his biting criticism of Gaddafi's regime in Saif's new media organization. Ali Tarhouni was the first and for a time the only person within the council to hold the title of minister (most of the others were named heads of committees, making decisions and statements about specific issues). Tarhouni had been in exile in the US since 1973 and had been condemned to death for sedition in absentia by a Gaddafi court. In March, he left his position as a professor of economics at the University of Washington in Seattle to serve the just-formed NTC.[45] The head of the council, Mustafa Abdeljalil came to the attention of the West through his previous efforts as minister of justice (from 2007) to moderate Gaddafi's stance on the Benghazi nurses. Abdeljalil's vice president-to-be, Abdelhafiz Ghoga was no stranger to Libyans, if less well known to the West. A lawyer and son of an ambassador, he oversaw the Libyan Bar Association for many years.

Mahmoud Shammam, a journalist living in exile in Doha until recently, headed the communication committee. General Omar el Hariri, one of Gaddafi's companions in arms in 1969, participated in the attempted coup of 1975 and was subsequently imprisoned until 1990. He became Abdelfattah Younes's chief of staff after Younes's defection to the rebel side and was then made nominal defense minister. Other members included Abdalla al Mayhoub (former dean of the faculty of law of the University of Benghazi), and Ahmed Al-Zubeir Al Senussi (the past political prisoner and focal point of the future Cyrenaican "autonomy" movement in 2011). In the early days of the NTC, there were thirty-one members, many of whom remained anonymous because of their connections in the west, which was of course, still under Gaddafi control.

On the military side, there were two personalities of note, as of mid-March, Khalifa Hifter and Abdelfattah Younes. Khalifa Hifter had spent many years in the US helping train Libyan dissidents for possible future action against Gaddafi. Hifter returned to Libya on March 14 to "take charge of the rebels' chaotic military campaign."[46] Abdelfattah Younes named head of the rebel army–Libyan Free Forces shortly after his defection on February 22, had been well known—a bit too well known for the comfort of many—as a longtime confidante and zealous partisan of Gaddafi, who held the posts of minister of public security and then minister of interior.

Younes's long service to Gaddafi was the reason Gaddafi sent him to crush the Benghazi insurrection in February. His delayed but dramatic defection to the rebel side was a significant blow to the regime, and was deemed greater than that of former head of external security Musa Kusa in March and his calls for intensified bombing critical to sustained NATO action. In the spring, Younes traveled by car to convince a group of tribal leaders near Sirte to turn from Gaddafi, instructing his bodyguards to kill him immediately if he was captured by loyalist troops. Ironically, he was ultimately killed by members of the opposition.

According to a *Telegraph* obituary:

> Younes's defection was crucial in helping the ragtag rebel forces mount an effective resistance during the early days of the fighting, and his command of the Interior Ministry brigade was believed to have been key to the decision by the rebel leaders to appoint him commander of their forces.[47]

Many continued to hold Younes responsible for Abdullah Senussi's escape from Benghazi.

As early as late March, and in the subsequent months, however, cracks began to appear in the NTC. Abdelhafiz Ghoga, then chief NTC spokesman, and others in the council seemed to contradict each other in public statements; members of the council accused Mahmoud Jibril, interim foreign minister, of spending most of his time outside the country and being "out of touch" with the people.[48]

Militarily, a clear chain of senior command was often not evident. Abdelfattah Younes entered the fold as chief rebel commander after February, while an NTC military spokesman said a few weeks later that Hifter had been appointed to the same post. Younes and Hifter feuded publicly through early April. Ghoga, then interim vice president, said: "We defined the military leadership before the arrival of Hifter from the United States. We told Mr. Haftar [sic] that if he wants, he can work within the structure that we have laid out."[49] In part to allay fears the NTC was falling apart, on May 5, the organization announced it had created an executive council, composed of ten individuals, including Mahmoud Jibril, Ali Essaoui (former minister of the economy and ambassador to India), and Ali Tarhouni.[50]

Younes' inability to command uniform respect among the disparate rebel forces (in Misurata, the Jebel Nafusa, and the east) may have sealed his fate, as it was clearly a factor in his inability to make decisive gains on either the western or eastern fronts. Lack of movement gave those who felt he was the wrong man for the job room to complain louder. The rebel military campaign reached a critical inflection point with Younes's assassination on July 28 along with two of his lieutenants, under circumstances best described as "murky" (by now a favored term in the international media for much of what was happening in Libya). Abdeljalil admitted to calling Younes in for "questioning" about possible evidence of double-dealing with the regime. As of the time of writing, it remains unclear whether Younes was killed before or after this questioning, a somewhat critical distinction.

In the days that followed, various theories emerged attempting to explain Younes's murder. But the most credible (both in the immediate aftermath, and at the time of writing) held that he was killed by Islamist elements, perhaps with the knowledge of members of the NTC, in revenge for his oversight of anti-Islamist or opposition groups in the east while working with the regime. In November 2011, Ali Essaoui, former interim deputy prime minister, was fingered by the NTC's chief military prosecutor as the source of the order to kill Younes. Essaoui, who continues to deny any connection to the assassination, was dismissed, along with several other NTC members at that time.[51]

At a press conference on the day of the assassination, *salaat al Janaza* (funeral prayers) broke out either directly outside or, according to one witness, within the Tibesti Hotel, forcing guests to crawl upstairs to the first and second floors on their hands and knees to an empty room to seek shelter from the ensuing crossfire. Word on the street was that this had been, in fact, an assassination attempt against Abdeljalil, who had delivered remarks at the hotel.

In the following days, "Oswald-like conspiracies" spread through the city, with some identifying a "Gaddafi Fifth Column," and others insisting it was an inside job.[52] Most in Benghazi seem to be willing to give Younes the benefit of the doubt. Four months later, the Tibesti Hotel was flanked by two billboards bearing larger-than-life images of Younes in military attire, above the words "Libya will not forget you." Across town, a particularly artistic piece of graffiti depicted Saif Al Islam as a small devil perched on his father's shoulder, offering him a gun (a clear play on the good Saif/bad Saif dichotomy, with the bad Saif ascendant).[53]

Younes's death—and the implication of Islamist factions within the NTC—signaled the emergence of religious agendas in the conflict. Ali Sallabi, whom we previously saw as the principal mediator between the regime and the LIFG, had called upon the US and the European Union on March 11, 2011, to aid the rebel cause by recognizing the council, providing weapons and supplies and imposing a no-fly zone, even as he tried to assure the West that the Libyan LIFG members and their associates posed no threat to Western interests.[54] Several months later, and around the time of Younes's death, he returned to Libya with access to Qatari money, attempting to beef up the Islamic credentials of the new leadership. His initiatives included the removal of "pagan" symbols—flags of coalition partners—from the main squares where daily group prayers were held, as well as encouraging local imams to issue fatwas discouraging rape victims from reporting the crimes. There was a palpable reaction against Sallabi in the commercial and NTC circles for the above reasons as well as his previous mediation role and the fact that he had openly remained in communication with the Gaddafi regime long after the conflict had started.

The situation in Benghazi in the immediate aftermath of Younes's murder was, in any event, extremely tense. Without a charismatic leader of the caliber of Younes, some felt the rebellion might collapse. Others saw his assassination as the first of a series of necessary reckonings with dissenting, armed groups, both secular and Islamist, which the NTC had been putting off for fear of forcing or exposing further divisions. These fears were exacerbated by the approach of the month of Ramadan, which meant that a lull in the fighting would offer an advantage to loyalist forces. On this basis, and given increased chafing by member nations regarding the length of commitments, NATO and the West were exerting pressure on the rebels to "wrap it up." The NTC was seen to have poorly concealed its dirty laundry. Abdeljalil quickly appointed one of Younes's cousins (and member of the Obeidat tribe) as interim successor, used the occasion to demand that the various militias within Benghazi lay down their weapons and submit to central control or face "severe consequences" and subsequently "fired" the NTC executive committee.[55] When one of the militias refused to comply with NTC orders, the latter sent units to disarm them, provoking a seven-hour gun battle on the outskirts of the city, which left plumes of dark smoke over the city in the morning light.

Yet even while chaos seemed, for a few days, to threaten to overtake Benghazi and the rebel leadership, Younes's death coincided with a decisive end to the military stalemate, whether by accident or something in the command structure that had been dislodged. The way was suddenly clear for rebel forces, those based in the east moving west, and those in the west (effectively under separate leadership) to regroup and make a decisive move on Tripoli.

PART IV

RECONCILIATION AND RECONSTRUCTION

CHAPTER 12

The End and a Beginning

Listen well, children, after seven days and seven nights, the wind abated, and, as the Fagih had said it would, Jalo was decimated. God did then forgive its sins and transgressions, and the caravans did return, and the souks buzzed anew with trade in slaves and spices, all as the Fagih said they would. But the Sultan did not return, for the ships could not sail on the surface of the desert. Know thee well: if you turn your back on Jalo, Jalo will turn its back on you.

SADIQ NEIHOUM[1]

Many expected Gaddafi's end to come as a result of a precision bomb, a suicide attack, or even an assassination by one of his inner circle within Bab Al Azziziya. This did not happen. First, he had to be dislodged from his stronghold.

Abdelhakim Belhaj led the unit that ultimately sacked Gaddafi's compound in Bab Al Azziziya. He was the same Belhaj the CIA had delivered to Gaddafi in 2004. Belhaj had been released in March 2010 as part of Saif's amnesty program for Islamists, in return for promises of good behavior. As soon as the revolution broke out, Belhaj and several others with similar backgrounds were given intensive training in Qatar and the UAE, and sent back to fight. To the embarrassment of the US (given the past relationship), Belhaj was promoted to head of the Tripoli Military Command. After militias from Zintan and Misurata—acting in concert with NATO—made the final assault on Tripoli on August 21 to 23, Belhaj was widely credited with helping "flip" Tripoli to the rebel side.[2]

Mahmoud Jibril, then alternating NTC foreign and prime minister, in an interview in *Asharq Al Awsat* on October 18,[3] insinuated that the US and NATO had purposefully delayed the quasi-coordinated rebel attack on Tripoli. He did not offer a motive. Some Libyans speculated that NATO was hoping Gaddafi might thus be flushed out to a neighboring state, where the

International Criminal Court (ICC) warrant could be served (thus avoiding a trial in Libya). An alternate speculation was that NATO and/or the US were trying to hedge their bets with respect to a possible takeover by Islamist elements, thereby preserving the possibility that Saif Al Islam or some other regime figure might be brought in at the last minute to restore the status quo if things got too messy.

Jibril said the liberation of Tripoli had been delayed three times, the third time specifically by NATO. The original date of the assault on Tripoli was to have been July 14, but, as Jibril noted, "many unexpected things happened, forcing us to delay because the necessary weapons had not arrived." NATO moved D-Day to August 17, then August 20.

For the final assault, Tripoli was divided into quarters. Each neighborhood was assigned three or four commanders, supported by groups of armed men. On August 20, NATO yet again asked for a delay, just four hours before the action was to begin. The original list of targets within Tripoli proper included eighty-seven sites, which were then winnowed down to twenty-seven, given impracticality of hitting some of them (individual apartments within high-rise buildings, for example). Two months later, Jibril linked this narrowing of targets and the fact that NATO struck only twelve of the final twenty-seven sites, to Gaddafi's escape. He suggested that details of the impending attack on Bab Al Azziziya had been leaked, just as the Italians and Maltese were said to have leaked the attack on Bab Al Azziziya in 1986.[4] "In the world of politics nothing is either impossible or unlikely," Jibril told *Asharq Al Awsat*. "The world of intelligence has rules of its own and sometimes the State says one thing and, the intelligence goes in the opposite direction."[5]

Between the fall of Tripoli on August 20 and the fall of Sirte two months later, Libya was gripped by a powerful ambivalence: a sense of relief on the part of the rebels and most of the population that the regime was done, balanced by a foreboding that arose from the fact that Gaddafi—and most of his family members—were still at large. Gaddafi had proven that he was still able to amass considerable support, in the West and South, at least, and was presumed to have access to substantial assets, through in-country loyalist networks and foreign accounts. (Many of Gaddafi's closest aides were said to have transferred currency out of the country and from known accounts outside the country into yet other accounts, for weeks before the outbreak of the revolution.) The South African government was widely rumored to have sent two cargo planes to Tripoli just before the fall of Bab Al Azziziya to pick up cash and gold bullion.[6]

Early rebel reports suggested that Gaddafi had made it to the southwestern desert oasis of Ghadames and was preparing to cross the border to Algeria, as many other members of the family would in later weeks. Saif and Mu'tassim were reported to be in the region of Bani Walid and Sirte, both loyalist strongholds. The three—Gaddafi, Mu'tassim, and Saif—exploited the environment of paranoia, calling in bold threats via satellite phone to a Syrian radio station. Few imagined that behind these threats, the Gaddafis were living a very precarious existence, traveling in small convoys from safe house to safe house.

The Gruesome End: October 20

Gadafi . . . lived and died in fear.

ASHARQ AL AWSAT, OCTOBER 21, 2011

Mahmoud Jibril recalled that "[a]nxiety was the principle motivator in [Gaddafi's] personality, and continues to be. . . . [I]t was an anxiety [rooted in fear for personal] security. I recall one time [Gaddafi] summoned me to meet with him. [I told him] the regime needed to provide for the development of the people, as this was the only path to true security. By acting otherwise, the regime was moving against the course of history."[7]

Through early October, Gaddafi was still at large. The push to take his final redoubt in his hometown of Sirte was threatening to become an embarrassment. Sirte's resilience seemed an affront to both the rebels' conception of increasing potency and the myth that Gaddafi had no support left in the country. But his time was running short; on the early morning of October 20, as rebel forces took control of the last corners of the city, Gaddafi made or was pushed to make his final move.

The NTC appeared uncertain of Gaddafi's whereabouts almost to the end. In an interview on October 18, Jibril said he believed Gaddafi was himself "safely" well hidden in the southern Ubari Sand Sea, somewhere between the oases of Ghadames and Ghat.

> I am sure he will try to return to power through the path of the Tuareg tribes in the north of Niger and South Libya, and Southern Algeria and Mali, and I believe that he has carefully prepared much of this matter. . . . He has a retributory stance and will not accept defeat, and will do anything possible to harass the new regime in Libya.[8]

Yet NTC forces on the ground sensed they were getting closer. Field reports noted "particularly strong resistance" in Sirte in the waning days of the battle for the city, leading some to suspect that "high-value" targets—perhaps Gaddafi himself—were present. Rebel officials indicated that Mu'tassim had been sighted in Sirte more than three weeks previously.[9] A few days before Gaddafi's death, rebel commanders claimed to have narrowed Saif's location to an area of desert southeast of Tripoli.[10] All the same, the fact that Gaddafi was not far away, in Sirte, seemed to come as a great surprise to many, just as unlikely as the notion that Saif would become "lost" in the desert, with a few aides, disguised as a camel-herder.

According to sources in communication with members of Gaddafi's entourage in the hours and days before his death, the circumstances behind Gaddafi's last days were less than heroic. His minders had been reduced to foraging through abandoned houses to feed Gaddafi, who by this point was virtually incoherent. Gaddafi was said to have wandered through rubble of Sirte with his satellite phone, speaking mostly to his daughter Ayesha.[11]

The atmosphere within Gaddafi's traveling circle had been contentious for days, if not longer. Most of those present or in communication with Gaddafi, including Abdullah Senussi, Gaddafi's driver Huneish Nasr, and bodyguard Mansour Dao, pleaded with the Leader to leave. Sirte would inevitably be taken, they said, and there was no easy exit.[12] Mu'tassim meanwhile insisted that the group stay in Sirte on the grounds that this would be the last place rebels and NATO forces would look for them.

As the rebel militias came closer—and fighting was raging around them—the decision was made. Gaddafi and a number of the remaining loyalist forces left Sirte proper before dawn on October 20.

Disarray in the camp forced a delay until 8:30 a.m. Many of the remaining loyalist forces banded together in this convoy, which was far larger and thus more obvious than the four or five 4x4s Gaddafi had traveled in since leaving Tripoli September 20. Britain's Sky News reported 175 cars in the convoy.[13] The events that followed, leading up to the demise of Colonel Muammar Gaddafi, came quickly, brutishly, and in the eyes of many on the outside, distastefully.

A US Predator drone, piloted from a control site in Las Vegas, spotted Gaddafi's convoy. A French Mirage received the drone's information and bombed the group, destroying one or two cars out of literally dozens. Gaddafi and key members of his group—including Mu'tassim and former Minister of Defense Abu Bakr Younes—exited their vehicles to seek cover on foot.

According to eyewitnesses, members of one of the Misuratan militias who had led the push for Sirte, set upon the remaining stragglers, executing most of them—by one account, more than a hundred people—on the spot.[14] Among the few survivors were two of Abu Bakr Younes's sons, who were severely beaten but spared, only to wind up in a Misuratan detention center for months.[15] Eyewitness accounts differ from official reports, which claim that most of those in the convoy were killed by aircraft-launched weapons.[16]

Some of what happened next was broadcast via numerous cellphone recordings. Gaddafi was said to have found refuge in a drainage pipe, when a group of young rebels found him and killed one or more of his bodyguards. In characteristic defiance or confusion, he said, alternately, "What's happening?" "You are my sons." "Show me mercy." "Don't kill my sons." Then, "*Haram Aliekum*" (shame on you all), to which one of the rebels present responded, "You don't know the meaning of shame."[17] Gaddafi was then jostled around by excited rebels, at one point touching his hand to his chest and appearing to be shocked by the sight of his own blood. The mob pulled his hair and hit him. One of his tormenters yelled, "This is for Misurata," before delivering a blow. According to the cellphone videos, Gaddafi put up a weak fight, stumbling as he went, until he was hoisted onto the hood of a 4x4. An unidentified rebel fighter pinned him down, while pressing against him with shoes, a sign of high disrespect in Arab culture.[18] Someone said, "We need him alive," and he was taken toward a waiting ambulance to be transported to Misurata. The last images available publicly show a beaten Gaddafi, a bullet hole clearly visible in his forehead.

The driver of the ambulance later said Gaddafi was dead when he first saw him. Others claimed later to know who shot him. NTC members subsequently all but acknowledged that rebels had killed him, perhaps in a dispute between members of different units, one from Benghazi and one from Misurata, each of whom wanted to take him to their leaders. Others claimed less convincingly that Gaddafi was shot on orders from abroad in order to make sure he did not reveal embarrassing information at a prospective trial. After the deed was done, one of the militiamen picked up Gaddafi's satellite phone—Ayesha was said to have been on the other end—and announced "Abu Shafshufa (a rebel moniker for Gaddafi, meaning, effectively, man with the wild hair) is dead!"

In a display of poor taste, which was defended by several senior members of the NTC, for nearly a week, the bodies of Gaddafi and son Mu'tassim were displayed side by side in a frozen-foods locker at a butcher shop in a

Misurata shopping center. A long line of visitors, including many children, came to view the bodies, perhaps seeking some sense of closure.

"We have been waiting for this historic moment for a long time. Muammar Gadhafi has been killed," Mahmoud Jibril announced on October 20. Some Libyans said they detected a note of sadness in his voice. Speaking from Benghazi, Abdeljalil expressed his regret that Gaddafi had not been brought to trial. President Barack Obama said to the Libyan people, "You have won your revolution."[19] While NTC officials expressed some regret over the circumstances of Gaddafi's death, the vast majority of the population did not seem concerned for the details, other than to say they were relieved that this chapter in their history was finally over.

Even so, the battle for Sirte continued. Pacifying Sirte remained important for several reasons; first and foremost it was Gaddafi's *muscat ra's*, his hometown and home base. Libya thus could not be considered free of Gaddafi or his influence until Sirte also fell. This focus on Sirte conveniently sidestepped the problem of ongoing violence in other pro-Gaddafi strongholds, such as Bani Walid, which would be dealt with later.

In death, as in life, Gaddafi continued to sow dissent—as his family demanded the NTC force the Misuratan militias to turn his body over to his tribe. Ultimately, four religious leaders were chosen to preside over a burial ceremony held somewhere in the Sahara, after swearing never to reveal the location.

While some details of Sadiq Neihoum's fable, the Sultan's Flotilla, the last paragraph of which is quoted at the start of the chapter, are irrelevant to Gaddafi's end—Gaddafi did not escape on a boat, nor is Sirte anywhere near Jalo—the fable continues to resonate on multiple planes: The Sultan's flotilla is a striking metaphor for Gaddafi's failed reform process; it had a positive result, from the perspective of the revolutionaries, but not for those to whom it was packaged as a solution. The desert storm (the revolution) was catastrophic, but it passed, and Jalo was left standing. The Sultan and his circle, however, were no more. As per the moral of the story, Gaddafi had indeed turned his back on the people of Libya (Jalo), and they, in the end, and euphemistically, turned their back on him.

Grim Findings

Any doubt about whether loyalist forces had perpetrated atrocities was definitely laid to rest with the discovery of a series of mass graves, some fresh, some older. According to one source, a large number of youth were discovered—many still alive—soldered inside shipping containers in the coastal town of Homs and Tripoli, and left to asphyxiate. Human Rights Watch documented eighteen deaths in this case, along with the apparent execution of forty-five detainees by members of the Khamis Brigade just before the fall of Tripoli in August.[20] Mass graves were discovered in the upscale Gargaresh neighborhood, containing two hundred to three hundred bodies; according to a rebel commander, another seven hundred had been found near Abu Selim prison.[21] More newly dug graves were discovered in Derna, east of Benghazi. In late February, early March, 157 bodies, civilians and armed rebels, were discovered in the eastern town of Bin Jawad, on the coastal road to Benghazi.[22] Mohammed Bin Lamin, the artist captured early in the conflict, described his eight-month detention and testified to HRW that only a fraction of those apprehended and placed in Abu Selim at the beginning of the conflict survived to the liberation of Tripoli. The extent of the tragedy of the *mafqoodeen*, or "missing" is highlighted by the fact that the NTC formed a Ministry of Martyrs, Wounded and Missing Persons, charged with finding and identifying officially seven thousand individuals still unaccounted for.[23]

While few Libyans—and few in the broader international community—expressed public regret for the manner in which Gaddafi died, questions arose quickly regarding the timing of Secretary Clinton's visit to Tripoli the day before Gaddafi's death. Clinton was asked in a subsequent interview if there was any connection between her visit and Gaddafi's demise. She said no, followed by a sarcastic "I'm sure it did." A YouTube video captured the moment when Clinton was informed Gaddafi had been killed. "We came, we saw, he died," the secretary quipped.[24]

It is certainly possible that the US or NATO knew Gaddafi was in Sirte: his satellite phone communications would have left some trace. Various possible motivations have been given for a conscious delay in capturing Gaddafi and his children, including the desire to push them out of Libya so they could be arrested and put into custody of the International Crisis Group. Another strategy was to hedge or buy time to arrange a deal if the situation—particularly that with the Islamists—seemed to be getting out of hand.[25] As with almost everything related to the situation in Libya over the previous nine months, mild conspiracy theories surfaced that were supported by high-level Libyans and some of the more credible international media. Mahmoud Jibril was quoted as saying he was reasonably sure Gaddafi's killing had been ordered from outside Libya.[26]

Planning Lost to Chaos

The question of what to do with Gaddafi when and if he was captured was something to which both the NTC and various bodies within the US government (and presumably, the EU and NATO) had given some advance thought, with the idea of trying to avert some of the mistakes of Iraq. There was similar dissent; many on the ground felt that a trial would be too much distraction from the pressing matter of recovery and reconstruction; others questioned whether Libya's legal system could ensure a fair trial. At the same time, many saw the ability to deal with Gaddafi and his family humanely and according to a procedure as a mark of order and a new respect for rule of law.

Given that those within Tripoli connected to Gaddafi had been increasingly hunted down and pursued in previous weeks—not to mention what happened to Gaddafi himself—as well as the supercharged and chaotic nature of the battleground and the rebels themselves—mainly youth under the age of twenty-five—made this outcome unlikely.

Many grudgingly gave Abdeljalil credit for managing conflict until this point. However, disputes within the NTC and between the NTC and those outside its sphere were rife. Mahmoud Jibril was criticized for being out of the country for large periods during late spring and summer, and for making the liberation announcement from Benghazi, not from Tripoli. Many felt this implied that Benghazi was somehow superior to Tripoli (even though Jibril himself was from the west). One citizen noted that he could understand that Tripoli may not have been safe at this point, "but if it's not safe, they should not be declaring the country liberated."[27]

Disputes within the NTC, and between Jalil and Jibril, culminated in Jibril's announcement that he would resign as interim prime minister once Libya was "liberated."[28] Along with this statement and the actual resignation came complaints that he could no longer be effective, that his orders and indeed those of the NTC as a whole carried no impact. Jibril said,

> I put forth my resignation because I have no influence. We make decisions that are then put in the trash bin. The peoples' expectations are very high and believe it is their right to do such and such . . . [but] they trying to do [replicate] what Gaddafi accomplished in 42 years, 42 days or 42 months. Does the Majlis have a plan? We are not elected.[29]

As time moved forward, and the NTC continued to be unable to provide the services expected of a national government, from meeting government payroll to making sure those without food, water, electricity, and medical assistance had what they needed, tempers flared. Militias within the various regions—from Tripoli to Zintan in the West to Benghazi in the East—which were formed from a mixture of *thuwwar*, regional and neighborhood watch associations, and fortified by a liberal supply of stray weapons, began to assert increasing control. The cities and regions of Misurata, Zintan, Tarhouna, to cite prominent examples, became almost islands unto themselves, with their own governments and standing armies—Misurata, in particular, started to take on the air of a medieval city, with access and egress tightly controlled: anyone not able to prove connection to the city (as during the Lebanese civil war, access between regions was controlled by checkpoints and code words) was denied entry, or detained. As the militia and regions amassed more control, they increasingly served as their own judges and juries, going after suspected collaborators. As the months went on, the NTC would be dogged by accusations that it was not doing enough to rein in these militias, as organizations such as Human Rights Watch and Amnesty International collected evidence of rebel-instigated torture on a reasonably wide scale, or rebel "cleansing" of areas under their control of those known or believed to have been directly associated with the Gaddafi regime. A well-publicized report published by Amnesty International in February 2012 labeled the militias "out of control," accusing of a myriad of human rights abuses, including rape and murder.[30] Some of the mid-level regime associates still present in Libya during the Liberation were able to buy their way out of the country, applying for and receiving asylum in various European countries. Others, many of whom had never been involved in atrocities, found themselves on local hit lists.[31] Some of the worst revenge attacks took place in the vicinity of Sirte, where militias from Misurata and other regions most savagely hit by loyalist forces, razed entire city blocks in acts of collective punishment (the parallels with Gaddafi's past tactics are obvious).

In the months following Gaddafi's death, rebels discovered the bodies of fifty-three loyalists in the vicinity of Sirte, their hands tied behind their backs, suspected to have been killed by anti-Gaddafi fighters.[32] African workers and migrants trapped in Libya suffered greatly in the months after February 17. Many were summarily executed purely for the color of their skin, suspected of being among those African mercenaries Gaddafi hired to wage war on his own people.[33] A video circulated on YouTube showing rebels taunting a group of black Africans being held in a cage.[34] According to Human Rights Watch, rebel forces staged revenge attacks on the neighboring town of Tawergha, where many residents were allegedly sympathetic to or assisted loyalist fighters in their six-month siege of Misurata. These attacks forced nearly thirty thousand Tawerghan residents to flee their homes.[35]

In a case that attracted little attention outside Libya, Salma Al Gaeer, a cousin of Gaddafi, a PhD pharmacologist, and one of the first recipients of the US State Department International Visitor Fellowship (IV)—one of the few to receive such fellowships solely on her own merits—was shot and killed while trying to shield her adopted son from close-range rebel fire as she and others attempted to leave Libya through Tunisia. In the wake of Liberation, one heard testimonials from individuals whose lives were, to varying degrees, "accidentally" tied to the Gaddafis, i.e., they had been married off or were clan members, but were not known and had not the resources to attempt to protect themselves from hits ordered by former neighbors and friends.

The Militias Take Over

The militias themselves were not the only threat to public order. As Azza Maghur, a prominent Tripoli lawyer, put it, there are the "freedom fighters, freedom fighters with guns, and then there are the people who are not freedom fighters, but have guns. And there are lots of them."[36] Many violent criminals had been released by the regime in the early days of the conflict to fight alongside the loyalists, and others broke free in prison rebellions both before and during the fall of Tripoli. Informal criminal associations, some under the guise of freedom fighters or avengers, roamed the city acting on tips.[37]

As of late January, there was still pro-Gaddafi fighting in one of the last cities to be put down, Bani Walid.[38] On January 23, there were resignations and demonstrations against the NTC, and Abdeljalil warned of a looming "bottomless pit" of internecine strife.[39] On February 26, there were rumors that Khamis was, if wounded, still alive and directing insurgency elements.[40] The administrative chaos in Libya and fractious decision-making processes and fuzzy rings of authority framed the urgent need for the NTC to implement not more reform, but a foundation for judicial process and security within the country. Human Rights Watch pleaded with Libya's interim government and its international supporters to "make it urgent priority to build a functioning justice system and begin legal reform that protects human rights after Muammar Gaddafi."[41]

Regime Figures Lost and Accounted For

Of the Gaddafi clan, it appears that the Leader's youngest, Saif Al Arab, along with three of Gaddafi's grandchildren, were among the first to be killed, allegedly by a NATO strike against Gaddafi's compound on May 1, 2011, though there are conflicting reports as to what happened.[42] There had been early rumors that Saif Al Arab had been spotted in a rebel protest in Benghazi, with rebel elements intimating he may have been "stage killed" back in Tripoli, to serve Gaddafi propaganda, with three of Gaddafis grandchildren thrown in for good measure to discourage any other "defections." This is complete hearsay, as there is nothing obvious in Saif Al Arab's background that would suggest a defection was in his character or inclination. But given the more credibly documented stories of a similar nature, the possibility cannot be dismissed. We know the regime exhumed bodies of adults and children alike to place by NATO strike sites, and an attempt to claim NATO was itself killing civilians, not protecting them. (There were, of course, civilian casualties from NATO strikes, these have been confirmed, even as NATO has been highly criticized for not launching a thorough investigation into the circumstances of the known collateral casualties.) Khamis was rumored to have been killed several times during the uprising, most recently in fighting in Tarhouna in late August 2011 (Abdullah Senussi was alleged to have been killed in the same fighting—a rumor that also proved false).[43]

On November 18 an armed rebel division from Zintan captured Saif Al Islam in the southern desert, allegedly as he was close to crossing the border to Niger. (His brother Saadi had turned up in Niamey, Niger, more than a month earlier and was at the time of writing still being held under "observation" by the Nigerian government). Saif's Zintani guards appear to have cut the middle and index fingers from Saif's right hand—the same fingers he shook at viewers during his infamous September 20 speech. Saif's captors flew him to Zintan, where at the time of writing he remains sequestered, as the ICC, the NTC, and the Zintan militias wrangled over his fate. Gaddafi's infamous head of Internal Security, Abdullah Senussi—whose hand was apparent in most of the major state-sponsored atrocities of the previous two decades, was apprehended by Mauritanian officials mid-March 2012, as he arrived on a flight from Casablanca to Nouakchott, where at the time of writing, he also remained under state detention. (Mauritania is not a signatory to the ICC.)[44]

Fred Abrahams of Human Rights Watch is to date the only foreigner to interview Saif after his capture. Abrahams had followed Saif's interactions with Human Rights Watch in the years prior to the Revolution, had not met Saif previously but noticed tensions within Saif. On the one hand, he said Saif responded to him with courtesy and the self-assurance of someone accustomed to being in power. He also had the look of someone who steadfastly refused to acknowledge the severity of his situation. Saif asked Abrahams to have HRW look into the situation of ten thousand or so loyalists being held by the new government. Abrahams recounted that Saif spoke as if he were still in a position of authority. At the same time, he said he noted a marked change in intensity once Saif's captors were asked to leave the room. Saif held up his partially severed, bandaged fingers, and pointed to his teeth, indicating he was in pain. Abrahams said he felt as though occasionally Saif would lapse from a brave, even relaxed front, to someone who looked very much frightened, "completely lost." Generally, Zintani militia leaders supported Abraham's observations, saying that Saif was in "good shape" mentally and physically, but "for the most part, still clinging to his previous convictions . . . and grandiloquence."[45]

Shukri Ghanem, the most visible and vocal of Saif's aides, former Prime Minister, and NOC head, was the first high-level casualty of Saif's reform circle. Ghanem defected to the rebel side in May 2011—long after the first waves—and moved to Vienna, where he had started an energy consulting group. Ghanem was found drowned in the Danube on the morning of April 29, 2012—the NTC was at the time in the process of trying to summon him back to Tripoli for questioning related to an investigation into corruption in foreign oil contracts during his tenure. As NOC head, and a key figure in Saif's entourage, Ghanem had unusual access to the mechanics of the oil-related contracts and associated money flows. While foul play was not indicated, there were many who presumably would have had an interest in this information not being made public.[46] Ghanem's concerns over being pressured by Mu'tassim to transfer money into his personal accounts had been reported in cables released through Wikileaks, and articles in the Pan Arab press. Meanwhile, Musa Kusa, who for years was pegged as the mastermind behind Pan Am 103, but whose involvement was downgraded in the media in line with his role in negotiating the Libyan-West rapprochement, found asylum in Doha, Qatar.

On May 20, 2012, the Libyan most directly associated in Western minds with Lockerbie, Abdelbasset al Megrahi, died in his home in Tripoli, almost three years—not three months as predicted—after his release on compassionate grounds by Scottish authorities, who continued to insist that prospective UK energy deals had absolutely nothing to do with his release. (The latest scandal involved attempts by British Gas, not BP, to facilitate Megrahi's release in exchange for forward movement on contracts.)[47] The NTC continued to promise to work with US and European investigators to try to unravel the many remaining mysteries surrounding Libyan involvement in the Lockerbie bombing. It is likely that key pieces of the story died with Megrahi—and Gaddafi—though there was never any indication he was willing to offer any clarity into his role and who his direct handlers were, even after the regime had fallen. One month before Megrahi's death, Al Jazeera aired a documentary entitled "Case Closed," purporting to offer evidence that would exonerate Megrahi—this amounted to little more than rephrasing of the argument that evidence collected by Maletese witnesses had been tainted—charges that had been made previously. NTC head Abdeljalil had insisted early on in the Revolution that Gaddafi had personally ordered the Pan Am attack.[48]

The first of a series of trials of senior Gaddafi officials began in early June 2012, as Gaddafi's last Intelligence Chief, Bouzaid Dorda took the stand in a Tripoli courtroom to deny the charges against him.[49] At the time of this writing, the question of what would happen, legally and otherwise, to both Saif Al Islam and Abdullah Senussi—who represented the extremes of the Gaddafi regime—remained very cloudy. Saif's Zintani guards were holding three members of an ICC delegation—one Saif's lawyer-designate—for allegedly trying to pass him communications from "dangerous allies," along with "codes." After an apparent heart attack, Senussi was still sitting in Mauritania. The problem of how to handle Saif would appear to be more complex than that of Senussi, given his past reform associations, the notoriety provided by the Gaddafi name, and the fact that there was a far greater public record of criminal actions on the part of Senussi. Many in the international humanitarian community evidenced some noticeable sympathy for Saif, and while he had been abandoned by many of his erstwhile associates within Europe's jet set, many who knew him during his London days would also countinue to express sympathy for him and insist that he was effectively a victim of uncontrollable circumstance. Many hoped Saif would indeed be transferred to the ICC, and that he might in the future shed light on the period during which he was an important protagonist.

CHAPTER 13

Assessment

According to one popular theory of revolution, people rise up against their leaders not when social and economic conditions are at their worst, but when conditions start to improve to the point where people can imagine a better future. The 2003 WMD-for-lifting-of-sanctions deal, supported as it was by a slew of consultants, commercially oriented universities, intelligence agencies and multinational companies, did several things of particular significance: First, it created a narrative, on both sides, according to which subsequent actions were judged—and judged increasingly poorly, as there were few fixed (or enforceable) deliverables on either side, other than those that related to the payment of reparations or exchange of information, for which incentives were aligned. Second, and in accordance with the "War of the Worlds" theory (see chapter 3), the US-UK-Libya deal, and subsequent rapprochement, did expose Libyans to the world (and vice versa), providing both sides a better look at what was happening inside and outside of Libya—in the case of Libya, what was possible. Third, as part of Gaddafi's effort to implement limited economic reform while skirting the issue of political reform or human rights, certain dynamics were put in place via the makeover, which, over the period of seven years managed to create a class of quasi-reformists—some still strongly attached to the regime, others pushing for fundamental change, most of whom became household names in international diplomatic circles. Controversial as many of these individuals were—precisely for the fact that they were used by the regime—they played a significant role in pushing forward and consolidating the gains of the 2011 revolution.

A Mediated, Youth-Led Revolution

Benghazi residents, and indeed most of Libya, insist that theirs was a "spontaneous" action, driven by collective rage at outrageous acts the regime committed over the course of four decades. To a large degree this is true—the youth were the fighters, the risk-takers, taking to the streets chanting "freedom or death." They found freedom, and a lot of death. They risked (and gave) their lives in countless numbers to take out Gaddafi's thugs and mercenaries, with guns, rockets, and appropriated tanks and an aircraft or two, and their bare hands if necessary.[1] Why were the youth so angry, and so vested? With a median age of 24.2, Libyans had no clear indication in 2010 that their lot would be substantially better under a partially made over Libya, as under an unknown Libya without Gaddafi or the Gaddafi clan. Despite the new money and investment, unemployment was still officially at 30 percent (Abdelrahman Shalgam claims it was closer to 40 percent.)[2] While the educational and medical system improved slightly post-sanctions, this only meant that there were more, somewhat more qualified, youth entering the ranks of the unemployed or underemployed each year.

A key question, however, is whether the Libyan youth, the raw material of the revolution, could have sustained this uprising, without an added element, a cadre that could coordinate actions in the wake of the "Day of Rage" and resulting street battles, while articulating the rudiments of a plan—on both the military and diplomatic planes; people who could persuade the outside world that this was a sustainable cause, not the makings of a state led by Al Qaeda. Gaddafi's reformists, and the concentric circles of individuals who either found reformist dialogue profitable or believed it was possible, provided this critical ingredient. Ironically, then, many people who were "of the regime" and are currently criticized for their association, may have been a necessary transitional ingredient. Would the US have responded to the pleas for help from individuals about whom they knew absolutely nothing?

Partial Reform Led to Human Networking

While the human rights situation in Libya, and press freedoms, had improved slightly, the real change initiated by the opening with the West was the formation of human social networks that the limited reform dialogue had permitted—linking citizens (particularly in the East) around issues of common concern and outrage, from the Abu Selim massacre, to the child HIV infections in the late 1990s, pervasive corruption, even reparations for land illegally appropriated during the 1970s and 1980s. The regime found itself forced, by the opening, to respond to some of the demands for increased information and compensation—to a degree. Saif Al Islam, from the perspective of many of his immediate family as well as Gaddafi's long time clients, may have fallen too much in love with his public role as reformer.

The fact that Mustafa Abdeljalil, Gaddafi's former Justice Minister, emerged within days of the first protests as the leader of the Rebel movement, and ultimately the NTC, had much to do with these networks, and past outrages. Abdeljalil was from the heart of the East, Al Beida, and as past president of the Al Beida appellate court had gained the confidence of many Benghazi families through his interventions on behalf of the Abu Salim families. As Justice Minister, he had become known to the West as a possible ally (he was said to have urged Gaddafi not to make a political issue of the nurses, and to release them—despite the fact that much of Benghazi believed they were guilty).[3] In 2009 and 2010, Abdeljalil pushed Saif Al Islam and Gaddafi to release more political prisoners (most of whom were, as one would have expected, from the East). The path from Abdeljalil's past experiences to leadership was a case study in the forces driving much of the popular revolution, and linking the people together in revolt. While Dr. Mahmoud Jibril had been lambasted in certain circles within Libya for being unable to communicate effectively with the Libyan people ("too intellectual") and as someone who had been closer to the previous regime financially and politically than had been previously revealed, he emerged at a critical time to articulate Libya's plight in a form that the West (Hillary Clinton, particularly) could understand. Whatever Libyans thought of him at the time, from the West's perspective he had a number of strong pluses: he was articulate; held a PhD from a respected American university; and he did not present as an Al Qaeda sympathizer.

Fathi Baja had been previously a correspondent and editor for one of Saif's reform-minded newspapers, *Oea* (and, allegedly, one of those Benghazi academics drafted by Saif to assist with advising/writing of his PhD thesis). He wound up being one of the principal authors of the bayan, the statement of principles of the revolution. Fathi Terbil, a tireless advocate for the Abu Salim victims (several of his family members also died in the massacre), was also someone with whom Saif had dealt directly, and one might say enabled, by providing a modicum of protection for these efforts. It was his arrest that launched pre-February 17th protests that subsequently mushroomed.

The Islamist Opposition, Commercial Activists, and Dissident Groups

While it is not wholly politically correct to admit it, either within Libya or outside, the Islamists—that is, those who fought Gaddafi under the banner of Islam, and with training received fighting the US and its allies in Afghanistan and Iraq—also played a strong role in framing Gaddafi's end. While not numerous, and while their ideas were not particularly popular, their efforts had kept the pressure on Gaddafi for the previous twenty years, and they almost managed to kill him on a number of occasions. The Islamists, in many ways, were the black dog that Gaddafi feared would ultimately get him. They were one of the main reasons Gaddafi sought common cause with the West in the fight against terror in the first place.

As part of the rapprochement and attendant reform process, the Islamists, too, agreed to compromise with the regime. Belhaj was one of the beneficiaries, having been released in 2010 via a "truce" with the regime, mediated by Saif Al Islam and Libyan expatriate cleric Ali Sallabi. In exchange for laying down their weapons, many of these leaders pledged a (temporary, perhaps) truce with a new, perhaps somewhat kinder regime. The fact that the US was now a partner with Libya in rooting out the LIFG and its offshoots must have been a factor in this decision—despite the fact that there was still no overwhelming evidence that the Libyan extremists shared significant interests with or were connected strongly to Al Qaeda and its more direct affiliates in North Africa, such as Al Qaeda in the Islamic Maghreb (AQIM).

One can draw similar parallels with some of the commercial elites, who, while vehemently opposed to the regime, looked at the deals Libya was striking with the West and figured, essentially, their choice, yet again, was between collaboration to various degrees, and exile. If they were to continue to have any say in Libya's future, it had to be through some form of accommodation. Maybe Saif would win the internal power struggle with his father and brothers. Maybe he would be better. Some believed it; others did not.

In addition to recognizing the Islamists and a few outspoken businessmen, one has to give credit to the Libyan opposition in exile, especially the National Front for the Salvation of Libya (NFSL), which, while criticized for being old (they had been at it for some time) and disorganized, kept up outside pressure on the Gaddafi regime—the fact that few listened to their dissertations on the human rights situation in Libya was not entirely their fault.

It is clear in interviews with Libyans from the various groups mentioned above that the individuals and activist groups communicated with one another, and to some extent, coordinated actions. After all, whatever their specific agendas, they had a common cause. Direct human networks played a far greater role in advancing the Libyan revolution than did Facebook, or Twitter. Without these conversations and dialogues having taken place, without the language of reform having been implanted in these groups, it is hard to see how organizations such as the 17th February Coalition, and then the NTC, could have coalesced so quickly. The fact that these bodies were not fully representative, that the process was imperfect and messy, and marked by infighting and naïvete, should not detract from the fact that the revolution, the process by which Libya, with the help of key outside allies, managed to dislodge Gaddafi and set the foundations of a government, was a stupendous achievement. What happens next is both up to the Libyans, and to forces they cannot fully control—just as was the case with the Revolution.

The Spark

For all of the cumulative suffering and the unplanned consequences of the rapprochement with the West, there still had to be a spark. The 2006 riots might have turned into an even greater problem then, had the regime attempted to repress the street as they did when the Arab Spring started. Things were far different in 2011.

Libyans who experienced the revolution in Tripoli and Benghazi described a growing feeling of frustration mixed with impotence as events progressed in Tunisia and Egypt and as the Benghazi revolt succeeded, while the Tripoli uprising failed. One Tripoli resident attributes the success of the Libyan uprising, in all seriousness, to a saying attributed to the Tunisians and the Egyptians, which most in the east and in Tripoli seem to have heard: "Keep your heads down Libyans, we want to see the real men on the other side of you."[4] The riposte, which circulated in various versions: "Hold on Egypt, hold on Tunisia; we were only bending down to tie our shoelaces, so we could deliver a real revolution."[5]

Why Didn't the West See It Coming?

There are a number of reasons the West did not see Libya's revolution—as distinct from the Arab Spring—in motion. The most obvious of the reasons I have discussed at length, that is, the subjugation of Libya-focused analysis and observation to larger foreign policy agendas—Iraq and Iran, principally—to which Libya was essentially a footnote; and the reinforcement of this overly rosy view of the status quo, via a range of commercial deals in oil, arms, and infrastructure.

In the late 1990s and early 2000s, the amount and quality of information the US and other Western governments had on events in Libya were poor at best. While much more information was forthcoming in the years 2004–2008, the inner workings of the Libyan regime were still largely a mystery, as various Wikileaks cables demonstrate. Once the extremist-oriented intelligence-gathering collaborations between the US and UK clandestine services were underway, there appeared to be an added incentive not to know exactly what was happening within the country. Even before the release of Wikileaks cables on Libya in 2010, relations between Libya and the US appeared to be declining rapidly, which also clearly had an effect on the quality of information available to senior US policymakers. As General Carter Ham, who oversaw initial operations against Libya in the campaign Odyssey Dawn, said: "We didn't have great data. . . . Libya hasn't been a country we focused on a lot over the last few years."[6] Further, "As Colonel Qaddafi [sic] began his recent crackdown on the rebel groups, the American spy agencies have worked to rekindle ties to Libyan informants and to learn more about the country's military leaders."[7]

As much as the West wanted to believe its own narrative about Gaddafi's potential conversion, those academics and policy experts who knew Libya best were, to varying degrees, highly skeptical. Many believed that ultimately—and as long as Gaddafi was at the helm—Libya would fall apart, and when it did, it would likely be messy. As Lisa Anderson commented:

> After decades of deliberate efforts to destroy the state, even the elites of this state could carry a perverse success, as Libya itself could very well self-destruct after the departure of Gaddafi. The country will divide thus between armed camps, organized around provincial or religious affiliations, and the battle which will finish by engendering a regime recognized by all Libyans or, in any case, by most of them, could last years.[8]

On the whole, most academics focused on the Middle East were too far afield of Libya to offer much insight.

The broader, regional indicators of the effects of high and chronic unemployment, corruption, and poor educational and medical infrastructures were obvious. Both the World Bank and the United Nations had produced dire reports concerning the demographic-reform crisis facing the Middle East. A 1999 report pointed out that employment specifically in North Africa, but also throughout the Middle East as a whole, needed to grow by 3.6 percent to 5 percent in order to provide sufficient jobs for young people—a much higher rate than that in the Asian and Latin American powerhouses.[9] The National Economic Strategy and a host of other documents related to Libya stressed the need for both reform and creation of a robust social safety net to protect, engage, and educate the youth and the most vulnerable elements of the population.

What About Oil?

On May 24, 2011, several hundred people demonstrated outside Buckingham Palace, where President Obama was meeting with Queen Elizabeth. Placards carried familiar slogans: "No War for Oil," "Stop Bombing Libya Now." Bumper stickers started showing up in Liberal strongholds reading "US out of Libya Now" and "No War for Libyan Oil." Many assumed, and have argued vociferously, that US intervention in Libya was really about access to the oil and not much else.

This argument makes little sense. The US was not keen to get involved in the Libyan conflict directly, as evidenced by the multiplicity of views within the US government regarding intervention. Many of the US oil companies were, as of late 2010, indeed, fed up with Libya. US and Western companies and bureaucracies had invested much time and effort in reestablishing access to Libyan energy, and the financial terms offered by the Libyans continued to compromise the viability of a number of previous EPSA concessions. That said, even as some companies neglected to renew concessions, at least two US companies remained very bullish on Libya exploration prospects.[10] Edward Morse, Managing Director, Global Head of Commodity Research at Citi Group notes, "With respect to Libya, the calculations of one company often varied tremendously from those of another," depending on a variety of factors, from technology, to records of past finds in-country, to their global portfolio.[11] The political volatility surrounding Libya in 2009/2010 (including the rapid freeze in relations with the US post-Wikileaks, and other strange events described above) very likely fed into some of the oil companies' reticence to proceed with, or negotiate, new contracts with, Libya—how much, future studies may reveal. Gaddafi's expressed admiration for Venezuelan President Hugo Chávez and his efforts to renationalize Venezuelan oil and ports were certainly not well received in the industry, or the State Department.

Moncef Djaziri, a seasoned Libya analyst, speculates that the West was becoming increasingly nervous in 2010, not so much about the fate of Libyan oil and gas resources as about the degree to which Gaddafi was courting the BRIC countries to invest in Libya and to block Western access to mineral- and oil-rich countries in Africa.[12] According to Djaziri's thesis the Arab Spring provided the Western allies the perfect excuse to upend Gaddafi, while benefiting from a more malleable National Transitional Council, "obligated" by Western intervention to favor Western companies with new contracts. This argument was presumably endorsed by those who thought Obama's presidential finding with respect to covert operations in Libya suspicious. Djaziri suggests that Germany's underwhelming support for Resolution 1973 was related to the fact that German firms had already begun negotiations with the Libyans to create a vast solar power array in the Libyan desert capable of supplying up to 20 percent of Europe's industrial energy needs.[13]

With deference to Djaziri's excellent previous studies on Libyan state and society, just as much broader perceived interests had motivated the US rapprochement with Gaddafi several years earlier, the same was likely true in 2011; Western actions in Libya would never be wholly about Libya.

A Humanitarian Hook?

The fact that the UN, the United States, the UK, France, Italy, and others (including various Arab states) were ostensibly galvanized to intervene in Libya in a mission to protect Libyan civilians from human rights violations at the hand of Gaddafi must be one of the largest ironies of the Libyan revolution, given how low such considerations had been on the list of priorities in dealing with Libya over the previous seven years. Yet Gaddafi provided an almost perfect proving ground for Western leaders who had promised to change business as usual and side with the people against tyrants. Additionally, a group within the White House and National Security Council had been waiting for a suitable opportunity in which to develop the Responsibility to Protect (R2P) doctrine, in part based on previous objections to US inaction in the face of genocides in Bosnia, Rwanda, Darfur, and so on. Regardless, Gaddafi's epic miscalculation of the international community's willingness to respond to a threatened leveling of Benghazi provided a clear situation for humanitarian-based intervention.

Were humanitarian grounds a pretext, a fig leaf, to cover other agendas? Certainly many in Benghazi felt so: one elder resident said in July, four months after the city's liberation, "We appreciate what the Americans have done. We would have been killed here without their help, and that of the French. But we also appreciate that America has interests, and must stay true to those interests. We do not expect they will solve our problems—even though many feel they should do more."[14]

What's Iran Got to Do with It?

Lurking behind the 2003 WMD deal and rhetorical rapprochement with Gaddafi was always the notion that a reformed Libya would lead Iran to follow suit and abandon its nuclear ambitions. Iran would be comforted by the US demonstrating the capability to take regime change off the table, so long as the other side was willing to make compromises as well.

In the wake of UN Resolution 1973 authorizing the use of force to protect Libyan civilians, almost all the architects of the West-Libya rapprochement insisted that Western foreign support for NATO intervention in Libya would have the greatest (negative) impact on US-Iran relations, and at a critical time. In other words, Iran would observe how quickly the US and its allies abandoned Gaddafi and conclude that it was right to have resisted dialogue about its nuclear weapons program. Another argument against intervention post-Revolution expressed in a May/June 2012 *Foreign Policy* piece evaluating Obama's foreign policy to date: the idea that by stretching the limits of the original UN mandate (Resolution 1973) to include, de facto, regime change, "We the West and the Arab world lost the support of the BRIC countries to do much about Syria." Accordingly, "Libya was always a strategic sideshow Obama helped achieve the relatively low-cost overthrow of a brutal dictator there . . . by repeatedly calling for Muammar al-Qaddafi's (sic) overthrow when UN Resolution 1973 provided for no such thing."[15] Obama confirmed Chinese and Russian charges that the West would distort the intention of UN resolutions on the matter for its own purposes."[16] The authors (among them Martin Indyk) argue that the "unintended consequence" of the NATO operation against Libya was that the BRIC countries, plus South Africa, would not support future UN resolutions to intervene in Arab Spring countries, thus has "made it more difficult for Obama to isolate the Assad regime."[17]

Take Iran: popular as it was, the argument that Libya's conversation would have a major impact on US-Iran relations was dubious from the beginning. Iran presumably knew just as well as did the US that Libya's nuclear program was far inferior to its own, and that the WMD story was "overcooked" for political purposes. Further, rather than seeing itself as another Libya, Iran would instead see that the US was willing to gamble that a partnership with someone as unreliable as Gaddafi would produce a major policy success. Khameini would say of the partnership that Gaddafi was like a child, whom the US had pacified with a lollipop.[18] Whether the US-Libya relationship succeeded or failed had little to do with Iran, where the stakes were much higher and the incentives to negotiate far less obvious.

Besides, at the time of the first stirrings of the Arab Spring, the Obama administration had already pursued a range of policies that Iran had interpreted as hostile—most notably, the ever-increasing and targeted sanctions, and harsh condemnation of Iran's crackdowns during its own Green Revolution in 2009. As Hossein Mousavian wrote in an April 2012 *Foreign Policy* article, "The Obama Administration has done more to undermine Iran over the past three years than any US presidency in the 33 years since the Iranian Revolution. Under the shadow of a policy of 'engagement,' the United States and Israel have led a campaign of economic, cyber, and covert war against Iran."[19]

Further, the Iranians were certainly not blind to the fact that the US-Libya relationship had been going downhill long before the Arab Spring. Gaddafi had after all complained vigorously that he was not sufficiently rewarded for his actions, and that Libya "would not be a model for Iran."[20] Things might have been different, had the intervention in Iraq gone significantly better. As Karim Sadjadpour of the Carnegie Endowment noted: "[T]he situation might have been different vis à vis Libya, had the U.S. made a stunning success in Iraq, and Iran not been able to acquire leverage there."[21] As we have seen, the Libya rapprochement emerged in large part from failed policies in Iraq; thus the Iranian regime would tend to see it, again, as a move taken from a position of weakness rather than strength. In any event, the parties that were most incensed by US intervention in Libya were a different lot altogether: "frequent statements from both President Barack Obama and the US State Department angered . . . America's allies in the region, who saw in the US failure to support a staunch ally and long-time recipient of US aid a sign that the superpower was not to be trusted."[22]

Mousavian's notion of an increasingly hostile US approach to Iran was supported by policy experts who argued informally that Libya was now most useful, not as an inducement to better behavior by Iran, but as an implicit threat, and an opportunity to signal that any further crackdown on its homegrown opposition was unacceptable. Ayatollah Khameini, for his part, countered by exhorting the rebels not to trust their Western "friends": they were the same, he said, as those who used to "sit and drink with those who once suppressed the Libyan nation," and were now looking to "take advantage of the situation."[23]

A Moral and Practical Question

It was not an argument that would have gone over well with a mass audience, for it would open up too many other prickly questions—but there was a moral argument for intervention that never made it into the Western press; i.e., the fact that Gaddafi could avail himself of large amounts of weaponry, much of which can be traced directly to the US's assent to, and participation in, the 2003 rapprochement. If a minority can overpower a majority with the help of weapons provided by a third party, does that third party then have a moral obligation to intervene to "even the playing field?" If the first problem did not occupy the minds of Western policymakers, another certainly did: Did the US and the West want these weapons seeping out into the hands of extremists and revolutionaries around the world, or did we prefer them to be left in the hands of a victorious or wounded Gaddafi (and we have a good sense of what that might engender—perhaps a slew of Pan Am 103s). Gaddafi may be gone, but his weapons and money are clearly still funding spoilers within Libya, and there are somewhere between $200 and $800 billion in state assets unaccounted for (Libya has engaged a series of forensic accountants to try to locate this money, but one can surmise that ultimately only a fraction of this money will be found, let alone recovered).[24]

Counterfactuals Galore

In part because of the mystery surrounding Libya and its leader, the rapprochement, and the complexity of the regional environment during the Arab Spring, it is tempting to ask a series of "what ifs?"

What if Gaddafi had taken a different tack once the protests started, that is, following the actions of Jordan and Morocco by committing to specific reforms by specific dates? After all, the 17th February Coalition initially called for specific reforms, not for Gaddafi's removal. If Gaddafi had agreed to promulgate a new constitution and hold a referendum on that document, as Mohammed VI of Morocco did on December 25, 2011, or to specific economic and political reforms, as King Abdullah II of Jordan did in mid-January, would the revolution have been contained? While the rapprochement may have primed the ground for upheaval, in the near term, it is very likely that the Gaddafi clan could have controlled the chaos, with a few bold actions—had, for example, Saif delivered the alternate speech drafted by Al Houni (an apology, promises of immediate reforms, standing down of troops), rather than ad-libbed a rambling series of threats.[25] Certainly the odds of NATO intervention would have been far lower had Gaddafi not credibly threatened to flatten Benghazi.

What if Syria had erupted in revolt a few weeks before it did, or if Gaddafi had been successful in controlling the revolt, either through repression or accommodation, until Syria blew up? The standard wisdom on this score is that the addition of new and more complex variables in the Arab Spring would have strengthened the hand of those who felt the US simply could not afford to get involved on multiple "hot" fronts in the Arab Spring.

What was really going on in Saif's head in February 2011? Was his fate sealed the moment he decided to return to Libya from London at the start of the conflict—i.e., he did not have the power to resist the forces aligned against him—or was he, as many Libyans insist, simply "his father's son, no more, no less?" Regardless, it is fascinating to watch Saif's public transformation taking place just as his father looked most vulnerable and alone—delivering his "zenga zenga" speech to an empty courtyard, looking forlorn sitting on a go-cart in light rain, holding up an oversize umbrella. It was as if the magnetic charges were reversed: those factors which impeded his decision-making abilities and led some to call him soft were no longer relevant.

Some choices are indeed too large for one person—many Libyans see Saif as indistinct from the mafia apparatus run by his father, and object to any additional attention given him over the thousands of martyrs. Others give him a bit more credit, empathizing with his situation, but expressing their view that, regardless of his personal views, resistance was futile. Yet others say that Saif was, to borrow the phrasing of Sawani, just too close to the fire—Saif's apolitical older half-brother Mohammed was a far less polarizing figure. While Saif's February 20th speech sent his erstwhile supporters running for cover, did the West cut itself off from him too soon, or did he perceive that the US was determined to see him pay? (Recall Lévy's interaction with Saif's emissary in Paris in mid-April 2011, who pointed to Egyptian President Mubarak's fate as an anti-inducement to Saif's believing he might be accorded safe passage.)[26] The number of unanswered questions, the tortuous psychodrama with the father, the good Saif–bad Saif dichotomy illustrated in the piece of Benghazi graffito, the charisma and the anti-charisma, the questions about his relationship with his current "jailers," and his ultimate fate, these make Saif's story a tantalizing psychodrama, but in a way detract from two far more interesting, and significant, issues: The role of "a Saif" (a person playing his role, vis-à-vis the West) in creating conditions that helped launch the revolution; and the even larger question of what might have happened had the US (and the West in general) exercised its influence in a more systematic, intelligent manner, starting with the initial negotiations around converting a rogue state.

What if, instead of letting external policy issues drive Libya policy, the US had paid more attention to the terms under which Gaddafi was let out of the "sanctions jail"—with advances tied not to reparation payments and counterterror compacts, but to substantive, verifiable improvements in human rights, political reform, and, yes, WMD (in which context Libyan reparations to victims of past terror might have been a side product of policy, and not a driver)? After all, counter to the post-9/11 US narrative, Gaddafi was well-documented to have been desperate for a solution, and, as former Assistant Secretary Indyk mentioned, the attitude of the Libyans in the early negotiations was one of high willingness to accommodate.

A better structured deal might have been a better deal for Gaddafi as well, to the degree it gave him the political cover against those who had, literally, done his dirty work for the previous decades and would never feel safe in a kinder, friendlier Libya. This construct, combined with some far better outcome in Iraq (i.e., no war, or a war that was prosecuted with a far greater degree of competence), might have served as a bona fide model for Iran, to the extent that the rewards to both sides (Libyan and American) were real and lasting. Most discussions regarding the failings or benefits of sanctions are framed in terms of WMD, not political reform or human rights. Most of the formal conclusions regarding sanctions are that they failed in Libya, and at the same time, they might have worked better had there been a road map, had advances in the relationship been more closely linked to verifiable moves. Several analysts, and the former head of the IAEA, Mohammed El Baradei, argued strenuously that the West did not take yes for an answer. As far as bringing Gaddafi to the negotiating table, the UN, EU, and unilateral US sanctions may be said to have worked brilliantly—it did not take long at all for Gaddafi to sue for peace (Gaddafi's first diplomatic approaches date to 1992, the same year UN sanctions were imposed). The failure was not in the sanctions regime, per se, but the overall strategy regarding how to convert sanctions to a stable equilibrium in West-Libya relations. This may have been impossible, as long as Gaddafi was in power.

The real problem, of course, comes back to the fact that Libya, and Libya's internal situation, were not the primary motivator behind the relationship—Iraq, the War on Terror, the need for a nonproliferation success, European pressure, access to oil, Israel-Palestinian relations—all of these elements had a role to play. Looked at from 2012, however, the most stark evidence of failure was the sheer amount of weaponry that the US consented to be sold to Libya. Since the US normalized relations with Libya, and the EU arms embargo was lifted in 2004, Libya purchased enormous amounts of riot control gear, small arms, ammunition, electronic surveillance equipment, military planes, and helicopters (documented to have been used on demonstrators). Russia concluded a $1.8 billion arms deal in 2010 that included "tanks, fighter jets, and air defense networks."[27] Italy exported UK£276 million worth of military equipment between 2006 and 2009. Belarus served as a "one-stop arms, banking, and transportation hub for Libya's dictator,"[28] and even sent mercenaries during the early days of the revolution. Much of these munitions were used fruitlessly in the end to try to repel the rebels.

While the US did not become a major supplier of weapons to Libya either before or after the lifting of the arms embargo in 2004, it appears this was mostly a matter of timing, as a number of US munitions and IT surveillance companies were discussing sales with the Libyans just before February 15.[29] US companies had already sold armored vehicles, later modified by Gaddafi loyalists to carry antiaircraft guns and other matériel.[30] An order for fifty US-made personnel carriers was in the works, part of a $77 million, Pentagon-approved transaction completed in late 2010, which allegedly included a contract to provide counterterrorism training for Libyan officers, as the British were doing.[31] The link between sanctions and arms sales is quite clear: In the early 1980s, Gaddafi regularly imported billions of dollars in arms.[32] By one estimate, after the UN arms embargo went into effect in 1992 and until 2003, Gaddafi was able to import no more than $10 million in arms per year from EU countries.[33] One has to assume that the Libyan revolution would have been much less bloody, and likely shorter, had this equipment not been present in country.

How "Marginal" Became "Central"

Relations with Libya seldom had any significant influence on U.S. foreign or domestic policy and seldom gained the attention of the American public. Consequently, what was good for Libya not only was not necessarily good for the United States, but often was of no interest to the United States.

RONALD BRUCE ST. JOHN[34]

The Arab Spring presented the US with a number of related, stark dilemmas. The president had promised in 2009 a new beginning with the people of the Arab world, support against tyrants, and a return to "American values." The administration clearly (to all but the most ardent conspiracy theorists, most of whom reside in the Middle East) was not expecting to be called upon to redeem its commitments immediately—but that was what happened. The US was caught hesitating on the issue of support for the Egyptian protestors versus standard assumptions of what was best for the number one ally in the region, Israel, and worst for the number one enemy, Iran. What would life without Egypt's Hosni Mubarak and Syria's Bashar al Assad look like? As the Arab Spring unfolded, the US, along with most of the world, waited on the sidelines, presumably hoping the anchor allies in the region—Egypt and Saudi Arabia, principally—would reassert control with as little bloodshed as possible, leaving the status quo intact.

Still, while France appeared to be actively supporting its client Ben Ali in Tunisia, the US did little for its own friends in the region. Tunisia, despite its deplorable human rights record, had been an ally in the war on terror. As late as January 7, 2011, the US was still urging all parties to resolve their disputes amicably.[35] The Egyptian uprising, officially dated to the January 25 Day of Rage, was under way for a week before the US administration finally tepidly called for Mubarak to leave office. This was preceded by calls for an "orderly transition," which assumed Mubarak as the steward of that process.[36] While the decision to let go of its former allies (of which Egypt was unquestionably one) and friends of convenience took some time to make, it was nevertheless a momentous move, as it no doubt played into the (largely self-interested or self-defensive) resolve of countries like France and the UK, which almost certainly would not have acted alone.

In the final calculation, the US (and more broadly, key members of the EU and the Arab League) intervened in Libya not for pure humanitarian reasons, although these were a factor. They intervened because Libya was one of the few Arab Spring countries in which the US had freedom to act without upending long-standing and economically and politically valuable relationships. At the time of the 2011 Benghazi uprising, the notion of Revolution was still more an idea than a reality in Syria, whose internal structure and sectarian divisions were far more analogous to Iraq than Libya—and thus far more concerning. Furthermore, Syria had been for decades at the core of some crucial US policy interests in the Middle East: the Arab-Israeli conflict for one, and the relations with Iran, via support for the Shiite Hezbollah in Lebanon.

In effect, Libya's famous "irrelevance" to US policy became the greatest impetus for action. As of mid-March, the Western leaders had the choice either of allowing Gaddafi to crush the uprising or of appearing impotent in front of the Arab Street and Arab leaders who had never understood why the US had ever taken Gaddafi seriously. The riposte was clear, as President Obama told the nation (and the world) after the start of the US-backed NATO campaign: "So for those who doubted our capacity to carry out this operation, I want to be clear: The United States of America has done what we said we would do."[37]

The Limitations of the Libyan Model

Not surprisingly, those who advocated US intervention in the Libyan conflict attempted to make that exercise a model for helping other Arab states caught in the throes of the Arab Spring. The most notable example was Syria, where the conflict grew for months in the shadows of Libya's uprising (and taking no little inspiration from it; there were even Libyan fighters who travelled to Syria—again, to assist). The West, and the Arab World as a whole did not respond as they did in Libya, despite the fact that the Syrian regime was clearly killing its own people on a massive scale. The main problem, of course, was that the consequences of a disintegrating Syria were potentially far higher than was the case with Libya (speaking to Gareth Evan's "proportional consequences" criterion for an R2P implementation, mentioned in chapter 10). Syria, unlike Libya, is made up of a patchwork of minorities and sects, all of whom have internal and external patrons. Further, there were no obvious internal mediators in the Syrian context, no cohesive reformist camp, no coherent statement of intentions.

Less than three months after Libya's liberation, Secretary Clinton told the UN Security Council that the world needed to stand with the Syrian people or be "complicit" in a crackdown.[38] Sarkozy echoed Clinton, proclaiming, "[W]e will not be silent at the Syrian opening."[39] This was in January. At the time of writing, in late June 2012, the crisis in Syria continued to take up the first pages of the Arab dailies and appeared to be no closer to resolution. The Russians were still backing Assad, while the US, EU, and Turkey were still talking about various ways of assisting Syrian rebels, literally at the margins, through establishing safe havens along the border with Turkey, for example, and military training. With Yemen rapidly descending into a no-man's land and Libya under Western cover, the Alawite regime represents Russia's last true client in the region (and, not insignificantly, its last unfettered access to the Mediterranean). The situation will undoubtedly evolve, as the US elections pass and the Russians and

Chinese likely realize they cannot prop Bashar al Assad's regime up indefinitely. The much talked about "Yemen solution," after the exit deal struck by Yemen's former President Ali Abdullah Saleh (according to which Assad might be granted safe passage to Moscow in exchange for a pro-Russian transitional government) might ultimately become viable, but likely not before many more are killed. Ten years hence, the Libyan revolution will likely be seen to have been an anomaly of sorts, not only with respect to its proximate causes, but also—hopefully—its success, in evolving Libya.

CHAPTER 14

Toward the Precipice

In the months immediately following liberation from the Gaddafi regime, polls showed much optimism among the Libyan people in general. When asked whether Libya was better off before or after the revolution, 34 percent of Libyans said the situation was "much better now" and 41 percent, "somewhat better." Only 11 percent felt it was either somewhat or much worse. Ninety-three percent said they believed the situation would be either somewhat or much better in a year. When asked if the revolution was "right" or "wrong," a full 82 percent of Libyans said they felt it was "absolutely right" and 2 percent, "absolutely wrong."[1] About half the respondents felt no distinction should be made between religion and politics, while only 21 percent felt the new Libyan government should make a distinction between the two spheres. Security was very much on respondents' minds: a large majority felt the government's top priorities should be to fight crime and disorder, rebuild infrastructure, and create jobs, in that order.

The National Transitional Council, now composed of some eighty members, relocated from Benghazi to Tripoli, symbolically starting a new era in a unified Libya. It brought with it not only the world's attention, but a fair degree of baggage (from the point of view of those in western Libya) due to being a product of the east.

As the days and months have gone by, however, one senses, through anecdotes, a creeping despair. One young female Libyan academic said that while she herself was optimistic by nature, she noticed what seemed to her a twenty-eighty pattern, whereby 20 percent of the people, some of them teachers, housewives, or otherwise "normal" people, had become activists, forming small associations to feed the poor, pick up trash, form neighborhood watch associations, assist with the search for the *mafqoodeen* (the war missing), or start a newspaper; 80 percent of the others, she continued, spent much of their time complaining that the nascent government was not meeting their needs.

As the militias continued to sit in Tripoli, pressing for salaries, jobs, and concessions, the NTC found itself severely challenged to maintain order. The various militias strove to strengthen their hand by taking control of key assets—like Tripoli Airport, which was held by a Zintani militia for over a month—and people, like Saif Al Islam, whom the Zintanis also held as a bargaining chip to trade for positions of political influence, such as interior minister.[2]

Meanwhile, the outlines of a transition process had been set. The NTC, still the primary executive and legislative body in Libya, named a transitional government on November 22, headed by US-educated Abdelrahim Al Keeb (at the time, unknown in Libya), and announced that elections would be held in the summer of 2012. They would not elect a new government directly, but a two-hundred-member *Mu'tammar al Watani* (National Conference), effectively another, larger transitional government. Its primary responsibilities would be to write a new constitution, which would set the overall political framework for the country, and to appoint the next (transitional-transitional) government.

While the NTC, and some of its senior members, were roundly criticized for inaction, favoritism, cronyism, inefficiency, and so on, it faced the same gargantuan tasks in attempting to satisfy pressing postwar needs in relation to ensuring medical services, creating or recreating government infrastructure, paying salaries, establishing order from mayhem, disarming the militias, and so on. Meanwhile, no one was able to tell if Abdeljalil was a strategic genius or just barely muddling through. The new government certainly had no easy time. At one point, Abdeljalil announced Al Keeb had been sacked, then retracted that announcement. Al Keeb, for his part, accused the NTC of "impeding" the process of preparing the country for elections.[3]

Chaos versus Progress

It would have been unrealistic to believe that Libya's post-Gaddafi path would be anything but turbulent—for all the reasons outlined in previous chapters. In addition to the myriad internal interests, Libya is an easy target for foreign manipulation. Qatar, while widely credited by the rebels with helping enable the revolution, is also known to be supporting the Islamist groups with money and weapons. The Algerians are providing sanctuary for the Gaddafi family members and allegedly still enable loyalist elements. The Chinese and Russians can be expected to stir the pot in Libya (as a future market and distraction from other interests, such as Syria). Within Libya, Egyptians are suspected of trying to promote discord as a means of grabbing some oil-rich lands along the Libyan-Egyptian border. As of June 2012, Tripoli remained hostage to four or five main militias from Zintan, Misurata, and Tarhouna, which doggedly refused to disband and occasionally made grand plays to wrest control of major civic assets—like the airport, again.

Attacks on the NTC offices, members of the transitional government and symbolic foreign targets, fed the sense of insecurity. A bomb was thrown at the convoy of UN envoy Ian Martin in Benghazi on April 10 (with no casualties). On May 8, militiamen stormed Al Keeb's office while he was meeting with his defense minister. An improvised explosive device was dropped outside the US consulate in Benghazi on June 6 (also with no major damage or casualties), supposedly in retaliation for a US drone attack in Pakistan that killed Abu Layth al Libi, a Libyan-born fighter and number-two Al Qaeda leader.[4] On June 10, the UK ambassador's convoy was hit by a rocket-propelled grenade, causing injuries but no fatalities. A few of these incidents have been attributed to or claimed by hitherto unknown extremist groups.

All this noise overshadows some real accomplishments, such as the fact that 50,000 and 70,000 ex-militiamen and former *thuwwar* have been integrated into a quasi-standing army, salaries are starting to be paid regularly, banks are reopening, and a number of early regional elections were held without major incident.

While most of the attention is focused on the northern population centers, the vast south remains a major concern; borders remain unsecured and intratribal fighting continues to flare up. The southern borders are entry and exit points for smuggling of all manner of military equipment, guns, drugs, and people. Problems in Libya have had repercussions in Niger and Mali, where extremist elements, backed by munitions smuggled out of Libya, have effectively staged an extreme Islamic coup.[5] Further, the south is home to a good portion of Libya's water and oil resources. The sheer number of weapons loose in Libya—and that have left Libya—remain a very serious concern. Internationally sponsored buyback programs within Libya have recouped some of the loose handheld missile launchers, but have made little progress in reducing the overall number of weapons to the point where it would actually be difficult for anyone to obtain munitions.

For those looking for a worst-case scenario with respect to the influence of extreme religion in Libya, there are certainly plenty of potentially scary stories. The eastern town of Derna reemerged in the spring and early summer of 2012 as a poster child for the lurking "Great Somalia": on March 4, the newly appointed head of the security committee for Derna, Mohamed al-Hassi, was assassinated in broad daylight at a petrol station in the city center; Abdel Hakim Al Hasadi, a former LIFG member, who had joined the revolution and denounced Al Qaeda, was attacked in Derna some days later. There have been a few car bombs, attributed to a hitherto unknown local Islamist group, *Ansar Sharia*. "Derna is not without al-Qaeda presence," one resident noted. "Al-Qaeda even has a presence in several areas in Libya, and this could be very dangerous if the National Transitional Council (NTC) doesn't pay attention and put an end to it."[6] At the same time, it is well worth noting that large groups of Dernawi residents have staged sit-ins at local mosques to protest what they feel is a foreign-instigated attempt to blacken their names and hijack their traditional, but moderate values dating back to the early days of the 2011 revolution.[7]

Managing Expectations

If one considers that the Libyan revolution began in February 2011 and continued for more than eight months, causing enormous physical and psychological casualties in addition to what the Gaddafi regime had inflicted for forty-one years, the fact that Libya is still reeling is not a surprise. Libyans have tremendously high expectations for the future in the wake of liberation. The Western media have a tendency as well to put Libya under a microscope. Libyans outside the country tend to bemoan how the country has left so many promises unfulfilled. The fact is, Libya is at the start of a long process, and, as one activist noted, "there are no guarantees."

Provisional Prime Minister Al Keeb felt compelled to address this "artificially short horizon" during a speech to the Carnegie Endowment in Washington, DC, in March 2012, "There are some who chose to dwell today on our challenges, on our differences and on our mistakes. I have no problem with that. But I believe that in so doing, they lack both perspective and an understanding of history and of the human spirit in Libya . . . and we have all the institutions of the state to rebuild from scratch, a huge challenge but a truly exciting one."[8]

As the date of the general elections approaches, the mood seems to be rising again, as reflected in mass voter registrations and an increased interest in the actual process behind the elections (as of May 15, 1,833,000 of Libya's 6 million odd citizens, close to 80 percent of those eligible, had registered to vote).[9]

Preparing for a Constitutional Assembly

Not in the manner anyone had envisioned it, but a full eight years after Saif Al Islam broached the notion, Libya has a draft constitution, whose articles appear designed to satisfy all the major interest groups. Article 1 states that "Islam is the religion of the State and the principal source of legislation is Islamic jurisprudence (*Shari'a*)" (without specifying whether the final draft would be formally based on Shari'a or merely be "in spirit" with it).

Article 4 of the NTC's draft constitution reads: "The State shall seek to establish a political democratic regime to be based upon the political multitude and multi-party system in a view of achieving peaceful and democratic circulation of power."[10] These parties, as necessary now as they were in 1951, did not spring full-blown from the Libyan dust. Predictably, the Muslim Brotherhood was one of the first to develop a formal structure, reconstituting itself as the Justice and Development Party on December 24, 2011. The *I'tilaf quwwaat al wataniyya*, or Alliance of National Forces, a coalition of "44 political organizations, 236 NGOs, plus more than 280 independent national figures," elected Mahmoud Jibril, former NTC foreign minister and prime minister, its head on March 13, 2012.[11] The alliance's platform includes "support for moderate Islam" and the "establishment of the foundations of a democratic, civil state"—something that sounds much like the Turkish model. Ali Tarhouni, the former oil and finance minister, founded his own center party about the same time.[12] While at the time of writing, both Tarhouni and Jibril were said to be discussing an alliance, the situation calls attention to many critical deficiencies in the "non-Islamist" camp—a leadership gap and organizational and capacity gaps. A third secularist alliance had been forming, but its leaders, lacking sufficient funds, decided to toss their support to the existing centrists so as not to further dilute the liberal opposition.

Advocates of the NTC say it has done its best under highly difficult circumstances, but seen from the outside, the process seems a complete mess. In a stab at political correctness, one of the first electoral laws set a quota for women candidates to reflect the active role of women in the revolution. That decision was reversed after a few weeks.

In the winter of 2011, Libya's political intelligentsia and external analysts stressed the need to encourage the formation of political parties and to reserve a certain proportion of seats for party lists as a counterweight to individual candidates, who were seen to be more susceptible to tribal influence and moneyed interests. *Asharq Al Awsat* warned that deemphasizing political parties would "open the door to a repetition of the Gaddafi experience in power, as moneyed classes, tribal interests and armed elements [militias] would have undo influence in the new state."[13] In January 2012, the NTC lowered the party quota from 136 seats to 80 seats, and increased seats available for individual competition from 64 to 120—then later reversed this allocation.

The next and perhaps deeper minefield related to regional representation: in late spring, the NTC caused a stir in the east by proposing to allot the sum of seats on a regional basis, but with quotas set according to population. In practice, this meant awarding the east 60 seats, against 102 for the west, raising the specter of renewed Tripolitanian dominance over national decision making. (Just as in 1951, the majority of Libya's 7 million people live in the west. However, much of the oil and gas resources are concentrated in the Sirte Basin, which is technically east.)[14]

This, of course, was completely unacceptable to the easterners, who saw the NTC's actions as a reversion to Gaddafi-era dominance by western interests, at their expense. In the view of those in the east, they were the ones who initiated the revolution, and furthermore, they were the ones with most of the oil. The southern regions, more disadvantaged than Benghazi to the west in terms of population, added their voices against proportionality. Thus came calls—largely from the east—for "federalism," which meant widely different things to different people. In the east, many federalist advocates pointed to the United States and the United Arab Emirates as possible examples. In any case, this was a solution, used in the 1950s, according to which the regions would secure their own interests until such time as the national government could stand on its own. In the west, federalism elicited the specter of outright secession in many, with South Sudan as a case in point. Again, the NTC reversed itself. Not only was the amendment reversed to accommodate equal representation, further plans were mooted to divide regions into smaller units, in a move that would end the anachronistic east-west-south setup that had prevailed during the monarchy.

This process of enacting and retracting electoral laws continued when the NTC outlawed participation by any party based on tribal, religious, or ethnic grounds, which, of course, sent the religious parties into a rage. Even for secularists, the idea that "parties might be good, but Islamist parties were bad," conjured up the aborted Algerian elections of 1991, when a military countercoup caused a ten-year bloodbath.

The Federalist Debate—A Red Herring?

As wrangling over representation continued at the NTC and transitional government, the people started to show signs of serious impatience; "we will take matters into our own hands," many former *thuwwar* could be heard saying. The word *federalism* reentered the political arena like a stray grenade, conjuring up, at best, images of the early monarchy period when Libya was divided into three provinces, each with its own capital. Federalism had become something approaching an obscenity for many, representing either a return to the anachronistic Libyan Federation of King Idris, which was hardly a success, or a prelude to outright secession. In March and April 2012, weeks after the first anniversary of the revolution, the entire country appeared to be consumed by talk of the evils or benefits of federalism, without really agreeing on what the term meant or what underlying regional grievances fed the argument.

Arguments over federalism heated up further after a group of three thousand Benghazi residents, nominally led by former political prisoner Ahmed Al-Zubeir Al Senussi (a direct descendant of King Idris), declared on March 6 their intention to proclaim an independent state, under Senussi's leadership. In short order, federalism came to be seen as code for an attack on the sacred notion of a unified Libya, for which the 17th February

Coalition and the NTC been fighting all along. The NTC saw calls for federalism as a manifestation of a popular no-confidence vote on its ability to govern, which was certainly deepening across the country every day. By March 6, 2012, Abdeljalil said that he would be prepared to enforce unity by force, despite the fact that NTC at this point barely controlled the Tripoli airport. The dean of an academic department at a major Benghazi university called the efforts of the "autonomy-seekers" crazy, and suggested that Senussi had Alzheimers.[15]

In an attempt to diffuse the growing talk of disunion, Prime Minister Al Keeb announced in early March 2012 that his government would pursue a strategy of "decentralization"—a concept that had been floating about since Gaddafi and Jelloud tried to devolve some limited budgetary authority back to local administrative districts (*sha'abiyat*) in the early 1990s.[16]

Not everyone was convinced of the evils of federalism or even of decentralization. Civic leaders within cities like Misurata and Barqa Benghazi said that they did not necessarily believe federalism was the optimal path for Libya, but that some form of robust local governance had simply become necessary, given the NTC's lack of control (here again, the issue may be one of semantics, as this could be called "temporary local governance").[17] As of May 17, Misurata, Zintan, and Benghazi had all held elections for local governing councils, meaning the process of decentralization had already begun, with regions electing local councils to replace those that formed organically during the revolution. Self-identified proponents of federalism argued that a weak center would be far worse than a number of stronger regional governments—again, in the interim.[18] Many pointed to Somalia and Yemen as the "next step" for Libya; after all, in the wake of its revolution (flawed, in that Saleh still has not completely relinquished power), provinces in Yemen's south have been saying they would accept nothing less than a federal structure for Yemen. They were being infiltrated by Al Qaeda.[19] (Of course, in the case of Yemen, South Yemen was previously an independent country, and since a flawed union in 1993, many in the south have been actively pushing for secession, which is not exactly the situation between eastern and western Libya.)

A principal complaint from those living outside Tripoli was that, under the current version of centralization, for any basic transaction involving a national identification, bank transfer, passport, and so on, people had to travel to Tripoli, often at considerable expense in time and money. Once there, they experienced the instability of a city under siege by representatives of every possible regional interest group, using whatever influence they could to exact services from a ruling apparatus in a city whose own administration had trouble ensuring that the trash was collected regularly.

The Future Role of Political Islam in Libya

"Whatever happens in Egypt and Tunisia, we will likely follow," proclaimed one Benghazi resident in late 2011. An Islamist government, led by the Ennahda ("revival") party in Tunis, was elected in January 2012,[20] and Islamist parties took 72 percent of the parliamentary seats. The same month, in Egypt's parliamentary elections, the Muslim Brotherhood took 47 percent of the seats, and Al Noor and other extremist or Salafist parties took 25 percent. The Muslim Brotherhood's Mohammed Morsi was elected president over former air force general Ahmed Shafiq in Egypt on June 17.[21] Thus, the diverse Islamist movement clearly has an advantage, even as suspicions of backroom deals with the military council and the supreme court, which dissolved the Egyptian parliament on June 14, left in doubt the question of exactly who will rule Egypt.

Yet Libya has always been different. Gaddafi saw to it that the Salafis[22] and even the Brotherhood never had a formidable presence in Libya, despite the fact that whatever happened across the border in Egypt had a strong impact on subterranean political discourse in Libya. At the same time, according to a prominent centrist activist, "The people are very simple, they don't think much nor do they think big, and will support simple people who suit their taste. They also, as in Egypt, would rather be in the shade of what they know, i.e., Islam and the Muslim Brothers, rather than venture into the new world of unknown parties like that of Jibril's."[23]

Libya in the 1980s and 1990s had followed the same trends as the rest of the Muslim world, with increasing numbers of educated women donning the *hijab* (headscarf). Many local women articulated this as an expression of a preference for Islamic values, in defiance of a leadership that used the vocabulary of Islam but were nonetheless thoroughly corrupt, as well as what they perceived as an encroaching materialism and the intrusion of foreign values through satellite media. An October 2011 poll by the International Republican Institute (IRI) found that 68 percent of residents in eastern Libya preferred that the national government have some religious affiliation.[24] Turkish Prime Minister Recep Erdoğan frequently attributes the success of his moderate Islamic Justice and Development Party (Turkish initials AKP) to its moderate Islamic morals and social platform, fused with recognition of the secular nature of the state.[25] Turkey's experience, born of a particular (and successful) historical experiment launched by the founder of modern Turkey Kemal Atatürk in the wake of World War I, is a concept alien to Libyan tradition and unlikely, at least in the near term, to be a practical model, despite a large number of self-defined secularists or liberals who have expressed admiration for Turkey's experience.

On the other hand, even for those with a more conservative view of the role of religion in politics, the Algerian example (where the military's cancellation of an imminent Islamist victory at the polls in 1991 led to a decade of particularly bloody civil conflict) remains very much in mind, as was seen in the framing of the struggle between the military command council and the Muslim Brotherhood in Egypt. There is no Libyan military to speak of, but the NTC and the future government cannot afford to dismiss the organized Islamic movements, the extremists, or the Gaddafi loyalists. Some feel the process underway in Libya is fundamentally flawed: "Libya does not need another provisional government," they say. "It needs a constitution."[26] The same activist echoed others interviewed, "We actually had hoped the elections would have been postponed until after we wrote our constitution and elect a parliament—and not another transitional government that is already mapped by the NTC and will do either the same or worse. I look at Iraq and fear the long-term transitional governments and what their impact can do."[27]

On May 28, Mustafa Abdeljalil suggested, then confirmed a few days later, that the National Assembly elections might indeed be delayed, citing the need to address appeals from previously disqualified candidates (which satisfied few, particularly among the Islamists and those who felt that a snap election was the fastest path to near-term stability). Some said this was yet another ruse by the NTC—and Abdeljalil himself—to hang on to power or consolidate their own influences over electoral candidates. The foreign press admonished the NTC president not to push his luck: "The NTC, which has been overseeing the country's affairs since the end of Col. Gaddafi's rule, had long promised to exit politics for five years once a permanent government was in place. But many have doubted it from the beginning and any delay is likely to feed conspiracy theories."[28]

Many in the liberal camp, however, welcomed the delayed opportunity to expose the Islamists as having hidden agendas and foreign backing, and to close liberal ranks, particularly through one yet-to-be-named party.

Reconstruction

If it were not for the problem of institution building, Libya's overall macroeconomic situation looks good (as it always has). Gaddafi did not, like Saddam, set afire or booby-trap the oil fields and pipelines (though loyalist forces did attempt to blow up the Tubruk pipeline early in the conflict). The Libyan oil infrastructure emerged from the uprising reasonably intact. Output fell to 22,000 barrels per day (bpd) in July 2011, but Libya was able to get its oil production up to half preconflict levels by the end of the year,[29] and more or less preconflict levels (1.29 million bpd) by May 16, 2012.[30] The Eastern Crescent refinery at Ras Lanuf is still not on line at the time of writing, as feedstock is sought from the Sarir and Messila fields.

While liquidity was the major issue as late as January 2012, it is no longer the country's major concern. As of April, there were no foreign exchange shortages, and most of the assets frozen by Western countries had been released to the NTC by December 16, though many billions were still missing and potentially at the disposal, although not en masse, of elements loyal to the previous regime. Foreign banks have bought into the Libyan system, increasing liquidity. Libya's Bank of Commerce and Development, based in Benghazi, approved the Qatari National Bank (QNB) Group as strategic partner. This would increase the bank's capital, which could support growth.[31]

Financial outflows are and will be large, and must be managed. Compensating the fighters, healing the war wounded, and rebuilding the basic infrastructure are necessarily top priorities. On March 15, the NTC approved an annual (2012) budget of approximately €42 billion—Libya's largest budget ever. Consistent with the need for normalization of key civilian enterprises, the largest single line item in the budget was for "Project and Development Programmes and Reconstruction." A bare majority of these funds were allocated to salaries and food and fuel subsidies, with the remainder for reconstruction and development. In the context of a raging debate over the relevance—and meaning—of federalism, the government tacitly acknowledged with its 2012 budget that, given the state of current administrative capacity, much of the decision making would of necessity need to be devolved to the regions.

As perhaps expected, given the scale of these efforts and what the NTC had to deal with, scandals emerged in short order, with tales of individuals who had not fought flying to Jordan and Europe on full government expense for non-urgent surgeries. Another plan to compensate former fighters with basic stipends with which to cover basic necessities was abruptly cut off after the NTC accused the fighters (*thuwwar*) and the leaders of various militias of embezzling large amounts of money by collecting payments on behalf of deceased or fictitious persons. Abdeljalil's decision to temporarily suspend payments until the system could be reformed created an enormous outcry, which led to further calls for him to step down and to direct attacks by the *thuwwar* on the NTC headquarters.

Addressing the Resource Curse

One of the main responsibilities of the future nontransitional Libyan government is to create a sound plan for investing in and stewarding Libya's oil resources. To avoid future wrangling over who owns what Libyan oil, the new government would do well, as suggested in a piece broadcast by National Public Radio, to look at the case of Norway, one of the few countries that did manage its oil transition well.[32] Farouk Al-Kasim, the Iraqi geologist who proposed the idea to the Norwegian government in the 1960s, said, "The Norwegian miracle is that . . . all the parties in parliament agreed on a policy, and they agreed among themselves that they will never use oil policy as a subject during elections." In Norway's case, this was made possible by an initiative that predated knowledge of just how extensive the country's hydrocarbon resources really were. In Libya, the magnitude is known, but the rebuilding of government apparatus and the rewriting of the social contract could offer an opportunity for Libya to address one of the fundamental sources of instability head on. Al-Kasim is not sanguine about Libya's chances in this regard—purely on the historical record—but the idea keeps coming up in other guises: the International Monetary Fund recommends that Libya needs to urgently "set up a clear macro-fiscal policy framework with a consistent fiscal rule reflecting the country's economic objectives and the volatile nature of hydrocarbon based revenues, and to integrate this plan assets controlled by the Libyan Investment Authority, Libya's largest Sovereign Wealth fund."[33]

One of the most urgent needs for Libya, as a wide-scale and massive retraining/retooling effort gets underway, is to provide for a social safety net for those injured, without jobs, and without access to essential services. Tribal and religious affiliations and regional militias are filling this role and, as in other such situations, will continue to gain strength in providing for basic needs. Early proposals by private businessmen to get money back into the hands of the people and to provide basic stipends for *thuwwar* were greeted enthusiastically, of course. The proposals soon proved to be major bones of contention as the lack of a system for identifying (voter rolls, so much for BPCS) eligible persons and distributing this money led to corruption, which then led the NTC to stop payments, which led to retaliation and more outrage.

One thing is painfully clear. Libya is at a crossroads: substantial progress has been made, yet serious problems remain. If these problems continue, and people continue to loose faith, the door is wide open for internal and external forces to roll back hard-won gains. It is easier to destroy institutions and political and knowledge-driven gains than to build them up.

Freedom to Speak

For anyone who spent time in Libya prior to February 2011, surely one of the most encouraging, heartening results of the February 17 revolution was the explosion of free speech and the strong participation of activist women. Throughout the revolution, youth and women joined men in support, becoming the equivalent of World War II's "Rosy the Riveter," working as lookouts, cooks, logistics agents, and medics. Afterward, women were heavily involved in creating the first NGOs, whether in the field of medicine, advocacy for the rights of women (particularly with respect to war-related and domestic violence), and their own community assistance groups and newspapers.

Reading copies of *Miyadeen,* one of the first postrevolutionary magazines (printed in Cairo, as Gaddafi had bombed the radio stations and printing presses), *Al Libi* (*The Libyan*), or *Sawt,* one is struck by the fact that the turgid, meaningless language of the Revolutionary Committees, which controlled practically all media before the revolution, has been replaced by thoughtful, eloquent, provocative articles criticizing NTC members, and debating the relevance of the Muslim Brotherhood and the Salafists. The newspaper *Arus Al Bahr,* launched in August 2011, announces itself as a publisher of direct commentary and brazen criticism "even if it hurts or shocks."[34] Attempts to control speech, whether through intimidation by militias or individuals, or even members of the government unhappy with what people are writing (there have been a few cases of militia members showing up at the editorial offices of publications that have printed unflattering stories about them), have been met with a flurry of editorials insisting that Libya's healthy political future is intimately and inextricably bound with freedom of speech.[35]

In another of many inspirational acts, a group of teenage youth (boys and girls) in Benghazi created a radio station called Tribute FM that broadcast messages and songs to the rebel frontlines, as Gaddafi's troops were at the city limits. Within a month of the fall of Benghazi, the first fourteen radio stations, the majority of which were centered in Benghazi. There are now twelve TV stations (originally in Benghazi, most now based in Tripoli) and forty-three newspapers in Libya, covering a range of topics, but still very much focused on the revolution and postrevolution.[36] While some complain that the militias are emerging as a new force to threaten press freedoms, on the whole this seems to be a minor consideration for those who write. Those who run most of Libya's new crop of printed media say that the main barriers are cultural and technical—creating a culture of reading, not just for critical information—as well as the availability of printing presses and technical assistance.

For an outsider, this media renaissance is one of the most inspiring and hopeful consequences of the Libyan revolution. Where previously, one had a choice between reading one of two turgid government-run papers, *Al Zahf al Ahdhar* (*The Green March*), run by the Revolutionary Committees, and *Al Jamahiriyya*, there are now several high-quality, highly informed publications, which—reports of militia interference notwithstanding—express a range of views and challenge almost everything. Though many in the current climate might prefer temporary stability to chaos, and security to freedom of speech, these are freedoms Libyans wanted for decades and that many died to obtain, both before and after the revolution.

Benghazi Rises—Again

Despite Western-Libyan fears of Benghazi going rogue, in early June 2012 the city appeared to have undergone a transformation or maturing process that the rest of the country had yet to experience. National and local papers pointed to Benghazi as a sign of the country coping and as a model for national elections and the process of educating people about the political process. The skittishness and nervousness that pervaded the city in the wake of the killing of Abdelfattah Younes—still unsolved—are largely gone and replaced by a determination among large segments of the people to get their own affairs and municipal affairs in order, while waiting for the center to sort itself out.[37] Prominent citizens dismissed the so-called Benghazi autonomy movement as marginal or even crackpot, while stressing that foreign interests were behind much of it—from Egypt coveting Libyan oil and real estate by encouraging federalism, to Qatar funding Islamist elements.

In the lead-up to elections for Benghazi's local governing council, held May 17, there were fears in both the west and the east that Benghazi might see deeper violence. Two car bombs went off near the Benghazi courthouse, which had acquired fame as the kitchen of the revolution. There was an attempted assassination of NTC member Khalid Assayih (another member, Fathi Baja, was in the car), as they drove into Benghazi from the airport on May 15.[38]

On May 17, Benghazi held the first ever elections for its local council, electing forty-four representatives to run the administrative affairs of the city—eleven of these will be seconded to the NTC until it is disbanded after the National Assembly appoints a new government, when they will return to serve the local council. To the surprise of many, elections proceeded in a peaceful and orderly fashion, with only isolated acts of violence and minimal need for oversight or protection of polling sites. The top vote getter was a female university professor, Najat Al Kekhia, a cousin of Mansour Al Kekhia, a former Libyan minister of foreign affairs-turned-dissident whom Gaddafi had "disappeared" in Cairo in 1993. A political novice, Al Kekhia beat forty-three candidates from the region of Berka, to become, effectively, the first female mayor of Benghazi.

It was rare to see anyone in Benghazi whose right index finger was not stained with the residue of voting ink.[39] The national (former dissident) paper *Libya Al-Youm* ran an article on May 28 extolling the Benghazi elections as a case study for the national elections.[40] This kind of positive story was dwarfed by the coverage of a homemade bomb that exploded near the US consulate in Benghazi a few days later.

The Engagement Imperative

Libya's position is somewhat anomalous to that of the other states of North Africa; rich in oil, it does not need grants and international loans, at least in the mid- to long term. This is reflected in the fact that international lending organizations, like the European Bank for Reconstruction and Development (EBRD), have not allocated assistance budgets for Libya, which they have for Tunisia and Egypt. Libyans are the first to say they do not need money; they need expertise.

Several initiatives have been set up to provide technical assistance to the Arab Spring states, in particular, Tunisia, Libya, Morocco, Jordan, and Egypt. These include the G8's Deauville Partnership created in May 2012, and a number of small-scale USAID-funded initiatives to support such priorities as employment creation, economic and social inclusion, private-sector expansion growth, regional and global integration, governance, rule of law, anticorruption, and postconflict health (rehabilitation, emergency medicine, etc.), some of which are funded by the US State Department's Middle East Partnership Initiative (MEPI). G8 countries have also committed to form a Financial Services Advisory Corps, to advise states in transition (including Libya) on good governance and fiscal management.

A USAID circular published in summer 2012 says the US government is "particularly focused on engaging marginalized populations, youth, and women, and increasing opportunities for their voices to be heard and their interests to be considered in decision-making that will shape Libya's future."[41] As of summer 2012, USAID had committed $29 million of a total of $91 million spent specifically on humanitarian assistance—about a tenth of the total US contribution to the military component of the NATO effort.[42] Press releases aside, the record of international, postconflict humanitarian interventions is often mixed. Before the end of the campaign to oust Gaddafi, nascent Libyan NGOs and institutions in transition complained that a large percentage of the international consultants were not useful, as they had neither the requisite language nor technical skills. The US government did bring a small number of war wounded to a Boston hospital (the effort was not an unmitigated success).

Some foreign entities have developed strong local followings. Creative Associates—one of the USAID contractors running MEPI grants and capacity-building programs in Tripoli and Benghazi, and agencies engaged by USAID to support small-scale rehabilitative and governance trainings—appears to have made a strong name for itself, in terms of the usefulness of its grant-making processes and outreach. Karama, a Cairo-based women's rights organization, has been supporting a number of democracy-awareness-building, lobbying, and organization campaigns in Tripoli, Misurata, Benghazi, and Derna, through local partners such as the women's platform for peace (*manbar al marrat al libiyya min ajl assalaam*).[43] These efforts are important for giving women and youth the strategic communication tools required to articulate individual and party platforms, but also to lobby on behalf of legislation relevant to the electoral process itself, such as the geographic spread of National Conference seats.

Despite pockets of foreign goodwill, many mainstream Libyans feel they are fighting a simultaneous battle against time and money they cannot win. As the head of a Benghazi community group complained, "Most of the NGOs are very weak and not properly managed—they are not getting sufficient support from the government, which of course is preoccupied with a million other crises, and they all want to become political parties, which means they're not doing the work they set out to do."[44]

In the two weeks before July 7, 2012, however, the national mood seemed to lift, as reflected in mass voter registrations and a rise in interest in the actual process behind the elections. As of May 15, 2012, roughly 1,833,000 of Libya's 6-million-odd citizens, close to 80 percent of those eligible, had registered to vote.[45] On election day itself, the polling experience largely mimicked what took place in Benghazi a month and a half before: 62 percent of voters cast their ballots for more than 3,000 candidates in a process that appeared to be both free and fair—and, a few incidents notwithstanding, orderly. There were reported instances of Libyans forming human cordons to protect polling places from possible attacks or disruptions to the vote.[46]

For many Libyans, both inside and outside the country, the election was one of, if not *the* most emotional experience they had had since the outbreak of the Arab Spring. Many said they felt it was a tangible sign that Gaddafi was gone and that the country had a future as a result. To the surprise of many, Mahmoud Jibril's self-described "centrist" party—Jibril took pains not to say "secular"—the Alliance of National Forces, took a plurality in the National Assembly, thirty-nine seats, versus seventeen seats for the Muslim Brotherhood, and none for Belhaj's Nation Party. At the time of this writing it appeared Libya would be "unique" in being the first Arab Spring country to elect a non-Islamist-dominated government.[47] One commonly heard explanation in Libya for why the Islamist parties did not do better was that many Libyans felt the Muslim Brotherhood and similar groups were trying to present themselves as "more Islamic" than everyone else, while allowing themselves to become instruments of the Qataris and the Saudis. While it will take weeks if not months to parse the character of the new government, given the large number of individual candidates with unclear tribal and religious affiliations—not to mention connections to the former regime—developments are positive, and appear to confirm the "uniqueness" of Libya's experience.

The chief medical officer at the Benghazi Medical Center, Dr. Laila Bugaighis, an MD and longtime advocate for women's rights in Libya, stresses the importance of Libyans reaching out to the outside world, expressing both their needs and understanding the outside countries' interests: "We will only move out of this drama if we start communicating with USA, UK, and France and know what they exactly want. Also we need to have our constitution written; otherwise we will not get out of this vicious circle of chaos we are in."[48]

Challenge from an Ex-Guantanamo Islamist

Abu Sofiyan Bin Qummu, the ex-Guantanamo detainee, has been tagged in the foreign press as one of the most extreme of Derna's West-hating Salafists. Yet in May, he gave an extensive interview in a local Derna paper in which he insisted he had no overt sympathies with Al Qaeda. "There was huge oppression of Derna during the Gaddafi reign," he said. "We do not want to repeat all that again—it is necessary not to marginalize Derna. We need good education, and solid housing; we need to assume our rights, meaningfully, and materially along with the rest of the Libyan cities."[49]

The United States and the West would be wise to respond to this challenge in force: helping the transitional and eventual permanent government rebuild and reengage the areas where desperation rules would do much to counter the proliferation of extremist ideologies. Relatively small actions can have big impact—a new clinic in a place like Derna, financed and staffed by Western organizations, a national diabetes campaign, greater connectivity, and so on. These are all things that are relatively cheap, for which the Libyans themselves can certainly pay and could demonstrate to the citizens of Derna and elsewhere in Libya who oppose extremism (currently, the majority) that they have national and international support.

A Return to Exceptionalism?

Libyans weakly acknowledge the efforts of the US government. Most Benghaziites recognize French assistance, before American. The reasons for this include the fact that the French and British have talked about their political roles substantially, while the US "led from behind." Further, European companies are closer to Libya, have longer commercial relationships, and are far more willing to operate under conditions of uncertainty. This was true during the rapprochement, as it is now.

Regardless, the situation in Libya currently screams of opportunity for the United States and US firms and individuals to pick up traces of the "American exceptionality" that was created in the 1960s from an odd mutual respect (if imbalance) between the United States and the nascent Libyan state. That exceptionality continued to be exemplified and sustained by projects such as the more than two hundred Esso-sponsored fellowships for graduate study in the US, which created a kind of "fifth column" within the Libyan establishment during the rapprochement: a group that would mouth lines from Gaddafi's *Green Book*, while reminiscing about football games at Louisiana State.

Apathy is not universal. A number of US firms, some familiar to the Libyan scene, some very new, have been looking for ways to contribute to local welfare. Amerada Hess, for example, has attempted to adopt the cause of diabetes prevention and treatment (the company recently sponsored a STEPWise survey, supervised by the World Health Administration).[50] Two Harvard-affiliated teaching hospitals and the Benghazi Medical Center (a twelve-hundred-bed facility, originally built in 1984 and mothballed by Gaddafi until 2009, as part of his collective punishment of Benghazi citizens), are discussing the possibility of developing BMC into a hub for emergency medicine in eastern Libya—a multimillion-dollar effort.

The situation is ripe for the United States, in particular, but the West as a whole, to reinvigorate that notion of American exceptionalism. Do we collectively want to repeat the mistakes of the past and find ourselves facing a Gaddafi in other garb? Postrevolutionary Libya has demonstrated courage and the desire for active participation in government and civil society. Yet enormous obstacles and well-funded spoilers remain. In order for the many Libyans at home and in the diaspora to contribute effectively, they must feel that the chances of success are at least as good as those of the revolution itself.

While there was a solid rationale behind the US strategy of "leading from behind"—militarily—this does not or certainly should not apply to reconstruction and organizational, technical, and commercial engagement. Libyans never responded well to offers of charity, even in hard times. Yet Libyans have historically been tremendously appreciative of the efforts of those who showed up during difficult times with the tools they needed. While the Obama administration is right in saying it will deal with moderate Islamists if they play by the rules of the game—we may have no choice—the best way to ensure Libya does not retreat into intolerance and isolation is to engage wholeheartedly in commerce, culture, education, and medicine.

CONCLUSION: THE WEIGHT OF THE PAST

Make the Revolution a parent of settlement,
and not a nursery of future revolutions.

EDMUND BURKE
REFLECTIONS ON THE REVOLUTION IN FRANCE

If there is one theme that runs through the story of the Gaddafi regime and the colonel's exit, it is the role of the past, that is, to what extent countries and individuals are shackled by their previous experiences. If there is hope for Libya—and indeed, Western policy in the Middle East—it is contained in the fact that time and human interactions produce discontinuities, which like genetic mutations, contain opportunities for adaptation. Looked at from a different perspective, Libya is not a near-failed state, but a fresh canvas. As a prominent Libyan businessman said recently, "If we Libyans truly want it, Libya can be fixed in no time. We are just 6 million people—a modest multiple of General Motor's global workforce. We are wealthy, and we are not extreme by nature."[1]

Popular discontent with King Idris and the still-fresh memories of the Italian occupation gave a poor, undereducated but singly focused person such as Gaddafi the opportunity to stage an unlikely coup; Gaddafi's early experience and deprivations conditioned his half-baked worldview, as well as the tools and strategies he used to maintain power and provoke the West. The Lockerbie (and UTA) bombings appear to be manifestations of Gaddafi's burning desire to right what he saw as past wrongs committed upon him by the outside powers, not only for ordering the raids against him in 1986 but for any number of slights to his person and policies.

The United States decided to engage with Gaddafi after a separation of over twenty years, for reasons that had far less to do with Libya per se and any of Gaddafi's idiosyncrasies, but more with a fixation on the recent past: What to do about a horrendously planned and incompetently executed invasion and reconstruction of Iraq, which itself followed from 9/11, which itself can be linked to US support for the Afghan *mujahideen* against the Soviets back in the late 1970s, through the creation of Al Qaeda.

Due to a collection of historical anomalies, the 2003 deal with Libya—notwithstanding its context—afforded an opportunity for both sides, Libya and the West, to make a break with the past, to refashion the relationship into something more mature and potentially sustainable. That Gaddafi did not rise to the occasion is not a tremendous surprise. By the same token, one would have expected the more stable, advanced, knowledgeable bureaucracies of the West to understand Gaddafi's game and inoculate themselves against it. They didn't.

The fact is that, fundamentally, neither side saw the potential of the deal, understood what it represented to the other, or made particular effort to parse it. Thus, historical factors and other pressing policy issues blinded both sides to potential discontinuities. Gaddafi, by accounts, was briefly surprised by his success in springing his country from sanctions, but was too enamored of himself (and paranoid) to consider that his future might be brighter if he actually went faster with a reform plan, rather than sticking to the superficial makeover. The United States and the West were, generally, too distracted by the apparent low-cost media distractions and financial benefits to think beyond the short term.

Halfway measures on both sides and, equally important, the absence of any precise commitments to actuate or (more importantly) enforce reform, in the form of a unified Western approach to sanctions, led to a situation in which each party—the West and Libya—could (and did, loudly) claim the other had reneged on original terms of the deal, whether these had to do with Lockerbie payments, the disposal of parts related to Libya's WMD efforts, the disposition of convicted Pan Am bomber Megrahi, and so on, thus effectively invalidating the deal and creating opportunities for new kinds of side deals and creative misunderstandings. Gaddafi, further, was (perhaps literally) like a schizophrenic who had gone off his medications—without a strong structure to enforce good behavior, relapse was practically assured.

One moment Gaddafi was celebrating his amazing success and a few new titles (King of Kings of Africa, for one), and the next he was face to face with a major catastrophe. True to his nature, and to history, instead of doing something different, he offered a knee-jerk reaction, when a more progressive touch might still have saved him (or at least bought the regime time to make more considered decisions). The window for a potential resolution in favor of a live exit for Gaddafi appeared to have been open for some months. When he was finally pulled from a drainpipe in Sirte in October, Gaddafi was Neihoum's Sultan, facing the black dog, cast as a Misuratan militia, twice-victimized: once by Gaddafi's past policies, and a second time by relentless loyalist shelling of their hometown. One of the most intriguing cases in the Libyan saga of history conditioning the present lives in the Leader's self-styled diplomat son, Saif Al Islam, his role in the rapprochement and remake of Gaddafi's Libya, and subsequent turn against a process he claimed to champion. Saif may, or may not, have been a reformist at heart. Some who knew him insist he was, and would have done great things for Libya had he been given the chance. Others (themselves not in a position to cast stones) claim to have seen evidence of a dark side, years before February 2011: simmering anger and resentment at the position his father (and History, with a capital H) had put him in and a proclivity for violence that may have, until that point, been sublimated to a far greater extent than in his brothers, but was not fully under control, either.

While most commentators attributed Saif's dramatic transformation to the circumstance of war and the possibility of the loss of privilege, one might just as well tie his change in behavior to a sudden, twisted change in psychological orientation vis-à-vis his father. As we have seen, Saif was not able, over the course of several years (though he appeared willing at various points), to push reform into the realm of politics. He was certainly not able to convince his father or brothers to ease up on the uprising once it began, whether or not he tried. Once Gaddafi had made the decision to fight to the last man, Saif went from what former Assistant Secretary David Welch called "somewhat soft," to exhibiting exactly the kind of qualities that might have enabled him to retain the Gaddafi dynasty, had it not been too late—decisiveness, perhaps ruthlessness, a clear vision of what he wanted, or needed, to accomplish. From all of this emerges, however, a question for any prospective judge and jury: does the fact that Saif's actions had a positive effect in loosening the media and human rights climate in Libya prior to the Arab Spring—and in creating this new class of "regime-enabled, half-in, half-out reformists," who would play such an important role during and after the revolution—mitigate whatever crimes he may have committed shortly before, or after, February 17, 2011? Ironically, the Iraq debacle conditioned both the US and Western involvement in Libya since 2004, and also conditioned the desire of President George W. Bush's successor, Barak Obama, to try to reassure the people of the Middle East that the United States was, in fact, capable of change and a return to its founding values, which he attempted to do through the 2009 Cairo address. While many in the region dismissed the speech at the time as eloquent talk, it clearly played a key role in the US response to Libya's spring.

On the Libyan side, there were those who wanted to convince the world (the Libyan people, and themselves, presumably), that Gaddafi's Libya could change. When the Revolution arrived, these people—former regime officials, regime interlocutors, Saif's direct associates (about whom much has been written here), and others who served as regime mediators—convinced the Libyan people that they were sufficiently "anti-Gaddafi" that they could be trusted to guide the revolution. All said, collectively, they did a pretty good job.

While many would challenge Washington lobbyist Randa Fahmy Hudome's pre-Revolution statement that Saif deserved a Nobel Prize for his role in the West-Libya rapprochement, without a "Saif-like figure" and "his people," the Libyan version of the Arab Spring would likely have taken a very different course—and not necessarily a better one. When Saif chose to stand with his family and regime, his previous protégés stepped in to fill the void. With Saif now playing the role of his father, they collectively became, and did, what Saif perhaps could not have been, or done.

With Libya's liberation from Gaddafi's regime, it arrived at a new, odd, and—with hefty recognition of the personal sacrifice made by the Libyan people—fairly accidental, discontinuity. Ten years from now, we may find that the contours of history have been redrawn, or re-traced: a new strongman, a repressive Islamic state. Or, one might find that all, or parts, of North Africa has reached a more or less comfortable equilibrium under a collection of representative governments in which moderate Islam is the principal political currency; or Libya will continue to prove its "uniqueness" in safeguarding its Islamic character under a more or less secular, representative government. It is too early to tell. The fact that, as of July 7, Libya had succeeded in holding free and fair elections, one national and several local, and that an alliance of "non-Islamist, culturally conservative moderates" had won 80 and 60 percent, respectively, of the vote in Tripoli and Benghazi—and a majority in the infamous city of Derna—vindicates those who insisted a year earlier that Libya was a "wholly different animal" from Iraq, Somalia, and Afghanistan. Despite the very real constraints facing the United States and the West with respect to intervention in other Arab Spring states (Bahrain and Syria are the two most obvious cases), the fact is the West *did* intervene in Libya; the United States did *not* repeat the mistake it made in buying off the Karamanli warlord before William Eaton and his Benghazi soldiers could overthrow him (nor, for that matter, did the US repeat the "watch and see" approach pursued during massacres in Rwanda or Bosnia). The Secretary of State has reinforced US willingness and interest to deal directly with moderate Islamic groups, wherever they gain power through popular mandate, and as long as they "follow the rules."[2] This would all seem to be very reasonable and evolutionary. At the same time, it is important to ask, given how much history was ignored in the formulation of the West's recent policies toward Libya: What have we learned? What are we doing now to assure that the subterranean "American exceptionalism," the bonds formed by the United States with Libya in the late years of the monarchy and the early years of Gaddafi's reign, is unearthed and restored in a manner that helps Libya avoid falling back into dysfunction, which, if it resurfaces, will inevitably come back to bite the West again?

While Gaddafi was the cause of most of his and his people's problems, the United States and the West made some truly gargantuan mistakes in their dealings with the Great Jamahiriya and its leader: some were errors of omission and neglect. The US policy apparatus tends to be a reactive, not a proactive, organism. Thus, once Libya (and to a large extent, Iran) disappeared behind their respective sanctions-sealed curtains, the requisite American expertise disappeared with it. US foreign policy pays dearly for such discontinuities, some of which date back to Henry Kissinger's notion, somewhat crudely put, that diplomats should be generalists, lest they be at risk of "going native." The Middle East during the Arab Spring provides stark examples of the costs of this short-termism. When a country deemed unimportant or isolated from frequent diplomatic commerce suddenly becomes critically important, the necessary expertise is simply not there—whether political, linguistic, or historical. The blank whiteboard leaves policy further open to manipulation by organizations and individuals whose interests are not necessarily at one with those of the nation.

In the case of Libya, the information gap with respect both to Libya and Iraq, and the Middle East writ large, allowed Gaddafi to run circles around many of his American and European interlocutors, while appealing to the venal interests of individuals and organizations everywhere. The pure scope of postrapprochement extortion by the Gaddafi *after* his so-called redemption shows that many politicians and governments, in many countries, either were not paying attention or did not find it in their interests to pay attention. One cannot afford to be naive, but the sheer speed and size of the revolving doors between government, lobbyists, individual politicians, oil companies, arms dealers, and their counterparts in the Libyan government is truly astounding.

While the Libya case may be—and is being—explained as a kind of passive neglect, the relationships between the United States and Western Libya exhibited far more active abuses. While the US preached "good governance" under the administration of George W. Bush, it was simultaneously an egregious violator of these same principles, selling arms (or, practically as bad, allowing arms to be sold) to Libya, and worse, literally delivering individuals to Gaddafi's front door with all but the weakest of caveats against torture—without really knowing much about these people or their motives. The fact that so many weapons were sold with zeal by the West to Gaddafi in the lead-up to the revolution, and that the US, the UK, and other countries actually participated in a program to deliver some of Gaddafi's enemies to him on a plate for torture, should by rights be cause for far greater outrage by the American public than has hitherto been the case.

As the Libyan revolution unfolded, many argued that the United States had no business intervening militarily in Libya. Few, however, were aware of the scale on which "we," the West, had been intervening in support of Gaddafi for the previous seven years. Is it better not to intervene or to try to level the playing field to correct past wrong? There are those who would argue that the Bush administration was right; the "War of the Worlds" thesis proved accurate. New ideas seeped in, and a revolution was born. This may be true, but at what cost in human lives? As I have argued in this book, the rapprochement with the West—and the US in particular—combined with Gaddafi's particular paranoid worldview, very likely sent the Gaddafi regime hurtling toward a nasty end. The problem, of course, is that it also led to huge casualties across the Libyan population. The estimates vary widely, but even on the low end, at the time of writing, top the single-country tallies in the Arab Spring: 25,000–50,000 dead, between 1,000 and 10,000 missing, and between 20,000 and 50,000 wounded, with a substantial number seriously wounded.[3] The US was the last hinge in Libya's acceptance back into the international community, with commensurate rights and privileges, including the right to buy massive amounts of weaponry.

Many contradictory statements have been made about Libya's role in US foreign policy, the importance of the rapprochement process, and the Arab Spring. The WMD agreement has been called "[p]erhaps the greatest counter-proliferation success of our time," yet the US intervention in Libya, part of a "strategic sideshow."[4]

Regardless of the motivations behind such claims, what happens in Libya over the next ten years will likely prove to be very relevant to the new Middle East, as it was to perceptions of the US support for limited change in the Middle East during the Arab Spring. While, again, nothing is certain, Libya has already shown its ability to produce discontinuities; if it continues on this path, change can be celebrated and used to motivate new changes in the region.

The US and the West do not have to wait to implement change—they should deliver as much technical assistance as Libya is able, and willing, to accept (and pay for). And they should accept the lesson Libya's recent history offers with respect to the link between human rights and international security. As the late Soviet dissident Andrei Sakharov said, "A country that does not respect the rights of its own people will not respect the rights of its neighbors."[5]

ACKNOWLEDGMENTS

THIS BOOK WOULD NOT HAVE BEEN POSSIBLE without the assistance of literally hundreds of people—Libyans, Americans, and others—who took real personal risks in speaking with me, both before and after the Revolution. I would like to thank, in particular, Maria Sturgis for her patience and support, innumerable conversations about related experiences, and extremely helpful challenges to my arguments over the course of the year it took to write this book; my father and my good friend David Grudoski for their patient readings and helpful comments on numerous drafts; my trusted partner Omar Benhalim, with whom I embarked on a complex and emotional series of return trips to Libya while the revolution was still under way. I am greatly indebted to Professor Dirk Vandewalle of Dartmouth College, who encouraged an interest in Libya since we were both residents at the American Institute for Yemeni Studies in Sana'a in the late 1990s, and whose work is the basis for any study of modern Libyan politics and economy.

In no particular order: Khaled Mezran, Karim Mezran, Safa Naili, Professor Saad Al Ghariani, the Hon. Abdelmoula Lenghi, Ambassador Aref Nayed, Husni Bey, Jalal Husni Bey, Adel Husni Bey, and Najat Husni Bey, for their interest and conversations on Libyan politics and commerce; Sandra Charles for her immense help with referrals and for speaking with me at length about her own experiences and impressions of Libya pre-2004; Ahmed Ibrahim Al Fagih, whose fiction served as an inspiration for my first book on Libya. Basem Tulti, Maged Mahfouz, Fawzi and Ali Tweni, Nurredin Tulti, Mohammed Binlamin, Shaib Agila, Ibrahim Sahad, Ahmed Shebani and Youcif Megaryaf. Professor Robert Springborg, Professor Chris Taylor, Dr. Laila Bugaighis and Dr. Fathi Jehani at Benghazi Medical Center, Professor Claude Ghez; Dr. Issam Hajjaji, Burhannedin Al Muntasser, Allaedin Al Muntasser, Khaled Mezran, Hafed Alghwell, Professor Tarik Yousef, Professor Grigory Barenblatt, The Volk family, Dr. Diana Pickworth, Judy Schalick, Peter Michael Kuchkovsky, Peter Lenhardt, and Anne O'Leary, for their long-term friendship, support, and encouragement.

I appreciate conversations with Assistant Secretary Elliott Abrams, Assistant Secretary David Welch, Tom Sams, Cherie Loustaunau, Assistant Secretary Martin Indyk, Assistant Secretary Richard Murphy, Ambassador Charles Cecil, Ambassador David Mack, Alan Makovsky, Ambassador Chris Stevens, Dr. Martin Quinn, Wayne White, Dr. Greg Berry, Anne O'Leary, Robert Waller, Leslie Tsou, Cecile Sakla, Virginia Ramadan, Rashidah Ellis, and Heather Kalmbach. A word to honor Dr. Salma Al Gaeer, a friend who was killed during the Revolution by people who knew nothing of her personal sacrifices, only their own; and my friend, Mohammad Binlamin, who spent most of the Revolution incarcerated in Abu Selim prison. At Human Rights Watch, Fred Abrahams and Sidney Kwiram were both particularly helpful, and inspirational; Andrew Feinstein, Karim Sadjadpour, Dr. Claudia Gazzini, Dr. Igor Cherstich, Gordon Church, Will Ward, and the inimitable and highly resourceful JF Hulston.

Writing this book was a constant struggle against time, inconsistent reports, and a subject that kept moving and twisting from the date I started research, in April 2011, to submission of the final manuscript in July 2012. There will necessarily be mistakes and omissions, for which I alone bear full responsibility. I hope that this book will encourage others to look into aspects of the US-Libya relationship in even more detail, and ask even tougher questions.

On the production side, sincere thanks are due my editor at PublicAffairs, Brandon Proia, for his insight and skill in helping shape the book, and Lisa Kaufman, Melissa Raymond, and Jaime Leifer, for both their hard work and navigation of a range of unforeseen complications. Last but not least, I would like to thank my excellent research assistant, Bashir Megaryaf, upon whose resourcefulness I relied on many occasions; W. Scott Chahanovich, for assistance with formal transliteration of Arabic sources; and Omer Abu Saleh at the Saudi Research and Publishing Company, for his archival assistance.

Appreciation goes to Lynn Gaspard at Saqi Books, for her interest in the then-just-begun Libyan Revolution, during an interval when many were not sure how interesting a story it would be, to Rukhsana Yasmin at Saqi for comments on an early draft, and to Professor Tony Sheldon and the Yale School of Management, for hosting me on an unrelated project but accommodating a trip to Libya during that time.

I spent many hours in many places writing this book. In that context, I'd like to thank for their hospitality the very friendly and indulgent staff in Berkeley at Teance, Imperial Tea Court, Café Strada, O Chamé, and Nefeli; and Gale Garcia, who rented me an exceptionally pleasant space to write for several months.

Ethan Chorin
Berkeley, California, July 2012

NOTES

INTRODUCTION

1. aṣ-Ṣādiq an-Nayhūm, The Sultan's Flotilla ('An Markab Assultan') in *Translating Libya*, Ethan Chorin, trans. (London, England: Saqi Books, 2008), p. 95–102.

CHAPTER 1

1. Projected capital and running costs for fifty years. See http://www.temehu.com /great-man-made-river-gmmr.htm.
2. Chorin conversations with Dr. Sa'd al-Ġariyānī in 2005.
3. This was a variant on a set of proposals dating back to the 1960s to divert the Ubangi to create new agricultural regions from reclaimed land.
4. Which puts the $1 trillion US expenditure on the Iraq War in some context.
5. See http://205.254.135.7/countries/cab.cfm?fips=LY.
6. *CIA World Factbook*, 2012–2013.
7. Judith Gurney, *Libya: The Political Economy of Oil* (Oxford, England: Oxford University Press, 1996), p. 87.
8. Danielle Bisson, Jean Bisson, and Jacques Fontaine, *La Libye: A la Decouverte d'un Pays*, Tome 1: Identite Libyenne, L'harmattan Paris, 1999, p.21.
9. Ibid., p. 26.
10. Ibn Ḫaldūn, *Muqaddimah*.
11. John Wright, *A History of Libya* (New York: Columbia University Press, 2010), p. 67.
12. Ibid., p. 93.
13. Samuel Edwards, *Barbary General: The Life of William H. Eaton* (Englewood Cliffs, NJ: Prentice Hall, 1968), p. 61.
14. Russell D. Buhite, *Lives at Risk* (Wilmington, DE: Scholarly Reources Books, 1995), p. 11.
15. Ibid., p. 12.
16. Gregory Fremont-Barnes, *The Wars of The Barbary Pirates* (Oxford, England: Osprey Publishing, 2006), p. 39.

17. Edwards, *Barbary General: the Life of William H. Eaton*, p. 89.
18. Barnes, *The Wars of the Barbary Pirates*, p. 41.
19. *Ahlam Abu Zeida, and Abdulrizaq Qarira, Mabnā al-Qunṣuliyyah al-Amrīkiyyah, Manšurāt Mašrū' Tanẓīm wa Idārāt al-Madīnahal-Qadīmah bi-Ṭarāblus.* Idārat at-Tawṯīq wa ad-Dirāsāt al-Insāniyyah, Tripoli, 2004.
20. Edwards, *Barbary General: the Life of William H. Eaton*, p. 28.
21. Joshua E. London, *Victory in Tripoli: How America's War with the Barbary Pirates Established the U.S. Navy and Shaped a Nation* (Hoboken, NJ: John Wiley & Sons, Inc., 2005), p. 113.
22. Ibid., p. 219.
23. Ibid., p. 117.
24. Barnes, *The Wars of The Barbary Pirates*, p. 41.
25. London, *Victory in Tripoli*, p. 233.
26. Dirk Vandewalle, *A History of Modern Libya*, 2nd ed. (Cambridge, England: Cambridge University Press, 2012), pp. 16–18.
27. Ibid., p. 21.
28. Ibid., p. 22.
29. Wright, *A History of Libya*, p. 112.
30. Ibid., p. 128.
31. Ibid., p. 133.
32. Ibid., p. 130.
33. Ibid., p. 131.
34. Issam Hajjaji, "Healthcare in Libya," unpublished, January 2012.
35. Bisson, Bisson, and Fontaine , *La Libye*, p. 86.
36. John Wright, *The Emergence of Libya* (London, England: Silphium Press, 2008), p. 330.
37. Ibid., p. 333.
38. Issandr El Amrani, "Is There A Libya?"*London Review of Books* 33, no. 9, 2012, pp. 19–20.
39. Wright, *The Emergence of Libya*, p. 333.
40. Ibid., p. 336.
41. Bisson, Bisson, and Fontaine, *La Libye*, p. 90.
42. Mustafa Ben Halim, *The Years of Hope*, English trans. (London, England: AAS Media Publishers, 1994), p. 119.
43. Not altogether different from US concept of "transformational democracy" more than fifty years later, according to which development assistance would go to countries that had made substantial progress toward democracy and the war on terror.
44. Ben Halim, *The Years of Hope*, p. 129.
45. Muḥammad Yūsuf al-Maqaryaf, *Lībīyā bayn al-Māḍī wa al-Ḥāḍir*, al-Qāhirah: Maktabat Wahbah, 2006, p. 95.
46. Gwyn Williams, *Green Mountain*, Dar Al Fergiani reprint (orig. London, England: Faber & Faber, 1963), p. 83.
47. Richard Goodchild, *Benghazi: The Story of a City*, Department of Antiquities Cyrenaical Libya, 1962 (Reprint), p. 26.
48. Gurney, *Libya: The Political Economy of Oil*, p. 42.
49. Dennis Gidney, "Esso Standard Libya Inc (ESL) Training and Development Program pre-1982," unpublished.
50. aṣ-Ṣādiq an-Nayhūm, *al-Ḥaqīqah*, 1969, unknown publisher.
51. El Amrani, "Is there a Libya?"
52. Libyan human rights lawyer Azza Maghur, in the wake of the 2011 uprising, posted to Facebook rare photos of masses of women marching through downtown Benghazi in the early 1960s, demanding the right to vote—another sign of the unexpected mix of liberal and conservative currents coexisting in the east at this time.

53. Nicholas Hagger, *The Libyan Revolution* (Johannesberg, South Africa: Alternative Books, 2009), p. 56.
54. Musa Kusa, "The Political Leader and His Social Background: M. Qadafi, the Libya Leader" (University of Michigan, Ann Arbor, 1978), unpublished MA thesis in sociology, p. 143.
55. Hagger, *The Libyan Revolution*, p. 54.
56. Mohammed Hassanein Heikal (then editor-in-chief of *Al Ahram* newspaper and a trusted advisor to Nasser and Sadat), arriving in Benghazi shortly after the coup, was said to have remarked famously: "Where is Abdulaziz?" (a reference to Shalhi), a remark many saw as a subterfuge to disguise Nasser's involvement and/or knowledge.
57. The year of Gaddafi's birth is unknown; he may have been twenty-six at the time.
58. This thesis evidences more than a little forethought on Kusa's part—and would certainly have been noticed by, and appealed to, Gaddafi for its well-articulated but still obvious praise for Gaddafi's "charismatic personality" and comparisons with Gandhi, Ataturk, and (indeed) Hitler as a leader able to forge powerful sociopolitical movements.
59. Kusa, "The Political Leader and His Social Background," p. 142.
60. Douglas Kiker, *The Atlantic*, June 1970, quoted in Kusa, p. 60.

CHAPTER 2

1. See http://www.youtube.com/watch?v=5dqn9Hwf-H0; Agnelli: Fiat and the Network of Italian Power; Alan Friedman, New American Library, 1989, New York, p 194
2. Stephen Dorril, *MI6: Inside the Covert World of Her Majesty's Secret Intelligence Service* (New York, NY: Touchstone, 2000), pp. 793–794.
3. Ibid., pp. 736–737.
4. Chorin interview with Ahmed Ibrahim Fagih, November 21, 2011.
5. Chorin interview with Ambassador David Mack, November 2011.
6. ʿAbd ar-Raḥmān Šalġam, *Ašḫāṣ ḥawl al-Qaḏḏāfī* (Dubai: Dār al-Farğiyānī/Madārik Publishers, 2012), p. 11.
7. Chorin interview with Omar Benhalim, October 2011.
8. Fāṭimah Ḥamrūš, "Hal Kān bi-Imkān Wālidī an Yuğannib al-ʿĀlam Diktūriyyat al-Qaḏḏāf'i?" (Was it possible that my father could have averted Gaddafis dicatorship?) *al-Kalimah*, November 20, 2011.
9. Ḫālid Maḥmūd, "Lībīyā: al-Istiqālāt taʿṣif bi-l-Mağlis al-Intiqālī . . . wa Ḥakūmat al-Kīb Taltazim aṣ-Ṣamt," *aš-Šharq al-Awsaṭ*, January 23, 2011.
10. Ibid.
11. Ġāzī bin ʿAbd ar-Raḥmān al-Qusaybī, *al-Wazīr al-Murāfiq*, 2nd ed. (Beirut: Arab Center for Studies and Publishing, 2001), pp. 125–126.
12. Chorin interview with Ahmed Ibrahim al-Fagih in Cairo, November 25, 2011.
13. Chorin interview with Wayne White, April 2, 2012.
14. See http://www.dailymail.co.uk/news/article-1336783/WikiLeaks-Colonel-Gaddafis-phobias-flamenco-dancing-voluptuous-blonde-nurse.html.
15. Bob Woodward, *Veil: The Secret Wars of the CIA, 1981–1987* (New York, NY: Simon and Schuster, 1987), p. 441.
16. Ḫālid Maḥmūd, "ad-Duktur Maḥmūd Ğibrīl yukaššif li-aš-Šharq al-Awsaṭ ʿan Muḫaṭṭat al-Qaḏḏāfī li-l-ʿAwdah ʾilā as-Sulṭah," *aš-Šarq al-Awsaṭ*, October 18, 2001.
17. Dirk Vandewalle, "The Failure of Liberalization in the Jamahiriyya," in *Qadhafi's Libya 1969–1994*, Dirk Vandewalle, ed. (New York, NY: St. Martin's Press, 1995), p. 209.
18. Yahia Zoubir, *Islamisme Radical et Lutte Antiterrorist: Maghreb-Machrek*, no. 184 (Summer 2005): 53–66, p. 55.
19. Mohamed El Jahmi, "Libya and the U.S.: Qadhafi Unrepentant," *Middle East Quarterly*, vol. XIII, Winter 2006, pp. 11–20.

20. Not to be confused with the United Arab Republic, linking Egypt and Syria from 1958 to 1961.
21. John Wright, *The Emergence of Libya* (London, England: Silphium Press, 2008), p. 347.
22. Issam M. Hajjaji, "Healthcare in Libya," unpublished article, January 2012.
23. Waniss A. Otman and Erling Karlberg, *The Libyan Economy: Economic Diversification and International Repositioning* (Springer: Berlin, 2007), pp. 146–147.
24. Hajjaji, "Healthcare in Libya."
25. This achievement should be measured against what he did *not* do, given the vast resources at the regime's disposal, and the fact that within twenty years of his assumption of rule, more than 20 percent of the population would be either below international development institutions' measures of poverty, or unemployed, or both.
26. Dirk Vandewalle, *Libya Since Independence: Oil and Statebuilding* (Ithaca, NY: Cornell University Press, 1998), p. 81.
27. Ibid., p. xxiv.
28. Ibid., p. 66.
29. Ibid., p. 67.
30. Omar El Fathaly and Monte Palmer, "Institutional Development in Qadhafi's Libya," in *Qadhafi's Libya 1969–1994*, Vandewalle, ed., p. 171.
31. Ibid., p. 161.
32. George Joffe, "Qadhafi's Islam in Historical Perspective," in *Qadhafi's Libya 1969–1994,* Vandewalle, ed., p. 149.
33. Musa Kusa, "The Political Leader and His Social Background: M. Qadafi, the Libya Leader," unpublished master's thesis in sociology, University of Michigan, Ann Arbor, 1978, p. 81.
34. Chorin interview with Benhalim, May 31, 2012.
35. Vandewalle, *Libya Since Independence*, p. xxvi.
36. Vandewalle, "The Failure of Liberalization in the Jamahiriyya," in *Qadhafi's Libya 1969–1994,* Vandewalle, ed., p. 210.
37. Moncef Ouannes, *Militaires, Elites et Modernisation dans la Libye contemporaine* (Paris: L'Harmattan, 2009), pp. 102–109.
38. Hanspeter Mattes, "The Rise and Fall of the Revolutionary Committees," in *Qadhafis Libya 1969–1994*, Vandewalle, ed., p. 97; *ʿAbd ar-Raḥmān Šalġam, Ašḫāṣ ḥawl al-Qaḏḏāfī*, p. 470.
39. Aḥmad Ibrāhīm al-Faqīh, *aṭ-Ṭāġiyyah fi-t-Tarīḫ, Muqaddimah fi Tašrīḫ aṭ-Ṭāġiyyah*, unpublished, 2011, p. 46.
40. See http://www.mongabay.com/history/libya/libya-the_revolutionary_committees .html.
41. See http://sijill.tripod.com/victims/.
42. Woodward, *Veil*, p. 367.
43. Aḥmad Ibrāhīm al-Faqīh, *aṭ-Ṭāġiyyah fi-t-Tarīḫ, Muqaddimah fi tašrīḫ aṭ-Ṭāġiyyah*, unpublished, 2011, p. 57.
44. Otman and Karlberg, *The Libyan Economy*, p. 54.
45. The International Court of Justice gave the Aouzou strip back to Chad in 1994.
46. "Aseer harb Tchad yarwi hikayatih," Abdelaziz ʿIsa in *Wifaq Libya*, October 29, 2011, p. 6.
47. al-Faqīh. *aṭ-Ṭāġiyyah fi-t-Tarīḫ*, p. 26.
48. William J. Foltz, "Libya's Military Power," in *The Green And the Black*, René Lemarchand, ed. (Bloomington, IN: Indiana Universtiy Press, 1988), pp. 62–66.
49. See http://memory.loc.gov/service/mss/mssmisc/mfdip/2005%20txt%20files /2004jos01.txt.
50. Ġāzī bin ʿAbd ar-Raḥmān al-Qusaybī, *al-Wazīr al-Murāfiq*, 2nd ed. (Beirut: Arab Center for Studies and Publishing, 2011), p. 123.

51. Moncef Djaziri, "La Crise de Lockerbie," in *L'annuaire de l'Afrique du Nord* (Paris: CNRS, 2000), p. 187.
52. Michael J.Graetz, "Energy Policy: Past or Prologue?," *Daedalus*, Spring 2012, p. 32.
53. Larry Collins and Dominique Lapierre, *The Fifth Horseman* (New York, NY: Simon and Schuster, 1980).
54. Chorin interview with Ambassador David Mack, December 2011.
55. Djaziri, "La Crise de Lockerbie," p. 184.
56. Ronald Bruce St. John, *Libya and the United States: Two Centuries of Strife* (Philadelphia, PA: University of Pennsylvania Press, 2002), p. 10.
57. Ibrāhīm al-Faqīh, "aṯ-Ṯawrah aš-Šaʿbiyyah al-Lībīyyah Tataḥawwil ʾilā Ḥarb Taḥrīr," *al-Mušāhid*, (unknown date), pp. 25-26.
58. al-Faqīh. *aṭ-Ṭāġiyyah fi-t-Tarīḫ*, p. 82.
59. Moncef Ouannes, *Militaires, Elites et Modernisation dans la Libye contemporaine* (Paris: L'Harmattan, 2009), p. 261.
60. al-Faqīh, *aṭ-Ṭāġiyyah fi-t-Tarīḫ*, p. 82.
61. See http://soundcloud.com/rebeccakesby1/khaled-mattawa-poem-after-42.
62. Otman and Karlberg, *The Libyan Economy*, p. 380.
63. Ibrahim, an uncle of Information Minister Ibrahim Musa, was captured in Sirte with Gaddafi on October 20, 2011; see http://vivalibya.wordpress.com/2011/12/02/urgent-appeal-for-the-life-of-ahmed-ibrahim.
64. Brownbook, Issue 22, Dubai.
65. John Biewen and Ian Ferguson, "Shadow Over Lockerbie," American RadioWorks, March 2000.
66. Milton Viorst, "The Colonel in His Labyrinth,"*Foreign Affairs*, March-April 1999.
67. French investigative journalist Péan argues the motive for the UTA bombing was "non-respect of promises made by France for Iran's assistance in freeing three French hostages in Lebanon," a charge made by a correspondent for the Lebanese newspaper *aš-Šūrā* subsequent to the the attack.
68. *ʿAbd ar-Raḥmān Šalġam, Ašḫāṣ ḥawl al-Qaḏḏāfī*, p. 430.
69. Chorin interview, source requested anonymity.
70. Mustafa Ahmed Benhalim, "Muthakiraat ra'is wuzara' Libya al asbaq" (London, England: Alhani publishers, 1992), dedication.
71. Chorin interview with Ahmed Ibrahim al-Fagih, November 21, 2011.
72. Ouannes, *Militaires*, p. 104.
73. Ammar Al Mabruk Iltif, *Libya: National Report on Human Development* (Tripoli, Libya: National Authority of Information and Documentation, 2002).
74. Ibid., p. 163.
75. Ibid., p. 81.
76. ʿĀdil al-Ǧawǧirī, "al-Ḫaṭar ʿalā an-Niẓām min ad-Dāḫil, Lā min Muʿāraḍat al-Ḫāriǧiyyah," *al-Wasaṭ*, February 8, 1993.
77. Ibid.
78. Ibid., p. 33.
79. Chorin interview, 2005, source requested anonymity.
80. "Libyan Arab Airlines flight 1103—Freedom opens up abuses of Libya's past," see http://www.youtube.com/watch?v=6rLt_LbAx0c.
81. Luis Martinez,"Libye: Transformations socio-Economiques et mutations Politiques sous l'embargo," (p. 211) in *Annuaire de l'Afrique du Nord*, tome XXXVII, CNRS Editions, 1998, pp. 205–225.
82. Meghan L. O'Sullivan, Shrewd Sanctions: Statecraft and State Sponsors of Terrorism (Washington, DC: Brookings, 2003), p. 195.
83. Danielle Bisson, Jean Bisson, and Jacques Fontaine, *La Libye: A la Decouverte d'un Pays*, Tome 1: Identite Libyenne, L'harmattan Paris, 1999, p. 140.
84. Ouannes, *Militaries*, p. 279.

85. See http://nanyang.academia.edu/JamesMDorsey/Papers/1056600/Libyan_rebels_investigate_Qaddafi_son_for_murder_of_soccer_player.
86. The National Transitional Council is currently investigating these charges.
87. Luis Martinez, *The Libyan Paradox* (New York, NY: Columbia University Press, 2007), p. 63.
88. Said Haddad, "La Politique Africaine de la Libye: de la Tentation Imperiale à la Strategie Unitaire," *Monde Arabe Maghreb-Machrek*, no. 170, October–December 2000, p. 32.
89. While the US praised Gaddafi for his assistance in applying pressure on the Sudanese government to end the conflict in Darfur, he was also linked to financing of the Janjaweed, the Muslim bands that razed southern Sudanese Christian villages.
90. Alexandre Najjar, *Anatomie d'un Tyran: Mouammar Kadhafi* (Paris: Actes Sud, 2011), p. 217.
91. See http://www.oilibya.com/?Id=15&lang=en.
92. Robert P. Baird, "Qaddafi's Dream," *Boston Review*, May-June 2011. See http://bostonreview.net/BR36.3/robert_baird_qaddafi_mosque.php.
93. Haddad, "La Politique Africaine," p. 33.
94. Abū Bakr Hāmid Kaḥal, *Tītānīkāt Afrīqiyyah* (Beirut: Saqi Books, 2008), p. 70.
95. Ouannes, *Militaires*, p. 283.

CHAPTER 3

1. Waniss A. Otman and Erling Karlberg, *The Libyan Economy: Economic Diversification and International Repositioning* (Springer: Berlin, 2007), p. 409.
2. Allan Gerson and Jerry Adler, *The Price of Terror* (New York: HarperCollins, 2001), p. 265.
3. Gary Hart, "My Secret Talks with Libya and Why they Went Nowhere," *Washington Post*, Sunday, January 18, 2004, http://www.washingtonpost.com/ac2/wp-dyn/A23872-2004Jan16?language=printer
4. Farrakhan claims to have received millions in support from Gaddafi since 1971. See http://www.suntimes.com/4600486-417/louis-farrakhan-defends-gadhafi-as-a-brother.html.
5. Meghan L. O'Sullivan, *Shrewd Sanctions: Statecraft and State Sponsors of Terrorism* (Washington, DC: Brookings, 2003), p. 200.
6. Judith Gurney, *Libya: The Political Economy of Oil* (Oxford, England: Oxford University Press, 1996), p. 82.
7. André Martel, "La Libye, Vingt ans Apres (1986–2005)," *Maghreb-Machrek*, no. 194 (Summer 2005): 24.
8. Moncef Djaziri, "La Crise de Lockerbie," in *L'annuaire de l'Afrique du Nord* (Paris: CNRS, 2000), p. 191.
9. See http://www.eurasiareview.com/01042011-libya-business-as-usual-but-what-about-tamoil-oped/.
10. Alan Friedman, *Agnelli: Fiat and the Network of Italian Power* (New York: American Library, 1989), p. 199.
11. O'Sullivan, *Shrewd Sanctions*, p. 216.
12. The identity of Fletcher's assassin was disclosed after the 2011 revolution; he was found dead shortly thereafter. See http://news.bbc.co.uk/onthisday/hi/dates/stories/april/17/newsid_2488000/2488369.stm.
13. Otman and Karlberg, *The Libyan Economy*, p. 410.
14. Jeffrey Steinberg and Scott Thompson, "An Imperial Love Affair," *Executive Intelligence Review*, March 11, 2011.
15. Stéphane Lacroix, *Awakening Islam* (Cambridge, MA: Harvard University Press, 2011), p. 206.
16. Chorin interviews, sources requested anonymity.
17. Chorin interview with former Assistant Secretary Martin Indyk, December 2012.

18. Lyn Boyd Judson, "A Medal of Good Hope: Mandela, Qaddafi, and the Lockerbie Negotiations," Pew Case Studies in International Affairs, no. 273, 2004, p. 5.
19. Bandar quipped famously in 2001, in connection with questions about the "British Aerospace" scandal, that "we [the Saudis] did not invent corruption." See http://www.guardian.co.uk/baefiles/page/0,,2095831,00.html.
20. Judson, "A Medal of Good Hope," p. 6.
21. Ibid., p. 7.
22. Ibid., p. 9.
23. Ibid., p. 6.
24. Ronald Bruce St. John, "Libya and the United States: A Faustian Pact?" *Middle East Policy* XV, no. 1 (Spring 2008).
25. The US opened a channel with the PLO, as a means of verifying what the Saudis were doing and to make sure, according to Martin Indyk, that "Bandar was straight" and that the Libyans were complying with closing the the Palestinian training camps.
26. See http://www.chron.com/news/nation-world/article/Gaddafi-calls-Israelis-Palestinians-idiots-1479401.php.
27. St. John, "Libya and the United States."
28. Chorin interviews with ambassadors David Welch and Martin Indyk, November-December 2011.
29. Chorin interview with Indyk, December 2011.
30. Judson, "A Medal of Good Hope," p. 11.
31. Chorin interviews, sources requested anonymity.
32. Chorin interviews, sources requested anonymity.
33. Chorin interview with Indyk, November 29, 2011.
34. Gerson and Adler, *The Price of Terror*, p. 292.
35. Ibid., p. 293.
36. Ronald Bruce St. John, *Libya and the United States: Two Centuries of Strife* (Philadelphia: University of Pennsylvania Press, 2002), p. 187.
37. Daya Gamage, "Intelligence Partnership between Libya and the CIA on Counter-Terrorism," *Asian Tribune*, March 21, 2011. See Asiantribune.com.
38. Gerson and Adler, *The Price of Terror*, p. 198.
39. Chorin interview with David Welch, November 2011; and with Sandra Charles, February 2012.
40. See http://www.huffingtonpost.com/2011/02/27/paul-wolfowitz-obama-libya-pan-am-families-bush-gaddafi_n_828797.html.
41. In 2004, the Libyans, via Saif's charity, settled with the families of the UTA bombing for a collective $170 million. A French court found Gaddafi's son-in-law Abdullah Sennusi, head of internal security; his right-hand man, Abdelsalam Hammouda; and four others guilty *in absentia* of the attack.
42. Robert G. Joseph, *Countering WMD: The Libyan Experience* (Fairfax, VA: National Institute Press, 2009), pp. 63–65.
43. "Bush Doctrine," November 15, 2011, accessed in November 2011, http://en.wikipedia.org/wiki/Bush_Doctrine.
44. Otman and Karlberg, *The Libyan Economy*, p. 408.
45. Rumors current in Libya at this time held that Gaddafi's wife, Safiya, was hysterical after the killing of Saddam's sons Uday and Kusai on July 22, 2003, and pleaded with her husband to save their sons from the same fate.
46. Condoleezza Rice, *No Higher Honor* (New York: Crown Publishing Group, 2011), p. 248.
47. See http://www.washingtonpost.com/wp-srv/politics/debatereferee/debate_1005.html.
48. Martin Indyk, "The Iraq War Did Not Force Gadaffi's Hand," Brookings, March 9, 2004, http://www.brookings.edu/opinions/2004/0309middleeast_indyk.aspx.
49. Chorin interview with Wayne White, former deputy director of the State Department's Near East/South Asia Intelligence Office, March 5, 2012.

50. Rice, *No Higher Honor*, p. 251.
51. Chorin interview, source requested anonymity.
52. Chorin interview with Wayne White, March 5, 2012.
53. Rice, *No Higher Honor*, p. 249.
54. Abdul Qadeer (A.Q.) Khan is a senior Pakistani nuclear scientist responsible for creating global nuclear proliferation network that included China, North Korea, Iran, Iraq, and Libya.
55. Wyn Q. Bowen, "Libya and Nuclear Proliferation: Stepping Back from the Brink" (London: International Institute for Strategic Studies, 2006), p. 44.
56. Ibid., p. 44.
57. Jean-François Daguzan, "De L'ennemi No. 2 au Premier de la Classe, Analyse de l'Abandon Reussi d'une Politique de Proliferation," *Maghreb-Machrek*, no. 184 (Summer 2005): 76.
58. Ibid.
59. Mohammed El Baradei, *The Age of Deception: Nuclear Diplomacy in Treacherous Times* (Doha: Bloomsbury Qatar Foundation Press, 2011), p. 158.
60. Ibid.
61. Daguzan, "De l'ennemi," pp. 74–75.
62. See http://georgewbush-whitehouse.archives.gov/news/releases/2004/07/images/20040712_p42133-103-515h.html.
63. Daguzan, "De l'ennemi," p. 72; El Baradei, *The Age of Deception*, p. 177.
64. El Baradei, *The Age of Deception*, p. 177.
65. O'Sullivan, *Shrewd Sanctions*, p. 229.
66. Unattributed, "Paul Wolfowitz Hits Obama on Libya, Blames Pan Am Families for Bush Policy Toward Gaddafi," video, February 27, 2011, http://www.huffingtonpost.com/2011/02/27/paul-wolfowitz-obama-libya-pan-am-families-bush-gaddafi_n_828797.html.
67. Glen Segell, *Axis of Evil and Rogue States: the Bush Administration, 2000–2004*, Google Books, p. 143.
68. TIFA = Trade and Investment Framework Agreement, typically used as an intermediary step to more formal or expansive trade agreements. The US and Libya signed a TIFA on May 20, 2010, after two years of negotiations. See http://libya.usembassy.gov/news-events/news-from-the-embassy2/united-states-and-libya-sign-trade-and-investment-framework-agreement.html.
69. Chorin interview with Assistant Secretary Elliott Abrams, September 2011.
70. O'Sullivan, *Shrewd Sanctions*, p. 208
71. Chorin interview with Assistant Secretary David Welch, November 2011.
72. Natan Sharansky, *The Case for Democracy* (New York: PublicAffairs, 2004), p. 273.
73. Chorin interview with Wayne White, April 2012.
74. Chorin interview with Ibrahim Sahad, former head of the National Front for the Salvation of Libya (NFSL), January 2012.
75. Chorin interview with Fred Abrahams, April 2012.

CHAPTER 4

1. See http://articles.cnn.com/2004-02-06/world/us.libya_1_libyan-government-libyan-officials-travel-ban?_s=PM:WORLD
2. Chorin interview, source requested anonymity.
3. Chorin interview with Wayne White, March 8, 2012.
4. Ibid., April 2012.
5. For most of the first year, US diplomats were confined to a twenty-mile cordon around Tripoli and could only travel outside those limits with express approval from the Ministry of Foreign Liaison.

6. Chorin interview, source requested anonymity.
7. See http://www.nbcphiladelphia.com/news/politics/Former-Pa-Rep-Curt-Weldon-Invited-to-Libya-119326809.html.
8. Wyn Q. Bowen, "Libya and Nuclear Proliferation: Stepping Back from the Brink" (London, England: IISS, 2006), p. 79.
9. Ethan Chorin, "The Future of the U.S.-Libyan Commercial Relationship," in *Libya Since 1969: Qadhafi's Revolution Revisited*, Dirk Vandewalle, ed. (New York, NY: Palgrave Macmillan, 2008), pp. 153–171.
10. Chorin interview, source requested anonymity.
11. Chorin, "The Future," p. 166.
12. Paul Blumenthal, "U.S. Companies Lobbied To Keep Libyan Market Open For Business," February 23, 2011; see http://sunlightfoundation.com/blog/2011/02/23/u-s-companies-lobbied-to-keep-libyan-market-open-for-business-2.
13. "US receives 1.5 billion dollars in compensation from Libya," *Agence-France Presse*, October 31, 2008.
14. See http://www.worldfocusgroup.com/reports/libya2/main.htm.
15. Nayed would later distinguish himself as the head of the National Transition Council's (NTC) Stabilization Committee, and subsequently as Libyan ambassador to the UAE.
16. Chorin interview with Burhaneddin al Muntasser, February 2012.
17. Chorin interview with Husni Bey, July 2011.
18. Ibid., June 2012.
19. Qureena/Oea: rajulal a'maal al libii Husni Bey: Khufitu wa Ujbirt ala tawqi' sheek bi milieen li ifraj 'anni, November 14, 2007.
20. Chorin interview with Husni Bey, March 28, 2012.
21. See www.alarabiya.net/ articles/ 2011/03/06/140415.html.
22. Chorin interview, sources requested anonymity; and Otman and Karlberg, *The Libyan Economy*, p. 409.
23. Chorin interviews, sources requested anonymity.
24. Elizabeth Douglass, "Occidental CEO's 2006 paycheck: $460 million," *Los Angeles Times*, April 7, 2007.
25. Michael Erman, "Libya probing local, foreign oil companies," *Wall Street Journal*, April 8, 2012.
26. See http://www.ai-cio.com/channel/NEWSMAKERS/UK_Prosecutors_Team_Up_With_SEC_to_Investigate_Bribery_Among_SWFs.html.
27. Chorin interview with David Grudoski, April 2012.
28. Chorin interview, source requested anonymity.
29. Chorin interview with Ambassador Charles Cecil, June 2012.
30. Chorin interview, source requested anonymity.
31. One reliable source speculated this was on Gaddafi's behest, to understand better how the international prosecution system worked, lest Gaddafi wind up in the same position at some point in the future.
32. Mustapha Sandid, "Hannibal Kadhafi le Sulfereux," *L'Express*, July 25, 2008.
33. Chorin interview with Ambassador David Welch, November 27, 2011.
34. Luis Martinez, *The Libyan Paradox* (New York, NY: Columbia University Press, 2007), p. 51.
35. Ibid. p. 52.
36. *Caesar's Return* ('Awdat Caesar') in Chorin, *Translating Libya*, pp. 150–152.
37. Abdel Raziq Al-Mansuri, *My Friends When I Die*, pp. 59–61, in Chorin, *Translating Libya*.
38. See http://www.keia.com/SPOTGuide.pdf.
39. *Al Jazeera* coverage, see http://www.youtube.com/watch?v=RjfLSPVZqHU (The Footage).

40. Chorin interview with David Welch, November 27, 2011.
41. See http://www.aljazeera.net/news/archive/archive?ArchiveId=1174222.
42. Chorin interview, source requested anonymity.
43. Chorin interview with Sandra Charles, August 2011.
44. David Rose, "The Lockerbie Deal," *Vanity Fair*, January 27, 2011.
45. "Libyan takes chair of UN human rights commission," *The Guardian*, January 20, 2003.
46. See http://www.nytimes.com/2003/01/23/opinion/payoff-for-colonel-qaddafi.html.
47. See http://www.guardian.co.uk/world/2003/jan/21/3.
48. Ibid.

CHAPTER 5

1. Chorin interview with Sandra Charles, October 2011.
2. Michael Isikoff, "Lobbying for Libya—and Bush," *Daily Beast*, October 27, 2004.
3. Chorin interview, source requested anonymity; see http://www.huffingtonpost.com/2011/02/24/muammar-gaddafi-us-business-lobby_n_827769.html.
4. Henry Porter and Annabel Davidson, "Colonel Qaddafi—Dictator Chic: A Life in Fashion," *Vanity Fair*, August 12, 2009.
5. ʿAbd ar-Raḥmān Šalġam, *Ašḫāṣ ḥawl al-Qaḏḏāfī* (Dubai: Dār al-Farǧiyānī/Madārik Publishers, 2012), p. 51.
6. Ḫālid Maḥmūd, "Ahar muder li mu'assisa Al qadhafi al alimiyya: tawajasat haifat min al amal ma'a mu'tassim lama sama'tuhy 'anhu min ghalta wa Jufa'a fi al ta'amul" PART II, Asharq Al Awsat, October 9, 2011,
7. One of Saif's friends related that when Freddo, one of the tigers, escaped his cage at one point, Saif "ran like hell." Upon Freddo's death, Saif had him stuffed.
8. Saif Al Islam, *Libya and the XXI Century* (One 9 Media, July 2002), from a university thesis presented to the faculty of California State University, Hayward IMADEC-CSUH, in partial fulfillment of the requirements for the degree of Executive Master of Business Administration by Saif al Islam M Al Qadhafi, March 2000. Diamond Theory is a standard "cluster, or comparative advantage model" of competitiveness that postulates why certain industries grow quickly at certain times and places.
9. Ibid., p. 127, citing Moammar el Gaddafi, *The Green Book*, Part III, p. 182.
10. Ibid.
11. Ibid., p. 273.
12. Chorin interview, source requested anonymity.
13. Chorin interview, source requested anonymity.
14. "The Woolf Inquiry: An Inquiry into the LSE's Links With Libya and Lessons to be Learned," (London, England: London School of Economics, October 2011).
15. See http://www.dailymail.co.uk/news/article-2068183/Blair-government-tried-Saif-al-Islam-Gaddafi-place-Oxford.html; and "The Woolf Inquiry," p. 28, n12.
16. London School of Economics, "The Woolf Inquiry," p. 86.
17. Fred Halliday, *Political Journeys* (London, England: Saqi Books, 2011), p. 225.
18. London School of Economics, "The Woolf Inquiry," p. 22.
19. Alexandre Najjar, *Anatomie d'un Tyran: Mouammar Kadhafi* (Paris: Actes Sud, 2011), p. 181; London School of Economics, "The Woolf Inquiry," p. 66.
20. See http://www.telegraph.co.uk/news/newstopics/mandrake/8472413/Cherie-Blair-eyes-up-the-top-job-at-the-London-School-of-Economics.html.
21. London School of Economics, "The Woolf Inquiry," p. 136.
22. Michael Seamark, "The Day that LSE Sold its Soul to Libya: *Daily Mail*, March 2, 2011; see http://www.dailymail.co.uk/news/article-1363222/The-day-LSE-sold-soul-Libya-BP-chief-makes-oil-deal-Gaddafi—drags-prestigious-university-disrepute.html.

23. London School of Economics, "The Woolf Inquiry," p. 65.
24. Ibid., p. 22.
25. Doug Flahut, see http://www.amconmag.com/article/2003/mar/24/00007/.
26. Chorin interview, source requested anonymity.
27. Yehudit Ronen, "Libya's Rising Star: Saif Al-Islam and Succession," *Middle East Policy* XII, no. 3 (Fall 2005).
28. Ibid.
29. Chorin interview with Ambassador David Welch, November 27, 2011.
30. Chorin interview, source requested anonymity.
31. Chorin interview, source requested anonymity.
32. Chorin interview, source requested anonymity.
33. Original source removed from Internet, http://www.cs.purdue.edu/about_us/annual_reports/95/AR95Book-13.html.
34. Michael E. Porter, "Competitiveness Issues for Iran, Institute for Strategy and Competitiveness," Harvard Business School, Teheran, by video link, June 24, 2008.
35. National Economic Strategy, Assessment of the Competitiveness of the Libyan Arab Jamahiriya, Monitor Group, and CERA, The General Planning Council of Libya, 2006.
36. Monitor Group, "Libya at the Dawn of a New Era: Improving Competitiveness in the Global Economy," internal PowerPoint, February 9, 2006.
37. National Economic Strategy, 2006.
38. Chorin interview with Maria Al Zahrani, December, 2010.
39. It is no surprise that Singapore, with its corporatist approach to governance, was seen as a reform model in other parts of the Middle East, notably Dubai, whose leadership seemed to idolize former Singaporean Prime Minister Lee Kuan Yew.
40. See http://www.washingtonmonthly.com/features/2004/0411.hirsh.html; and Dirk Vandewalle, *A History of Modern Libya*, 2nd ed. (Cambridge, England: Cambridge University Press, 2006), p. 202.
41. Monitor Company Group, LP, Draft Proposal for Qadhafi Manuscript, Confidential, 2007, p. 3.
42. Ibid.
43. Chorin interview, source requested anonymity.
44. See http://www.motherjones.com/mojo/2011/03/monitor-group-lobbying-libya-disclose; http://feb17.info/news/massachusetts-consulting-firm-aiding-libya-did-not-register-as-foreign-lobbyist.
45. Jeffrey Goldberg, "The World's Greatest Book Proposal, Courtesy of the Monitor Group," *The Atlantic*, November 1, 2011.
46. Chorin interview with senior Monitor official, April 2012.
47. Ibid.
48. Chorin interview with Sandra Charles, September 2011.
49. Chorin interview, source requested anonymity.
50. Ḫālid Maḥmūd, interviews with Yusuf Sawani, PART I-III aš-Šarq al-Awsaṭ, October 8–10, 2011.
51. Ibid.
52. Ibid.
53. Chorin interview with Dr. Salma Al Gaeer Al Gaddafi, Summer 2005.
54. Ḫālid Maḥmūd, interviews with Yusuf Sawani, PART I-III aš-Šarq al-Awsaṭ, October 8–10, 2011.
55. Ibid.
56. Ibid.

CHAPTER 6

1. Ahmed Ibhrahim Fagih says he believes that Gaddafi was behind a plan to infect "more than a thousand" Benghazi infants with HIV. In line with this assertion, Fagih says Gaddafi was "surprised" by the strength of the local (Benghazi) reaction and demands for accountability from the regime, and was forced to look for scapegoats. Gaddafi appeared to be mildly obsessed with the epidemic, at various times alleging AIDS was a CIA or Mossad plot against Africa. Gaddafi said "Islamists" were "worse than AIDS." Yahia Zoubir, "Islamisme Radical et Lutte Antiterroriste," *Maghreb-Machrek*, no. 184 (Summer 2005), p. 60.
2. Marc Pierini, *Le prix de la liberté* (Paris: Actes Sud, 2008), pp. 19–20.
3. Ibid., p. 22.
4. Ibid..
5. Ibid., p. 27.
6. Ibid., p. 57.
7. Ibid., pp. 57–58.
8. Ibid., p. 68.
9. Ibid., p. 69.
10. Valya Chervenyashka and Nikolay Yordanov, *Notes from Hell, A Bulgarian Nurse in Libya* (Durban, South Africa: 30 Degrees South, 2010), p. 64.
11. Chorin interview, source requested anonymity.
12. See http://www.novinite.com/view_news.php?id=83986.
13. Pierini, *Le prix de la liberté,* p. 132.
14. Ibid., p. 133.
15. While no conclusive evidence has surfaced tying Sarkozy to a Gaddafi donation, Saif Al Islam's allegations and demand that he "return the money" to the Libyan people after the start of the 2011 revolution have been cited as contributing factors to Sarkozy's electoral loss in May 2012.
16. David Rose, "The Lockerbie Deal," *Vanity Fair*, January 27, 2011; see http://www.vanityfair.com/politics/features/2011/01/libya-201101.
17. Hussain Solomon and Gerrie Swart, "Libya's Foreign Policy in Flux," (Oxford, England: (Oxford) Journal of African Affairs, July 2005), p. 491.
18. Ibid.
19. See http://www.telegraph.co.uk/news/worldnews/africaandindianocean/libya/8771192/Libya-Tony-Blair-and-Col-Gaddafis-Secret-Meetings.html.
20. See http://www.telegraph.co.uk/news/worldnews/africaandindianocean/libya/6073643/Swiss-governments-apology-over-Hannibal-Gaddafis-arrest-sparks-angry-backlash.html.
21. Helena Bachmann, "Gaddafi's Oddest Idea: Abolish Switzerland," *Le Matin*, September 25, 2009.
22. Asharq Al Awsat: Almania: Jadal howl manh Saif al Arab al Qaddafi imtiazaat diplomasiyya, editors, January 17, 2012.
23. Chorin interview with Fred Abrahams, Human Rights Watch, January 10, 2012.
24. The Italians had helped build the original road and effected improvements to it from 1955 to 1958. See http://www.nytimes.com/2008/08/31/world/europe/31iht-italy.4.15774385.html.
25. "Il Grande Gesto Dell'italia Verso La Libia," LIMES (Italian Review of Geopolitics), June 30, 2009; see http://cornellsun.com/node/31317.
26. Alan Friedman, *Agnelli: Fiat and the Network of Italian Power* (New York, NY: New American Library, 1989), p. x.
27. Andrew Feinstein, *The Shadow World: Inside the Global Arms Trade* (New York, NY: Farrar, Straus and Giroux, 2011), p. 492.
28. Jean-Marc Tanguy, *Harmattan: Récits et Révélations* (Paris: Nimrod, 2012), p. 21.
29. Ibid., p. 20.
30. Ibid., pp. 20–21.

31. Feinstein, *The Shadow World*, p. 489; and see http://www.telegraph.co.uk/news/worldnews/africaandindianocean/libya/8743226/MI6-caught-Libyans-lying-about-nuclear-weapons-documents-reveal.html.
32. See http://www.guardian.co.uk/world/2011/aug/31/us-firms-torture-flights-rendition.
33. See http://www.nytimes.com/2011/09/06/world/europe/06britain.html.
34. Ibid.
35. Owen Bowcott, Ian Cobain, and Richard Norton-Taylor, "Gibson inquiry into MI5 and MI6 torture collusion claims abandoned," *The Guardian*, January 18, 2012.
36. Jane Mayer, "Outsourcing Torture, the Secret History of America's 'Extraordinary Rendition' Program," in *The United States and Torture*, Marjorie Cohn, ed. (New York, NY: NYU Press, 2011), p. 141.
37. Ibid., p. 146.
38. Abdelhakim Belhaj, "Du Djihad a la Revolution," *Jeune Afrique*, no. 2643, September 4–10, 2011, p. 26.
39. al-Kašf, "ʿan Waṯīqat Muwāfaqat Lundun ʿala Taslīm Bal-Ḥāǧ ʾilā Lībīyā," aš-Šarq al-Awsaṭ, April 10, 2012.
40. See http://www.cbsnews.com/2100-3480_162-20101324.html.
41. Andy Worthington, "The Death of Rendition Victim Ibn al-Shaykh al Libi," in *Commentaries, The Future of Freedom Foundation*, May 11, 2009; Dana Priest, "Al Qaeda-Iraq Link Recanted," *Washington Post*, August 1, 2004.
42. And a prime example cited by those who argue that torture fails to produce reliable information (and indeed often produces either useless or counter-productive data), independent of any moral considerations.
43. See http://www.ennaharonline.com/en/international/1151.html.
44. "as-Siǧīn as-Sābiq fī Ġuāntānāmū Sufyān bin Qūmū: 'Anā Lastu min al-Qāʿidah . . . sa-ʾUqātil Rayʿ ar-Rāyāt as-Sawdaʾʾ," al-Aḥwal, May 16, 2012.
45. See http://www.state.gov/j/drl/rls/hrrpt/2005/61694.htm.
46. Phillipe Sands, "Terrorists and Torturers," in *The United States and Torture*, Cohn, ed., p. 277.
47. At this point, there is no indication that the US or other countries complied with Algerian suggestions or requests. Chorin interview with Wayne White, March 8, 2012.
48. See http://www.telegraph.co.uk/news/worldnews/northamerica/usa/5208701/Condoleezza-Rice-approved-torture-techniques.html.
49. Ben Hubbard, "Documents Show Ties between Libyan Spy Head, CIA," Associated Press, September 4, 2011.
50. The stain metaphor was repeated in President Obama's 2009 "New Beginnings" speech and Samantha Power's subsequent remarks during the 2011 uprising.
51. Stéphane Lacroix, *Awakening Islam* (Cambridge, MA: Harvard Universtiy Press, 2011), p. 206.
52. Daya Gamage, "Intelligence Partnership between Libya and the CIA on Counter-terrorism," *Asian Tribune*, March 21, 2011; see Asiantribune.com.
53. Ironic, given that the main focus of LIFG activity was unseating Gaddafi—both before and during the upcoming revolution.
54. Chorin interview, source requested anonymity.
55. Chorin interviews, sources requested anonymity.

CHAPTER 7

1. According to Hussein al Shafa'i, interviewed by a Human Rights Watch witness.
2. See http://www.hrw.org/news/2012/06/27/libya-abu-salim-prison-massacre-remembered.
3. Chorin interview, source requested anonymity.
4. "Muḏakkirāt Bū Slaym," *al-Lībī*, July 26, 2011, pp. 12–14.

5. Ibid.
6. Claudia Gazzini, "Talking back: Exiled Libyans Use the Web to Push for Change," *Arab Media & Society*, February 2007.
7. CNN, "In Libya, 11 reportedly die in cartoon protests," February 18, 2006.
8. Spiritual leader behind the International Muslim Brotherhood and host of a widly popular religious program, As-sharia wa al-Hayat (Shari'a and Life), on Al Jazeera.
9. See http://www.reuters.com/article/2011/03/11/us-libya-scholar-idUSTRE72A4FG 20110311.
10. Mathieu Guidère, *Le Choc des Revolutions Arabes.* (Paris: Editions Autrement, 2011), p. 104.
11. Chorin interview with Fred Abrahams, April 2012.
12. Aisha al-Rumi (pseudonym), "Libyan Berbers struggle to assert their identity online," *Arab Media & Society*, Spring 2009, p. 6.
13. Ibid., pp. 4, 6.
14. Chorin interview, source requested anonymity.
15. Dirk Vandewalle, *A History of Modern Libya*, 2nd ed. (Cambridge, England: Cambridge University Press, 2012), p. 200.
16. See http://www.hrw.org/sites/default/files/reports/libya1209webwcover.pdf.
17. Ibid.
18. ʿAbd ar-Raḥmān Šalġam, *Ašḫāṣ ḥawl al-Qaḏḏāfī* (Dubai: Dār al-Farğiyānī/Madārik Publishers, 2012), p. 495.
19. See http://www.hrw.org/sites/default/files/reports/libya1209webwcover.pdf.
20. David Rose, "The Lockerbie Deal," *Vanity Fair*, January 27, 2011.
21. Ibid.
22. Timeline: Lockerbie Bomber's Release, August 29, 2011.
23. See http://www.nationalreview.com/corner/242497/what-s-letter-obama-s-al -megrahi-culpability-kathryn-jean-lopez.
24. See http://www.telegraph.co.uk/news/wikileaks-files/libya-wikileaks/8294627 /MEGRAHI-RETURNS-TO-LIBYA-ACCOMPANIED-BY-SAIF-AL-ISLAM -QADHAFI.html.
25. Wikileaks source withdrawn from Web.
26. See www.nationalreview.com/corner/242497/what-s-letter-obama-s-al-megrahi -culpability-kathryn-jean-lopez.
27. See http://www.reinventinglibya.org/index.php.
28. See http://www.amnesty.org/en/region/libya/report-2011.
29. See http://uk.reuters.com/article/2010/11/08/libya-media-idUKLDE6A60AB 20101107, November 9, 2010.
30. Saif Gaddafi, "Now Indistinguishable from his Father," *New York Magazine*, May 22, 2011; see http://nymag.com/news/politics/saif-qaddafi-2011-5.
31. See http://www.dailymail.co.uk/news/article-1208434/Gaddafi-son-buys-10m -Hampstead-mansion.html.
32. Mohamed Eljahmi, "Bad Decision 101: Columbia embraces Qadhafi—and so do we," see http://old.nationalreview.com/comment/eljahmi200603200808.asp.
33. See http://www.libya-watanona.com/adab/maljahmi/mj20036a.htm.
34. See http://www.nysun.com/new-york/columbia-partner-in-gadhafi-parley-has-grim /29810.
35. Due to technical difficulties, Gaddafi's call from the Arab League Conference in Damascus (where, ironically, he predicted his own demise at the hands of NATO) was canceled.
36. See http://www.freerepublic.com/focus/f-news/2034881/posts.
37. See http://www.telegraph.co.uk/news/worldnews/africaandindianocean/libya /8129254/Gaddafi-hosts-20-Italian-models-on-all-expenses-paid-trip.html.
38. See http://www.youtube.com/watch?v=9rtCC9Yw1kc.
39. See http://kenyastockholm.com/2009/09/24/mohammed-gaddafis-full-un-speech.
40. Ibid.

41. Alexandre Najjar, *Anatomie d'un Tyran* (Paris: Actes Sud, 2011), p. 126.
42. See http://www.thecuttingedgenews.com/index.php?article=11556&pageid=37&pagename=Page+One.
43. See http://www.thenational.ae/news/world/middle-east/prominent-britons-scramble-to-repudiate-links-with-saif-qaddafi#page2.
44. See http://in.reuters.com/article/2011/09/09/idINIndia-59244320110909.
45. Ḫālid Maḥmūd, "'Āḫar Mudīr li-Mu'assasat al-Qaḏḏāfī al-'Ālamiyya: Mašru' Sayf al-Islām al-Iṣlāḥī Muğarrad 'Wahm'," *aš-Šarq al- Awsaṭ*, October 8, 2011.
46. Ḫālid Maḥmūd, "'Āhar Mudīr li-Mu'assasat al-Qaḏḏāfī al-'Ālamiyya: Tawağğasat Ḫayfah min al-'Amal ma' Mu'ṭaṣim Lamā Sama'ithu 'anhu min Ġilẓah wa Ğafā' fī at-Ta'āmul." PART II, *aš-Šarq al-Aswaṭ*, October 9, 2011.
47. Ibid.
48. Fatḥī Bağa', "Lībīyā 'ilā 'Ayn? al-Maqālah allatī Kaššafat Wahm al-Iṣlāḥ," *Miyādīn*, May 22, 2011, pp. 4–5.
49. Ibid., p. 4.
50. Chorin interview, source requested anonymity.
51. Ḫālid Maḥmūd, "'Āḫar Mudīr li-Mu'assasat al-Qaḏḏāfī al-'Ālamiyya: Mašru' Sayf al-Islām al-Iṣlāḥī Muğarrad 'Wahm'." *aš-Šarq al- Awsaṭ*, October 8, 2011.
52. Mustafa Ben-Halim, *Libya: The Years of Hope: The Memoirs of Mustafa Ahmed Ben-Halim* (London: AAS Media Publishers, 1998), p. 96.
53. Ibid., p. 94.
54. Alexandre Najjar, *Anatomie d'un Tyran: Mouammar Kadhafi*, (Paris: Actes Sud, 2011), p. 152.
55. Chorin interview, source requested anonymity.
56. 'Abd ar-Raḥmān Šalġam, *Ašḫāṣ ḥawl al-Qaḏḏāfī*, p. 58.

CHAPTER 8

1. Daniel Kaufmann, *Control Risk Assessment*, cited in "Libya's Starting Failure: Unforeseen or Ignored" (Washington, DC: Brookings), February 25, 2011.
2. Heba Saleh, "Libya Looks to the Future," *Financial Times*, June 8, 2010.
3. See http://www.imf.org/external/pubs/ft/dp/2012/1201mcd.pdf.
4. For years, Tripoli had a Ministry of Railroads—despite the fact that there were no railways anywhere in the country.
5. Chorin interview, source requested anonymity.
6. Chorin interview, source requested anonymity.
7. Unattributed, interview with Maḥmūd Ğibrīl in aš-Šarq al-Awsaṭ; "ad-Duktur Maḥmūd Ğibrīl yukaššif li-aš-Šharq al-Awsaṭ 'an Muḥaṭṭat al-Qaḏḏāf'i li-l-'Awdah 'ilā as-Sulṭa," *aš-Šharq al-Awsaṭ*, October 18, 2011.
8. Chorin interview, source requested anonymity.
9. Unified Protector, Quels Parametres pour une Operation Lance sans Filet?, DSI, p. 40, footnote 2.
10. Chorin interview, source requested anonymity.
11. Chorin interview, source requested anonymity.
12. Wikileaks leaked cable containing a missive to Washington from Ambassador to Tripoli, Gene A. Cretz, September 29, 2009.
13. See http://www.guardian.co.uk/world/us-embasssy-cables-documents/227491.
14. John Hamilton, "Libyan Promise Falters," *The Africa Report*, no. 26 (December 2010–January 2011).
15. See http://blogs.reuters.com/globalinvesting/tag/emerging-markets-libya-gadaffi-frontier-markets.
16. See http://www.npr.org/templates/story/story.php?storyId=9937606.
17. Ali Shuaib, "Libya says Chevron and Oxy Exit Licenses," Reuters, October 2, 2010.
18. Vaughan O'Grady, "Why Libya Needs a New Oil Law," *Oil Review Africa*, issue 3 (2010).
19. Ibid.

20. Editors, "Libya: Family, Friends and neighbors," *The Africa Report*, no. 26 (December 2010–January 2011): p. 289
21. Daniel Yergin, "Libyan Oil in the Global Context," Libyan Academy for Graduate Studies speech, Tripoli, January 2006.
22. ʿAbd ar-Raḥmān Šalġam, *Ašḫāṣ ḥawl al-Qaḏḏāfī* (Dubai: Dār al-Farǧiyānī/Madārik Publishers, 2012), p. 474.
23. See http://www.asharq-e.com/news.asp?section=1&id=23231.
24. ʿAbd ar-Raḥmān Šalġam, *Ašḫāṣ ḥawl al-Qaḏḏāfī*, p, 55; and see http://www.aawsat.com/details.asp?section=4&article=597431&issueno=11690.
25. Maghreb Confidential source, cited in Heinz Duthel, "Duthel Intelligence Report-2011: Libyan Civil War," self-published on Amazon.com, p. 98; see also http://www.reuters.com/article/2007/12/11/us-france-libya-idUSL1153657420071211.
26. Najjar, Alexandre, *Anatomie d'un Tyran* (Paris: Actes Sud, 2011), p. 243.
27. "Fin de parties pour Mismari," *Jeune Afrique* no. 26045, December 11, 2010.
28. ʿAbd ar-Raḥmān Šalġam, *Ašḫāṣ ḥawl al-Qaḏḏāfī* (Cairo, Dar al Madarek, 2012), p. 474.
29. Najjar, *Anatomie*, p. 243.
30. Luis Martinez, "Luis Martinez: Il sera difficile de contraindre le régime de Kadhafi a une retenue dans la repression," *Le Monde*, February, 21-21, 2011.
31. Ibrahim Sharqieh, "Even a weakened Libya can avoid civil war," *Financial Times*, March 3, 2011.
32. Farağ Nağam, "al-Qabaliyyā wa Ṭabīʿatuha fī Lībīyā," al-Ḥayāt, March 12, 2011.
33. Shabakat Corporation, International Republican Institute Survey of Public Opinion in Eastern Libya, October 12–25, 2011; see www.shabakat.se, quoted in Marbo3a.
34. Bernard-Henri Lévy, *La Guerre sans l'Aimer* (Paris: Bernard Grasset, 2011), p. 69.
35. Joseph Felter and Brian Fishman, "Al-Qa'ida's Foreign Fighters in Iraq: A First Look at the Sinjar Reords," Harmony Project, Combating Terrorism Center, West Point, December, 19, 2007; see http://tarpley.net/docs/CTCForeignFighter.19.Dec07.pdf.
36. Of the sample, 41 percent were from Saudi Arabia, and 18.8 percent from Libya; of the Libyan fighters, 60.2 percent were from Derna, and 23.9 percent from Benghazi.
37. Richard Oppel, "Foreign Fighters in Iraq are Tied to Allies of the US," *New York Times*, November 22, 2007.
38. Kevin Peraino, "The Martyr Factory: Why One Libyan Town Became a Pipeline for Suicide Bombers in Iraq," *Newsweek*, April 20, 2008.
39. See http://www.principiadiscordia.com/forum/index.php?topic=29127.5;wap.
40. Abdelhakim Belhaj, "Du Djihad à la Revolution," *Jeune Afrique*, no. 2643, September 4–10, 2011, p. 26.
41. "al-Kutub allatī Manaḥaha al-Qaḏḏāfī Talqi rawāğan fī Manāṭiq al-Muʿāraḍah al-Lībīyyah," al-Ḥayāh, May 19, 2011; "Neglected Libyan city battles al-Qāʿ idah," Reuters, May 12, 2011.
42. Lévy, *La Guerre sans l'Aimer*, p. 41.
43. Luis Martinez, *The Libyan Paradox* (New York, NY: Columbia University Press, 2007), pp. 64–67.
44. Muḥammad Muḥammad al-Muftī, *Sahārī Dirnah*, Binġāzī: Dār al-Kutub al-Waṭaniyyah, 2007, p. 152.

CHAPTER 9

1. (Part III opening page) Lisa Anderson, "Qadhafi's Legacy: An Evaluation of a Political Experiement," in *Qaddafi's Libya, 1969-1994*, Dirk Vandewalle, ed. (New York, NY: St. Martin's Press, 1995), pp. 223-237.
2. Hannah Arendt, *On Revolution*, Jonathan Schell, intro. (New York, NY: Penguin, 1963), p. 8.
3. "Another Arab Regime Under Threat," *The Economist*, January 28, 2011.

4. Heinz Duthel, Duthel Intelligence Report, 2011 Libyan Civil War, Timeline for the 2011 Libyan Civil War, self-published.
5. James Dorsey, "Wikileaks Disclosures about Gaddafi Spark Cancellation of Libyan Soccer Matches," Bleacher Report, February 1, 2011.
6. Colin Freeman, "How Britian Courted, Armed and Trained a Libyan Monster," Tripoli, September 25, 2011.
7. Chorin interview, source requested anonymity.
8. Fatḥī Baġaʿ, "Lībīyā ʾilā ʾAyn? al-Maqālah allatī Kaššafat Wahm al-Iṣlāḥ," *Miyādīn*, May 22, 2011.
9. Ibid.
10. Ibid.
11. See http://www.bbg.gov/broadcasters/mbn.
12. Chorin interview with Mohammed Bin Lamin, December 2011.
13. Laura Rodríguez Rojas, "Pintor libio sufrió ocho meses de tortura," *Nacionales*, September 17, 2011.
14. See http://en.rsf.org/surveillance-libya,39717.htm.
15. Ibid.
16. Chorin interview with Ibrahim Sahad, January 26, 2012.
17. Ibid.
18. Chorin interview with Rida Husni Bey, November 2011.
19. Chorin interview, source requested anonymity.
20. Alanoud Al Sharekh, "Reform and Rebirth in the Middle East, in Survival," The International Institute for Strategic Studies, April-May, 2011, p. 56.
21. Ibid., p. 53.
22. Mathieu Guidere, *Le Choc des revolutions arabes* (Paris: Editions Autrement, 2011), pp. 106–107.
23. Chorin interview, source requested anonymity.
24. Duthel, Duthel Intelligence Report, p. 13.
25. See http://feb17.info/news/saadi-gaddafi-addrssed-the-people-on-a -benghazi-radio -station/Febraury 17th.
26. Chorin interview, source requested anonymity.
27. Chorin interview, source requested anonymity.
28. ʿAbd as-Salām Mismārī, "Dūrunā Ḥimāyat aṯ-Ṯawrah wa Istimrār Ahdafaha," *Berenīq*, May 23, 2011, p. 3.
29. Asmāʾ Faraǧ al Fitūrī, Binġāzī: as-Safīr Press/al-Wikālah al-Lībiyya li-t- Tarqīm ad-Dawalī al-Muwaḥḥad li-l-Kitāb, *Binġāzī min 1911 ʾilā 2011*, 2011, p. 126.
30. Ibid.
31. Fatḥī Baġaʿ, "Lībīyā ʾilā ʾAyn? al-Maqālah allatī Kaššafat Wahm al-Iṣlāḥ," *Miyādīn*, May 22, 2011.
32. Asmāʾ Faraǧ al Fitūrī, Binġāzī: as-Safīr Press/al-Wikālah al-Lībiyya li-t- Tarqīm ad-Dawalī al-Muwaḥḥad li-l-Kitāb, *Binġāzī min 1911 ʾilā 2011*, 2011, p. 126.
33. Ibid., p. 127.
34. Chorin interview, source requested anonymity.
35. Mehdi Ziu, "We Win or We Die," documentary video posted to Feb17.info, December 29, 2011; see http://feb17.info/news/video-we-win-or-we-die -documentary-about-the-hero-mahdi-ziu.
36. ʿAbd as-Salām Mismārī, "Munassiq Iʾtilāf 17 Fabrāyīr, Dūrunā Ḥimāyat aṯ-Ṯawrah wa Istimrār Ahdafaha," *Berenīq*, May 23, 2011.
37. Ibid., p. 3.
38. See http://feb17info/news/masses-of-protesters-flood-to-benghazi-north-court.
39. See http://feb17info/news/eye-witness-describes-libyan-crackdown-on-protesters-in -benghazi; Armed Men Kidnap Wounded Protesters from Hosptial in Benghazi, Posted Feb 18, Feb17Info.
40. ʿAbd as-Salām Mismārī, "Dūrunā Ḥimāyat aṯ-Ṯawrah wa Istimrār Ahdafaha," *Berenīq*, May 23, 2011, p. 3.

41. Ibid.
42. Asmā' Farağ al-Fitūrī, Binġāzī: as-Safīr Press/al-Wikālah al-Lībiyya li-t- Tarqīm ad-Dawalī al-Muwaḥḥad li-l-Kitāb, *Binġāzī min 1911 'ilā 2011, 2011*, p.128,
43. Ibid., p. 127.
44. Duthel, Duthel Intelligence Report, p. 14.
45. Ibid., p. 15,
46. Asmā' Farağ al-Fitūrī, Binġāzī: as-Safīr Press/al-Wikālah al-Lībiyya li-t- Tarqīm ad-Dawalī al-Muwaḥḥad li-l-Kitāb, *Binġāzī min 1911 'ilā 2011*, 2011, p.128.
47. Chorin interview with Dr. Abdelnasser Saadi, May 29, 2012.
48. See http://www.tripolitimes.com/archives/96, from behind the walls of the battalion of Fadeel Bu Omar in Benghazi; Asmā Farağ al-Fitūrī, Binġāzī: as-Safīr Press/al-Wikālah al-Lībiyya li-t- Tarqīm ad-Dawalī al-Muwaḥḥad li-l-Kitāb, *Binġāzī min 1911 'ilā 2011*, 2011. p. 128; Ziu, "We Win or We Die," December 29, 2011.
49. Ibid.
50. Fatḥī Baġa', "Lībīyā 'ilā 'Ayn? al-Maqālah allatī Kaššafat Wahm al-Iṣlāḥ," *Miyādīn*, May 22, 2011, pp. 4–5.
51. Chorin interview with Christopher Stevens.
52. See http://www.scribd.com/doc/49221707/Full-Text-of-Saif-Gaddafi-s-Speech.
53. Insider report: Saif Al-Gadaffi attempts to flee Libya, denied access to airport; see http://feb17.info/news/insider-report-saif-attempts-to-flee-libya-denied-access-to-airport. Posted on February 18, 2011.
54. See http://www.guardian.co.uk/world/2011/feb/21/saif-al-islam-gaddafi.
55. See http://www.benjaminbarber.org/Benjamin%20Barber%20Qaddafi%20Foundation%20Press%20Release%202-22-11.pdf.
56. Chorin interview with Maged Mahfouz, London, December 23, 2011.
57. Chorin interview, source requested anonymity.
58. See http://www.bbc.co.uk/news/world-africa-13927208.
59. Phillipe Sands, "The Accomplice," *Vanity Fair*; see Vanityfair.com/ politics /features/2011/08/qaddafi-201108.
60. Ibid.
61. Dr. Issam Hajjaji, "Healthcare in Libya," January 2012 (unpublished copy).
62. Wayne White, "Fighting in Libya: the Military balance," MEI Policy Watch #1768, March 3, 2012.
63. *aš-Šarq al-Awsaṭ*, Spring 2011 (unknown date).
64. 'Abd as-Salām Mismārī, "Munassiq I'tilāf 17 Fabrāyīr, Dūrunā Ḥimāyat aṯ-Ṯawrah wa Istimrār Ahdafaha," *Berenīq*, May 23, 2011.
65. "Libya's Ambassadors to India, Arab League Resign in Protest Against Government," *RIA Novosti*, February 21, 2011; see http://wn.rian.ru/worldl/20110221/162698818.html.
66. Chorin interview with Ahmed Ibrahim Fagih, Cairo, November, 2011.
67. Duthel, Duthel Intelligence Report, p. 30.
68. "Ğābir 'Uṣfūr Yatanazzil 'an Ğa'izat al-Qaḏḏāfī Iḥtiğāğan 'alā al-Mağāzir fī Lībīyā," *al Ḥayāh*, February 27, 2011.
69. See http://www.un.org/apps/news/story.asp?NewsID=37633.
70. Colin Freeman, "How Britain Courted, Armed, and Trained a Libyan Monster," Tripoli, September 25, 2011.
71. See http://www.mashhadlibya.com/index.php?option=com_content&view=article&id=4144:-22-2011&catid=1:2010-03-09-10-35-20&Itemid=50.
72. The location of Mecca, relative to a Muslim's current position, and direction of prayer.
73. See http://www.mashhadlibya.com/index.php?option=com_content&view=article&id=4144:-22-2011&catid=1:2010-03-09-10-35-20&Itemid=50.
74. The US State Department also arranged a flight to follow the sealift. The ferry was stranded in Tripoli harbor for a few days due to rough seas.

75. "Libya's Humanitarian Crisis—As Protests Continue, Medical Supplies, along with Fuel and Food Are Running Dangerously Short," Al Jazeera English, February 28, 2011.
76. Chorin interviw with Maged Mahfouz, London, December 23, 2011.
77. "Thousands Flee Across Libya-Tunisa border," *Globe and Mail*, February 24, 2011; see www.theglobeandmail.com.
78. Humanitarian Situation Deteriorates, February 25, 2011; see www.icrc.org.
79. Chorin interview with Dr. Issam Hajjaji, October 2011.
80. Chorin interviw with Maged Mahfouz, London, December 23, 2011.
81. Wayne White, "Fighting in Libya: the Military balance," MEI Policy Watch #1768, March 3, 2012.
82. Duthel, Duthel Intelligence Report, p. 21.
83. Dayer Barbou; see www.globalsecurity.org.
84. Delphine Minoui, *Tripoliwood* (Paris: Bernard Grasset, 2011), p. 130.
85. See http://libyanfreepress.wordpress.com/2011/09/02/manifesto-of-the-libyan-tribal-council; and see http://www.mathaba.net/news/?x=628458.
86. Mathieu Guidère, *Le Choc des Revolutions Arabes* (Paris: Editions Autrement, 2011), pp. 97–114.
87. Chorin interview with Ambassador David Welch, November 2011,
88. Jon Lee Anderson, "Sons of the Revoluton," *The New Yorker*, May 9, 2011.
89. *The Economist*, February 26, 2011.
90. Guidère, *Le Choc*, p. 106.
91. David Kirkpatrick, "Tripoli residents tell of terror," *International Herald Tribune*, March 4, 2011.
92. Michael Peel, "Distrust Pervades Streets of Tripoli," *Financial Times*, August 8, 2011.
93. Wayne White, "Fighting in Libya: the Military balance," MEI Policy Watch #1768, March 3, 2012.
94. See http://www.voanews.com/content/clinton-us-far-from-decision-on-libya-no-fly-zone-117257118/135886.html.
95. "al-Qaḏḏāfī Yuʿlin Istirǧāʿ Mudun . . . wa al-Muʿāraḍah Tanfi," al-Hayāt, March 7, 2011.
96. "The colonel charges ahead," *The Economist*, March 19, 2011.
97. Ibid.
98. See http://abcnews.go.com/ThisWeek/week-transcript-saif-al-islam-saadi-gadhafi/story?id=13012239&page=4.
99. Editors, "'Unified Protector' Quels Parametres pour une Operation Lance sans Filet?" *Defense et Sécurité Internationale* (DSI), no. 70, May 2011, pp. 27–40.
100. "Libya mass rape claims: using Viagra would be a horrific first," posted June 9, 2011, Feb17.Info.
101. See http://www.google.com/hostednews/afp/article/AleqM5i-gZI_6hGmnPbI1MLAMXWSppP05g.
102. Human Rights Watch, Libya Report 2012.
103. Ibid.
104. Louis Charbonneau, "Strong proof of Libya crimes against humanity," ICC, posted to Feb17.info, May 2, 2011.
105. "Gaddafi Addresses Benghazi Residents," LibyaInfo.com, March 17, 2011.
106. See http://www.youtube.com/watch?v=ULw5lUG5wl0.
107. Chorin interview with Heather Kalmbach, December 21, 2011.
108. Michael Hastings, "Inside Obama's War Room," *Rolling Stone*, October 11, 2011.

CHAPTER 10

1. Barack H. Obama, "Remarks by the President on a New Beginning," June 4, 2009, transcript, http://whitehouse.gov/the _press_office/remarks-by-the-president-at_cairo_university.

2. Ibid.
3. Ibid.
4. Michael Hastings, "Inside Obama's War Room," *Rolling Stone*, October 11, 2011.
5. See http://www.nytimes.com/2011/03/03/world/africa/03military.html?pagewanted=all.
6. See http://www.nytimes.com/2011/04/03/opinion/03kristof.html?ref=nicholasdkristof.
7. See http://www.nytimes.com/2011/09/01/opinion/kristof-from-libyans-thank-you-america.html?_r=1&ref=nicholasdkristof.
8. Dirk Vandewalle, "How Not to Intervene In Libya," *Wall Street Journal*, March 10, 2011.
9. Ibid.
10. "Libya's no fly zone: The Military Balance," *The Economist*, March 3, 2011.
11. International Crisis Group, "A Ceasefire and Negotiations: the Right Way to Resolve the Libya Crisis," March 10, 2011; see http://www.crisisgroup.org/en/publication-type/media-releases/2011/a-ceasefire-and-negotiations-the-right-way-to-resolve-the-libya-crisis.aspx.
12. See http://www.crisisgroup.org/en/publication-type/media-releases/2011/a-ceasefire-and-negotiations-the-right-way-to-resolve-the-libya-crisis.aspx.
13. Richard McGregor and Peter Spiegel, "US split on response to Tripoli," *Financial Times*, March 10, 2011.
14. See http://www.ft.com/intl/cms/s/0/da6865be-4aa8-11e0-82ab-00144feab49a.html#axzz1z2eRESB9.
15. Joseph Berger, "U.S. Senators Call for No-Flight Zone Over Libya," *New York Times*, March 6, 2011.
16. See http://theamericanideal.wordpress.com/2011/03/10/wh-chief-of-staff-bill-daley-says-violence-in-libya-is-not-americas-problem-rather-a-human-problem.
17. Feb17.info (reference was removed from site).
18. See www.ft.com/intl/cms/s/0/da6865be-4aa8-11e0-82ab-00144feab49a.html .
19. CNN, "Paul Wolfowitz Hits Obama On Libya, Blames Pan Am Families For Bush Policy Toward Gaddafi," *Fareed Zakaria GPS*, video, February 27, 2011.
20. Michele Bachmann, "Obama 'Put Us in Libya. He Is Now Putting Us in Africa'" video, October 18, 2011. Bachmann was referring to a recent announcement that the US would be sending 100 American troops to Uganda.
21. "Herman Cain Stumbles on Libya Questions," *Huffington Post*, November 14, 2011.
22. See http://www.tnr.com/blog/plank/103782/start-the-attack-then-work-backwards.
23. Elliott Abrams, "Qaddafi's Fall: No, Obama Was Not Right," *National Review*, August 22, 2011.
24. See http://www.nationalreview.com/corner/262674/way-forward-libya-john-hannah.
25. Abrams, "Qaddafi's Fall: No, Obama Was Not Right," National Review, August 22, 2011.
26. Condoleezza Rice, *No Higher Honor* (New York, NY: Crown Publishing Group, 2011), p. 703.
27. See http://www.nytimes.com/2011/03/03/world/africa/03military.html?pagewanted=all.
28. Chorin interview, source requested anonymity.
29. Chorin interview, source requested anonymity.
30. Mark Mazzetti and Eric Schmitt, "CIA agents in Libya Aid Airstrikes and Meet Rebels," *New York Times*, March 30, 2011.
31. David Bromwich, "The CIA, the Libyan Rebellion, and the President," *Huffington Post*, March 31, 2011.
32. See http://www.reuters.com/article/2011/03/30/us-libya-usa-order-idUSTRE72T6H220110330.
33. Mazzetti and Schmitt, CIA agents in Libya Aid Airstrikes and Meet Rebels.

34. See www.dsi-presse.com/?p=3065.
35. Josh Rogin, "How Obama turned on a dime toward war," *Foreign Policy*, March 18, 2011.
36. Stephanie Funk, "The Domestic Context and Policy Process that Created an Unprecedented U.S. Policy to Libya," unpublished paper, National Defense University, National War College, Summer 2011, p. 4.
37. Robert Dreyfuss, "Obama's Women Advisers Pushed War Against Libya," *The Nation*, March 19, 2011.
38. Funk, "Domestic Context and Policy," p. 4.
39. Samantha Power, *A Problem from Hell: America and the Age of Genocide* (New York, NY: Harper Perennial, 2002), p. 261.
40. See http://www.thealtlantic.com/daily-dish/archive/2011/03/obama-and-r2p/174146.
41. Samantha Power had called Clinton a "monster" in an interview with UK media during the presidential campaign.
42. Rogin, "How Obama turned on a dime toward war."
43. See http://www.bangkokpost.com/lite/breakingnews/222970/libya-live-report.
44. See http://www.businessweek.com/news/2011-02-26/qaddafi-son-says-libya-at-risk-of-becoming-like-somalia.html.
45. Samantha Power, in *A Problem from Hell*, claims that President Bush Sr. intervened in Somalia mainly to deflect attention from atrocities in Bosnia, and to demonstrate that lack of action there was not a "Muslim thing". [Samantha Power, *A Problem from Hell* (New York, NY: Basic Books, 2002), p. 285.]
46. The piracy analogy went the other way as well: a recent book by Martin N. Murphy on Somalia-based piracy was titled: *Somalia: The New Barbary?: Piracy and Islam in the Horn of Africa* (New York, NY: Columbia University Press, 2010).
47. See http://en.trend.az/regions/met/arabicr/1839151.html; "Clinton: US Worried about Libya becoming 'giant Somalia,'" Deutsche Presse-Agentur, March 3, 2011; see http://abcnews.go.com/blogs/politics/2011/03/clintons-biggest-fear-libya-as-a-big-somalia-says-al-qaeda-affiliates-are-biggest-threat.
48. See http://in.reuters.com/article/2011/03/08/idINIndia-55392520110308.
49. See http://www.bbc.co.uk/news/mobile/uk-13044846; Mas'a arabi li iqna' al qadhafi bi 'al manfa' wa amreeka takhshi min 'Sumal Kabir.'
50. Gianandrea Gaiani, "The Leader in Tripoli's Method's to Isolate the Islamists," Sole-24 Ore, March 4, 2006.
51. "Al-Qaeda in N. Africa Backs Uprising," Agence France Presse, February 23, 2011.
52. "Cameron's lead of Libya sows Confusion," *Financial Times*, March 3, 2011.
53. See http://www.thenational.ae/news/world/middle-east/prominent-britons-scramble-to-repudiate-links-with-saif-qaddafi#page2.
54. See http://www.sify.com/news/france-puts-diplomatic-relations-with-libya-on-ice-news-international-lc1gEgecbic.html.
55. See http://af.reuters.com/article/libyaNews/idAFPISQDE72H20110226.
56. Editors, "'Unified Protector' Quels Parametres pour une Operation Lance sans Filet?" *Defense et Sécurité Internationale* (DSI), no. 70, May 2011, p. 34.
57. See http://www.guardian.co.uk/world/2011/mar/27/libya-bernard-henri-levy-france.
58. Bernard-Henri Lévy, *La Guerre Sans l'Aimer* (Paris: Bernard Grasset, 2011), p. 81.
59. Ibid., p. 100.
60. *Le Nouvel Observateur* (unknown date).
61. Marc Pierini, *Le prix de la liberté* (Paris: Actes Sud, 2008), p. 139.
62. See http://www.economist.com/blogs/newsbook/2011/03/frances_role_libya.
63. Editors, "'Unified Protector,'" p. 28.
64. Ibid., p. 28.
65. See http://frenchpolitics.blogs.france24.com/article/2011/04/05/saving-president-sarkozy-0.

66. See http://www.rt.com/news/sarkozy-gaddafi-campaign-contribution-238.
67. Ibid.
68. See http://www.reuters.com/article/2011/02/28/us-libya-usa-clinton -idUSTRE71Q1JA20110228.
69. See http://www.reuters.com/article/2011/02/28/us-libya-usa-clinton -idUSTRE71Q1A20110228.
70. See http://www.guardian.co.uk/world/2011/mar/03/libyan-leader-stand-down -obama.
71. Stephanie Funk, "The Domestic Context and Policy Process that Created an Unprecedented U.S. Policy to Libya," unpublished paper, National Defense Universtiy, National War College, Summer 2011.
72. See http://frontpagemag.com/2011/03/23/samantha-power-the-troubling-woman -behind-the-curtain-of-obama's-libya-policy.
73. See http://www.nytimes.com/2011/03/30/world/30power.html.
74. Obama, "Remarks by the President on a New Beginning."
75. See http://www.washingtonpost.com/world/national-security/the-libyan-war -clintons-role/2011/10/30/gIQArixGXM_gallery.html.
76. Hastings, "Inside Obama's War Room."
77. Ibid.
78. Musa Kusa was named foreign minister in a cabinet shuffle in 2009, replacing Abdelrahman Shalgam.
79. Jon Lee Anderson ,"Sons of the Revolution," *New Yorker*, May 9, 2011.
80. Chorin interview with Adel Husni Bey, July 21, 2012.
81. Chorin interview with Youcif Mgarief, April 2012.
82. Lévy, *La Guerre aans l'Aimer*, p. 121.
83. See www.ipotnews.com/index.php?jdl=UAE_condemns_Libya_violence _offers_aid&level2=newsandopinion&level3=&level4=LIBYA&news_id= 433297&group_news=ALLNEWS&taging=subtype=LIBYA&popular+&search= y&q=LIBYA.
84. Ibid.
85. "Masā' al-Arbiʿā' li-Iqnāʿ al-Qaḏḏāfī bi-l-Manfā wa Amrīkā Taḫša min 'Sumāl Kabīr, *Al Hayat*, March 3, 2011.
86. See http://dawn.com/2011/02/23/ahmadinejad-tells-arab-leaders-to-respect -protesters.
87. See http://www.guardian.co.uk/world/2011/mar/17/un-security-council-resolution.
88. Hastings, "Inside Obama's War Room."
89. "Libya Thanks Qatari Task Force at Honoring Ceremony in Doha," Tripoli Post, May 26–June 1, p. 5.
90. Lancement d'une Chaine de Television par L'opposition Libyenne depuis Doha, *Moyen- Orient*, July-September 2011, p. 75.
91. Pierini, p. 116.
92. Hugh Eakin, "The Strange Power of Qatar," *Financial Times*, October 27, 2011.
93. Laurent de Saint Périer, "le Qatar mise et gagne," in *Jeune Afrique*, September, 4–10, 2011.
94. Laurent de Saint Périer, "Le Qatar Mise en Gagne," in *Jeune Afrique*, September 4-10, 2011.
95. "No Illusions," *The Economist*, March 19, 2011.
96. Editors, "Unified Protector," pp. 26–40.
97. Jean-Marc Tanguy, *Harmattan: Récits et Révélations* (Paris: Nimrod, 2012), p. 42.
98. Joby Warrick, "Clinton credited with key role in success of NATO airstrikes, Libyan rebels," *Washington Post*, October 28, 2011; see http://www.washingtonpost.com /world/national-security/hillarys-war-how-conviction-replaced-skepticism-in-libya -intervention/2011/10/28/gIQAhGS7WM_story.html.

99. See http://www.guardian.co.uk/world/2011/jun/21/arab-league-chief-libya-air-strikes?INTCMP=SRCH.
100. "A United front against Gaddafi," *Financial Times*, March 21, 2011.
101. Charles Clover, "Tripoli's anti Gaddafi Voices reemerge," *Financial Times*, March 23, 2011.
102. "Allies will allow dictator to Leave Libya," *The Times* (of London), March 29, 2011.
103. See http://www.independent.co.uk/news/world/middle-east/americas-secret-plan-to-arm-libyas-rebels-2234227.html.
104. Chorin interivew with Hunsi Bey, May 2011.
105. See http://feb17.info/news/algerian-regime-shows-itself-to-be-a-true-friend-to-qaddafi.
106. More-junior State Department officials expressed doubts about the "criticality" of Power's role, saying she was not in evidence at early sub-principal Libya meetings.
107. Gareth Evans , "Responding to Mass Atrocity Crimes: The 'Responsibility to Protect' After Libya," transcript, Chatham House, October 2011; see http://www.chathamhouse.org/publications/papers/view/178795.
108. Matthew Moran, "Saving President Sarkozy?," April 5, 2011; see http://frenchpolitics.blogs.france24.com/article/2011/04/05/saving-president-sarkozy-0.
109. Duthel, Duthel Intelligence Report.
110. See http://www.nytimes.com/2011/03/29/us/politics/29prexy-text.html?pagewanted=all.

CHAPTER 11

1. "Binġāzī Tasta'idd li-z-Zaḥf Ġarban," *al Hayāt*, March 3, 2011.
2. See http://www.washingtonpost.com/world/national-security/the-libyan-war-clintons-role/2011/10/30/gIQArixGXM_gallery.html.
3. See http://www.hrw.org/world-report-2012/time-abandon-autocrats-and-embrace-rights.
4. See http://www.nytimes.com/2011/06/16/us/politics/16powers.html?pagewanted=all.
5. Jon Hilsenrath, "Gates Says Libya Not Vital National Interest," *Wall Street Journal*, March 27, 2011; see http://www.youtube.com/watch?v=2Ev7TyrP08k.
6. Steve Chapman, "Robert Gates and our 'interest' in Libya," *Chicago Tribune*, March 28, 2011.
7. Woodward, Bob, *Veil: The Secret Wars of the CIA, 1981–1987* (New York, NY: Simon and Schuster, 1987), p. 364.
8. Hilsenrath, "Gates Says Libya Not Vital National Interest."
9. "Lugar Challenges Obama Administration on Libyan War Authorization," May 13, 2011; see http://lugar.senate.gov/record.cfm?id=332842&.
10. State Department, State of Continuing Emergency Release, February 2012.
11. Michael Young, "Promising Clarity on Libya, Obama delivers confusion," *The National*, March 31, 2011.
12. Editors, "De l'importance des Fondamentaux," DSI, no. 70, May 2011, p. 25.
13. See http://www.nytimes.com/2011/03/30/opinion/30friedman.html?ref=thomaslfriedman.
14. Editors, "Unified Protector," pp. 26–40.
15. Ibid., p. 30.
16. Chorin interview, source requested anonymity.
17. Chorin interview with Maged Mahfouz, November 25, 2011.
18. Shabakat Corporation, International Republican Institute Survey of Pubilc Opinion in Eastern Libya, October 12–25, 2011; see www.shabakat.se, quoted in Marbo3a.
19. Editors, "Unified Protector," pp. 26–40.

20. International Crisis Group, "A Ceasefire and Negotiations the Right Way to Resolve the Libya Crisis," ICG website, March 10, 2011; see https://www.google.com/#hl=en&sclient=psy-ab&q=international+crisis+group+right+way+to+resolve+Libya&oq=international+crisis+group+right+way+to+resolve+Libya&gs_l=hp.3...771.10870.0.11126.75.49.10.13.14.5.390.8332.0j40j8j1.49.0...0.0.lAGEYx2Pf4s&pbx=1&bav=on.2,or.r_gc.r_pw.r_qf.,cf.osb&fp=6b20fd341076c19f&biw=1366&bih=622.
21. Nick Meo, "Col Gaddafi refuses to step down, playing chess instead," *The Telegraph*, June 13, 2011; see http://www.telegraph.co.uk/news/worldnews/africaandindianocean/libya/8573080/Col-Gaddafi-refuses-to-step-down-playing-chess-instead.html.
22. Bernard-Henri Lévy, *La Guerre sans l'Aimer* (Paris: Bernard Grasset, 2011), p. 217.
23. "Libye: Crise libyenne—Museveni portraiture Kadhafi," *Jeune Afrique*, April 19, 2011.
24. See http://allafrica.com/stories/201103240033.html.
25. See http://www.huffingtonpost.com/doug-noll/another-international-med_b_872106.html.
26. See http://www.nytimes.com/2011/04/06/opinion/06Weldon.html.
27. Verini, James, "The Good Bad Son," in *New York Magazine*, May 22, 2011; see http://nymag.com/news/politics/saif-qaddafi-2011-5.
28. Michael Hastings, "Inside Obama's War Room," *Rolling Stone*, October 11, 2011.
29. Lévy, *La Guerre sans l'Aimer*, p. 279.
30. Dirk Vandewalle, *A History of Modern Libya*, 2nd ed., (Cambridge, England: Cambridge University Press, 2012), p. 207.
31. "Assistant Secretary Of State Jeffrey Feltman Discusses Libya, Syria, and Lebanon During an Interview on Alhurra Television," July 27, 2011.
32. Lévy, *La Guerre sans l'Aimer*, p. 123.
33. Rafāīl Lūzan, "Lā Astabaʿad an Yakūn al-Qaḏḏāfī Saʿī li-l-Ḥuṣūl ʿalā Musāʿadah min Isrāʾīl," *aš-Šarq al-Aswaṭ*, October 12, 2011; Waṯāʾiq, "Alāqāt Istiḫbārāt al-Qaḏḏāfī Tuṯīr Ǧadalan Dawliyyan," *aš-Šarq al-Awsaṭ*, September 4, 2011.
34. "Gaḏḏāfī Yuwaffid Mabʿūṯīn ʾilā Israʾīl," reprinted from Aljazeera.net in Ṣawt, July 14, 2011.
35. See http://wee.aljazeera.com/indepth/features/2011/08/2011831151258728747.html; Minā al-ʿArabī. "Ǧadal Ḥawl Waṯāʾiq Lībīyyah tarbuṭ David Welch bi-l-baḥṯ ʿan 'Muḫriǧ' li-l-Qaḏḏāfī." *aš-Šarq al-Awsat*, September 1, 2011.
36. Minā al-ʿArabī, "Ǧadal Ḥawl Waṯāʾiq Lībīyyah Tarbuṭ Dafīd Wīlš bi-l-Baḥṯ ʿan 'Muḫriǧ' li-l-Qaḏḏāfī," *aš-Šarq al-Awsat*, September 1, 2011.
37. See http://wee.aljazeera.com/indepth/features/2011/08/2011831151258728747.html; al-ʿArabī, Minā, "Ǧadal Ḥawl Waṯāʾiq Lībīyyah tarbuṭ David Welch bi-l-baḥṯ ʿan 'Muḫriǧ' li-l-Qaḏḏāfī," aš-Šarq al-Awsat, September 1, 2011; and see http://thecable.foreignpolicy.com/posts/2011/08/31/state_department_we weren't_ part_of_the_qaddafi_welsh_meetings.
38. Minā al-ʿArabī, "Ǧadal Ḥawl Waṯāʾiq Lībīyyah Tarbuṭ Dafīd Wīlš bi-l-Baḥṯ ʿan 'Muḫriǧ' li-l-Qaḏḏāfī," *aš-Šarq al-Awsat*, September 1, 2011.
39. Ibid.
40. Chorin interview with US Department of State Libya Desk Officer, January 2012; Victoria Nuland, State Department spokesperson, said, "David Welch, a former assistant secretary, is now a private citizen. This was a private trip. He was not carrying any message from the U.S. government." See http://thecable.foreignpolicy.com/posts/2011/08/31/state_department_we weren't_ part_of_the_qaddafi_welsh_meetings.
41. Chorin interview with Assistant Secretary Welch, July 2011.
42. See http://www.state.gov/r/pa/prs/ps/2011/09/171603.htm.
43. Chorin interview with Dirk Vandewalle, November 2011.
44. Chorin interview with Assistant Secretary Indyk, November 29, 2011.
45. Profile of Ali Tarhouni in *The Atlantic*, November 2011, p. 64.

46. See http://articles.cnn.com/2011-04-04/world/libya.rebel.leader_1_wadi-doum-libyan-exiles-libyan-pows?_s=PM:WORLD; see http://www.theaustralian.com.au/news/world/new-rebel-commander-khalifa-haftar-aims-to-build-disciplined-fighting-force/story-e6frg6so-1226032915918.
47. See http://www.telegraph.co.uk/news/obituaries/politics-obituaries/8671455/General-Abdel-Fattah-Younes.html.
48. See http://www.guardian.co.uk/world/2011/sep/08/libya-mahmoud-jibril-growing-unrest.
49. See http://www.guardian.co.uk/world/2011/apr/03/libya-rebel-leadership-split.
50. *Jeune Afrique*, April 10-16, 2011.
51. See http://www.telegraph.co.uk/news/obituaries/politics-obituaries/8671455/General-Abdel-Fattah-Younes.html.
52. "Assassination attempt on Benghazi official: said to be linked to Younis killing," *Libya Herald*, March 5, 2011.
53. Chorin interview, source requested anonymity.
54. Ethan Chorin, "The Graffiti of Benghazi;" see http://wordswithoutborders.org/dispatches/article/the-graffiti-of-benghazi.
55. Samia Nakhoul, "Libyan Scholar Urges Help for Rebels Fighting Gaddafi," Reuters, March 11, 2011; see http://www.tripolipost.com/articledetail.asp?c=1&i=6600.

CHAPTER 12

1. aṣ-Ṣādiq an-Nayhūm, "Qiṣaṣ Aṭfāl," *Lībīyā* (Tala Books/Arab Diffusion Company, 2002), reprinted and translated in Chorin, *Translating Libya*.
2. Abdelhakim Belhaj, "Du Djihad a la Revolution," *Jeune Afrique*, no. 2643, September 4–10, 2011, p. 26.
3. Ḫālid Maḥmūd, "ad-Duktur Maḥmūd Ğibrīl Yukaššif li-aš-Šharq al-Awsaṭ ʿan Muḫaṭṭat al-Qaḏḏāfī li-l-ʿAwdah ʾilā as-Sulṭah," *aš-Šarq al-Awsaṭ*, October 18, 2011.
4. Claudia Gazzini, "Who Tipped Off the Libyans?," blog post, November 3, 2008; see http://claudiagazzini.com/website/blog/index.php?p=27.
5. Ḫālid Maḥmūd, "ad-Duktur Maḥmūd Ğibrīl Yukaššif li-aš-Šharq al-Awsaṭ ʿan Muḫaṭṭat al-Qaḏḏāfī li-l-ʿAwdah ʾilā as-Sulṭah," *aš-Šarq al-Awsaṭ*, October 18, 2011.
6. Chorin interview, source requested anonymity.
7. Ḫālid Maḥmūd, "ad-Duktur Maḥmūd Ğibrīl Yukaššif li-aš-Šharq al-Awsaṭ ʿan Muḫaṭṭat al-Qaḏḏāfī li-l-ʿAwdah ʾilā as-Sulṭah," *aš-Šarq al-Awsaṭ*, October 18, 2011.
8. Ibid.
9. "Masʾūl Lībī: Sayf al-Islām fī Banī Walīd wa Muʿtaṣim fī Sirt," aš-Šarq al-Awsaṭ, Sept.ember 29, 2011.
10. "Qiyādī fī Ğibhat aṯ-Ṯūwwār: Tamm Taḥdīd Mawqiʿ Sayf al-Islām fī Ṣaḥraʾ Ğanūb Šarqi Ṭarāblus," *aš-Šarq al-Awsaṭ*, October 20, 2011.
11. Chorin interview, source requested anonymity.
12. "Muammar Gaddafi Dead: Mansour Iddhow, Former Servant, Recounts Colonel's Final Days;" see http://www.huffingtonpost.com/2012/02/21/muammar-gaddafi-dead-mansour-iddhow_n_1290789.html.
13. See http://news.sky.com/home/world-news/article/16095070.
14. Chorin interview, source requested anonymity.
15. Chorin interview, source requested anonymity.
16. Chorin interview, source requested anonymity.
17. *aš-Šarq al-Awsat*, October 23–24, 2011.
18. Kim Gamel, "Gadhafi's burial delayed for further investigation," Associated Press, October 21, 2011.
19. Chorin interview, source requested anonymity.
20. Human Rights Watch, World Report 2012; see http://www.hrw.org/world-report-2012.

21. Aḥmad Ibrāhīm al-Faqīh, *aṭ-Ṭāġiyyah fi-t-Tarīḫ, Muqaddimah fi tašrīḫ aṭ-Ṭāġiyyah*, unpublished 2011, p. 73.
22. "Libya unearths largest mass grave of civil war dead with 157 bodies in battleground town," Associated Press, March 4, 2012.
23. Chorin interview, source requested anonymity.
24. Corbett B. Daly, "Clinton on Qaddafi: 'We Came, We Saw, He Died,'" CBS News, October 20, 2011.
25. Chorin interview, source requested anonymity.
26. See http://wfol.tv/index.php?option=com_k2&view=item&id=246:jibril-foreign -elements-ordered-gadhafi-dead.
27. Adam Nossiter and Kareem Fahim, "Revolution Won, Top Libyan Official Promises Elections and a more Pious State," *New York Times*, October 23, 2011.
28. Ḫālid Maḥmūd, "ad-Duktur Maḥmūd Ğibrīl Yukaššif li-aš-Šharq al-Awsaṭ ʿan Muḫaṭṭat al-Qaḏḏāfī li-l-ʿAwdah ʾilā as-Sulṭah," *aš-Šarq al-Awsaṭ*, October 18, 2011.
29. "ad-Duktur Maḥmūd Ğibrīl yukaššif li-aš-Šharq al-Awsaṭ ʿan Muḫaṭṭat al-Qaḏḏāf'i li-l-ʿAwdah ʾilā as-Sulṭa," interview with Maḥmūd Ğibrīl in aš-Šarq al-Awsaṭ, October 18, 2011.
30. "Libya: 'Out of Control' Militias Commit Widespread Abuses, a Year On from Uprising," press release, Amnesty International, February 16, 2012; see www.amnesty.org.
31. Chorin interview, source requested anonymity.
32. Nossiter and Fahim; "Revolution Won, Top Libyan Official Promises Elections and a More Pious State."
33. Human Rights Watch, World Report 2012; see http://www.hrw.org/world-report -2012.
34. See http://www.youtube.com/watch?v=SPTTkNstS58.
35. Human Rights Watch, World Report 2012; see http://www.hrw.org/world-report -2012.
36. Chorin interview with Azza Maghur, January 19, 2012.
37. Chorin interview, source requested anonymity.
38. "Lībīyā: Maqtal 5 wa Iṣābat 20 fī Ištibāqāt bayn Anṣār al-Qaḏḏāfī wa Ṯūwwār fī Banī Walīd," *aš-Šarq al-Awsaṭ*, January 24, 2012.
39. "Lībīyā: Istiqālāt wa Iʿtiṣāmāt wa ʿAbd al-Ğalīl Yuṯār min "Huwa bi-lā Qarār," *aš-Šarq al-Awsaṭ*, January 23, 2012.
40. "Anba' howl Dhuhur mufaji' li-Khamees Al Qadafi bi saaq mubtawara," *aš-Šarq al-Awsaṭ*, February 26, 2012.
41. Human Rights Watch, World Report 2012; see http://www.hrw.org/world-report -2012.
42. See http://www.bbc.co.uk/news/world-africa-13251570.
43. "22 people killed in Libya in clashes between rival towns in country's West," Associated Press, April 3, 2011.
44. See http://www.bbc.co.uk/news/world-africa-17413626.
45. "Qiyadi bilZintan: Saif ma zal 'ala qina'atihi al qadima'..wa tartibaat limuhakimatili 'alaaniyya : Abdel sitar hatita," *aš-Šarq al-Awsaṭ*, January 31, 2012.
46. Šukrī Ġānim, "Ṣunduq Aswad Aḫar Yatawārī," *Lībīyā al-Yawm*, May 7, 2012.
47. "Mawt al-Maqrāhī...wa Ḥaqīqat al-Muʾāmirah," *Lībīyā al-Yawm*, May 28, 2012, p. 7.
48. See http://www.guardian.co.uk/uk/2011/feb/23/gaddafi-lockerbie-bombing -minister-libya.
49. See http://www.nytimes.com/2012/06/06/world/africa/libya-trial-opens-for-ex-spy -chief.html.

CHAPTER 13

1. Chorin interview with Dr. Laila Bugaighis, May 28, 2012.
2. ʿAbd ar-Raḥmān Šalġam, *Ašḫāṣ ḥawl al-Qaḏḏāfī* (Dubai: Dār al-Farğiyānī/Madārik Publishers, 2012) p. 53.

3. Chorin interview, source requested anonymity.
4. Chorin interview with Rida Bey, November 22, 2011.
5. Chorin interview with Maged Mahfouz and others, Winter 2011.
6. Mark Mazzetti and Eric Schmitt, "C.I.A. Agents in Libya Aid Airstrikes and Meet Rebels," *New York Times*, March 30, 2011. The article implies that Libya fell "out of focus" as an object of intelligence gathering itself, after the rapprochement.
7. Ibid.
8. Lisa Anderson, "La Libye de Kadhafi," *Monde Arabe Machrek*, no. 170, October–December 2000, p. 15.
9. See http://www.google.com/url?sa=t&rct=j&q=&esrc=s&source=web&cd=8&ved=0CGUQFjAH&url=http%3A%2F%2Flnweb90.worldbank.org%2FCAW%2FCawdoclib.nsf%2FvewCrossCountryStudies%2F87F59BE2E95BC9B285256D0A004C1D91%2F%24file%2Fwp0041.pdf&ei=A72JT9-UIIX6tgeLnZDGCQ&usg=AFQjCNHMaVfDi9rEYrEtYmPyNu77d3HgFw&sig2=Fg1Tdzf41t3Jaf9aQF7nhw.
10. Chorin interview with Ed Morse, Citibank, June 27, 2012.
11. Ibid., July 1, 2012.
12. Moncef Djaziri, "Libye: Les enjeux economiques de la "guerre pour la democratie," *Moyen-Orient*, October-December 2011, pp. 78-83.
13. Ibid, p. 81.
14. Chorin interview, source requested anonymity.
15. Kenneth G. Lieberthal and Michael E. O'Hanlon, "Scoring Obama's Foreign Policy," *Foreign Affairs*, May/June 2012.
16. Ibid.
17. Ibid.
18. See http://www.leader-khamenei.com/khamenei-lectures/1779-haram-emamreza90.html.
19. See http://www.foreignpolicy.com/articles/2012/04/13/backed_into_a_corner?page=full.
20. See http://www.sudanvisiondaily.com/modules.php?name=News&file=article&sid=19413.
21. Chorin interview with Karim Sadjadpour, March 4, 2012.
22. Alanoud Al Sharekh, "Reform and Rebirth in the Middle East, in Survival," International Institute for Strategic Studies, April–May 2011, p. 53.
23. See http://www.euronews.com/2011/08/31/iran-leader-tells-libya-rebels-to-beware-of-west.
24. Chorin interview with Ahmed Sheibani, July 4, 2012.
25. Chorin interview, source requested anonymity, but also see Andrew Feinstein and Jean-Marc Tanguy in Bibliography for more information.
26. Bernard-Henri Lévy, *La Guerre sans l'Aimer* (Paris: Bernard Grasset, 2011), p. 279.
27. Andrew Feinstein, *The Shadow World* (New York, NY: Farrar, Straus and Giroux, 2011), p. 492.
28. Ibid., p. 491.
29. Chorin interview, source requested anonymity.
30. See http://jalopnik.com/5793212/libyan-blood-on-american-trucks.
31. Daya Gamage, "Intelligence Partnership between Libya and the CIA on counter-terrorism," *Asian Tribune*, Washington, DC, March 21, 2011; see Asiantribune.com.
32. Dirk Vandewalle, *A Modern History of Libya*, 2nd ed. (Cambridge, England: Cambridge University Press, 2012), p. 146.
33. Feinstein, *The Shadow World*, p. 490.
34. Ronald Bruce St. John, *Libya and the United States: Two Centuries of Strife* (Philadelphia, PA: University of Pennsylvania Press, 2002), p. 10.
35. Shadi Hamid, "Tunisia: Birthplace of the Revolution," in *The Arab Awakening* (Washington, DC: Brookings, 2011), p. 115.

36. See http://www.nytimes.com/2011/01/31/world/middleeast/31diplo.html.
37. See http://content.usatoday.com/communities/theoval/post/2011/03/obama-live-on-libya/1#.T-6yCZj7X3A.
38. Laura Rozen, "Hillary Clinton to UN: Stand with Syrian people or be 'complicit' in crackdown," *The Envoy*, January 31, 2012.
39. "Sarkozy: 2012 'Aam al Makhatir..wa lan naskat ala "al Fathihat assooriyya,'" *aš-Šarq al-Awsaṭ*, January 21, 2012.

CHAPTER 14

1. 2012 National Survey of Libya, Shabakat Corporation, International Republican Institute Survey of Public Opinion in Eastern Libya, October 12–25, 2011; see www.shabakat.se, quoted in newslist Marbo3a.
2. Some still insist it is the opposite, i.e., Saif is paying off the Zintanis to keep him from both the ICC and the NTC.
3. Chorin interview, source requested anonymity.
4. See http://www.almanaralink.com/press/2012/06/18024/; Declan Walsh and Eric Schmitt, "Drone Strike Killed No. 2 in Al Qaeda, U.S. Officials Say," *New York Times*, June 5 2012; see http://www.nytimes.com/2012/06/06/world/asia/qaeda-deputy-killed-in-drone-strike-in-pakistan.html?pagewanted=all.
5. "Libya: The Uncalm South," *The Economist*, May 12, 2012.
6. Asmaa Elourfi, "Libya: Al-Qaeda elements surface in Derna," *Magharebia*, April 5, 2012; see http://www.uruknet.info/?p=m87084&fb=.1
7. "Dirnah Madīnah Lībīyyah Mahmūlah Tukāfiḥ li-Tabdīd Sūratiha' Kama'Qāl li- 'al-Qāʿidah'," *al-Ḥayāt*/Reuters, May 7, 2011. p. 5.
8. See http://www.carnegieendowment.org/files/030912_transcript_libyapm1.pdf.
9. "Irtiya' fi As-Shaari'a li tamdid fitrat al tasjeel," *Libiyya*, May 15, 2012, p. 1.
10. See http://www.al-bab.com/arab/docs/libya/Libya-Draft-Constitutional-Charter-for-the-Transitional-Stage.pdf; the original drafters of the *bayan* (Baja et al.), perhaps taking a lesson from former Prime Minister Mustafa Ben Halim (one of whose main regrets from the 1960s was his failure to encourage political parties, a situation that he felt created vulnerabilities that Gaddafi all too deftly exploited.), felt the new constitution should encourage the creation of political parties.
11. Mahmoud Jibril, elected head of Alliance of National Forces, *Libya Herald*, March 14, 2012; see http://www.libyaherald.com/mahmoud-jibril-elected-head-of-alliance-of-national-forces.
12. Ibid.
13. "Ahzab al libiyya tu'aani min al tahmeesh wasat tusaa'id dowr qaadat al qaba'il wa milisheeaat," *Asharq Al Awsat*, January 31, 2012.
14. Judith Gurney, *Libya: The Political Economy of Oil* (Oxford, England: Oxford University Press, 1996), p. 85.
15. Chorin interview, source requested anonymity.
16. See http://english.alarabiya.net/articles/2012/03/05/198799.html.
17. Christopher Stephen and Caroline Alexander, "Libya's Post-Qaddafi Government is Hobbled as Misrata's City State Thrives," Bloomberg, February 28, 2012.
18. Mohamed Eljarh, "Federalism Would Preserve Libya's Unity," *Fikra Forum*, April 3, 2012.
19. Ḫālid Maḥmūd, "Raʾīs al-Mağlis al-Ahlī fī Ḥaḍramūt:Lan Naqbil illā bi-Iqlīm Fadarālī fī al-Ḥadd al-adnā," *aš-Šarq al-Awsaṭ*, January 20, 2012.
20. See http://www.mepc.org/articles-commentary/commentary/islamic-party-wins-tunisia?print.
21. See http://www.nytimes.com/2012/01/22/world/middleeast/muslim-brotherhood-wins-47-of-egypt-assembly-seats.html.

22. *Salafism* and *Islamism* are highly imprecise terms, encompassing various strains of thought. Those who call themselves Salafis range from eschewing politics entirely (the "quietists") to those who advocate violence to achieve their objectives (the "Jihadists").
23. Chorin interview, source requested anonymity.
24. Shabakat Corporation, International Republican Institute Survey of Public Opinion in Eastern Libya, October 12–25, 2011; see www.shabakat.se.
25. Chorin interview, source requested anonymity.
26. Chorin interview, source requested anonymity.
27. Chorin interview, source requested anonymity.
28. Borzou Daragahi, "Delays to Libya elections spark concern," *Financial Times*, May 30, 2012; see http://www.ft.com/intl/cms/s/0/19487524-aa63-11e1-8b9d-00144feabdc0.html.
29. Ralph Chami, "Libya beyond the revolution: Challenges and Opportunities," International Monetary Fund, Washington, DC, 2012.
30. See http://www.libya-businessnews.com/2012/04/16/libyan-oil-exports-to-total-1-29-million-bpd-in-may.
31. "Qatar's QNB acquires 49% stake in Libyan Bank," Arabianbusiness.com, April 14, 2012.
32. Alex Blumberg, "How to avoid the oil curse," *NPR Planet Money*, September 6, 2011.
33. See http://www.imf.org/external/pubs/ft/dp/2012/1201mcd.pdf, p. 13.
34. Fathi M. bin Issa, "Some of us fight with guns, others with pens;" see http://www.reinventinglibya.org/index.php.
35. ʿAbd al-Qādir al-Aǧtal, "Ḥurriyyat al-Intiḫābāt wa Ḥurriyyat al Iʿlām Lā Yaktamil Aḥaduhumā bī-dūn al-Āḫar," *Lībīyā al-Yawm*, May 28, 2012..
36. Compilation of Libya's print and broadcast media, MICT, January 2012; see http://www.reinventinglibya.org/index.php.
37. The judge who ordered Younes's arrest was found dead in Benghazi in late June 2012.
38. "Lībīyā: Maqtal 5 wa Iṣābat 20 fī Ištibāqāt bayn Anṣār al-Qaḏḏāfī wa Ṯūwwār fī Banī Walīd," *aš-Šarq al-Awsaṭ*, January 24, 2012.
39. Gada Mahfud, "Go Bengo Go!" *The Tripoli Post*, May 26–June 1, 2012, p. 6.
40. Editors, "intikhabaat Benghazi duruus fi al amaliyyat al intikhaabiyya," *Libya Al Yowm*, May 28, 2012.
41. Libya Country Profile 2012, USAID.
42. Ibid.
43. See http://el-karama.org/content/libyan-women's-platform-peace-kicks-strategic-communications-trainings-tripoli-misrata-and-benghazi, May 17, 2012.
44. Chorin interview, source requested anonymity.
45. "Irtiya' fi As-Shaari'a li tamdid fitrat al tasjeel," *Libiyya*, May 15, 2012, p. 1.
46. "Libya's election: A big step for a battered country," *The Economist*, July 14, 2012, p. 43,
47. Ḫālid Maḥmūd, "Lībīyā: al-Istiqālāt taʿṣif bi-l-Maǧlis al-Intiqālī . . . wa Ḥakūmat al-Kīb Taltazim aṣ-Ṣamt," *aš-Šharq al-Awsaṭ*, July 9, 2012.
48. Chorin interview with Dr. Laila Bugaighis.
49. Assijin Assabiq fi Guantanamo Sufyaan bin Qummu, "Ana lastu min al Qaeda . . . sauqaatil ria al raayat assuda," *Al Ahwal*, May 16, 2012.
50. Chorin interview with Dr. Issam Hajjaji, June 10, 2012.

CONCLUSION

1. Chorin interview with Libyan businessman Husni Bey, July 2011.
2. See http://topics.nytimes.com/top/news/international/countriesandterritories/egypt/index.html.

3. Most of these figures come from NTC and Ministry of Health sources in 2011 and 2012; http://www.nytimes.com/2011/09/17/world/africa/skirmishes-flare-around-qaddafi-strongholds.html?pagewanted=all.
4. Martin S. Indyk, Kenneth G. Lieberthal, and Michael E. O'Hanlon, "Scoring Obama's Foreign Policy," *Foreign Affairs*, May/June 2012, p. 39.
5. Natan Sharansky, *The Case for Democracy: The Power of Freedom to Overcome Tyranny & Terror* (New York: PublicAffairs, 2004), p. 3.

BIBLIOGRAPHY

Periodicals

IN ARABIC

Aḫbār al-Ān (Libya)
al-Ahrām (Egypt)
al-Aḥwāl (Libya)
al-Hayāt (Pan Arab)
al-Kalimah (Libya)
al-Lībī (Libya)
al-Manār (Libya)
al-Mušāhid (BBC publication)
aš-Šarq al-Awsaṭ (Pan Arab)
Lībiyah al-Yawm (Libya)
Miyādīn (Libya)
Quraynah (Libya)
Sawt (Libya)

IN ENGLISH

Daedalus
Dissent
Financial Times
Foreign Affairs
Foreign Policy
New York Times
The Africa Report
The Atlantic
The Economist
Tripoli Post
Wall Street Journal
Washington Post

IN FRENCH

Défense et sécurité international (DSI)
Jeune Afrique
Le Monde
Le Monde diplomatique
Manière de Voir
Moyen-Orient

Monographs

IN ENGLISH

Bowen, Wyn Q., *Libya and Nuclear Non-Proliferation: Stepping Back from the Brink* (Adelphi Paper 380). London, England: Routledge Press, IISS, May 2006.

Chorin, Ethan, *Country Commercial Guide, Libya 2006*. Washington, D.C.: U.S. Liaison Office, U.S. Department of State, 2006.

Hightower, Barrett, *Libya Guide to an Emerging Market*. Washington, D.C.: Corporate Council on Africa, December 2004.

International Monetary Fund, with Ralph Chami, *Libya Beyond the Revolution: Challenges and Opportunities*. Washington, D.C.: International Monetary Fund, 2012.

Monitor Group and CERA, *National Economic Strategy: Assessment of the Competitiveness of the Libyan Arab Jamahiriya*. Tripoli, Libya: General Planning Council of Libya, 2006.

Moss, Dana, *Reforming the Rogue: Lessons from the U.S.-Libya Rapprochement* (Policy Focus #105). Washington, D.C.: Washington Institute for Near East Policy, August 2010.

Vandewalle, Dirk, *Libya: Post-War Challenges* (African Bank for Development Economic Brief). Tunis, Tunisia: African Bank for Development, September 2011.

Woolf, Right Hon. Lord Harry, *The Woolf Inquiry: An Inquiry into the LSE's Links with Libya and Lessons to Be Learned*. London, England: LSE, October 2011.

IN FRENCH

Annuaire de l'Afrique du Nord. Paris: CNRS Editions, 1998, 2000, 2001.

Daguzan, Jean François (ed.), "Libye: Vers le Changement?", Paris: *Maghreb-Machrek*, No. 184, Spring 2005.

Martinez, Luis (ed.), "La Libye Après l'Embargo," Paris: *Maghreb-Machrek*, No. 170, October–December 2000.

Books

IN ENGLISH

Al Gaddafi and Saif Al Islam, *Libya and the XXI Century*. Tripoli, Libya: One 9 Media, 2002.

Al Mabruk Iltif, Ammar, *Libya: National Report on Human Development, 2002*. Tripoli, Libya: National Authority of Information and Documentation, 2002.

Arendt, Hannah, *On Revolution* (introduction by Jonathan Schell). New York, NY: Penguin, 1963.

Ben Halim, Mustafa, *The Years of Hope* (English trans.). London, England: AAS Media Publishers, 1994.

Buhite, Russell D., *Lives at Risk*. Wilmington, Delaware: SR Books, 1995.

Chervenyashka, Valya, and Yordanov, Nikolay, *Notes from Hell: A Bulgarian Nurse in Libya*. Durban, South Africa: 30 Degrees South, 2010.

Chorin, Ethan, *Translating Libya*. London, England: Saqi Books/SOAS, 2008.

Cohn, Marjorie (ed.), *The United States and Torture: Interrogation, Incarceration and Abuse*. New York, NY: New York University Press, 2011.

Collins, Larry, and Lapierre, Dominique, *The Fifth Horseman*. New York, NY: Simon and Schuster, 1980.

Duthel, Heinz, *Duthel Intelligence Report, 2011 Libyan Civil War: Timeline for the 2011 Libyan Civil War*. Self-published, 2011.

Edwards, Samuel, *Barbary General: The Life of William H. Eaton*. Englewood Cliffs, New Jersey: Prentice Hall, 1968.

Elbaradei, Mohammed, *The Age of Deception: Nuclear Diplomacy in Treacherous Times*. Doha, Qatar: Bloomsbury Qatar Foundation Press, 2011.

Feinstein, Andrew, *The Shadow World: Inside the Global Arms Trade*. New York, NY: Farrar, Straus and Giroux, 2011.

Fremont-Barnes, Gregory, *The Wars of the Barbary Pirates*. Oxford, England: Osprey Publishing, 2006.

Friedman, Alan, *Agnelli, Fiat and the Network of Italian Power*. New York, NY: New American Library, 1988.

Gerson, Allan, and Adler, Jerry, *The Price of Terror*. New York, NY: HarperCollins, 2001.

Goodchild, Richard, *Benghazi: The Story of a City* (reprint). Benghazi, Libya: Department of Antiquities Cyrenaical Libya, 1962.

Gurney, Judith, *Libya: The Political Economy of Oil*. Oxford, England: Oxford University Press, 1996.

Hagger, Nicholas, *The Libyan Revolution*. Johannesburg, South Africa: Alternative Books, 2009.

Halliday, Fred, *Political Journeys*. London, England: Saqi Books, 2011.

Ismail, Salwa, *Rethiniking Islamist Politics: Culture, the State, and Islamism*. London, England: I.B. Taurus, 2003.

Joseph, Robert G., *Countering WMD: The Libyan Experience*. Fairfax, Virginia: National Institute Press, 2009.

Kusa, Musa, *The Political Leader and His Social Background: M. Qadafi, the Libya Leader* (unpublished MA thesis in sociology). Ann Arbor: University of Michigan, 1978.

Lacroix, Stéphane, *Awakening Islam*. Cambridge, Massachusetts: Harvard University Press, 2011.

Lemarchand, René, *The Green and the Black*. Bloomington, Indiana: Indiana University Press, 1988.

London, Joshua E., *Victory in Tripoli: How America's War with the Barbary Pirates Established the U.S. Navy and Shaped a Nation*. Hoboken, New Jersey: John Wiley and Sons, 2005.

Martinez, Luis, *The Libyan Paradox*. New York, NY: Columbia University Press, 2007.

Matar, Hisham, *In the Country of Men*. New York, NY: Dial Press, 2007.

Mayer, Jane, *The Dark Side: The Inside Story of How the War on Terror Turned into a War on American Ideals*. New York, NY: Anchor Books, 2009.

Neihoum, Sadiq, *An Markab Assultan* (trans. Ethan Chorin, in *Translating Libya*). London, England: Saqi Books, 2008.

O'Sullivan, Meghan L., *Shrewd Sanctions: Statecraft and State Sponsors of Terrorism*. Washington, D.C.: Brookings Institution Press, 2003.

Otman, Waniss, and Karlberg, Erling, *The Libyan Economy*. Berlin, Germany: Springer, Heidelberg, 2007.

Power, Smantha, *A Problem from Hell: America and the Age of Genocide*. New York, NY: Harper Perennial, 2002.

Rice, Condoleezza, *No Higher Honor*. New York, NY: Crown Publishing Group, 2011.

Segell, Glen, *Axis of Evil and Rogue States: The Bush Administration, 2000–2004*. Self-published, Google Books.

Sharanksy, Natan, *The Case for Democracy: The Power of Freedom to Overcome Tyranny & Terror*. New York, NY: PublicAffairs, 2004.

St. John, Ronald Bruce, *Libya and the United States: Two Centuries of Strife*. Philadelphia, Pennsylvania: University of Pennsylvania Press, 2002.

St. John, Ronald Bruce, *Libya: From Colony to Revolution*. Oxford, England: Oneworld, 2011.

Vandewalle, Dirk (ed.), *Qadhafi's Libya: 1969–1994*. New York, NY: St. Martin's Press, 1995.

Vandewalle, Dirk, *Libya Since Independence: Oil and Statebuilding*. Ithaca, New York: Cornell University Press, 1998.

Vandewalle, Dirk, *A History of Modern Libya*. Cambridge, England: Cambridge University Press, 2006, 2012.

Vandewalle, Dirk (ed.), *Libya Since 1969: Qadhafi's Revolution Revisited*. New York, NY: Palgrave MacMillan, 2008.

Williams, Gwyn, *Green Mountain* (reprint Dar Al Fergiani). London, England: Faber & Faber, 1963.

Woodward, Bob, *The Veil: The Secret Wars of the CIA, 1981–1987*. New York, NY: Simon and Schuster, 1987.

Wright, John, *The Emergence of Libya*. London, England: Silphium Press, 2008.

Wright, John, *A History of Libya*. New York, NY: Columbia University Press, 2010.

IN FRENCH

Bisson, Danielle, Bisson, Jean, and Fontaine, Jacques, *La Libye: A la Decouverte d'un Pays* (Tome 1). Paris, France: Identité Libyenne, L'Harmattan, 1999.

Djaziri, Moncef, *Etat et Société en Libye*. Paris, France: L'Harmattan, 1996.

Haimzadeh, Patrick, *Au Coeur de la Libye de Kadhafi*. Paris, France: JC Lattès, 2011.

Lévy, Bernard Henri, *La Guerre sans l'Aimer*. Paris, France: Bernard Grasset, 2011.

Minoui, Delphine, *Tripoliwood*. Paris, France: Bernard Grasset, 2011.

Najjar, Alexandre, *Anatomie d'un Tyran: Mouammar Kadhafi*. Paris, France: Actes Sud, 2011.

Otayek, René, *La Politique Africaine de la Libye*. Paris, France: Editions Karthala, 1986.

Ouannes, Moncef, *Militaires, Elites et Modernisation dans la Libye Contemporaine*. Paris, France: L'Harmattan, 2009.

Péan, Pierre, *Manipulations Africaines*. Paris, France: Plon, 2001.

Pierini, Marc, *Le Prix de la Liberté*. Paris, France: Actes Sud, 2008.

Staub, Vincent, *La Libye et les Migrations Subsahariennes*. Paris, France: L'Harmattan, 2006.

Tanguy, Jean-Marc, *Harmattan: Récits et Révélations*. Paris, France: Nimrod, 2012.

Vincent, Pierre Marie, *Journal d'un Médecin en Temps de Guerre: Libya HURRA!* Paris, France: Editions les Nouveaux Auteurs, 2012.

IN ARABIC

ʿAbd al-Hādī, Yūsuf, *Ṣuwwar min Hayāt Idrīs as-Sanūsī*. Dār bin Šitwān (unknown location/year).

Abu Zeida, Ahlam, and Qarira, Abdulrizaq, *Mabnā al-Qunṣuliyyah al-Amrīkiyyah, Manšurāt Mašrūʿ Tanẓīm wa Idārāt al-Madīnahal-Qadīmah bi-Ṭarāblus*. Tripoli, Libya: Idārat at-Tawṯīq wa ad-Dirāsāt al-Insāniyyah, 2004.

Bin Nafīsah, Sārah, and Distrimou, Blandine (eds.), *Ihtiğāğāt al-Iğtimāʿiyyah wa aṯ-Ṯawrāt al-Madaniyyah*. al-Qāhirah: al-Ahrām Publishers, 2011.

Buẖayt, Ramaḍan ʿAdb Allah, *Ḥikayāt al-Maḍī wa al-Qarīb*. Dār al-Kutub al-Waṭaniyya (unknown location), 1996.

Imām, Ḥamādah, *Abnāʾ ar-Ruʾasāʾ: Min al-Quṣūr ʾilā as-Suğūn*. al-Qāhirah: Kunūz li-n-Našar wa at-Tawziʿ, 2012.

Kaḥal, Abū Bakr Ḥāmid, *Tītānīkāt Āfrīqiyyah*. Beirut, Lebanon: Saqi Books, 2008.

al-Faqīh, Aḥmad Ibrāhīm, *aṭ-Ṭāġiyyah fi-t-Tarīẖ: Muqaddimah fi tašrīẖ aṭ-Ṭāġiyyah*. Unpublished manuscript, 2011.

al-Maqariyaf, Muḥammad Yūsuf, *Lībiya bayn al-Māḍī wa al-Ḥāḍir*. al-Qāhirah: Maktabat Wahbah, 2006.

al-Muftī, Muḥammad Muḥammad, *Sahārī Dirnah*. Binġāzī, Libya: Dār al-Kutub al-Waṭaniyyah, 2007.

an-Nayhūm, aṣ-Ṣādiq, *Qiṣaṣ Aṭfāl*. Tala Books/Arab Diffusion Company.

al-Qusaybī, Ġāzī bin ʿAbd ar-Raḥmān, *al-Wazīr al-Murāfiq (The Accompanying Minister)*. Beirut, Lebanon: Arab Center for Studies and Publishing, 2011.

Quwaydar, Ibrāhīm, *Lībīyā: Irādat at-Taġyīr*. Cario, Egypt: Dār al-ʾUmum, 2011.

Šalġam, ʿAbd ar-Raḥmān, *Ašẖāṣ ḥawl al-Qaḏḏāfī*. Cairo, Egypt: Dār al-Farğiyānī, 2012.

al-Fitūrī, Asmāʾ Farağ, *Binġāzī min 1911 ʾilā 2011*. Binġāzī, Libya: as-Safīr Press/al-Wikālah al-Lībīyyah li-t-Tarqīm ad-Duwalī al-Muwaḥḥad li-l-Kitāb, 2011.

Iġtiyāl Lībīyā. al-Qāhirah: Maktabat Madbūlī, 1993.

GENERAL REFERENCES

Amghar, Samir, *La Salafisme D'Aujourd'hui*, Paris, France: Michalon, 2011.

Arab Human Development Report 2002. United Nations Development Programme, 2002.

Fuller, Graham E., *The New Turkish Republic*. United States Institute of Peace Press, 2008.

Ibn Khaldun, *The Muqaddimah*. Princeton, New Jersey: Princeton University Press, 1967.

Ightiyal Libya. Cairo: Maktabat Madbouli, 1993.

Khoury, Philip S., and Kostiner, Joseph (eds.), *Tribes and State Formation in the Middle East*. Berkeley, California: University of California Press, 1990.

Lynch, Marc, *The Arab Uprising*. New York, NY: PublicAffairs, 2012.

Missouri, Moftah, *La Libye des Voyageurs (1812–1912)*. Lausanne, Switzerland: Editions Favre, 2000.

Nafisa, Sarah bin, and Distrimou, Blandine (eds.), *Ihtijajaat Al Ijtimaiyya wa Al thowraat al madaniyya* (Nabil Abdelfatah, ed., Arabic version). Cairo, Egypt: Al Ahram Publishers, 2011.

Osman, Tarek, *Egypt on the Brink*. New Haven, Connecticut: Yale University Press, 2010.

Ottaway, Marina, and Hamzawy, Amr (eds.), *Getting to Pluralism: Political Actors in the Arab World*. Washington, D.C.: Carnegie Endowment for International Peace, 2009.

Pliez, Olivier (ed.), *La Nouvelle Libyae*. Paris: Editions Karthala, 2004.

Pollack, Kenneth, Byman, Daniel, et al., *The Arab Awakening*. Washington, D.C.: Brookings Institution Press, 2011.

Pope, Nicole, and Pope, Hugh, *Turkey Unveiled*. New York, NY: Overlook Press, 2004.

Rutherford, Bruce K., *Egypt After Mubarak*. Princeton, New Jersey: Princeton University Press, 2008.

Schmitt, Eric, and Shanker, Thom, *Counterstrike: The Untold Story of America's Secret Campaign Against Al Qaeda*. New York, NY: Times Books, Henry Holt and Company, 2011.

Tezcur, Gunes Murat, *Muslim Reformers in Iran and Turkey*. Austin, Texas: University of Texas Press, 2010.

Wallace, Jonathan, and Wilkinson, Bill (consultant eds.), *Doing Business with Libya, CWC Associates Limited*, 2nd ed. Kogan Page, 2004.

Websites and Newslists

Feb17.Info
Libya Al Mustakbal
Libya Al Yowm
Marbo3a
The Huffington Post

INDEX